Kate Smith

Kate Smith

*A Biography, with
a Discography, Filmography
and List of Stage Appearances*

by RICHARD K. HAYES

with a tribute by HELEN HAYES

McFarland & Company, Inc., Publishers
Jefferson, North Carolina, and London

Frontispiece: Kate Smith singing sweetly in an NBC publicity closeup. "Evening Hour," 1952.

British Library Cataloguing-in-Publication data are available

Library of Congress Cataloguing-in-Publication Data

Hayes, Richard K., 1934–
    Kate Smith : a biography, with a discography, filmography and
list of stage appearances / by Richard K. Hayes.
      p. cm.
    Includes bibliographical references and index.
    ISBN 0-7864-0053-6 (lib. bdg. : 50# and 70# alk. paper) ∞
    1. Smith, Kate, 1907–1986. 2. Singers—United States—
Biography. 3. Smith, Kate, 1907–1986—Discography. 4. Smith,
Kate, 1907–1986—Filmography. I. Title.
ML420.S67H39 1995
782'.0092—dc20
   [B]   95-6056
                                       CIP
                                     MN

Manufactured in the United States of America

McFarland & Company, Inc., Publishers
 Box 611, Jefferson, North Carolina 28640

This book is dedicated to the many
friends of Kate Smith who have inspired me
over the years; to the memory of my dear friend
and favorite star, the subject of this book;
and to my long-suffering mother

Contents

Acknowledgments

I am indebted to many people, both living and deceased, for helping to make this a far more thorough, accurate, and entertaining true story than I ever could have written alone. The late F. Winfrey Carter of Richmond made a trip to Greenville, Virginia, to investigate Kate Smith's alleged place of birth. John W. Brake, unofficial Greenville historian, conducted exhaustive research regarding her alleged birthplace and the circumstances of her birth. Charles P. Gernand II researched her girlhood in Washington, D.C. Helen Hayes, late great star of stage and screen, related her memories of appearing with Smith, first when they both were girls in the nation's capital, and later on Smith's radio program.

James E. Stettler of Los Angeles provided details and background for Smith's early years as a professional on stage, screen, and radio. Dr. Howard B. Gotlieb, director of special collections at Boston University, and his staff were most cooperative during the many days I spent there researching the Kate Smith collection. Smith had arranged many years ago to leave most of her career memorabilia there. Her scrapbooks of press clippings and her photograph collection proved very valuable.

Arthur Tracy, the Street Singer, provided some insights into both his and Smith's early days at CBS. David W. McCain of New Orleans permitted me to view a rare 1932 Vitaphone movie short subject. Jim Stettler, Father Raymond Wood, and I spent a delightful evening at the Los Angeles home of actress Sally Blane, who was in the cast of Smith's one feature picture, *Hello Everybody!* and told us about the making of the movie.

Jack Miller's daughter Dorothea Civitarese reminisced about her father, Smith's orchestra leader for a quarter century. Kathryn (Klinge) Christie gave me her mother's precious diaries of visits with the Songbird in the halcyon days of the Thirties in New York City, while Bessie (Phillips) Allen shared her memories of twice visiting Smith at the radio studio during that era. Allen also gave me her letters and postcards from Kate, as well as her scrapbooks.

André Baruch, famed announcer on the "Kate Smith Hour" and many other CBS radio programs, along with his famous wife of over fifty years, Bea Wain (vocalist with the Larry Clinton orchestra and "Your Hit Parade"), granted me a touching, enlightening, and amusing telephone interview from their home in Beverly Hills.

I am grateful to Irving Berlin's daughters for reading Chapter 5, correcting several errors of fact.

The late Ezra Stone (Henry of radio's "The Aldrich Family") and Jackie Kelk (his sidekick Homer and a radio and television comedian) consented to tape an interview with me and Father Wood. Jack Kelk led Jim Stettler and me to the Studio City, California, apartment of actress Betty Garde, who appeared many times in the drama segment of the "Kate Smith Hour," and who gave Smith her favorite dog Freckles. Garde proved tremendously insightful about both Smith and her manager-partner Ted Collins. Comedian Henny Youngman gave me a revealing telephone interview.

Cynthia Hoffman of Saugerties, New York, not only told me of her many meetings with Smith between 1942 and 1969, but also gave me access to her impressive and detailed log books of nearly every one of Smith's radio and television appearances from 1940 to the end of her career in 1976. John Behrens of CBS Archives provided me with a wealth of information about Smith's radio programs when I visited the archives in New York City. Michael R. Pitts, author of *Kate Smith: A Bio-Bibliography*, researched the contents of the "Kate Smith Sings" broadcasts of the early thirties, and Albert F. Koenig, Jr., provided additional radio data.

Ken Roberts, an early CBS radio announcer, spoke to me about announcing for Smith in 1932, while George Ward reminisced about being a child actor on the "Kate Smith Hour" on radio.

Peg Lynch, creator, writer, and star of the radio and television situation comedy program *Ethel and Albert,* invited me, along with several friends, to her home in the Berkshire Hills of western Massachusetts to talk about her association with Smith and Collins and their live television shows in the Fifties. Denman (Gabe) Meinhardt of Port Charlotte, Florida, told about being a member of the chorus on that NBC show and of his affection for Smith.

Glenna Durkin of Lake Placid, New York, widow of one of Smith's caretakers at her island Camp Sunshine, led me to B. J. Cook, who was Smith's caretaker from 1940 to about 1955. Father Wood and I traveled to Wilmington (near Lake Placid) one beautiful early spring day to visit "Beejie." The colorful and candid nonagenarian told us fascinating stories about Smith, whom he loved and respected, and Collins, whom he did not.

Sound engineer Harold F. Schneider, who worked with a host of celebrities during a long career with NBC radio, gave me an insight into Smith and Collins at Lake Placid, as well as a description of her penthouse apartment on Park Avenue and the radio programs they broadcast from it.

Musician Lyn Duddy spoke with me about rehearsing songs with Smith at his East Side apartment, about her Carnegie Hall concert in 1963, and also about Collins. Two young men with whom Smith corresponded when they were teenagers in the sixties shared their letters from her and their meetings with her. They are Bill Freeh, Jr., now an NBC-TV sound engineer, and Chuck D'Imperio, now a radio personality in Oneonta, New York.

Bill Byrge, a combination librarian and movie actor of Nashville, Tennessee, and Dorothy Mull of Ellenton, Florida, told of meeting with Smith at her concerts in those southern states in the later years of her career.

I am most grateful to Paul Williams, vice president for international product development for BMG/RCA Records, and to Columbia Records, for providing discographical information from their files.

I owe a special debt of gratitude to Patricia Castledine of Clifton Park, New York, for keeping me informed of developments in Raleigh, North Carolina, when she was Smith's resident companion during her final debilitation, a long and sad period of nearly seven years. Few came to know the real Kathryn Smith as well as did Castledine, nor loved her as much.

I offer my thanks to Pat Castledine, Sue and Lou Sann, Father Wood, James Robert Parish, Marie Marchesani, Albert F. Koenig, Jr., Jim Stettler, Charles K. Stumpf, Frederic Goldrup, and William T. Anderson, for reading part or all of my manuscript at various stages. I am grateful to such thoughtful friends as John J. Campbell of Staten Island, New York, Harry J. Lednum, Jr., of Newark, Delaware, Charles Stumpf, Brian Wiggin of Conway, New Hampshire, and Charles Prynne of St. Ives, England, for providing articles and photographs. My deep appreciation is extended to Luisa M. P. Landi for her diligence in manuscript typing and to Sarah A. DiNatale for typing the index.

I, of course, accept all responsibility for the pitfalls of this volume, whether errors of omission or commission.

RICHARD K. HAYES

Kate Smith and I were both members of St. Patrick's in Washington, D.C. Our pastor, Father Hurney, had a variety show every year in which the youth of his church performed.

Kate and I were on a couple of times together—she, of course, the star turn; I, just a modest reciter. Years later, when I went on Kate's radio show, we talked about Father Hurney and we switched roles. I sang, she recited. It was good for a laugh.

I loved her as a person and, of course, as a great performer. What a blessing she was to our country!

HELEN HAYES

CHAPTER 1

Half a Moon Is Better Than No Moon

Kate Smith did few things in moderation. When she ate, it was a banquet. When she drove, it was full throttle. When she sang, it was with all the power her voice could deliver, and that was a great deal. She was a decisive person. I never heard her say, "I don't know." If she was not sure of the answer to a question, she made one up. She was one of a kind.

As I DROVE FROM RHODE ISLAND toward Cherry Hill, New Jersey, with three friends on a pleasant Saturday in December 1974, we considered the possibility that this might be our last chance to see our famous friend, Kate Smith, on stage. We knew her health was not nearly as robust as the public was given to believe. She suffered from cardiovascular problems and complications from a late but difficult case of diabetes, among other ailments. This week-long theatre engagement was a tour de force for her. We were exuberant at the prospect of being in the audience and meeting with her backstage afterwards.

Upon our arrival in this Philadelphia suburb, we met other friends, freshened up in our hotel rooms, and then were off for the dinner show at the swank Latin Casino. Smith's bodyguard, an ex–Marine named Salvatore Gelosi, had reserved a front-and-center table for us and for Kathryn's sister, Helena Steene, and Helena's nephew. (Kate Smith's friends and relatives always called her Kathryn.)

There was a capacity crowd in this large and splendid dinner room. After everyone had finished dining, comedian Soupy Sales was the opening act. Then came the familiar strains of "When the Moon Comes Over the Mountain," Smith's perennial theme song. She walked onstage briskly, radiant in the spotlight as always, clad in a pink chiffon gown with loose pleated sleeves. Looking ageless, she sang perhaps more beautifully than ever. Her audience listened in rapt attention and applauded with enthusiasm after each number. She had the Kids Next Door with her, a lively and talented group of some twenty young folks who sang and danced and added an element of "now" to her shows. "God Bless America," her final selection, evoked the customary standing ovation.

After the dinner show, Sal Gelosi motioned to us to follow him to Smith's dressing room. She greeted us as warmly as ever. If some of her friends had not been there she would have been disappointed. We could see that she was exhausted and needed time to rest before the later show. Gelosi made it clear to us that we would have only a few minutes to visit. That was one of his duties, and he performed it well. Smith loved to talk, and he eventually had to step in and tell her she would have to let us go so she could get some rest.

I told Smith I was pleasantly surprised that she had added "These Foolish Things Remind Me of You" to her medley of standards. Her quick reply was, "And that may be the last time you'll hear it, too. You know, Richard, sometimes when you've sung a song so many times over the years, you just don't ever want to sing it again." I could tell from that remark that she was tired, so I quickly changed the subject by introducing two of my friends whom she had not met. She greeted them graciously, thanking Alan for the lovely roses he had sent earlier in the day. She happily consented to pose for pictures with them. Then all of us except her sister Helena departed to await the second show. It was amazing that at age 67 and with all of her medical problems she had the stamina to perform as well as she did in two long stage shows every evening for a week.

At the dinner show I sat beside Helena, whom I had not met. The two Smith sisters bore little resemblance physically, in personality, or in their chosen careers. Helena was a reading specialist in the schools of Easton, Connecticut. As I was also a teacher, we had that much in common. As editor of the journals for Smith's "Friends" club, I seized the opportunity to ask Helena to write a story about their childhood in Washington, D.C., for our next issue. She chuckled and replied, "I'd be glad to, but I don't know whether my sister would approve of what I'd write." That was my first experience of the longtime sisterly friction I had heard about.

KATHRYN SMITH ALMOST ALWAYS CLAIMED to have been born in the small town of Greenville, in the Blue Ridge Mountains of Virginia. Her birth certificate, however, makes it clear that she was born at home in Washington, D.C. The date was Wednesday, May 1, 1907 (not 1909, as she always claimed in interviews), and the attending physician was Dr. N. R. Jenner. Home was 211 First Street, in the northwest quadrant of Washington, not far from the Capitol.

Smith's parents were William H. and Charlotte Yarnell (Hanby) Smith. Her father's occupation was listed as "News Paper Agent." He was a native of Washington, D.C., while her mother was born in Delaware. Her sister Helena was born November 17, 1904. Between Helena and Kathryn there was a sister named Martha who died in infancy, a not uncommon occurrence in those times before modern medicine.

Bill Smith was owner of the Capitol News Company, which distributed out-of-town newspapers (big business in Washington), as well as such magazines as *The Saturday Evening Post, Ladies' Home Journal,* and *Country Gentleman.* His office was at 227 B Street, also a short distance from the Capitol. Lottie Smith's parents, Mr. and Mrs. Benjamin Franklin Hanby, lived at 2152 F Street, four blocks away. They were a close-knit family with old-fashioned ideals.

One day in 1917 a young man named Hugh Melton of Greenville, Virginia, came to work at the Justice Department. Melton, age 25, bought newspapers from Bill Smith and told him that he was looking for a room to rent. The Smiths decided to rent him their spare room, and Hugh Melton roomed with them for several years. Thus he knew Kathryn from the time she was ten. Later he lived with the Hanbys for many years. Hugh and Kathryn remained lifelong friends until he died in 1976. He visited her at her New York apartment and always spent two weeks in August at her Lake Placid summer home. She always called him "Uncle Hughie."

Although Hugh Melton maintained that Kate Smith was born in Washington, not in his hometown of Greenville, a folklore developed that she was indeed born in Greenville. In her 1960 autobiography, *Upon My Lips a Song,* she referred to her birthplace, saying that in an interview early in her career, she had replied to a question by telling a reporter she was born in Greenville. After the interview, her manager, Ted Collins, asked why she did not say she was born in Washington, D.C. He is supposed to have added, "Now we'll have you claimed by Greenville as a native daughter and you don't know a soul there. I bet you don't even know what the main street looks like." Smith goes on to say, "Greenville did try to claim me, and I felt very uncomfortable that I had no ties there. And in some reference books my birthplace is given as Greenville, some as Washington." She never does commit herself. As late as 1974, when she cohosted "The Mike Douglas Show" on television, Douglas asked where she was born and she said, "Greenville, near Staunton, Virginia."

The question of Kate Smith's birthplace is a strange matter. If both her birth certificate and the "Report of a Birth" to the Health Department of the District of Columbia state that it was indeed Washington, then this city must be her birthplace. In an attempt to get a clarification, I wrote the only living person I knew of who would know the true story, her sister, but she refused to help. I presented two hypothetical versions of her birth in Greenville, based in large part on the folklore. She simply said, "I can assure you that neither of your versions is even close to 'correct.'" Apparently not, if she was born in Washington. Smith's mother backed up the Greenville story in an article she wrote for *Screen and Radio Weekly* in 1938. The article contains the statement "We moved to Washington when Kate was just a few weeks old." This would appear to be untrue, as the birth certificate was filed May 9, 1907.

The question of the birthplace of the Songbird of the South has been a bone of contention among residents of Greenville for many years. While many deny she was born there, others will name the building where the birth took place. Some claim it was in the colonial Smith estate (no relation) or the three-room log cabin on the Smith property. Others maintain it was in the Melton Hotel, owned and operated by Hugh Melton's parents, John and Ellen. The town physician, son of the doctor resident in 1907, is not saying anything. It seems clear that Kate Smith was not born in Greenville, Virginia.

One fact appears to be set in concrete, and that is that on her summer visits to the Meltons in later years, Kathryn Smith always had at least one meal at Howard Johnson's two miles north of Greenville. She would have a fried clam plate and then three or four scoops of ice cream (different flavors). She would buy little jars of ice cream topping and open the jars at the table so she could eat the topping with the ice cream, using her finger to get the topping from the jar.

Smith used to delight in telling of when and how she first began to speak. Her mother sang and played the piano at the local Presbyterian church. One day, when Kathryn was three years old, she was standing beside Lottie at the piano when she suddenly began to sing with her mother. Lottie was so relieved and happy that she ran downstairs to tell Bill the good news. Little Kathryn was not a mute after all. Smith enjoyed embellishing her stories a bit, so she claimed she was four years old. She added that whenever her mother related the story she quipped, "And she hasn't stopped since."

Smith's father was an amateur singer too. He and his father were members of a men's chorus. Bill Smith attended the Immaculate Conception Catholic Church. Young Kathryn joined a group there called the St. Pat's Players. As she wrote in her first autobiography, *Living in a Great Big Way*, "I was something of a tomboy, climbing trees, playing the rougher games, racing after fire engines, and roller-skating." She was the only girl in a little club some of the neighborhood children had when she was six. She loved to stage vaudeville shows in her backyard.

The neighborhood gang Smith belonged to was called the Midnight Riders, though she did not know why, as they were all tucked into bed by eight o'clock. She recalled, "I was the president, secretary, treasurer, and initiator. My fees were bags of marshmallows, chocolate sundaes with whipped cream and nuts or something of that sort. Whenever a new member was brought into our club I'd drag him out to the clubhouse in the backyard, jab a pin into his thumb and put his thumb-prints in blood at the top of our law book. It was great fun."

To hear Smith recall her childhood, one would be led to believe she was the original Baby Snooks, full of mischief and forever up to no good. Not long after she began talking and before she was old enough to go to school she earned a good spanking for taking a pair of scissors and snipping off all of the tail feathers from her father's beautiful stuffed bird on the mantel. Then she proceeded to snip the tassels from her mother's table scarf. She got another spanking for cutting off most of her hair one day.

One Easter morning young Kathie Smith was wearing a new melon pink linen dress. As she waited for the family to go to church services, the boy next door asked her for a push on his coaster wagon. She obliged, then jumped on for a ride. In doing so she soiled her brand new Easter dress.

On her first day of school, Smith remembered, she ran away four times. Finally her mother lured her back to the schoolroom with a bag of caramels and the promise of an ice cream soda after school. She played hookey whenever she could and would hide out from the family and the truant officer. In a large pear tree in her backyard, she built a cozy bower that was hidden by the tree's foliage. She hoisted a chair into the crotch of the tree and would sit for hours while a frantic search was taking place before her very eyes.

Smith always loved fire engines. "I used to shock everybody by riding to fires on the fire engines," she reminisced gleefully. "The chief was an old pal of mine and he would stop and pick me up on the way to a fire. What fun tearing through the streets on a careening fire wagon behind a three-horse hitch! Mother couldn't break me of the habit. I just grew out of it."

Another of Smith's childhood interests was pets. "We had every kind of pet imaginable," she recalled fondly. "There were rabbits, guinea pigs, chickens, pigeons, dogs, cats—oh, everything. The family stood it until I insisted on keeping all the young ones. Father just made me get rid of them. Our yard looked like a branch of the SPCA!"

Surprisingly, Smith adored her dolls, and she also liked nice dresses. Her favorite childhood dress was one her mother sewed: a blue crepe-de-Chine dress with beautiful velvet and satin flowers around the sash.

But Smith preferred playing rough-and-tumble games such as cops-and-robbers with the boys. Once during a game of hide-and-seek she hid in the back of a furniture truck. Before she could jump out, the truck drove to nearby Virginia. The truckers found Smith when they opened the back and phoned her father, who came and took her home.

Smith also liked automobiles. She remembered being tempted at age 13 by her uncle's car, which was parked in front of the Smith house. She climbed into it and started the engine. When she could not stop it, she became panic-stricken, but a neighbor came to her rescue.

Three years later Smith's father gave her a roadster. That was the term used for a sporty convertible, which was quite a gift. She took it for a ride, speeding down a narrow street. A trolley car soon came alongside and clanged for the right-of-way. Challenged, Smith sounded her horn in happy defiance and held the road. The motorman ordered her back, but she laughed at him through the glass, howling at the scowl on his face. She raced the trolley for a block. Then as she slammed on the brakes, the roadster slid askew, bouncing to a stop with its radiator over the tracks. The street car lunged against the automobile, ruining the left front mudguard. Smith was determined to have her revenge. She found a five-pound rock, waited forty-five minutes for the trolley to return, and then heaved it through the motorman's window and ran. Her punishment for that incident must have been severe indeed.

Kathryn Smith was bitten by the show business bug at an early age. The Rev. Francis J. Hurney was pastor of the Immaculate Conception Church in Washington, which Smith's father attended. He was also chaplain of the Catholic Actors' Guild and directed the St. Patrick's Players, an organization with a record for developing stars second to none. According to Father Hurney:

> Though she was never a member of the organization, it may surprise her to know how closely linked with her "great chance" was that old Player group. One spring . . . Eddie Dowling came to see one of the St. Pat's performances and was much impressed by several of the cast. . . . He said he had a spot [in his new New York play] for the girl whom he had seen the preceding year in a Keith [Theatre] benefit. He could not recall her name and he could give me only a description of her work. . . . Several hours afterward I happened to think of Kate. I called her on the phone, and after some checking, concluded that she was the girl, told her to report to rehearsal with the Dowling show at the Casino Theatre the following Monday at ten o'clock.

Each year Father Hurney would direct the St. Pat's Players in a variety show. Two of these annual productions included the future First Lady of Radio and the First Lady of the Theatre. Smith was about nine or ten years of age and Helen Hayes Brown was fifteen or sixteen. Miss Hayes also recalled that her father, Frank Brown, always ran the Elks' annual celebration in the District of Columbia and always had Kate Smith sing.

During the First World War, Washington was a hubbub of activity. Kathryn Smith's musical debut, so to speak, took place at a bond rally in 1917. The Blue Devils, a band of one hundred French soldiers, had come to Washington to take part in a Liberty Loan Drive. Smith was asked to sing a few war songs, perhaps because of her father's connections in his magazine business.

The rally was held in Peck Memorial Chapel. Smith's songs included "Over There," "Keep the Home Fires Burning," "Rose of No Man's Land," "I've Got My Captain Working for Me Now," and "There's a Long, Long Trail." Her nine-year-old voice tugged at the heartstrings of the audience gathered for the occasion. Several years later, quite unexpectedly, she received an order from General John J. "Blackjack" Pershing himself to attend a dinner at the White House, where she received a medal for her singing. Warren G. Harding was president at the time. It would not be the only time she was invited to the White House.

At age twelve Kathryn Smith entered vaudeville, singing at an amateur night at a local theatre. She received a five-dollar gold piece as winner of the contest. She returned the next week and for several weeks thereafter, each time coming away with the winner's gold piece.

As a high school student, Smith was mediocre at best. Latin and algebra were her worst subjects; she found geography and history "the most bearable." The most fun, she said, was when her music teacher was absent and she was allowed to take over the class. She was on the girls' basketball team. Perhaps some of her problems in high school were due to the fact that she was younger than most of her peers. When she graduated from Business High School in June 1923, she was barely sixteen.

Older sister Helena loved to read and excelled in school. (She received a Doctorate in Education at age 83.) Kathryn preferred the limelight. She was never happier than when performing before a receptive audience. During her high school years, she occasionally sang on radio station WRC, at the B. F. Keith vaudeville theatre, and at several roadhouses in the greater Washington area, including the Toll House Tavern. These activities displeased her parents and grandparents, especially in view of her mediocre schoolwork.

By the time Smith graduated from high school, she was quite buxom, though amazingly light on her feet, as many heavy-set people seem to be. Her family urged her to pursue a career in nursing, but she was adamant that she wanted to be an entertainer. One evening an especially fierce argument between Kathryn and her father resulted in his slapping her face. She then enrolled at George Washington School of Nursing and gave it a nine-month try, but her heart was truly in show business. Besides, her feet ached.

Smith found time to continue performing in and around Washington, especially after she left nursing school. (In later years she would say she attended medical school.) In February 1926, *Variety*, the newspaper of show biz, reviewed her engagement at the Earle Theatre. The review was prophetic: "Give Kate Smith about six months' experience and she will blossom out as a blues singer who will grace any man's bill." The reviewer noted that she had not only "a good voice, but one of much volume. She switches from a sentimental ballad to a 'Madame Sophie Tucker' with ease and with a wallop behind it. Then for good measure does a dance handling about 200 pounds with such grace as to take her away with a great finish." The booking at the Earle "follow[ed] the rapid rise of Miss Smith within but a very few weeks, she being so much in demand that local engagements are overlapping, with her name worth money at the boxoffice."

Smith's big break came early that summer when she was asked to fill in for a week at the Keith. She rehearsed the popular Charleston dance and incorporated it into her act; it delighted the audience. A. L. "Abe" Ehr-langer, an important New York producer, chanced to see her at the Keith and told playwright-actor-lyricist Eddie Dowling about her. Dowling and his partner, composer-pianist James Hanley, were working on a new musical comedy. That summer they had to go to Washington on business. They were involved in persuading Congress to extend the number of copy-right years for ASCAP songs before they entered the public domain. They had also arranged to try out the songs for the new show at the Keith.

Dowling spoke to the theatre manager, a Mr. Robbin, about the Smith girl. Robbin (according to Dowling in a 1969 radio interview) took him and Hanley to a barbershop where Smith was cutting hair. (Her sister denied that she cut hair.) Robbin explained that he had arranged for Smith to sing some of their songs on the stage. The idea was to have Dowling as the name star in the stage show. Robbin told Smith he had advised Dowling and Hanley that she was "pretty good." She is supposed to have replied in a loud and brassy tone of voice, "Well, I can do a Charleston better than anybody *they* ever saw." And she proceeded to give a demonstration then and there. Hanley loved it. They took her to their suite at the Washington Hotel, where they played "Jersey Walk," the tune to which she was to sing and dance the Charleston.

On stage at the Keith, Smith "killed 'em," as they say in the vernacular of show biz. Hanley and Dowling insisted she be in their show, *Honeymoon Lane*. Smith was skeptical, as she said she had been given similar promises by Al Jolson and Eddie Cantor and nothing had materialized. To prove their sincerity, Dowling handed her a $100 bill and told her to go tell her folks that if they would come to the barbershop for a meeting, he would ad-vance her the balance of $1,000. Her parents agreed, after a fashion, and she was given a contract. Incidentally, she flew to New York on the first commercial airplane, a flight that took three hours.

Following several weeks of rehearsals, *Honeymoon Lane* tried out in Atlantic City for a week beginning August 29. After a successful stand in Atlantic City, *Honeymoon Lane* moved to the Garrick Theatre in Philadelphia. While there, on September 16, James Hanley took Smith to nearby Camden, New Jersey, to the studios of the Victor Talking Machine

Company, where she made test pressings of three songs from the show: "The Little White House," "Mary Dear," and "Jersey Walk." Hanley accompanied her at the piano. They were rejected. They recorded the songs again on October 7, and they were again rejected. This time Smith and Hanley rejected Victor, and on October 28 they recorded the songs for the Columbia Phonograph Company in New York. The first two were released December 30; Smith's first record was Columbia 810-D.

As opening night at New York's Knickerbocker Theatre neared, rehearsals were rugged, with final changes being made. The excitement of it all possessed this talented girl who had had neither a singing nor a dancing lesson. That supreme confidence of youth was Smith's and cast in the comic role of Tiny Little, she never really experienced stage fright.

Eddie Dowling remembered with glee that opening night forty-three years later in a radio interview. He said, "I sat her through every scene in the show and never let her open her mouth, just this big, fat, 260-pound girl. People asked, 'What is this?' until this moment, about a quarter of eleven at night. Just before the finale of the show, when the boy meets the girl (which is me in this case) I turn her loose. And boy I want to tell you! I couldn't finish the play, by the way. They [the audience] wouldn't let the play finish."

Sidney Solomon, owner of the posh Casino Club in Central Park, wanted her for a midnight show there. Dowling told him he could have her, but first, " 'I've got to go out there. I've got to get this audience out of the theatre.' When she finished that chorus and came off, I came on and took her by the hand and said, 'Ladies and gentlemen, we've made a tremendous discovery. It's going to take precedence over the play and everything else. A new and great talent has been born tonight. And I want to tell you something else, too: she isn't going to sing any more. But I've got to tell you not to worry about the little white house (at the end of Honeymoon Lane) and the girl running out on me. I get her and she's got the white house. And the fat girl has got a contract. Good night!' "

Charlotte Cole of Upper Darby, Pennsylvania, attended one of the early performances. I asked her to recall it for our club magazine. She remembered that when she reached the theatre and read the marquee, "ALSO INTRODUCING KATE SMITH," she recalled having read in *Variety* in a column titled "New Acts" that they had reviewed "another youngster, predicting that she will go places — one Kate Smith." She recalled the gales of laughter that greeted Smith when she stepped out onto the stage. To the audience she was a buffoon, and Charlotte thought to herself, "Oh, give the gal a chance." She sang her song, "Half a Moon" (Is Better Than No Moon), and danced the Charleston. The audience loved it. For Charlotte there was not only the voice but a sincerity behind it. She followed Kate Smith's career from that time on.

The *New York Times* review the next morning was headlined:

"HONEYMOON LANE" IS COLORFUL AND LAVISH
Eddie Dowling Liked in Musical Role
Kate Smith, 250-pound Blues Singer, a Hit

The reviewer emphasized Smith's contribution to the show:

> According to advance notices it had a newcomer who stopped the show in a late specialty, and all the first nighters were told to be on the lookout for her. She is one Kate Smith and she weighs, according to a rough estimate, with all the returns not in, between 200 and 250 pounds. As a dancer and coon-shouting blues singer she proved unusually adept, and stop the show she did last night as predicted.

Mayor Jimmy Walker, who had been a songplugger and lyricist and was as much involved with show business as politics, predicted that the play would run two years. And that it did: 364 performances on Broadway and a second year on the road. And the ballad called "The Little White House" became a hit. It was, as we said, Kate Smith's first record. Although her nineteen-year-old voice sounds formal and high-pitched, each word is enunciated in clear bell-tones.

Smith's second record contrasts utterly with the first, consisting of two lively jazz tunes: "One Sweet Letter from You" and "I'm Gonna Meet My Sweetie Now." She was accompanied by the legendary Charleston Chasers, a jazz septet led by cornetist Red Nichols. The ensemble included trombonist Miff Mole, Jimmy Dorsey on clarinet and alto sax, banjoist Dick McDonough, Joe Tarto playing tuba, drummer Vic Berton, and pianist Arthur Schutt; each and every one was a jazz legend. Smith exudes confidence on these vocals. Had she continued along these lines she might have become a legendary jazz vocalist herself. Her delivery, however, was straight and forceful, a forerunner of the hundreds of commercial pop tunes she would record in decades to come.

Life offstage was not pleasant for Smith. She was shunned socially by her peers in the cast, so she spent many lonely hours crying herself to sleep in her small hotel room. Since she neither smoked nor drank, was offended by risqué jokes, and had a weight problem, she just did not fit in. In all these ways she would change very little during her long career. The "fat jokes" always smarted deep down inside, even as she would watch a late evening talk show many years later. She would ask, "Now why did they have to say that?" She never learned to live with it. Jokes about her weight were an inevitable part of the Kate Smith legend. As grateful as she was to Eddie Dowling for giving her that first big break as a professional, it is clear that she was exploited. There was even a clause in her contract stating that she must maintain a weight of over 200 pounds during the run of the play.

During the run of *Honeymoon Lane* at the Ehrlanger Theatre in Chicago (March 25–May 5), Smith headlined the bill at the Hotel Sherman's College Inn. She was billed as "Star of *Honeymoon Lane*, America's Greatest Popular Singer." And this was in 1928.

After *Honeymoon Lane* closed at the end of the summer of 1928, having played in many major cities from coast to coast, Smith returned home for a rest. She was downcast at the clear realization that her singing ability was not being taken seriously, but rather that she was regarded as a comic foil, an object of ridicule. One day, as she walked along the Potomac, brooding about her future, she contemplated jumping in and ending it all. Her despondency turned to amusement as she realized that she would surely float to the surface. And that is as close to suicide as she ever came.

Smith was called back to New York right after Christmas, as the Savoy Musical Comedy Company was planning a brief revival of the 1927 Vincent Youmans musical comedy *Hit the Deck*. They wanted her to play in blackface the role of Mammy Lavinia, a role originated by Stella Mayhew in the original New York production. She would be belting out the hit tune "Hallelujah." Well, it was a job, and she accepted it with reservations. The show opened at the Shubert-Belasco Theatre January 6, and Smith was given top billing. Two weeks later the company revived *Honeymoon Lane*, and she reprised the part of Tiny Little, again getting star billing. In later years she made light of *Hit the Deck*, perhaps embarrassed in retrospect. Still, she sang on radio and recordings in perfect black dialect. And soon she would be known as the Song Bird of the South.

Two striking events occurred the first week of April 1929 that would portend Smith's future success. She made her debut at the legendary Palace Theatre, mecca of all performers. True, she was at the bottom of the bill headed by vaudeville comedian Will Mahoney, but it was a sizable feather in her cap nonetheless. A *New York Times* review of the show commented, "Kate Smith, a generously proportioned and resonant-voiced singer of the 'coon-shouter' type, fetched most of the audience with her specialties. They included, among other matters, a revival of the Charleston."

Another feather in Smith's cap that week was her first network radio appearance. It was April 4 on an NBC nationwide remote broadcast with celebrities like Sophie Tucker (the Last of the Red Hot Mamas), bandleader Ted ("Is everybody happy?") Lewis, and smooth vocalist Nick Lucas. Quite a week it was.

The following July Smith resumed recording, now on the budget labels of Columbia: Harmony, Velvet Tone, and Diva (sold in W. T. Grant stores). She was good at imitating other vocalists, such as Ethel Waters, Sophie Tucker, and Ruth Etting. At times she even tended to imitate such male crooners as Bing Crosby, Russ Columbo, and Arthur Tracy. She was now recording with a Columbia house band called the Harmonians, often led by Columbia vice president/conductor Ben Selvin. Her voice could be powerful or sweet, sad or exuberant, and her records sold well in those days before the stock market crash.

Enter the tumultuous thirties. Smith signed for a more important role in a new George White musical comedy, *Flying High*. Again she was cast as a comic foil, playing opposite funny man Bert Lahr. *Flying High* opened in New York on Monday, March 3, at White's Apollo Theatre on 42nd Street, west of Broadway. Its opening was so eagerly anticipated, based on reviews from tryouts in Boston and New Haven, that it was the first show ever to command a $6.60 seat on Broadway. It became the biggest Broadway hit of 1930.

The story line involved a cross-country air mail race, with Lahr as pilot Rusty Krause. He played an incompetent mechanic who gets up in the air and cannot come down, thus winning the race. Smith, as his girlfriend Pansy Sparks, wants to fly with Rusty, but he turns her down, commenting, "Lindbergh wouldn't take his cat." She chases him offstage.

The next scene—Smith is not in it—contained what was considered a very risqué sequence. Rusty is having a medical examination for the flight. The doctor hands him a graduated glass for a urine sample. While the doctor turns to his desk, Rusty pulls a flask from his back pocket and measures three fingers of liquor into the glass. He staggers over to the doctor, hands it to him and says, "Here you are, boy. That's all I can spare." The writers had feared that it would be considered in bad taste, but instead it brought the house down, becoming the biggest laugh in the history of the stage. The laughter was clocked at sixty-two seconds. Reviewer Robert Littell wrote in the *World Telegram*: "George White's new musical is chiefly remarkable for three items, Bert Lahr, a fat girl named Kate Smith, and a very physical medical joke."

The *New York Times* review was unkind to Smith, while praising Lahr's comic talents: "In order to make Lahr's love life richly comic they have mated him with Kate Smith, whose proportions are mountainous and whose singing voice lacks that cathedral tone. 'Red Hot Chicago' she bellows in such volume that the orchestra swoons in despair. Collect all the brass instruments in New York and with one big invocation to 'Red Hot Chicago' she can blow all the men down."

Smith's big ballad in the show was "Without Love." It was passionate, it was rangy, it was gorgeous. Unfortunately, she never recorded it. She later vowed she would never sing any of the songs from that musical again, as it was the saddest time of her life. Her salary was $550 weekly, and she earned every penny of it in misery.

Bert Lahr made Smith's life miserable, but in her usual ladylike fashion, she was careful through the years not to mention his name. Despite what he had done to her, she did not want to say anything that might be damaging to his career—or libelous. When she cohosted the Mike Douglas television show for a week in May 1974, the subject came up. When Douglas asked Kate whether a musical comedy they were discussing was one in which she worked with Bert Lahr, she responded that it was. She said she had not intended to mention his name, but "he was not a person who kept things running smoothly." He resented other actors' getting any applause.

When Douglas asked how Lahr expressed his resentment, Smith explained that he would upstage her. Upstaging meant that Lahr would keep moving back, forcing her to turn the back of her head toward the audience. Stage hands tipped her off to go back with him, that when he hit the scenery he would have to stop. Smith added, "You know, he had a very powerful voice, with the 'hong-hong-hong' business, and he would do that at the end of my songs" to kill the applause. "And then he'd come off stage and use profanity at me as we came off, which hurt me very much because I thought it was so ungentlemanly."

John Lahr, Bert's son, wrote about this episode in his biography, *Notes on a Cowardly Lion*. Bert said that Smith's lack of experience grated on his professionalism. Born Irving Lahrheim in 1894, he was a veteran of burlesque and vaudeville, though he had performed on the Broadway stage for only two years. He admitted, "I was feeling my oats then," but said that Smith hurt many of his laughs. Lahr, by his son's admission, used coarse language and was a womanizer. His sordid affair with a woman named Rachel, while his wife was mentally ill, became a public scandal during tryouts in New Haven. This in itself must have embarrassed Smith. A few weeks after *Flying High* opened in Manhattan, Mercedes Lahr was committed to a sanitarium.

Lahr admitted to calling Smith "Etna" under his breath on the stage, an obvious reference to Italy's volcanic Mount Etna. He said: "Laughs are very sensitive and having been in burlesque I knew what to do and what I was contending with. Kate and I didn't work well together and she inadvertently hurt many laughs. She could have fed me lines much better." John Lahr writes that his father's comic moment "played on the buffoon's innocence in the face of experience."

It is said that the hour is darkest just before the dawn. A few weeks after *Flying High* opened, Smith received a telegram from the family physician saying that her father was desperately ill and advising her to come home. Bill Smith had been in failing health from diabetes and its complications for some time. According to Helena, he had disregarded his doctor's advice to avoid sweets. George White flatly denied Kate permission to leave, explaining that she had a contract and that the show would have to be cancelled if she left, resulting in a large financial loss. Apparently she did not have an understudy. So she stayed, leaving for Washington directly after the performance, but was too late; she drove up behind the hearse. She never forgave George White.

Smith's emotional nadir was reached one evening in the summer of 1930 when Granny and Grandpa Hanby came to see the show. Though she had pleaded with Lahr to go easy on her that one evening, he treated her more unmercifully than ever. Kathryn could see her grandparents in the front row, even with her blurry nearsightedness, embarrassed and refusing to join in the laughter at their granddaughter's expense. In her dressing room after the show, she burst into sobs as her grandfather implored her to leave the show as soon as possible. She explained that she was under contract and would have to remain until it closed, but that she would go home after that. It was a bitter disappointment to all of them that things went so miserably. Poor Kathryn had "half a moon"; she was singing on the stage, but she was utterly lacking in self-respect and personal happiness.

CHAPTER 2

The Moon Comes
Over the Mountain

A knock on Smith's dressing room door at the Apollo Theatre after an August performance of *Flying High* was to herald a reversal of her unhappy existence. The usher passed her a business card which read: "Ted Collins, Columbia Phonograph Company."

Turning the card over, she read the scribbled message "Important business." Weary and despondent, she feared it was just another man asking to take her to dinner to win a wager as to how much she could eat. Reluctantly, she agreed to see him, or so the story goes. She tore the card in half and threw it into the waste basket, an act she would later regret. It would have made such a nice souvenir of the occasion.

Smith was immediately disarmed by the man's friendly smile. Collins explained that he had missed the train to his home on Long Island and had come to see the show to pass time. He told Smith he was charmed by her singing voice: it had a glorious quality. He had to have been familiar with her, as she was a recording artist with his company. Perhaps he had not fully appreciated her until he saw her in a live performance. He implored her to meet with him at his office to discuss her records and her future in recording. They set the appointment for eleven A.M., and he left.

Smith arrived for her meeting with this Columbia A and R (Artists and Repertoire) man at the appointed hour. Collins told her he had been listening to her records, and he praised the clarity and richness of her voice. He assured her that she had a great future, not on the stage but in records and on the radio. They arranged a second meeting. It was then that Smith burst into tears and confessed to this understanding young Irish-American gentleman her misery in *Flying High*. She told Collins how unkind Bert Lahr was to her and how disappointed her family was with the turn her career had taken. Collins took her hand and assured her that he personally would go to the theatre and speak to the proper officials to see to it that things would be more to her liking for the duration of the play.

Ted Collins, as Smith averred many times over the years, was the first person to take a serious interest in her vocal talent. Somehow she sensed that she could place her trust in him. Their brief meeting after the show that hot summer evening was to prove fateful for both of them. Not only would Collins shape Smith's career, but her popularity would provide him with opportunities he never would have dreamed of without her. Collins became Smith's great mentor, her confidant, her closest friend, indeed her Svengali.

Joseph Martin Collins was born on Columbus Day, October 12, 1899. In a 1933 magazine interview he gave some details about his early years:

> What do you want to ask about me for? Kate Smith is your real story. I could tell you that I was born in New York on 46th Street between 8th and 9th Avenues. I could tell you that I used to chase fire engines as a kid. I could tell you that I graduated from college [Fordham, with a prelaw major] here in New York City. I could tell you that phonograph records were a lifelong hobby and as soon as I got out of college I started selling them and eventually got to be vice president of the company but what would all that mean? I'm here as the manager of an artist.

A 1944 article in *Coronet* casts further light on Collins's life. He grew up in the Hell's Kitchen section of Manhattan, attending Holy Cross parochial school, where he served as an altar boy for Father Francis Duffy of New York's "Fighting 69th" fame in the First World War. At age seventeen Collins joined the navy, serving aboard the transport *Henderson* hauling doughboys to France. After graduating from Fordham, he was hired by Columbia as a record salesman. He was promoted to sales manager at age 23, and several months later was made recording manager, the youngest in the company's history. (The Columbia Phonograph Company was established in 1888 and made its first disc records in 1901.)

How did young Joseph Martin acquire the nickname "Ted"? His father was a physician and had attended some of the Roosevelts. He greatly admired Theodore (Teddy) Roosevelt, so when he saw his young son walking sturdily, the way Teddy walked, he dubbed him "Little Ted" and the name stuck. Ted's mother was a Kelly, and he married a beautiful woman named Jeanette. In 1930 they had an eight-year-old daughter, Adelaide. Collins was 30 when he met Smith; she was 23.

Ted Collins was endowed with a full measure of both Irish wit and Irish temper. He could entertain people of all ages with stories and shenanigans. But when things did not go his way—or Kate Smith's way—he could come down with an iron fist. Take, for instance, his confrontation with Lahr. He threatened to report him to the Actors' Equity Association if he did not lay off Smith. He set his goals and let no one stand in the way of his achieving them.

Within a few weeks of his first meeting with Smith, Collins made a momentous decision. He could see nothing ahead but trouble for the record industry in the Depression. Radio, on the other hand, was free and was rapidly gaining popularity. And Kate Smith was a ready-made talent for that medium. He asked whether she would like him to be her personal manager. He explained that he would arrange her bookings, manage the finances, select the songs. They would divide the work, and the profits, equally. Smith said, "All right, it's a deal," and they shook hands. The partnership lasted for a third of a century—"on a handshake," as Smith proudly proclaimed. Collins said, "You do the singing and I'll fight the battles." He was shrewd when it came to finances. It was customary for a manager to take between ten and twenty percent of the profits, not fifty. But Smith thought Collins was worth it, and she proved to be correct.

For a time Collins retained his position with Columbia Records. He was involved with getting a new budget label, Clarion, off the ground when they first met. Smith introduced the Clarion Music Corporation's first song, "You'll Never Know, Sweetheart," over the entire Columbia network on September 22, 1930. She recorded it the next day, under Collins's supervision, with "Maybe It's Love" on the flip side.

Smith's first radio series was a weekly quarter-hour Columbia feature heard at 5:45 P.M. Mondays during the winter of 1930-31. She sang with Freddy Rich's Rhythm Kings. On the first show she rendered "Laughing at Life" and "Tell Him What's Happened to Me." But her most important radio stints that season were on the brand new "Rudy Vallée Fleischmann Sunshine Hour" over NBC. Collins knew Vallée and had offered to become his personal manager at one time. Vallée later asserted in one of his books that one of the greatest mistakes he ever made was turning down that offer. Vallée was the current heartthrob, and his musical variety hour was very popular, aired from the studios of WRCA each Thursday evening at eight o'clock. Collins arranged three guest spots for Smith on Vallée's show, the first being October 30. She sang three numbers: "My Baby Just Cares for Me," "Just a Little Closer," and that latest recording, "You'll Never Know, Sweetheart." Four days later she was on "The Roxy Gang Program," singing Irving Berlin's "Who's Calling You Sweetheart Tonight?" She also guest-starred on the popular "Ludwig Baumann Hour."

While still starring in *Flying High,* Smith began an engagement at New York's prestigious Capitol Theatre on November 8, her third return engagement there in four months. With a seating capacity of 5,300, the Capitol was New York's largest theatre. Then on January 19, 1931, she opened at the coveted Palace, singing with Harry Richman's fine orchestra. This time she was not at the bottom of the bill. Two weeks later she headlined at the Earle, along with comedian Joe E. Brown. Her reviews were uniformly favorable. *Flying High* closed on January 3 after 357 performances. Her official reason for leaving the show as it went on the road was "a salary dispute." Charlotte Greenwood replaced her. When the musical was made into a movie, Greenwood played opposite Lahr, though the role was considerably altered.

Smith's second appearance on the "Vallée Hour" was January 8. Vallée tried to persuade her to sing her big ballad from *Flying High*, but she steadfastly refused. Vallée said, "To hear her sing 'Without Love' is to forget that the song was ever sung by anyone else." Actually Harry Richman's vocal recording of the number is a fine second best. Listening to Richman's powerful voice, one can imagine how Smith's rendition must have sounded. Vallée himself refused to sing the song, yielding to Smith's thrilling delivery. *Flying High* had completed its New York run just five days earlier, to Smith's great relief. She did sing four numbers on "The Sunshine Hour," including "(You) You're Driving Me Crazy," which would become a popular standard.

Kate Smith was the first artist to make a return appearance on "The Ludwig Baumann Hour." It was in response to thousands of letters, and it was at an annual ball at the Astor Hotel. She wore a sleeveless gown and sang on this broadcast benefit to equip city hospitals with radios for shut-ins.

Radio was still a relatively new communications medium in 1931. The first radio station of any consequence was Pittsburgh's KDKA, which began operations by broadcasting the 1920 presidential election returns. Other independent stations came onto the dial in the early twenties, and many are still going strong. There was no such thing as a network of stations until November 17, 1926, when the National Broadcasting Company was formed, with young David Sarnoff as its president. William S. Paley owned two stations: WCAU in his home city of Philadelphia and WABC in New York. In 1927 Paley decided to give NBC some competition, so he formed the Columbia Broadcasting System on September 9. These fledgling networks did not have many stations, and they did not extend from coast to coast. Both had their flagship stations in New York City. NBC's was WRCA (for the affiliated Radio Corporation of America) and CBS's was WABC (for Atlantic Broadcasting Company). In the radio guides of the day, each station carrying a particular program was listed, not the network.

Kate Smith "arrived" in radio early in 1931. The first "Kate Smith Sings" program was on March 17 (not May 1, as has frequently been reported), and it was on NBC, not CBS. The hour was 11:30 P.M., an hour when orchestras otherwise dominated the dial. Smith had taken a brief vacation back home in Washington and had had her tonsils removed. Ted Collins called her early in March to tell her he had arranged for her to have her very own singing program, thanks largely to her reception on the Rudy Vallée shows. NBC would see how she went over from week to week. She opened that St. Patrick's Day show with what would be her perennial theme song, "When the Moon Comes Over the Mountain." She had written part of the lyrics as a poem when a girl. Collins had composer Harry Woods write the melody and Howard Johnson add the verse. Woods had written such hit tunes as "Paddlin' Madeline Home," "When the Red-Red Robin Comes Bob-Bob-Bobbin' Along," "I'm Looking Over a Four-Leaf Clover," and "Side by Side." Curiously, the famous composer was born without a left hand; he would play the melody with his right hand and add a bass harmony line with his left wrist. The song became one of the major hits of the year.

> When the moon comes over the mountain
> Ev'ry beam brings a dream, dear, of you.
> Once again we stroll 'neath the mountain
> Through that rose-covered valley we knew.
>   Each day is gray and dreary,
>   But the night is bright and cheery.
> When the moon comes over the mountain
> I'm alone with my mem'ries of you.*

Smith's program was advertised as one of diverse song types: hillbilly songs, southern spirituals, and pop tunes. Collins selected an Irish classic of John McCormack's for this occasion: "A Little Town in Old County Down." Smith was introduced as the Song Bird of the South.

Smith's third and last appearance on the "Fleischmann Sunshine Hour" was on April 9, 1931. She sang Irish tenor Morton Downey's new hit ballad "Wabash Moon," a silly novelty called "(Hi-Hi-Hi) Just a Crazy Song," and the heartfelt "By the River Ste. Marie." Vallée claimed to his dying day (which was just sixteen days after Smith died) that he discovered Kate Smith by giving her her radio debut. A few years later their prime time variety hours would be pitted against each other on rival networks, with Smith's eventually forcing Vallée's off the air. Such was the competition of network radio, just as it is today with television.

Smith returned to the Capitol Theatre to give four performances daily for a week early in April. She was so enthusiastically received that the engagement was extended for eight more weeks, setting a longevity record. Ted Collins invited Bill Paley, along with a few more Columbia network executives, to take in one of Smith's stage shows. Paley loved her, as Collins expected he would. He asked Paley what he thought of putting her on his network. Since Paley had set aside the hour between 7 and 8 P.M. for promising new musical talent, he was more than happy to give Smith a spot and thought it was a splendid idea. At the moment the 7:45–8:00 P.M. spot was available.

An item in the entertainment sections of the New York newspapers announced on April 22 that Kate Smith had a one-year contract with CBS and would begin broadcasting for them on Sunday, April 26. This came as a surprise to the folks over at NBC, which caused Ted Collins no end of glee. All NBC would do was to continue her late-night show on a week-by-week basis. Now they had lost her to the opposition.

Smith replaced Morton Downey in that time slot. Downey had acquired a sponsor (Camel cigarettes) and was moving to the 7 P.M. time slot, opposite NBC's enormously popular "Amos 'n' Andy" program. Smith would now be heard over fifty-six stations, as opposed to the fifteen stations that picked up her NBC program.

Ted Collins saw this as Kate's big chance to succeed "on the airialto" as the radio waves were glamorously called in those early days. He suggested she continue with the same theme song and open each show with a simple "Hello everybody" and close with "Thanks for list'nin' and goodbye, folks." He hired a small studio orchestra fronted by Nat Brusiloff. Brusiloff also hailed from Washington, D.C., and had worked with Smith in her amateur days. When his orchestra was playing at Le Paradis there, Smith was his featured singer on several occasions. He also played a hot violin. This was a sustaining show (not sponsored) so CBS was willing to spring for only a seven-piece orchestra. Collins financed eight additional musicians. And what musicians they were. Smith later took pride in reciting the roster: trumpeter Bunny Berigan (later famous for his rendition of "I Can't Get Started"), trombonist Tommy Dorsey and his clarinet-playing brother Jimmy, Charlie Margulis on trumpet, drummer Johnny Williams, trombonist Jack Lacey, ace guitarist Eddie Lang, pianist Jack Miller. Smith's weekly salary was a whopping fifty dollars.

On that fateful Sunday evening Collins had arranged for a taxi to bring Smith from the Capitol Theatre, after her next-to-last show for the day, to the WABC studio. As the time approached she experienced a case of mike fright, she later admitted, because she realized the importance of this particular debut. As the red light went on at precisely 7:45, she stepped to the mike and sang a few bars of "When the Moon Comes Over the Mountain," said "Hello everybody" slowly, and introduced her first song, "Dream a Little Dream of Me." She then went into "By the River Ste. Marie," followed by a lively number, "Please Don't Talk About Me When I'm Gone," ending with a blockbuster rendition of "I Surrender Dear." She said, "Thanks for list'nin' and goodbye, folks," and sang a bit of her theme song again. As the "On the Air" light went out at 7:59:30, she breathed a sigh of relief. She turned to Collins and asked how she had done. He beamed and said simply, "Swell." Now the telephone switchboard began to light up. One of the first callers was Smith's mother, long distance from Washington. She told her daughter that she sounded "just swell" (*swell* was a popular word in those days) and that she, Granny and Grandpa Hanby, and sister Helene were all so proud of her. Fan mail began arriving Tuesday, to Smith's surprise and Collins's delight. The broadcasts had exceeded all expectations.

Following the special Sunday debut of "Kate Smith Sings" on CBS, Smith's regular broadcast days were Monday, Wednesday, Thursday, and Saturday. Soon two more days were added, and on May 24 she followed Morton Downey to the 7 o'clock spot, opposite "Amos 'n' Andy." It was a tough challenge, as "Amos 'n' Andy" was so popular that movie theatres stopped the picture to broadcast the program to their audiences. But Smith made inroads, and Paley and company were pleased.

NOT ONLY WAS SMITH SUCCEEDING in her career; her personal life had taken a turn for the better too. She was now earning enough—from her stage shows, not the radio programs—to lease a three-room apartment on the fourteenth floor of an exclusive Park Avenue hotel. Her address was 10 Park Avenue. Her living room furniture was eighteenth-century mahogany with English chintz fabric. She was enjoying robust health while weighing in at 215 pounds. She stood 5'10" tall, and her somewhat wavy auburn hair was very fine and hard to manage.

Because she was quite nearsighted, Smith wore glasses, except in public. She was sometimes taken for being "high hat" or snooty when she would pass somebody she knew without speaking. Arthur Tracy, the popular Street Singer of the thirties, reported that she had snubbed him at the radio station back then, or at least he thought she had. A few weeks later they were both playing in Syracuse when he called her on it. Both his party and hers were dining at the same restaurant one evening. He walked over to her table and asked why she had not spoken to him. Had he somehow offended her? She did not recall seeing him and explained her extreme myopia, apologizing for the apparent snub.

Smith had lovely white teeth, which she retained all her life. Perhaps part of her secret was that she had seven toothbrushes, one for each day of the week. She kept them in a sterilizer in the bathroom.

Smith's apartment was aptly described as a penthouse. She always had a maid/cook because with her busy schedule she did not have time for such chores. As much as she liked to cook, she seldom indulged in it, contrary to her public image. She loved sweets, as the world knows; she was in fact addicted to them. Chocolate ice cream sodas were her favorite. She neither drank alcoholic beverages nor smoked and took the best care of her precious vocal cords, having regular checkups with a throat specialist. Her vocal cords were very small, like Enrico Caruso's.

For relaxation Smith liked to play tennis and golf in the summer and enjoyed ice skating, skiing, and bobsledding in the winter. She loved attending sports events, whether basketball, football, baseball, or ice hockey. Collins was an avid sportsman, so she had many such opportunities. She loved swimming and speedboating, and she often drove to the Collins home in Neponset on Long Island in her LaSalle convertible coupe. She stayed with Collins's family for extended periods during those summers, which sometimes put Collins in an awkward position, being torn between the demands of his wife and his principal artiste. They lived two miles east of Rockaway Beach.

At home Smith enjoyed playing backgammon and card games with "the girls." Although her reading was largely confined to newspapers, magazines, fan mail, and radio scripts, she also found time to read novels in the late evening. She never lounged around in a kimono, but got fully dressed and corseted upon rising. In her dressing room at the theatre or studio, she wore a favorite smock. She kept that good luck smock for many years.

Kate Smith had little concern about money, nor much understanding of its management. She invested in government bonds and left most of the bill-paying to Collins and her business managers. Although she was not a spendthrift, she never deprived herself or her family of anything they might need. She really did not care how many millions she had, as long as she had enough to live comfortably.

Smith was not a jewelry collector. In 1931 she owned just four pieces: two large diamond rings and two broad diamond bracelets, all of which she bought herself.

What would Smith have liked that she did not have? In a 1932 newspaper interview she said, "I'd like to own a house, with a garden and a lake, a motor cruiser, and have a husband, a girl and a boy." Before the decade ended she would have all of these material possessions, though never a family of her own.

THE SONG BIRD OF THE SOUTH was such a hit in radio that in July 1931 she made her television debut. NBC had opened an experimental television station in July 1930. Not content to be outdone by the rival network, William S. Paley advised CBS to do likewise. On July 21, 1931, CBS made its television debut a gala occasion. Mayor Walker officially opened the station, whose call letters were W2XAB. Sportscaster Ted Husing was master of ceremonies. Composer George Gershwin played "Liza," the Boswell

Sisters sang "Heebie Jeebies," the Mills Brothers performed, and Kate Smith sang "When the Moon Comes Over the Mountain" and "Please Don't Talk About Me When I'm Gone." The program lasted forty-five minutes: from 10 to 10:45 P.M.

The primitive studio was on the top floor of the Columbia Building. The press described it as a "2×4 room," and in reality its dimensions were only 10 feet square. Smith said she felt embarrassed singing to a little red light and decided she would stick with radio for the time being. One writer quipped, "How Kate Smith, together with her accompanist, the announcer and two or three executives ever got into the miniature studio will remain a mystery forever." The studio was in total darkness except for a two-foot square of light. Smith remarked, "It was so hot I was swimming when I came out." Shortly afterwards she was seen eating a dish of chocolate ice cream.

The entire program was supposedly filmed, but this historic piece of film has disappeared. By the end of the year the networks were televising several hours a week—to an audience of dozens. The New York World's Fair of 1939 gave television a big boost. Then came the Second World War and progress was deferred for the duration.

The next day, July 22, Kate Smith was named Queen of the Air and Rudy Vallée was named King, in a ceremony conducted by Mayor Walker on the city hall steps. This came as a result of a radio popularity poll conducted by the *New York Mirror*. The radio critics selected her as their favorite in a poll conducted by critic Jack Foster in the *New York World-Telegram.*

On August 1, 1931, Smith began a record-breaking singing engagement at the famed Palace Theatre, thrilled to be replacing "the great Ethel Merman," as she called her. Merman was experiencing voice problems and needed a rest. The two contraltos had a mutual admiration, though they never shared the same stage. Day after day, show after show, Smith packed the Palace. Her run was held over again and again, for a record eleven weeks, at the end of which comedian Eddie Cantor presented her with a large loving cup. The previous record of ten weeks was held by comedian Lou Holtz; Smith's would not be exceeded for two decades, and then by Judy Garland. Smith is supposed to have remarked, "Judy lasted longer but I never missed a performance." A valid point.

Entertainment columnist Ed Sullivan attended Smith's opening show at the Palace, writing, "This is the first time I have ever heard Kate Smith sing in person and she is disappointing. . . . Her voice is just so-so." Two months later he retracted that statement, reporting, "For the first time since I heard her sing, Kate Smith actually sold me a vocal bill of goods. . . . I'll withdraw my original and deprecatory remarks and bend low in a sweeping apology. She can sing a song for my money." File that remark for future reference.

In years to come, whenever Smith's record-breaking engagement at the Palace was brought up by an interviewer, she would "correct" her interrogator, saying, "No, honey, it was fourteen weeks," or "Oh, no, I was there for sixteen straight weeks." Each time the duration grew a bit longer in her mind.

After four months as a sustaining program, "Kate Smith Sings" acquired a sponsor in September. The Congress Cigar Company of Philadelphia, owned by Bill Paley and his father Sam, signed a two-year contract to advertise its brand of cigars, LaPalina. Although Smith herself never delivered the commercials, her association with the product greatly boosted sales. It was said that one of her avid lady fans had even taken up cigar smoking. Smith was amused when reminiscing about her first sponsor many years later. She remarked, "I never smoked a cigar; I never even smoked a cigarette." Her salary increased to a handsome $1,500 per week. A young crooner named Bing Crosby succeeded Kate in the 7 P.M. sustaining time slot. Soon he also had a cigar sponsor, Cremo.

At this time many Kate Smith fan clubs were being formed by admirers with the encouragement of her cigar sponsor. Elaborate Kate Smith–LaPalina Club charters, signed by Kate, were printed and given to each new group, which was assigned an official number. Smith announced the chartering of each club over the air. LaPalina also sent pictures of their star to those who requested them.

Smith's quarter hour was now followed by Arthur Tracy, known as the Street Singer. Tracy's was a more formal show, with his theme song being "Marta (Rambling Rose of the Wildwood)." Tracy recalled one of his early programs that left a lasting impression on him both mentally and physically. On this evening Kate Smith was "holding court"—that is, gabbing with some of the crew—after her program, while he anxiously waited to get before the microphone. As there was only half a minute between shows, time was of the essence. He rushed in so fast that he banged his forehead into the microphone support, sustaining a painful and bloody gash. Now the show must go on, but at the commercial break crew members ran to him with handkerchiefs to sop up the blood. His impression of Smith as a person was that "She was peculiar, very heady." Tracy and Smith had minor roles in the Paramount feature picture *The Big Broadcast* in 1932. Incidentally, "Kate Smith Sings" was now heard at 8:30 P.M. with "The Street Singer" at 8:45.

When a magazine writer asked Smith what she did with all her money, she responded:

> I live on the comparatively small amount it takes to run a modest apartment, to pay for the services of a maid and a chauffeur, and my two secretaries. I like clothes and jewelry, but I think the simpler a fat woman dresses, the better. I own only four pieces of jewelry: a wrist watch, a ring,

a brooch, and a necklace. I own a roadster—I adore driving fast!—and a rowboat on a little creek on Long Island. I spend various amounts for my own personal charity, helping people in the vicinity of New York who really need help.

From the beginning Smith took her fan mail seriously. She was touched to think that people would trouble themselves to write to a radio voice. She tried to read every letter and answer them herself. Before long it became impossible, but even when she turned over many replies to her secretaries, she would make notes on the cards and letters indicating the nature of her response. The secretaries simply formalized her replies. There were many requests for money, both from those down-and-out and from those who hoped she would be a soft touch. Collins hired an investigator to check out certain requests. If he found them to be legitimate, Smith often made a donation to the petitioner.

In addition to these acts of charity, Smith found time to visit hospitals several times a week to bring some cheer to the patients. There were those who would insist that she did it to get publicity, but in reality she was as unobtrusive about it as possible. She remembered her months in nurse's training and had a soft spot in her heart for the infirm, especially war veterans. She once told me, "You know, Richard, I was to go into medicine, but the Good Lord had a different plan for me. He wanted me to use my voice to bring happiness to people." She considered her many hospital visits divinely ordained. It was part of her way of thanking God for her blessings.

After Smith had been broadcasting for the better part of a year and had become a genuine star, she was asked by the press how she was enjoying her fame. She admitted that despite the fact that Collins was "fighting the battles," her life was not without its burdens and pressures. Those who had snubbed her when she was relatively unknown now courted her friendship. Some months before she had her own radio program, she went to the office of a well-known music publisher on Tin Pan Alley seeking some songs to sing. The publisher told her he had nothing for her, that he could not waste his time on singers who might get into radio. Smith was humiliated. A year later that same publisher walked up to her in the WABC studio, asked how she was, then inquired as to her mother's health. Smith flushed, her eyes flashed, and she replied, "What do you care? My mother never asks for you." She cut him dead; now it was he who was humiliated. And she refused to sing any of his songs, to his great dismay.

Another problem the Song Bird was having was the theft of items of her clothing. Once when she sang at the Ambassador Hotel in Atlantic City, she laid her coat on a chair while she stopped to write a few penny post cards. When she went to pick it up, it was gone. A few days later a letter arrived at the studio explaining the mystery. It was from a man who signed it simply "An Admirer." He said he had been watching her for hours, looking for a chance to snag something of hers. He wrote, "I'm a loyal fan and I hope you won't be angry, but it was I who swiped your coat—and I'm going to keep it." That sort of fan was not appreciated.

The record industry was feeling the crunch of the economic depression. Smith remained with Columbia through mid–1932 and made some very unusual records during her first year on the radio. For instance, she recorded "When the Moon Comes Over the Mountain" twice in the summer of 1931, each time using her spoken introduction, "Hel-lo everybody, this is Kate Smith." She also used it on "I Don't Know Why" and never again. She was recording both on the 35¢ and the 75¢ Columbia labels. Often the same songs would be released on Harmony, Velvet Tone, Diva, and Clarion labels, sometimes with different takes. One example was "Shine On Harvest Moon," coupled with "I Apologize." But the maroon Harmony label gives the vocalist's name as Ruth Brown, not Kate Smith with her "Swanee Music." Perhaps an exclusive deal had been made with a chain of department stores to market the disc, so the name was changed for contractual reasons. At any rate, that record is a rare collector's item. Smith laughed at her *nom de disc* years later when bandleader Paul Whiteman asked her about it. In December 1931 she made a record with Guy Lombardo and his Royal Canadians: "River, Stay 'Way from My Door"/"Too Late." She also recorded "River" with her "Swanee Music" on the Clarion label.

Early in 1932 Smith interpolated a lovely chorus of "Blues in My Heart" into the middle of her recording of "Between the Devil and the Deep Blue Sea," with no indication of it on the label. About that time she took part in Columbia's first ten-inch "longer play" record, lasting about four minutes per side rather than the usual three. Each side contained a medley of three songs from a current hit musical. She sang the first song on each side. Her pianist, Jack Miller, a first rate vocalist in his own right, sang the last song. The smooth dance band was conducted by Ben Selvin. Her last record for the Columbia Phonograph Company, made May 12, 1932, was the first of a short series of five twelve-inch 78s. Titled "Kate Smith Presents a Memory Program," it plays like a miniature radio program, complete with opening and closing signatures and Smith introducing each of the four old-timers, including the favorite "Grandfather's Clock." At the end she mentions "my good friend Ted Lewis," whose band was on the flip side, featuring jazz legend Muggsy Spanier. That record brings a small fortune in the collectors' market.

Not long after Smith had completed her eleventh week at the Palace, Collins signed her for thirty-nine weeks with the various RKO theatres in the New York City area. Her starting salary was $3,000 weekly, working up to $5,400 per week. This, in addition to her $1,500 weekly salary for the LaPalina radio series, made her the highest paid radio personality.

On February 7, 1932, Smith sang "River, Stay 'Way from My Door" on Columbia's "Hello Europe" program, heard throughout the British Isles. Coincidentally, during the night the rain that had been causing Ireland's Shannon River to overflow had stopped. Skies cleared and valley dwellers were able to return home.

On April 12 Smith made her nightclub debut at the ultrachic Central Park Casino. Again she replaced Ethel Merman, singing with Eddie Duchin's society orchestra. Her contract was for five weeks. It was at this time that Collins formed a corporation called Kated (Kate-Ted), with himself as president and Smith as vice president. When owner Sidney Solomon tried to cheat Smith out of $5,500 in salary, Kated successfully sued him.

Smith celebrated her first anniversary on the radio (not counting her unsuccessful NBC program) on April 26 by singing the same four songs she had sung on her first show. She would continue this tradition for years to come.

On July 31 Smith's vaudeville production, *The Swanee Revue,* opened at the Palace. By now even the Palace was being affected by the Depression and on July 16 had begun showing movies. In addition to Smith's songs, the program included Cliff "Ukulele Ike" Edwards (who was also under Collins's personal management), dancer June Preiser, pianist Jack Miller, and conductor Nat Brusiloff. They gave six shows daily, with Smith's salary being $7,500 weekly. The next day she had the thrill of being made an honorary chief of the New York Fire Department.

Along with all this stage work, "Kate Smith Sings" continued on the air every Monday through Thursday at 8:30 P.M. Smith combined songs old and new, devoting Wednesdays to memory songs, which had proven popular with listeners. It is no wonder that with this rigorous schedule coupled with her hospital visits and other charity performances, she developed a nagging cold and laryngitis that September. Her doctor told her she had bronchitis verging on pneumonia and that she must rest. He ordered her to retreat to either a hot, dry climate or to a locale where the air was clear and cold. She cancelled a scheduled engagement at the Hippodrome in Baltimore and ventured some 250 miles north to the Adirondack Mountains, discovering the peaceful village of Lake Placid.

Lake Placid was a sleepy little town nestled in a picturesque location. It was built around two lakes, the smaller Mirror Lake and the much larger Lake Placid, with its three sizable islands. Looming above the lakes, only eight miles distant, was Whiteface Mountain, 4,876 feet high. The village had received worldwide fame the previous winter as the site of the 1932 Winter Olympics, at which Norwegian-born figure skater Sonja Henie had won a gold medal for the United States. (In 1980 it would again host the Winter Olympics, with Eric Heiden winning five gold medals.) The clean air, blue skies, and deep snow make it an ideal resort for skiing and skating. Summer tourists flock there for boating, water skiing, swimming, golf, tennis, and hiking. Smith fell in love with the area immediately.

Smith did not go alone. She took her mother, Collins and his wife, and the entire radio orchestra. She stayed at the plush and exclusive Lake Placid Club. The radio broadcasts continued, with Collins as announcer. Smith's rest was a relative thing. She sang at Lake Placid's charity ball, as did Jack Miller. The folks at nearby Saranac Lake had asked her to sing there too, but she turned them down. After all, she was supposed to be resting her vocal cords. They were understandably miffed.

Collins rescheduled Smith's week at the Hippodrome, and her mother and grandparents came to see her there. But the laryngitis persisted, and her physician ordered her back to Lake Placid for two more weeks of "R and R." Again her mother joined her, this time bringing along a pair of skis.

CHAPTER 3

Kate Goes Hollywood

Hollywood was eager to cash in on the radio boom of the early thirties, as financially hard-hit families opted to stay home and be entertained by the free medium coming into their parlors, rather than spend money at the movies. The hope of the movie studios was that radio fans would clamor to see what the people behind those faceless voices looked like on the screen.

Kate Smith had already made several movie short subjects when she was approached by Paramount to appear in a feature film. She had made a Vitaphone short in 1929 that was released in 1930. Titled "Kate Smith, the Song Bird of the South," the short is set in a drawing room. The Vitaphone catalog's description of item #817 reads: "A couplet of red hot songs from a red hot momma with a red hot voice. Kate Smith puts over her numbers—and how! In her first appearance on Broadway she stopped the show the opening night of Eddie Dowling's *Honeymoon Lane*. If a Vitaphone act could take encores you'd have to play this one all night." The songs she sang were the lovely "Carolina Moon" and a rousing "Bless You, Sister." The sound was recorded on a disc and synchronized with the silent picture.

In the spring of 1932, Smith appeared in the final scene of the first short in a series, also for Warner Bros. The series was called "Rambling Round Radio Row." Others in this short included comedian Sid Garry, bandleader Abe Lyman, the talented singing Boswell Sisters (Martha, Connie, and Vet), and comedians Stoopnagle and Budd. Smith's scene opens in her apartment with bandleader Nat Brusiloff and pianist Jack Miller anxiously awaiting her arrival to rehearse a new song for the Casino show. She appears at the door, having been horseback riding. Brusiloff asks her if she is reducing. Her good-natured retort is "No, but the horse is." Her song is the lively "Whistle and Blow Your Blues Away," written by Carmen Lombardo. After singing it, she asks Miller what time it is. When he replies, "8:20," she says, "Come on, we have a program to do," and the three of them make a hasty exit.

Soon after this short, Smith appeared in a Paramount "pictorial" containing three segments. In the first a naturalist does a show-and-tell with several animals of the Gobi Desert. The second shows autumn foliage (in glowing black-and-white). The third segment is titled "Ted Collins: Star-Maker" and opens with Collins seated at his desk. He makes a few comments about being a personal manager, walks over to what seems to be a portrait of Ukulele Ike, then the portrait comes to life and Cliff Edwards croons a little number with his uke. Collins shows a picture of singer/pianist Jack Miller, then picks up an autographed picture of his newest discovery, Kate Smith. Whereupon Smith appears in the doorway wearing a flowered dress and wide-brimmed hat. They engage in a little small talk, then she sings a chorus of a song dedicated to firemen (near and dear to her heart) called "When Work Is Through," accompanied by Jack Miller. After a few bars of her theme song, the pictorial ends.

In the summer of 1932, Paramount Pictures produced *The Big Broadcast,* with an all-star cast from radio. The 78-minute black-and-white film was an important picture, not only for its box-office success but also because it featured Bing Crosby in his first starring role. Costarred was Stu Erwin as the owner of a radio station. Leila Hyams and Sharon Lynne were the romantic interests. To save Erwin's station from financial ruin, Bing (as himself) agrees to star in a blockbuster special called "The Big Broadcast." Other big names in the picture are George Burns and Gracie Allen, the Boswell Sisters, the Mills Brothers, Vincent Lopez and his orchestra, Arthur Tracy, vocalist Donald Novis, Cab Calloway and his orchestra, and Kate Smith.

Smith's four-minute cameo was filmed at Paramount's Astoria studio in Queens. As she sings a few bars of her theme song, announcer William Brenton introduces her: "And now, ladies and gentlemen, we take great pleasure in presenting the greatest name in radio, the Song Bird of the South with her Swanee Music, your own Kate Smith, and here she is." Smith's song is the lovely and powerful Freed-Barris ballad, "It Was So Beautiful," which she had introduced at the Brooklyn Paramount Theatre. Oddly enough, she did not record it commercially until 1964, and then in a gently swinging arrangement. Ruth Etting did record it, and Frances Langford's picture appears on the sheet music. Bing Crosby's big hit from the picture was "Please." When he does a disappearing act and the finale of "The Big Broadcast" is about to take place without him, Stu Erwin decides to use a copy of Crosby's record of the song. He experiences all manner of difficulty in finding the record and getting it to the station. While the orchestra vamps in Crosby's absence, Erwin puts the record on the turntable. Alas, it is impossibly warped, so Erwin rushes to the mike and attempts to do an imitation of Bing, which is way off key. Crosby appears just in time to save the program, and everyone lives happily ever after.

Another Crosby song which appears from time to time in the picture is the lamentation "Here Lies Love," also sung nicely by the Street Singer early on. Smith sang it in a Paramount short subject released a year later.

Following the success of *The Big Broadcast,* Paramount was eager to engage several of the radio stars to make their own feature films, including Kate Smith. Fannie Hurst, a highly regarded author, wrote the story for Smith's movie, which was to be called *Moon Song.* The title was later changed to *Hello Everybody!* Smith agreed, Collins signed the papers, and the entourage departed for Hollywood on the midnight train on November 7, 1932. It would be Smith's first visit to the fabled movie capital, and she was thrilled and excited at the prospect. She thoroughly enjoyed the trip across the heartland of America, although Hollywood itself frightened her. Everything about it was foreign to her experience. Although Thanksgiving was not far away, the grass was green, flowers were blooming, and the orange and lemon trees were laden with fruit. And everything was so lavish. Though she was with Ted and Jeanette Collins, Smith became terribly homesick. In truth, she was so sickened by the phoniness of Hollywood that she took to her bed at the Ambassador Hotel for three days with a fever. Only when Collins told her that he, she, and Jeanette were going to look at a house to rent did she revive. The house was in swanky Beverly Hills, an elegant home with tennis courts, a swimming pool, and well-manicured lawns; it was owned by silent movie comedian Monty Blue.

The making of the film was hard work, involving long days and much waiting around. A typical day's work on the set would commence at 8 A.M. and last until 5 P.M. On broadcast days Smith would have to quit at 2:30 P.M. in order to rehearse for her radio program, which was broadcast from KNX, the famous station on the Paramount lot. It would be the first time that she was heard west of the Rockies in her own show.

Smith's contract called for Paramount to pay the $3,600 weekly to wire her programs to the East Coast, a heavy drain on the picture's budget. After the broadcast they would look at the day's rushes. Many parts of the picture were filmed at the Lasky Ranch in the valley, and it was those days that Smith enjoyed most. Her costars were handsome young Randolph Scott and glamorous Sally Blane, sister of Loretta Young. Charley Grapewin played the dependable farmhand Jed. Sally Blane's principal recollection nearly sixty years later was that Smith came on like Gang-busters and did not fit in at all with the Hollywood actors. She told me that Collins catered to her every desire and that, in her opinion, they were in love. She said that Smith was quite a good actress, in view of the fact that she never had a lesson. Blane recalled Randy Scott fondly, saying that he was a true Southern gentleman. In the picture she and Scott were lovers.

The picture itself has taken more than its share of criticism over the years. Smith herself called it corny. Actually its plot was way ahead of its time. A large power company wants to buy all the privately owned farmland in a northern California valley to build a vast hydroelectric plant. Smith leads the farmers' battle to retain their land. A fortuitous thing happens to her: she is called on to sing on a propaganda radio show put on by the company (they are trying to sweeten her up). Ted Collins, an important radio executive, just happens to catch the program back east in New York. He sends a telegram to Smith saying he liked her singing and would she come to New York for an audition? She ponders the move and prays about it. She decides to go, thinking of the money the farmers need to fight their court battle. She becomes a big success and ends up agreeing to pay half of the extra cost to move the project to another valley. So again everyone lives happily ever after (except the folks in the other valley), and Smith gets to sing some songs for the folks in the theatres.

Kate Smith plays Kate Smith, a buxom farm girl, with Sally Blane cast in the role of her slender, sexy sister Lily. Julia Swayne Gordon plays their rather pathetic mother, who is confined to a wheelchair. Randolph Scott, later a star of many Westerns, plays Hunt Blake, an agent of the power company sent to sweet-talk Smith into giving in. She becomes sweet on Hunt, only to discover him in an embrace with sister Lily. This occasions her lament, "Moon Song," one of the best songs in the picture. She also gets to sing the lilting and catchy "Twenty Million People" a couple of times. She reprises "Moon Song" in a scene on stage at the Central Park Casino, followed by a chorus of "Dinah" with a very memorable shot of her dancing the Charleston and running off stage. (Collins put a stop to that, deciding that it was more of an exhibition than anything else, and that it was unbecoming to a heavy-set young woman.)

Smith's other songs were the saccharine "My Queen of Lullaby Land," a cute but, in retrospect, offensive novelty called "Pickaninnies' Heaven," and "Out in the Great Open Spaces," the tune Collins hears her sing on the power company's program. Ted Collins has a minor part as Smith's manager and announcer on the fictitious Nationwide Broadcasting System (NBS, a perfect hybrid of NBC and CBS). The five original songs were composed by Arthur Johnston and Sam Coslow. It was their first collaboration for a motion picture score. Smith recorded all except the forgotten "Out in the Great Open Spaces" on Brunswick records the following February, with Victor Young's orchestra. Nat Brusiloff is seen conducting in the Casino scene. Young Edith Head designed the dresses.

The commercial success of the song "Moon Song" more than compensated for the financial loss suffered by Paramount in producing the picture. Filming was completed early in January and the picture was rushed into release, premiering at New York's Paramount Theatre on January 27, 1933. (The stage show that accompanied it featured comedians Willie and

Eugene Howard.) Reviews were mixed. According to the *New York Telegram:*

> It's all Kate Smith, and goodness knows, there's enough to go 'round and 'round and 'round. So if you're one of the millions—count 'em, millions—who tune in the radio wren's melodic efforts with moons and mountains, here's your chance to get an eyeful as well as an earful. But regarded as motion picture entertainment rather than a Kate Smith sideshow, there is less virtuosity in the piece itself, than in the star's practically continuous warbling. The plot is as antiquated as *East Lynne* and just as heavy with saccharine hokum. It is actually a relief when they forget about the story line and let Kate sing—even about "Mammy."

In the opinion of the *New York Sun:*

> The voluminous Kate Smith, fresh from networks and personal appearances, is presented in her first talkie at the Paramount. . . . It may be classified as slightly better than the usual first picture of a radio star. . . . Miss Smith's is a cut better than most, which still, unfortunately, leaves it an unimportant little program talkie. . . . The genial and excellent crooner—she really has a pleasant, if unimportant natural singing voice— must have been difficult to cast. Were producers to cast her as the large lady in the old custard pie comedies who went through such delicate and intricate situations as sliding down steps? Or as stopping pies? No, this could not be when Miss Smith's crooning demanded something more dignified. Thus Paramount has hooked her up to the highly prevalent themes of power companies and farm relief. . . .

In the important *New York Times* review we read:

> The picture is obviously designed for those special admirers who never tire of hearing Miss Smith describe the moon coming over the mountain. As such it is completely successful. The old songs are in it, and some new ones. Miss Smith gives an amiable portrait of Miss Smith, happily avoiding the more strenuous phases of dramatic expression. . . .
>
> On the sentimental side of *Hello Everybody*, its lyric heroine is made to illustrate the idea that nobody loves a fat girl. Although Kate loses her heart to a dashing young man from the city, she gallantly resigns when she discovers he is really interested in her more attractive sister. Thereafter she pours her heart out in her songs and lives vicariously in the happiness of others.

Finally, in the *Los Angeles Times* (the picture had also premiered at the United Artists Theatre there), Philip K. Scheuer concluded:

> Charles Grapewin is the most able of the cast, as Jed, a farm hand. The photography is nice, but there is nothing else about *Hello Everybody* to indicate that it could not have been made when singing talkies were a novelty.

The WOR nostalgia king, Joe Franklin, asked Smith in a 1968 radio interview what she thought of the picture. Her instant reply was, "Oh, it was terrible as far as I was concerned. . . . I went out to [Hollywood] to do a picture and, oh, it was horrible . . . it was a mess. I was so homesick for the East I couldn't wait to go back home again. I really didn't enjoy motion pictures. I thought it was a terrible picture. That's why I never made any more." After a short pause she added, "I wasn't asked!"

In her 1938 autobiography Smith wrote at some length about her Hollywood experience. Although she tried to make it sound glamorous, her basic honesty came through and her unhappiness was apparent. The happiest times were when her mother and sister surprised her by arriving to spend Christmas with her. Collins had undoubtedly arranged it. Given a few days off from filming, Smith was able to drive down the coast with them to the Mexican resort town of Aguascalientes, as well as to Palm Springs. They took a boat ride to Catalina Island and then traveled to the winter sports resort of Lake Arrowhead.

In a 1938 magazine story titled "No More Pictures!" Collins revealed that Smith had been offered a singing part in a picture at $15,000 a week but that he had turned it down. He admitted that they had erred in doing *Hello Everybody!* and asserted that "the best actress can be ruined by a slipshod production and a weak story."

Smith's voice was first heard from Hollywood on November 14, 1932, emanating from KNX. On her December 28 program she introduced three songs from the picture, with Collins doing the announcing. Al Jolson was set to introduce "Pickaninnies' Heaven," but he deferred out of professional courtesy to Smith. On several of those broadcasts she interviewed other actors and actresses in the picture. One evening she was to do a brief interview with a ten year-old extra. The lad spied the CBS microphone and froze, bursting into tears and burying his head in his mother's lap. After a moment of stunned silence, Collins stepped up to the mike and spoke, in a high-pitched voice, "Thank you, Aunt Kate. We're glad to have you in Hollywood and we hope you'll come again soon."

Smith and the Collinses arrived back in New York on January 9. Two days later she was on the air introducing a patriotic song called "Buy American," which was "dedicated to the future prosperity of the United States." The slogan was adopted by the Hearst newspapers in an effort to speed the return of prosperity. Smith pledged to sing the song on every program for the next twelve weeks. Six years later she would be singing another patriotic song on every program for over sixty weeks.

Rehearsals were taking place for performances of Kate Smith's Swanee Revue, which opened at the Paramount Theatre in New York City on January 20, a week before *Hello Everybody!* opened there.

Smith and Collins had plans to observe their second anniversary on the Columbia network May 2, 1933. Collins had prepared a congratulatory speech to read in place of the LaPalina commercial, but the sponsor balked. Collins handed them an ultimatum: "Either I pre-empt the commercial or you get yourself another announcer." The announcer that evening and for five months thereafter was young Ken Roberts, who would later be famous for the Blue Coal commercials on "The Shadow," among other things. When I questioned him about this incident he did not recall it, although he remembered well being Smith's announcer. It was quite a feather in his cap, since she was so popular. He did recall asking her to sing a particular favorite of his: "Without Love," from *Flying High*. Her curt reply was a firm refusal.

Smith often did answer song requests on the air. On August 10, 1933, she announced that somebody had asked for the oldie "Any Rags, Any Bones, Any Bottles?" but that they were unable to locate the music for it. Thirty-nine people sent in the music, with Grandpa Hanby's arriving first—Special Delivery.

There were several significant changes in "Kate Smith Sings" effective with the September 14 broadcast. The two-year contract with LaPalina Cigars had expired and the program was done on a sustaining basis. Collins returned as announcer. The show was now broadcast west of the Rockies, over a total of sixty-five stations in the network. Then on September 26 Jack Miller replaced Nat Brusiloff as conductor/arranger. Brusiloff had suddenly quit, even though Collins was paying for seven additional musicians. One report was that Collins and Brusiloff had had an altercation and Collins had fired Brusiloff. Another simply stated that Brusiloff was going to work for another artist. The first is the more likely story.

Because of Jack Miller's importance in the story of Kate Smith, it is worth presenting a brief sketch of maestro Miller. He was born in the Dorchester section of Boston on September 4, 1895, of Irish ancestry. Although an accomplished pianist, his talent came naturally; he never took a piano lesson. He did study musical composition, however. After the First World War, he formed a band. He discovered, quite by accident, that he was a pretty decent singer and eventually made records for Columbia. On one "Special Record" on the Metro-Goldwyn-Mayer label, "made exclusively for MGM theatres," Smith sings "Waiting at the End of the Road" on one side, and Miller sings "How Am I to Know?" on the other. Then there was their joint effort on the two recorded show medleys in 1932. Miller had his own fifteen-minute singing show on the Columbia network until October 1933, when he gave it up at the same time Smith's show ended, so that they both could go on the road with the *Swanee Revue*. In the summer of 1936 Miller resumed singing, while conducting the orchestra, as a summer replacement during Smith's vacation.

On Wednesday, October 11, 1933, Kate Smith went classical for an evening. She was invited to sing with the Philadelphia Orchestra, conducted by Leopold Stokowski. There was a gala dinner, held in the grand ballroom of the City of Brotherly Love's Bellevue Stratford Hotel. George Jessel served as toastmaster. Violinist Efrem Zimbalist and composer Deems Taylor participated in the evening's entertainment, as well as Secretary of the Treasury William H. Woodin, who played guitar with Stokowski. And there was Kate Smith, Song Bird of the South, clad in a becoming green gown.

During the afternoon rehearsal a couple of amusing things happened. As the orchestra began to play "When the Moon Comes Over the Mountain," Smith interrupted, telling them that it was entirely too stiff. She hummed a few bars and the arrangement was loosened up. Then she asked Maestro Stokowski to whistle the beginning of her big aria, "My Heart at Thy Sweet Voice," from the Saint-Saëns opera *Samson and Delilah.* Stokowski was astonished that she could not read music and had never had a singing lesson. He gave her a bit of advice, saying, "God gave you that voice. Don't let anyone change it." At one point during the actual performance, Smith subconsciously began to direct the symphony orchestra. Stokowski gave her a menacing look and the audience of six hundred invited guests gasped.

To sing her theme song, Smith leaned against the grand piano, which was piled high with greenbacks. The occasion was a benefit performance to raise funds to rescue the orchestra from the financial doldrums. It raised $1,500.

Smith's performance of that operatic aria was very well received, prompting her to sing it on her next broadcast. Surprisingly, she had sung it on the air the previous June, immediately followed by the rather irreverent "It Don't Mean a Thing (If It Ain't Got That Swing)." She probably did that for utter contrast and to assure her listeners that she was not going highbrow. She would continue to sing an occasional classical selection for the next year, one of her favorites being "O Promise Me."

SMITH'S SUSTAINING RADIO SERIES ENDED October 31. Ted Collins had another idea for her—an exciting one indeed. He thought it was time for her to take to the road and entertain as many of her twenty million fans as possible in person by touring many American cities with a vaudeville show. He put together an expanded version of the *Swanee Revue* that had played at the Palace. All told, the road company included fifty people.

Jack Miller would conduct the orchestra from coast to coast. Hilda Cole was press agent. Tony Gale was arranger and pianist, Steve Evans did impersonations of various pop characters, Don Cumming was the comedian, and there were the Seven Reillys, a tap-dancing family. Smith's personal secretary, Jane Tompkins, went along, too. She later recalled that ventriloquist Edgar Bergen and comedian Bob Hope were also in that troupe. The tour, originally slated for several weeks, proved so popular that it was extended to eight months. It was a grind, as each day's work involved four or five separate hour-long performances.

The troupe traveled by train, reserving three special cars. The *Swanee Revue* played in scores of large cities including Baltimore, Washington, Philadelphia, Boston, Buffalo, Indianapolis, Columbus, Des Moines, Sioux City, Louisville, Memphis, Dallas, and El Paso. Everywhere the entertainers went they were greeted with multitudes of floral pieces, proclamations, keys to cities, delegations from charitable organizations, and large, eager audiences.

In each and every city Smith took time to send postcards to family and friends, including a fourteen-year-old fan in DuBoistown, Pennsylvania, named Bessie Phillips. Bessie saved all those post cards. One said simply "Regards from Memphis, K.S.," another "Love from Houston, Kate," a third, from San Antonio, "I'm still travellin', K.S." It was "Best regards from Waco, K.S.," and a similar message from Fort Worth. They were only penny post cards, but the fact that the Song Bird remembered was worth a million dollars to young Bessie, and who knows how many others. Smith never forgot her devoted fans, although she preferred to call them friends.

Each performance of the vaudeville show opened with the band playing a rousing "Marching Along Togther." Then came Don Cumming with his lariat-twirling and storytelling, followed by Steve Evans's impersonations, then the Reilly children. Finally Smith stepped on stage, always to cheers, whistles, and wild applause. She sang a mix of old and new songs, ending with her song and dance routine to "Dinah," which never failed to surprise and amuse the audiences.

After each day's final performance there was a routine backstage. Smith's maid, Maria, would have her bathrobe ready so she could change and shower. After an alcohol rubdown from Maria, she would don street clothes and she and the Collinses would wind down for a time before retiring in the wee small hours of the morning. Eventually the grind would take its toll on Smith.

After she had played frigid Milwaukee in the dead of winter, Smith's throat problems came to a head in Omaha. She had been treated by eight different throat specialists to no avail. One evening the pain was so great that she asked Collins to reduce her part in the show. He eliminated her emcee duties and cut down the number of her songs. She walked onstage to the customary thunder of applause and sang "Did You Ever See a Dream Walking?" one of the top tunes of the day. Next was "A Shanty in Old Shanty Town," one of her most popular tunes during the tour. It was then that her voice cracked. She apologized and rushed offstage.

Smith sobbed hysterically, fearing that her career was ruined. Collins took her aside, reassuring her that everything would be all right. He told her that she would be able to return to do her closing number and that the entire staff was depending on her. Following the tap-dancing Reilly family, she ran out on stage and commented to the audience, "Folks, those frogs will get into your throat sometimes." They laughed and applauded her courage. Then she went into "When the Moon Comes Over the Mountain," which was followed by a tumultuous ovation.

Soon after that episode Collins announced that Smith would take a two-week vacation at a well-known resort in Hot Springs, Arkansas. The Collinses and Smith arrived February 18 and stayed in apartments in a bungalow adjoining the Mountain Valley Hotel. The main building contained fifty rooms with twenty-six bedrooms.

Unfortunately, the day after they arrived the hotel burned to the ground. Smith lost most of her luggage in the fire, as their bungalow also burned. Not one to miss an opportunity, she salvaged her camera and took pictures of the blaze. Some of her pictures appeared in the local paper, which pleased her greatly. Fortunately, there were no deaths or serious injuries.

Smith enjoyed the respite from the grueling tour; she watched race horses and the spring training of a professional baseball team that included such notables as Rogers Hornsby and Dizzy Dean. They left Hot Springs on March 1 to resume the vaudeville tour in Indianapolis.

It was springtime and troupe members sweltered in Tucson and Phoenix; they "killed 'em" in Los Angeles, Long Beach, and San Francisco. Then it was north to Portland, and finally to Seattle, where the whirlwind tour ended and the troupe disbanded. It was a sad parting, as such things always must be, but the immediate Kate Smith party were able to journey eastward at a leisurely pace, after taking a week's rest at the Banff Springs Hotel in the Canadian Rockies. They reached New York on June 19.

CHAPTER 4

Living in a Great Big Way

It was the middle thirties and Kate Smith was indeed living in a great big way. Her radio programs were thriving and prospering, and she was a true star. Her success enabled her to give generously to the needy, too, both financially and in personal appearances. And she was able to live an elegant, though uncomplicated, lifestyle.

The Smiths of Washington were very good friends with the Klinges (pronounced Cling). Mrs. Minerva Klinge, a woman of fifty or so, was invited to spend ten days with Kathryn Smith in New York in May 1933. Affectionately known as "Aunt Minnie," Klinge kept detailed diaries, not only of this visit but also of four others during the next few years. Through the generosity of her daughter, Kathryn (Klinge) Christie, who gave me her mother's diaries, we are enabled to peek into the private life of Kate Smith in that first exciting decade of her radio career.

Minerva Klinge traveled to New York on the Colonial, a streamline train, arriving at 7:45 P.M. Wednesday, May 3, 1933. We read from her diary:

> Well, here I am, all safe and sound. Kathryn met me and we drove to her apartment. Had a light lunch, as she had planned an early dinner. The day before, they celebrated her [26th] birthday at the studio, and she had an immense chocolate and vanilla cake: 3 tiers, 5 layers each. She had brought a piece home, so we had some of it. I then rested and we chatted until dinner.
>
> Mr. Collins came to dinner and he is fine—I like him immensely. You look for a man in his profession to be excited, but not him, very calm. Jack Miller came in later and K. and he went through a short rehearsal, after which they left for the studio. I remained at home, as I had had enough excitement for one day. Before her program came on, I wrote a letter to my [daughter] Kathryn, and while I am waiting for her return will describe her apartment.
>
> It is located on the 19th floor of a large apartment house on Park Ave.— a beautiful corner—three immense big windows in the living room—one in the bedroom—one in the kitchen (casement windows) with Venetian

blinds. Gorgeous drapes. The living room is entered from the entrance hall, three steps down, 17×25 feet — with a real built-in fireplace in one corner, with electric logs, andirons, etc. Over it hangs a lovely painting of Kathryn — her desk in another corner — grand piano in another — and the other corner is the entrance. Her divan is green figured silk tapestry, an immense chair to match, large loose pillows — Cogswell chair — exquisite coffee table and two beautiful end tables and radio. Pillows everywhere and lamps, five gorgeous ones in this room. On the piano she has a genuine rose quartz lamp with a hand-embroidered shade.

The room is so beautiful, as is the bedroom, which is green and peach color — twin beds with satin bedspreads embroidered in peach, with a large pillow to match. On each bed is a Lenzi doll, dressed in organdy. Gorgeous colors in the two shades cover the entire top of the beds — about 15 other pillows scattered about on cedar chest and easy chair and slipper chair. Chairs are covered with peach and green silk moire, peach silk voile casement curtains with green silk overdrapes.

Then the dinette-galley: gate-leg table and odd chairs — beautiful lamps — Chinese rugs. Kitchen and bathroom the latest in everything.

Kathryn was gone about an hour, and in the meantime I heard her voice over the radio — when the bell rang and there she was. It is raining, in fact a real storm with lightning and thunder. Kathryn brought the papers and we read and chatted until 12 o'clock. Then "Mother Bear" and "Baby Bear" went to the kitchen to see what we could find to eat. We were not really hungry but just a habit. We had such a grand dinner. Menu was:

Creamed pea soup
Prime roast beef — Potatoes — Creamed onions
Endive salad — Hot biscuits
Birthday cake and coffee

Everything tasted so good. You can readily see that Freda, the cook, knows her business. After our midnight lunch of crackers and anchovy paste we went to bed. Oh, what a bed. How good it felt after such a strenuous day.

On Saturday evening, May 6, Smith and Klinge went to the theatre to see one of the season's smash hits. Klinge recorded the evening in her diary:

[At 6 o'clock] we dressed to go see the musical comedy, *Strike Me Pink*. It has been here for months and still carries a crowded house. It was swell. Good music, good dancing, and pretty girls. Jimmy Durante and Lupe Velez take leading parts and they were swell. Some risqué things are pulled off. Girls in dancing costumes. The orchestra was conducted by Al Goodman, who is on the air with Will Rogers. As soon as we entered we had seats in the first row orchestra. The leader of the orchestra recognized Kate and leaned over to shake hands and ask how she felt after her recent sick spell. [She had had foot surgery, as infection and possible blood poisoning had set in from calluses caused by dancing.] Then others recognized her. Even when Jimmy Durante came out he would stand in front of Kate and smile at her and raise his hat. Lupe Velez blew her kisses and winked an eye as if to say "Hello." She was adorable, very pretty. Eddie Garr, a young man Kate had in her Revue, takes a prominent part. Hal LeRoy is great in tap-dancing. During intermission several young ladies came and asked her to autograph their programs.

After the show we had a chocolate milk shake, then walked a block to Times Square, and then I saw it in all its glory of electric lights, thousands and thousands of them. ... It has stopped raining and the streets are crowded—never saw so many people in my whole life. Everybody is well dressed and they look like they are having a good time. Took a taxi for home after a wonderful evening that I will never forget.

The following Thursday, May 11, the two women headed for the Kated offices at 1619 Broadway:

> On the 20th floor of a large office building is where all of Kathryn's fan mail and her business affairs are handled. She has two secretaries, whom I met. The main office is in a beautiful corner room with four large windows, two overlooking Central Park and the other two over the Hudson, where I could plainly see where all the [ocean] liners come in. Beautifully furnished, but best of all are the large silver cups that K. has been presented at different times for breaking records in theatres, and some when she was chosen Queen of the Air. Pictures of her all about, all framed alike, and many other gifts presented her by famous people. We spent almost two hours there, then went to a store where Kathryn bought my Kathryn a fountain pen, after which we took a cab home. When we reached there we were good and hungry and the dinner was thoroughly enjoyed by all. Menu:
>
>
>
> Tomato juice cocktail
> Roast pork with baked beans
> Combination salad—Sliced tomatoes
> Hot biscuits
> Sponge cake with hot chocolate fudge sauce
> Coffee—Nuts
>
>
>
> After dinner Jack Miller, her pianist, came in to rehearse a few songs, then off to the studio again. In honor of Mother's Day she sang "My Mom" and "My Queen of Lullaby Land." It made me a little homesick, but not for long.

Aunt Minnie was having the time of her life. Smith took her to see the new Radio City, even though it was part of NBC, the other network. They went to the top of the Empire State Building, then the world's tallest building, which opened to the public May 1, 1931. They went to the movies twice, took a bus tour of the city, and of course Klinge got to attend one of Smith's broadcasts:

> After dinner we changed our dresses and then for a real thrill. We left about 7:30 for the broadcasting studio as Kath wanted to rehearse for a

while with her orchestra. I went into the room, sat about ten feet away from the mike. They worked hard for about thirty minutes, then they were all set. When 8:30 approached you could have heard a pin dropped. The production manager is standing by the clock, arms raised. All eyes are on him. When 8:30 comes he drops his arms and Kate raises her hand as a signal for her orchestra to play the "Moon Song" ["When the Moon Comes Over the Mountain"] and then the program continues. It was a queer feeling, sitting there listening, as I had hundreds of times on the air, seeing her there before me, and knowing that all the folks at home were listening in also. Tears filled my eyes, and I would look at her and she would smile.

Well, it was just marvelous. Not a word spoken, only what is heard on the air. When 8:45 comes everyone draws a long breath. They are off the air. Then remarks are passed about the program among each other and then it's over. Jack Miller took us home and while [we were] waiting at the curb for his car, two policemen kept people from asking for autographs. "Such is the price of fame."

"KATE SMITH SINGS" RETURNED TO THE AIRWAVES July 16, 1934, complete with a new theme song, "Time to Dream." Although it was a very pleasant melody, Smith's listeners urged her to return to "When the Moon Comes Over the Mountain," which she eventually did. Smith's voice had a new vibrant quality now, which she attributed to the fact that she had met so many of her "friends" face-to-face through the *Swanee Revue* and she knew they loved her. After all, hadn't she been made an honorary Texas Ranger in Dallas by Governor "Ma" Ferguson herself? And wasn't she an honorary member of the Winnebago Tribe of Sioux Indians, with the name "Glory of the Morn"? And hadn't the *Swanee Revue* played to sellout crowds for sixteen weeks out of the thirty-two? Kate had a newfound confidence. And sponsors? They were clamoring for her program: Camel cigarettes, Vicks Vaporub, Sunshine Biscuits, LaFrance, and Fletcher's Castoria.

Bill Paley was aware of all of Smith's success. After all, he and Ted Collins were in regular communication. But Paley had a new idea. He wanted to bolster the daytime listening audience. He suggested to Collins that CBS hire Smith for a noncommercial afternoon hour on Wednesdays. She would pioneer a daytime variety hour. "The Kate Smith Matinee" went on the air September 12. It featured a comedy-mystery serial story with character actor Parker Fennelly, who would later become famous as Titus Moody, the New Hampshire hick of Fred Allen's Alley. There were a few songs by Smith and by Cliff Edwards. A human interest feature and a personality in the news were included, and a remote visit to a distant location completed the variety show. Bob Trout was the announcer.

There were sports figures, including Babe Ruth and Dizzy Dean; there were rodeo riders, artists, hillbilly singers, a town crier, and a visit to the zoo. It was a big show at an unlikely hour. The network allowed Collins much flexibility, so he employed his flair for originality and Smith became a skillful interviewer. One of the most memorable features was the man-on-the-street interview.

Meanwhile Smith's evening song programs continued, expanded to thirty minutes; a vocal trio called the Three Colonels was also added. In December she acquired a new sponsor, the Hudson Motor Car Company. The prime time show was entitled "Kate Smith's New Star Revue," as each week a talent contest was conducted in a different city and a promising new star would be given a debut. There was a 35-piece orchestra, and Smith's salary was $4,900 weekly. The show was due to premiere Christmas Eve, but for a few days it was touch-and-go whether Smith would be well enough, because she was again suffering from a grippe cold, bronchitis, and incipient pneumonia. She rallied, however, and the show went on as scheduled. Guests were comedians Pick and Pat and baritone James Melton. A highlight was Smith's rendition of "Silent Night."

On the New Year's Eve show Smith sang the Cole Porter sensation, "Night and Day." The Three Colonels were now the Three Ambassadors, a trio of young men from California. There was also a female vocal trio, the Wallace Sisters. Smith was advertising the 1935 Hudson and Terraplane, all the while driving a Lincoln Phaeton.

Each week the show was broadcast from the city in which the talent contest was conducted, an excellent advertising gimmick. The cities included Boston, Philadelphia, Rochester (New York), Akron, Pittsburgh, Cleveland, Columbus, Detroit, and Des Moines. By the end of March, however, it was decided to forgo the amateur contests in favor of more comedy. Apparently the novelty had worn thin. The series ended May 27, to be succeeded just three days later by a full-hour variety show.

It was 8:00 Thursday evening, and "The Kate Smith Hour" was for the first time—but not the last—pitted against NBC's "Rudy Vallée Hour." Although not sponsored, it was a high budget production and a successful competitor. On the Fourth of July all the stops were pulled out. There was a thirty-minute drama of the signing of the Declaration of Independence. There was a two-minute fireworks display (on radio) by using sound effects, with Smith urging folks not to use them because of the danger. Guests were Irish wrestling champion Dan O'Mahoney and swimming champ Annette Gellerman. The August 1 show was done live from Waikiki Beach, Hawaii, with Smith in the surf in an outrigger canoe. That week a new female trio, Three Little Words, replaced the Wallace Sisters.

KATE SMITH WAS OFTEN DESCRIBED AS "the big lady with the big heart." We have already mentioned her frequent visits to veterans' hospitals. She never forgot singing for the servicemen during the First World War, and she always had a soft spot for them, especially those who returned from the "war to end all wars" with debilitating injuries. Routinely, she would dedicate a song to vets in a particular hospital or sanitarium, to a group of orphan children, or to a shut-in.

On her way to Hollywood to film *Hello Everybody!* Smith stopped in Chicago for two hours to visit a seventeen-year-old boy who had been blinded in a bomb explosion. Once she drove from Lake Placid to Poughkeepsie to drop in on a boy in a respirator, a victim of infantile paralysis. She spent Saturday evening and Sunday afternoon with him and even persuaded two aviators to fly over the hospital for his amusement.

When the *Swanee Revue* played in Richmond, Virginia, she put on a show sponsored by the Rotary Club to raise money for undernourished children. The show raised $7,000, every penny of which was turned over to the Rotarians. Smith paid the troupe out of her own pocket. She supported four orphans in a home in Brooklyn and sent barrels of groceries to depression-starved families in the greater New York City area.

In 1934 Smith was named Chairman of the National NRA Committee of Radio, Stage and Screen. This was a position of importance in that it gave her a unique opportunity to aid in relieving the effects of the Great Depression. (The R of NRA stood for Recovery, not Rifle.) The committee's goals were to assist voluntary cooperation of business and industry in price control, while encouraging collective bargaining to raise workers' wages. Its symbol was the Blue Eagle, with the motto "We Do Our Part." Blue Eagle stickers appeared everywhere, on food and clothing, in shop windows, on cars, in homes. The success of the National Recovery Administration is debatable, however, and when the act was declared unconstitutional by the Supreme Court in May 1935, the Blue Eagle was dead.

BESSIE PHILLIPS, THE TEENAGE FAN from Pennsylvania, and Kate Smith kept up a correspondence over a five-year period. In the summer of 1935, Bessie, now sixteen years of age, had her fondest dream come true. She got to meet her idol in person. Fifty years later she recalled the event:

> Two ladies were friends of my mom's family. They both lived in Brooklyn. They were Emma and Mame but I called them Aunt Emma and Aunt Mame. . . . They used to come to the farm every summer to see the Ryan family. . . .
> In July they took me back with them. After a few days Aunt Mame said, "How would you like to go and visit Kate Smith?" The first thing I thought of was the pretty little organdy dress that my mom had bought for the trip. She said, "I've already contacted them." She must have called the studio office. In those days they didn't have any audiences, but they said it was all right for me to come. They told Aunt Mame where to bring me.

We went in and Kate was already in there. She showed us where to sit. She greeted me very warmly. Oh, she was so precious. She told us to take a seat and hoped we'd enjoy the broadcast. She was on only fifteen minutes at that time. I sat there looking at her, not believing I was in the presence of that great woman. She would look over when she was singing and she would wink at me and smile. And oh, this little girl's heart just went pi-ti-pat!

After the program she introduced me to Jack Miller, her orchestra leader, and to Ted Collins, and we visited a while. I had an autograph book and she wrote in that for me. We talked a bit and then she took us down in the elevator. I can remember two or three men going down at the same time. I was rather shy but I wished I could throw my arms around her and kiss her goodbye. There she was towering way above me. She was so big, tall, and beautiful. We got off the elevator and she just put her arms around me and literally lifted me off the floor and gave me a big kiss and a big bear hug! She thanked me for coming and said if I ever came back to feel free to come again, and to keep writing to her. She didn't need to tell me that.

IN SEPTEMBER 1935, MINNIE KLINGE and her teenage daughter visited Smith for a few days. When Smith had to leave them to go on a publicity tour for her new sponsor, the Great Atlantic and Pacific Tea Company, better known as A & P, Klinge received a letter from her, as she noted in her diary:

> I received a letter from Kathryn from Detroit and she said "just to let you know I am thinking of you." . . . She wrote us of her experiences in one day in Detroit, such a busy day one wonders how she can stand it. She left Monday at 7:30 P.M. and arrived in Detroit at 8:30 A.M. Tuesday, was met by a committee from A & P Company, cameramen and reporters. Then to the Book-Cadillac Hotel for breakfast. After that to the City Hall to meet the mayor (for the second time). Then to traffic court, as they broadcast the trials every day and she gave her opinion of the broadcast to the listeners. Then back to the hotel for a press luncheon. From there to WGY where she was interviewed on the air for fifteen minutes. And at 2:00 was in the A & P factory meeting the Detroit officials of the company, who escorted her through the entire plant. Then to the Masonic Temple to rehearse for the evening's affairs—then back to the hotel for a dinner given in her honor to meet the directors and their wives. Then she went to her suite of rooms and dressed for the concert. They received her with a great ovation and she sang in all eight songs. She had with her Jack Miller's orchestra and "Three Little Words." She said the girls made a hit also. Then back to the hotel to bed. What a strenuous day. . . . Imagine anyone putting in a day as busy as that and then to have the patience to write such a nice long letter. Today is another busy day for her, as she is going through the same routine for the A & P Company located in Boston.

A great Kate Smith gala was held at Madison Square Garden on Wednesday, September 30, 1935. The sensational promotional extravaganza was organized by A & P to publicize Smith's association with them. The Garden was packed to capacity, with many celebrities attending. Smith wrote to Aunt Minnie an enthusiastic description of this memorable event:

> Those A & P people have run me nearly ragged. Of course to begin with was the big affair at Madison Square Garden. Well all the people came that they predicted would come, and then some more. The Garden was packed to capacity (over 25,000 people) and they had to turn away over 5,000 more I understand. They were there to meet me face to face and welcome me into the A & P Family. Really I was never so thrilled as that before, I consider that affair the Crowning Event of my career so far. I'm so sorry that you all weren't able to be present. It was simply marvelous. The Garden was decorated in thousands of flags, banners, and huge "WELCOME KATE SMITH" streamers. The stage was all light green curtains and of course the huge replica of an A & P store front. There was a 36 piece orchestra on stage with Jack Miller conducting, they played for all the acts and for the dancing afterwards. The stage show started at 9:00 P.M. and was in two parts. The first half consisted of 6 very fine vaudeville acts and also a line of "Danny Dare Dancers" (6 girls and 6 boys) and they were excellent. Then the second half was presided over by me. My part included "The Three Little Words," "The Three Ambassadors," "The Three Wallace Sisters" and Katie herself. It ran 1 hour (I mean my part of the show). Also we had the Baer-Louis fight pictures for them and during the evening I introduced such Guest Celebrities as: Jack Dempsey, Al Roth, Toni Canzinari, Jimmie Braddock, Babe Ruth, and Vinnie Richards (the tennis champ). Vinnie and I autographed 4 dozen tennis balls and hit them out into the audience and the person getting the ball with a RED A & P marked on it also came up on the stage and received the tennis racket. There were many glowing speeches about me also by the different executives and the President of the A & P stores (Mr. John Hartford) presented me with a huge bunch of 6 dz American Beauties about 5 feet tall. They were simply glorious and in handing them to me he said, "Kate we sincerely hope that you will learn to love the A & P Family as much as they love and adore you," etc. I also received two large baskets and another bouquet on the same night. The stage show was over at 11:30 and from then on they danced until 1:00 A.M. It was a marvelous night and one that I'll never forget as long as I live. It was the first time a thing like that has ever been done for a celebrity and is probably the last, for only a huge concern like the A & P Company could afford to have a thing like that. They spent $30,000.00 for that one evening's entertainment. I am having Jane Tompkins send you (under separate cover) one of the lovely programs of the affair. Then the next night came the first broadcast, and I received four large boxes, two baskets of flowers and a corsage of 4 deep purple orchids with lilies-of-the-valley. That night right after the broadcast I had to attend a dinner given for me at the Waldorf-Astoria Hotel by Mr. Freeley (the Pres. of the American Coffee Co.) who are sponsoring the program. It was very grand and there were 24 guests in all. So that about winds up the A & P News up to date. By-the-way how have you liked the shows? You know all comments are cheerfully received. I am going out to Chicago the 18th of this month for them, will be there for a week during which time I will go out to the Edward Hines Hospital and put on

a show for the boys. Then the 18th of November I go to Pittsburgh for them to have the same kind of party as Detroit, Boston, New York, Chicago and also Philadelphia. They are talking about having me go down to New Orleans for them too. But at this time it isn't definite. They are going to put out in their stores a KATE SMITH NEWS also. I saw the first copy of it and it sure is cute. It will be on the counters for their customers. So much for A & P.

"Kate Smith's A & P Coffee Time" went on the air each Tuesday, Wednesday, and Thursday at 7:30 P.M., opposite NBC's "Lum and Abner." As before, she sang the top tunes of the day as well as "souvenir songs," as she called the oldies. She was advertising A & P's three brands of coffee: Bokar, Eight O'Clock, and Red Circle. She was doing it so well that sales were up 25 percent by the end of the year.

November 9, 1935, was another important day in the life of America's Song Bird. She appeared on the annual American Red Cross Program, "Red Cross Roll Call." The First Lady, Eleanor Roosevelt, was on it from Washington. Smith sang and was inducted into the Canteen Corps of the Red Cross by Chairman Cary T. Grayson.

That same month Ed Sullivan wrote about her in his "Broadway" column:

> Kate Smith [is worth] $900,000. Kate, withdrawing from every vestige of Broadway nightlife and romance, because her size has made her sensitive, finds the only outlet for her bottled-up emotion in welfare work. Other girls have husbands and families. Denied both, she has found a substitute. ... At Hartford, Connecticut, in a driving rainstorm, she slipped in the back door of a hospital to comfort a dying boy, and stayed with him until daylight. His parents had wired her that the youngster idolized her. She refused to pose for pictures. The next day the Hartford paper berated her, claiming that she was too high-hat to pose with the Mayor of the city. If she poses for pictures, she's roasted; if she doesn't pose she's roasted. Sometimes she thinks the world is a little crazy.

Collins now came up with another idea. Harking back to the success of Smith's sustaining evening variety hours of the previous summer, he decided he would like to see her return to that format for the 1936-37 radio season. CBS officials thought it might work, so they had Collins test the waters with a special on March 15. There was no need to "beware the Ides," as the show was an unqualified success. What nobody in the radio audience knew was that Smith had fallen down a whole flight of stairs just a few minutes before air time. She was shaken up, naturally, but uninjured, except for a sleeve of her gown and a heel of her shoe.

Four studios were used for this spectacular. At the outset Smith asked the audience to refrain from applauding. Collins engaged an impressive array of guests, including singer Dick Powell, comedian Bob "Bazooka"

Burns, Harry Reser's popular "Clicquot Club Eskimos" orchestra, Eva LaGallienne, Harry Horlick's Gypsies, baritone James Melton, "The Goldbergs," and Doc Rockwell. Ted Husing was the announcer. The next day one columnist said the whole town was raving over her show and that it had made the opposition sound like amateurs. (The opposition was "Major Bowes' Amateur Hour"!)

There were a couple of persistent rumors about Smith at this time. One was that she was going to make another movie, this time with child star Shirley Temple. It was not true. The other rumor was that she was looking for a new theme song and liked English composer-bandleader Jack Hylton's composition "She Shall Have Music." He denied permission.

Smith's thrice weekly quarter-hour "A & P Coffee Time" shows continued into the summer of 1936. On May 21 she wrote a letter to Bessie Phillips, the teenage fan from Pennsylvania, to say that she would be in New York through June and into the first week of July. She ended the letter with "I hope you do get your trip to New York again this year. It will be nice seeing you again." Bessie would be seventeen on July 6.

Not long after school let out for the summer, Bessie went to New York, this time traveling with her brother and his fiancée. She had written Smith to tell her they were coming and when. Smith wrote back and said to present her letter at the desk and they would be let in. There were still no audiences, so they were the only ones there.

Again there was the lovable, warm greeting and she sat them down. This time Bessie took one of her scrapbooks for Smith to write a note in. "After she was through singing," Bessie reminisced, "she wanted us to go with her to [the CBS commissary] where the stars went. She wanted to know if I could drink a chocolate ice cream soda. I said, 'You bet.'"

Smith told Bessie that if she went to the Kated office, Jane Tompkins, her secretary (with whom Bessie had also become a pen pal), would be there and would give her some items for her scrapbooks. Bessie said, "Did she ever! That's where I got a scrapbook of nothing but 8"×10" glossies. And then she gave me a great big one—it must have been nearly three feet high. It was just packed full of clippings, of her different concerts, of news items." Bessie was overwhelmed by this generosity. She just knew the kids in her little Kate Smith club back home would never believe it all, especially the *two* ice cream sodas she had with Kate Smith.

Kathryn Smith, Ted and Jeanette Collins, and their daughter Adelaide spent part of their summer vacation that year in the Canadian Rockies and part of it at Lake Placid. August was divided between business and pleasure, as the new hour-long "Kate Smith A & P Bandwagon" was slated to debut September 17. This was to be the name of Smith's variety hour, again opposite Rudy Vallée's variety hour on NBC: 8 o'clock Thursdays.

The three LeBrun Sisters of Rochester, New York, would be regulars, along with the Three Ambassadors male singing trio. Babe Ruth, newly retired from baseball, was to be a regular, too, doing a weekly comedy sketch with Smith. In rehearsals for the opening show, Smith and the Babe rehearsed singing "I'm an Old Cowhand," but the song turned out "Ruthless" on the air. There would be a segment in each show in which Smith would present a $500 reward to a person of great courage. Smith's big song on the premiere broadcast was the lovely new "These Foolish Things Remind Me of You."

On the December 3 show Smith missed a song cue because she was startled by an explosion and left the stage to investigate it. It was a rubbish fire below the stage. The next week the All-Collegiate Football Awards were presented for the first time. It was Collins's idea, and he was joined by Fordham coach "Sleepy" Jim Crowley. It became an annual tradition that was still strong at the time of this writing, with Bob Hope presenting the awards on a television special.

On January 14, 1937, Smith began to collect celebrity autographs, her first being from guest star Walter Huston. She had a golden opportunity, what with her star-studded show, and before long her book was filled with now-valuable signatures and notes.

One of the best remembered features of the "Bandwagon" is Smith's interview with champions. She became known as the "champion champion-finder." Each week she would interview someone who had set some sort of record, and some were truly far out. Her guests included a champion bridge player, ice skaters, aviators Jimmy Doolittle and Eddie Rickenbacker, the Olympic bobsled champion, pine tree choppers from Idaho, boxing champ James Braddock, a speed typing champ, a grade school speller, gliding champ Richard C. duPont, billiards champ Willie Hoppe, and tennis champion Bill Tilden.

Minerva Klinge visited her famous young friend Kate Smith for three weeks in April of 1937. This time they visited St. Patrick's Cathedral, went to the circus at Madison Square Garden, took the Radio City tour again, saw a rehearsal of the Fred Allen program "Town Hall Tonight," went on Smith's annual spring shopping spree to Macy's, took a Sunday drive to Long Island in her Lincoln (with Smith at the wheel), and saw Helen Hayes in her famous play, *Victoria Regina,* at the Broadhurst Theatre. Aunt Minnie attended not one but four radio broadcasts.

In her diary Klinge described a visit to the Columbia Broadcasting Theatre to see "The Kate Smith Bandwagon":

> I met Kathryn at the theatre at one o'clock, where a rehearsal was going on for her show. One would really have to spend an entire day with her to see how hard they all work to make a broadcast successful. Every song, every bit is timed minutely in order to get it complete in 60 minutes. There have to be several timings in order to cut some parts which can be

eliminated without notice to the radio audience, and to be within the sixty minutes.

After the first rehearsal she had dinner, served in her dressing room, and then another rehearsal. In the meantime something is going on all the time. Probably the drama being rehearsed or the Three Ambassadors going over their song before the final rehearsal at 5 o'clock. It is then put on just as if it were on the air, after which they all leave to dress for the evening. But Kathryn, Jack Miller, and Mr. Collins, and a few others dress at the theatre. Kay has the star's dressing room, a large cheerful room, private bath, etc. I assisted her in dressing and at 7:45 she called an usher to show me to my seat. She selected it during the day as a good location — 6th row on the aisle. By that time the theatre was packed and at 7:50 André Baruch comes before the curtain and tells about the show. He tells the audience to applaud only at certain times, as it interferes with the timing of the broadcast. He tells who the guest stars will be and then it is 7:58. The curtain rises and on the stage is Mr. Collins at the mike. And Jack Miller's band in uniform, a beautiful setting in the background with Kate's face amid stars — below it three packages of coffee and in large letters, "A & P Bandwagon."

Promptly at 8 o'clock the show begins. André Baruch starts the announcing, then Ted Collins introduces Kate — and then she introduces her show. It is done on a grand scale. The Kate Smith Singers are a group of twenty young ladies and men led by Mr. Ted Straeter. They were all in evening clothes, all the girls in black and white, flowers or head pieces which made them look grand, all grouped in one corner of the stage. On the other side were the Three Ambassadors in white with C. A. L. in red letters on their blouses (one letter on each), as they are originally from California. In the middle of the stage is a mike for announcing and for guest stars, and a little to one side is our beloved "Songbird," Kate Smith, with her own mike. She looked beautiful in a lovely black chiffon evening dress with a corsage of three immense deep purple orchids. (At the end of the broadcast an usher handed her a large bouquet of three dozen American Beauty roses, tied with American Beauty satin ribbon.) Her guest star was Miss Helen Menken, one of the theatre's foremost stage stars, with a supporting cast of six persons. Also Sheila Barrett, an impersonator, also Henry Youngman, the comedian whom Kate discovered and gave his first break on radio. He is very funny and I can well understand why he is gaining popularity so rapidly.

Everybody connected with the show is in evening clothes and during the entire hour there is not a delay of any kind, being well-timed. The theatre is one of New York's large theatres that the Columbia Broadcasting Company has taken over until their new building is completed, which will be located at Park Ave. and 7th, but it will be three years before completion. At 9 o'clock promptly the show is over, but the curtain does not go down. Then Kate takes the opportunity to thank the audience for coming and for their reception of her show, inviting them to come again. After about 15 minutes the curtain goes down, after a very fine performance by all.

I remained in my seat for about ten minutes to permit the visitors to say good-bye to Kate, but when I made an attempt to get to her dressing room, the corridor leading to it was packed. I finally made it, and there she was all smiles and waiting for me. I told her how grand the show was, when a knock on the door came. Someone asked her if she would pose for a picture for *Radio Stars* magazine. So out she went to the stage, where a small crowd was waiting to get her autograph. She told me to be sure and stay with her, as she wanted me in the picture. I did and am anxious to see it. We then went back to her dressing room, and she takes her time leaving. She removes her makeup, changes into her street clothes, and while doing this is interrupted time and time again by different people wanting to see her or say "Good-Night." Mr. Collins has the dressing room next to hers, and after the show the A & P officials usually drop in to say hello to Kay and Ted and tell them how they liked the evening's broadcast. Mr. Collins sent in a nice cold drink for both of us. I had Coca Cola and Kay had milk. It was after 10 o'clock when we left the theatre, and there were some of her fans waiting outside all that time. I carried her roses, as she was laden down with her silver fox furs and orchids. I walked on with Mr. Collins while she smiled and chatted a minute with an ardent admirer, a Miss Catherine Carruthers, who has never missed a broadcast and who keeps a scrapbook of all her clippings. We reached home about 10:30 and by 11:30 Kay was in bed. A very strenuous day for her. I have never met anyone with the pep she has. All during the rehearsal she directs the whole show, can tell if the least flat note is played.

BESIDES ATTENDING THE "KATE SMITH A & P BANDWAGON" on two successive Thursdays, Klinge was in the audience at "The Richard Himber Show" of April 26, when Smith was the guest hostess. As Himber was on NBC, the show was done at Radio City. Smith sang three songs: "Dedicated to You," "It's Swell of You," and a swing arrangement of "Way Down Yonder in New Orleans" with the Three Ambassadors. Klinge reported in her diary that Smith looked stunning in a Kelly green two-piece wool sport suit, with her gorgeous mink cape, antelope and mink hat, British tan shoes, bag and gloves. Smith even did a commercial skit for Studebaker automobiles with a fourteen-year-old boy.

Advertising was an important element in Smith's work; she had known for a week that she would be changing sponsors come fall. Collins came to dinner on the 19th and told her that she would be leaving A & P in June, would have a two-month summer vacation, then in September would go on the air for General Food Products. Same time, same stations, at $5,000 per week salary, with the orchestra and special talent being paid for by the sponsors. And her show would now be broadcast from coast-to-coast for the first time. That would mean that the entire program would have to be done live all over again for the Pacific time zone stations. Although each show was recorded on mammoth sixteen-inch transcription discs, the networks frowned on simply playing the discs. (It would not be until 1946 that transcribed shows would begin to be accepted, and then only because Bing Crosby refused to broadcast his "Philco Radio Time" unless the network consented to air the shows transcribed. That started a trend.) Smith was pleased with her new contract.

CHAPTER 5

God Bless America

"I felt, here is a song that will be timeless—it will never die—others will thrill to its beauty long after we are gone." Kate Smith uttered these prophetic words at 12:13 P.M. November 10, 1938, on her midday commentary program, "Kate Smith Speaks," and sang the song for the first time that evening on "The Kate Smith Hour."

A man named Israel Baline was responsible for this new direction in Smith's career that would forever alter her image. Born in Russia, May 11, 1888, Baline came with his family to America when he was four years old. When he published his first song in 1907, he changed his name to Irving Berlin. Already a composer of note, he enlisted in the U.S. Army in 1918 and was stationed at Camp Upton in Yaphank on Long Island. While there he had a brainstorm: why not produce a camp show utilizing the talent of the men at the base? He was granted permission, and the result was a soldier's show with the unlikely title of *Yip, Yip, Yaphank.*

By 1938, after two decades of peacetime, there were distinct undercurrents of war brewing in Europe. Ted Collins thought it was time for Smith to do something musically to unite Americans in an attitude of patriotism. That Armistice Day would mark twenty years since the end of the First World War. On that Thursday edition of "Kate Smith Speaks," Smith related the story behind the new song she would introduce that night. Before she began her account, she spoke of some current events overseas:

> In Germany, the Nazis are taking vengeance for the killing of an official by a Jewish youth. Mobs roamed the cities and towns last night, wrecking Jewish shops and setting fire to synagogues. It was a night of terror for German Jews.
>
> It's a different story in London. Prime Minister Chamberlain told the people he wants the British government to be a "go-getter" for peace. And he added that conditions in Europe are settling down to quieter times.

Shortly after the second Diamond Crystal Salt commercial, Smith began:

52

Tomorrow we pay tribute to our honored dead and to the millions of Veterans of World War who were spared to return to their native land following the Armistice of twenty years ago. ... It has been my privilege to be on the air on Armistice Day or Armistice Eve for the past eight years, and on each of these occasions I have tried to give a fitting salute to our heroes. This year, with the war clouds of Europe so lately threatening the peace of the entire world, I felt I wanted to do something special—something that would not only be a memorial to our soldiers—but would also emphasize just how much America means to each and every one of us. I wanted more than an Armistice Day song—I wanted a new hymn of praise and love and allegiance to America. ... So, several weeks ago, I went to a man I have known and admired for many years—the top-ranking composer in the music field today. ... I explained as well as I could what I was striving for. He said, "Kate, you want something more than a popular song. I'm not sure, but I will try." He worked day after day, night after night, until at last his task was completed. The other day he sent me his masterpiece, and along with it this little note: "Dear Kate: here it is ... I did the best I could, and it expresses the way I feel." The song is called "God Bless America"; the composer, Mr. Irving Berlin. When I first tried it over, I felt, here is a song that will be timeless—it will never die—others will thrill to its beauty long after we are gone. In my humble estimation, this is the greatest song Irving Berlin has ever composed. It shall be my happy privilege to introduce that song on my program this evening, dedicating it to our American heroes of the World War. As I stand before the microphone and sing it with all my heart, I'll be thinking of our veterans and I'll be praying with every breath I draw that we shall never have another war. And I'll also be deeply grateful to Mr. Irving Berlin for his beautiful composition, "God Bless America."

A remarkable essay, in retrospect, to be sure. Irving Berlin was born a Russian Jew. He had returned from a very sad trip to England shortly before Smith (or Collins) had come to him about a song. He described Europe as "hate-torn" and was more grateful than ever for the peace and freedom he had in his adopted country, the United States of America. How could he possibly turn down Kate Smith's request? He searched his brain for an idea and wrote lyrics, but was unable to come up with a suitable melody for them. Then he remembered a closing number he had written for *Yip, Yip, Yaphank* that had been rejected for the show.

Irving Berlin, like most composers, had a trunk full of unpublished, and in many cases untitled, compositions accumulated over the years. He asked his secretary, Mynna Granate, to locate the *Yip, Yip, Yaphank* file and find "God Bless America." It took some searching because it was untitled, but she eventually found it. Berlin made some changes in both lyric and melody, added a lovely introduction that expressed his current feelings, and sent it to Smith.

One lyric change that Irving Berlin felt was necessary was in the phrase "Stand beside her and guide her to the right with a light from above." In the time since 1918 "the right" had taken on a political connotation, so he replaced that phrase with "through the night." The line "From the mountains to the prairies to the oceans white with foam" had been "From the green fields of Virginia to the gold fields out in Nome." Smith did sing the earlier lyric in her first introduction.

The Pan-American Conference was scheduled to open a month later in Lima, Peru. A wave of isolationism was sweeping the country, led by transoceanic aviator Charles Lindbergh and others. Smith introduced the song this way on the air:

> And now it's going to be my very great privilege to sing you a song that's never been sung before by anybody, and that was written especially for me by one of the greatest composers in the music field today. It's something more than a song—I feel it's one of the most beautiful compositions ever written, a song that will never die. The author: Mr. Irving Berlin. The title: "God Bless America."

Columnist Nick Kenny reported in the *New York Sunday Mirror*, "I wonder if I'll ever receive as great a thrill as I did last Thursday night listening to Kate Smith's inspiring singing of Irving Berlin's new patriotic hymn, 'God Bless America.' We were listening to the broadcast with Mr. and Mrs. Berlin in Irving's office. You never saw a more nervous chap than America's number one song writer as he listened to Kate's glorious rendition of his song, nor a prouder wife than Mrs. Berlin when the telephones began to ring with messages from all parts of the country asking, 'Where can we get that song Kate Smith just sang?' Irving changed other plans he had for the evening and took a taxi to Times Square to catch the midnight rebroadcast for the West Coast audience."

After that show, at 1 A.M. eastern time, November 11, Smith called Irving Berlin to the stage. She gave him such a bear hug that it lifted his feet right off the floor. Just imagine great big Kate and little Irving; the audience roared.

Two sources indicate that the song failed to take the nation by storm after that first introduction. A friend in Los Angeles remembers listening to the show over KNX. And veteran *New York Times* radio writer Ben Gross confirms it in his book, *I Looked and I Listened*. Collins had invited Gross to the studio, as he was going to do a story about Smith in his column. Collins explained to him that Smith felt the song should have more of a martial air, but that Berlin disagreed, so she sang it as he wanted it sung, more as a ballad. The arrangement was altered for the November 24 broadcast to the one we all know so well. That night the impact was nothing short of sensational. Here are the finalized lyrics, as sung by Smith that Thanksgiving evening:

While the storm clouds gather far across the sea,
Let us swear allegiance to a land that's free.
Let us all be grateful for a land so fair,
As we raise our voices in a solemn prayer.

God bless America, land that I love,
Stand beside her and guide her
Through the night with a light from above.
From the mountains to the prairies
To the oceans white with foam,
God bless America, my home sweet home,
God bless America, my home sweet home.*

This version of the anthem electrified the nation, as evidenced by the number of telegrams, telephone calls, and letters that came in praising it. Smith sang it on nearly every broadcast from then until December 1940, a total of seventy-one times. For a few months it was her exclusive property, but there was no stopping others from performing it, from school choirs to great orchestras. She recorded it for RCA Victor on March 21, 1939, and this version has been reissued over the years countless times. The record sold like hotcakes and was being played on jukeboxes from coast to coast. The lyrics were inserted into the Congressional Record, and a movement was spawned to make it the national anthem. Smith addressed the Congress, imploring its members not to do that. She argued that "The Star Spangled Banner" was written during a battle but that "God Bless America" was composed (in part) during peacetime. In fact, she recorded the national anthem on the other side of "God Bless America." Berlin was also vehement that it not be a national anthem.

"God Bless America" was sung at both the Republican and Democratic national conventions in 1940, to rousing cheers from assembled politicians. It was recorded, in its ballad arrangement, by Bing Crosby, Barry Wood, the Horace Heidt orchestra, and, later, Gene Autry. But this one was Kate Smith's all the way and forever. Berlin asked her to introduce most of his published songs during the decade 1935–45, and she always regarded him as her favorite composer. At Carnegie Hall in 1963 she referred to him as "the dean of them all." He said of "God Bless America," "Those thirty-two bars of words and music are the most important I have ever written." It was his love song to his adopted homeland. In recent years the immortal anthem has taken on a renewed popularity and is often sung complete with the introduction.

In 1940 Berlin established a trust, the God Bless America Foundation, with all royalties earned from the song by either Berlin or Smith going to the Boy and Girl Scouts of America. This includes the sale of sheet music and records as well as live performances. These organizations were chosen because, to quote the agreement, "the completely nonsectarian work of the Boy Scouts and Girl Scouts is calculated to best promote unity of mind and patriotism, two sentiments that are inherent in the song itself."

On December 29, 1940, Smith electrified an audience of tens of thousands standing in the streets of New York City at an "I Am an American" rally as she sang "God Bless America."

On January 1, 1941, a ban on the radio performance of ASCAP songs took effect and Smith could no longer sing "God Bless America" on her shows. So she substituted "We're All Americans," which had a similar tempo, melody, and message, and caught on rather well. Sometimes she revived the pre–World War I song "America, I Love You." As soon as the ban was lifted, she resumed "God Bless America" and continued to sing it all during the Second World War as her radio troupe broadcast on location from military bases and centers of war production across the country. Much later, when she gave live concerts in the civic auditoriums of major cities, her audiences eagerly anticipated "God Bless America" as the finale. The reaction was totally predictable: an audible sigh in unison, then applause, and a standing ovation at its conclusion. Kate Smith had a built-in guarantee of a standing ovation at the end of every performance.

WHEN WORLD WAR II CAME ALONG, Irving Berlin wanted to somehow recreate an all-soldier show like *Yip, Yip, Yaphank.* It took a monumental effort but he did it. He even went back to Camp Upton in Yaphank to recapture the atmosphere of military life, this time as a 53-year-old civilian. The show was called *This Is the Army* and it featured over three hundred soldiers in the cast. Berlin chose 25-year-old Staff Sergeant Ezra Stone to assemble the company for the stage show. Stone had achieved fame as radio's teenage Henry Aldrich on "The Aldrich Family." Rehearsals were hectic as Berlin was determined that the show, all of whose profits would accrue to the Army Emergency Relief Fund, would make its debut on the stage of the Broadway Theatre on July 4, 1942.

This Is the Army made a radio debut as excerpts were broadcast on "The Kate Smith Hour" of June 26, the season finale. Guest stars were Berlin and Stone, as well as the Army show chorus of one hundred men. Incidentally, Smith and Stone were well acquainted, since "The Aldrich Family" had spent a season as a comedy spot on Smith's program in 1938-39 before it became the highly successful spin-off program that it was.

Smith's program opened with Berlin's rousing new patriotic song, "This Time," which would be the closing number of *This Is the Army.* Next

Smith sang the popular "We'll Meet Again," which England's Vera Lynn was singing to raves. The song would become one of Lynn's biggest hits. (Vera was known as England's Kate Smith, while Smith was known in England as America's Vera Lynn.) Next Berlin stepped to the mike to talk a bit about his new show, where and when it would open; then he announced that Kate Smith had bought the first two tickets for a handsome donation of $10,000. (Berlin had himself bought two at $2,000 each.)

After an "America Sings with Kate Smith" medley of favorites, there was a lengthy dramatic sketch with Smith, Berlin, and Stone, along with the military chorus, which opened with "This Is the Army, Mister Jones" (which would be a standout hit). Next Smith did a minstrel sketch to "Mr. Bones" with some of the soldiers. This was followed by Stone's comic rendition of "The Army's Made a Man Out of Me." Smith introduced the lovely ballad, "I Left My Heart at the Stage Door Canteen," which was destined to become one of the year's most popular songs. The Army Chorus sang "That Russian Winter," followed by a black soldier soloist rendering "That's What the Well-Dressed Man in Harlem Will Wear."

Now it was Berlin's turn to sing, in his own small, raspy voice, accompanied by the chorus, "Oh! How I Hate to Get Up in the Morning," one of the show's high points. Smith sang the spirited "With My Head in the Clouds" and then ended with "God Bless America," appropriately enough for the occasion.

This Is the Army was a smash hit, running until September 26, then going on the road to Washington, D.C., where a special matinee performance was staged for President Roosevelt at the National Theatre. (Eleanor had already seen it three times in New York and loved it.) It played in Philadelphia, Boston, St. Louis, San Francisco and other major cities, as Berlin was negotiating the sale of movie rights to Warner Bros. Studio. It would be an expensive Technicolor production, with profits again going to Army Emergency Relief.

The name Hollywood stars of the motion picture would be Lieutenant Ronald Reagan and George Murphy. Berlin insisted that Kate Smith be brought in to stage her radio introduction of "God Bless America." Ted Collins managed to have the filming of her five-minute cameo coincide with a transcontinental tour of her radio hour. It was filmed early in May, on or about her birthday. Producer Hal Wallis wrote in his autobiography that there was great excitement when Smith agreed to appear in the film. He met her at the train, a thing he had not done since the days of silent movies. Wallis found her to be a charming guest as he and his wife entertained her in their home. He said that Irving Berlin doted on Smith and that her song and Berlin's song were the two highlights of that picture, generally regarded as the most important World War II musical film.

In 1991 a restored version of *This Is the Army* was released by the AMC

(American Movie Classics) cable network, which had cosponsored the restoration work done by the University of California at Los Angeles (UCLA). The color is brilliant, all splices have been removed, and several "lost" minutes of film have been put back. It was also shown at selected theatres across the country at that time, hosted by actor Cesar Romero. Seeing it in a theatre causes one to realize why it was so entertaining and important in the midst of war. An amusing moment, in retrospect, occurs when Lt. Reagan speaks to the cast just before the performance for President Roosevelt, telling them to give it all "for the president." Little did he know that he himself would be president forty years later.

Ezra Stone had some recollections of the filming and of "God Bless America" when I interviewed him in 1988. He recalled: "'God Bless America' had a very checkered career. [Irving Berlin] wrote it in World War I for *Yip, Yip, Yaphank* and it didn't make it. He wanted it to be the finale of *This Is the Army*. Bill Horne was to sing it—beautiful voice, operatic tenor—and Berlin, almost every other day would ask, 'When are you going to stage "God Bless America"?' I'd kinda weasel out of it. I'd say, 'We've got so much to get rehearsed.' We had to open [the stage show] on the Fourth of July; that was a must and time was awasting and we were 310 men. I didn't think it was the effective way to close the show. That shows you how wrong I was. I felt the number that he wrote as the finale ['This Time'] for *This Is the Army* had more impact than 'God Bless America,' which at that time I felt was rather jingoistic, and obvious flagwaving. But it's become virtually our national anthem."

Stone, while not the stage director for the film version (he and Berlin had had some serious disagreements), was present when Smith made her cameo. (He had a bit part in the picture.) He recalled how Berlin catered to her. Her cameo takes place in a large simulated radio theatre, with the announcer saying, "And now the star of our show, Kate Smith." She strides on stage to great applause and announces, "Hello everybody! It is my happy privilege to introduce a new song, 'God Bless America.'" Then she launches into the charming, lovely, and seldom-heard verse, with Jack Miller conducting the orchestra. This is followed by two full choruses as the camera fades to scenes of World War I veterans listening in. George Murphy rebuts "son" Ronald Reagan's assertion that it is a brand new song when he recalls it from the Camp Upton show, saying, "I took that out of *Yip, Yip, Yaphank* twenty years ago. Sounds better now."

This historic cameo has been used many times since, on television shows with patriotic themes and in World War II retrospectives, and it was used in every TV obituary when Kate Smith died in 1986.

There are two factual errors regarding "God Bless America" in the film. In the 1918 scene at Camp Upton in which the songs are being rehearsed, the title is clearly shown on the sheet music, while in actuality it was untitled. And just before Smith is introduced, a radio newsman is reviewing countries conquered by the Nazis. Those invasions took place in 1939; the song was introduced a year earlier.

The stage troupe of *This Is the Army* went abroad in the fall of 1943, opening at the London Palladium in mid–November, complete with a new song designed to cement Anglo-American relations: "My British Buddy" ("He thinks he's winning the war and I think it's me"). This touching ballad was introduced on American radio by Kate Smith on December 3. The song was much parodied in versions such as "My Irish buddy, he's as neutral as can be" and "My Russian buddy . . . he says he's winning the war and that's okay with me." General Eisenhower, supreme commander of the European Theater of Operations, attended the last London performance. He congratulated Berlin after the show and asked him whether there was anything he could do to help out. Berlin asked him to grant permission for the show to play in the war zones. Eventually such permission was granted, and it played in such far-flung locales as Naples and Rome, Cairo, the Philippines, Saipan, and Okinawa. It closed in Honolulu on October 22, 1945, several weeks after the war's end. It had entertained 2.5 million G.I.'s and made over $10 million for the Army Relief Fund.

There was a down side to Kate Smith's association with "God Bless America." That song so overshadowed the other outstanding songs she sang that many actually believed she sang only two songs: that and "When the Moon Comes Over the Mountain." A great many powerful love songs, which she delivered with great feeling, were and are overlooked.

A POSTSCRIPT ABOUT THE MANUSCRIPT of "God Bless America" is of interest. In 1990 I received a letter from the president of the New York Sheet Music Society informing me, as secretary/treasurer of the Kate Smith/God Bless America Foundation, that the society knew where the original manuscript was, and were we interested? I replied that we were and the president called me, explaining that the document (with lyrics) was written by Berlin's underlings, except for a passage that he had crossed out and changed in his own handwriting.

I was informed that Ted Collins had had possession of the document and had turned it over to one Tommy Shattuck, with a letter (which still accompanies the manuscript) early in 1941. Shattuck was an acquaintance of Collins in Lake Placid; Collins knew of his interest in historic documents and realized by that time that "God Bless America" was destined to be an important song in Americana. Shattuck was a member of the family who owned the coast-to-coast chain of Schrafft's candy stores.

My inquiries in September 1990 led me to believe that William Cheadle of Clearwater, Florida, Shattuck's son-in-law, might have possession of the manuscript. When I called Cheadle, he told me he had sold it and Collins's letter to the Gallery of History in Las Vegas. He rued the fact that he had been unaware of the Kate Smith/God Bless America Foundation and its interest in the documents.

I called the Gallery of History and had an informative chat with Todd Axelrod, who said he had the framed manuscript in his office even as we spoke. He referred to it with enthusiasm as "the manuscript of manuscripts" and a most exciting piece of Americana. Axelrod said that the lines Berlin had changed became "From the mountains to the prairies / To the oceans white with foam." He changed them a few days after Smith's Armistice Day introduction of the song and returned them to Collins, along with a marginal note which reads, "Ted: what do you think of it now?"

As for the value of the manuscript, I was told that Cheadle had sold it to the Gallery of History for about $20,000. Axelrod said he had had it professionally photographed for a book about historic documents he was writing and that he had it for sale at $295,000. It clearly belongs at the Smithsonian Institution or some similar national museum, to be displayed along with other historic American documents.

CHAPTER 6

Kate, Radio,
and the Roosevelts

"The Kate Smith Hour" debuted on CBS radio in September 1937, sponsored by General Foods. Aired Thursdays from 8 to 9 P.M., opposite NBC's "Rudy Vallée Hour" just as her "A & P Bandwagon" had been, it quickly made inroads on the "Vallée Hour" in popularity polls. Because of the importance of this variety hour in the Smith career and in radio history, it is worth reviewing the program by focusing on one particular broadcast: December 9, 1937. This show has been chosen for two reasons: to date it is the only "Kate Smith Hour" whose transcriptions have survived the years and it contains a historic interview with First Lady Eleanor Roosevelt.

The program log for the evening listed the following items:

1. Sign-on: André Baruch, m.c., Ted Collins, announcer
2. "Every Day's a Holiday"—The Boys and Girls (led by Ted Straeter)
3. "You're a Sweetheart"—Kate
4. Swansdown Cake Flour commercial—André and Kate
5. "You Can't Stop Me from Dreaming"—Kate and the Three Ambassadors
6. Kate Smith's All-Collegiate Football Team—Ted Collins and Fordham coach "Sleepy" Jim Crowley
7. "The Sunshine of Your Smile"—Kate
8. Station Break
9. "Who?"—Ted Straeter and the Kate Smith Singers
10. Calumet Baking Powder commercial—Kate
11. "Bob White"—Kate and the Three Ambassadors
12. Women of America: Special Guest—Eleanor Roosevelt
13. Memory Medley of songs Kate introduced on the air:
    A. "I'm Getting Sentimental Over You" (1932)
    B. "Hold Me" (1933)
    C. "Wrap Your Troubles in Dreams" (1931)

14. Comedy segment: Henny Youngman, with Charlie Cantor as Uncle Max
15. Commercial: Calumet and Swansdown—Kate and Ted
16. "You've Gotta Have Oomph"—Kate and the ensemble
17. Sign-off—Kate and Ted

The master of ceremonies was André Baruch, one of the most distinguished and best remembered radio announcers. I interviewed Baruch and his wife of over fifty years, famed big band vocalist Bea Wain, in 1989. They told me they were both on the Fred Waring show in 1936, André as announcer and Bea as a member of a vocal octet called the V-8s ("Waring and His Pennsylvanians" was sponsored by Ford Motors). It was not until a year or so later that Baruch and Wain began to take a romantic interest in one another. At that time Wain was a member of Ted Straeter's chorus on "The Kate Smith Hour." She recalled that soprano Dorothy Kirsten stood beside her. "She thrilled me when she went for the high notes; my voice was so much lower." Kirsten later went on to fame in opera.

Bea Wain had an occasional four- or eight-bar solo, and her voice attracted the interest of bandleaders looking for a girl vocalist. One Thursday, right after the show, she received a phone call from Larry Clinton, who said he was organizing a band and would like to audition her as a vocalist. She joined his band and sang a number called "True Confession" at the band's first RCA Victor recording session. Soon the Clinton band was on the air, at an hour which conflicted with the rebroadcast of the "Kate Smith Hour" for the West Coast. She approached the kindly Ted Straeter, who advised her to go with Clinton, saying he would temporarily replace her in the chorus. She decided to take his advice and went on to record such standards as "My Reverie," "Martha," "I Dreamt I Dwelt in Marble Halls," and "Deep Purple." Later still she became a featured vocalist on the Saturday night fixture, "Your Hit Parade," with husband André Baruch doing the announcing.

Wain and Baruch were, as Smith was fond of stating it, "married on our show." Actually they were married on Saturday, May 1, 1938 (Smith's 31st birthday), at the St. Moritz Hotel, but Smith made a production of it on the radio two days before. She told the audience she had baked a wedding cake, and she had it brought out while on the air. She gave them a magnificent silver candelabra as a wedding gift.

Both Wain and Baruch spoke warmly about their memories of Smith. Baruch spoke of her tremendous vocal talent and the fact that even now she is admired and her memory is beloved by millions around the world. When I asked him what he thought of Ted Collins, he said, after a brief pause for the right word, "He had tremendous perspicacity." Collins had an ability to find talent and a great business acumen. He guarded Smith jealously, keeping one and all away from any close association with her.

One of Baruch's duties was to "warm up" the studio audience just prior to each broadcast. With the curtain closed, he would stand at the front of the stage and tell amusing stories to loosen them up so that they would laugh and applaud appropriately. In fact, he became a legend as radio's finest warm-up man.

One Thursday about 7:55 P.M., during the warm-up, the spotlight suddenly shone on a bulge near the left of the curtain about three feet from the floor. The bulge slowly made its way toward the right side of the stage, with the spotlight and Baruch following its progress. This helped immensely to loosen up the audience. Baruch recalled gleefully, "When it was about three-quarters of the way across, I hit the bump with the script. As the curtain opened to start the show I received two glares, one from Kate and the other from Ted." He later learned that it was Kate quietly making her way to the mike, bending slightly to avoid hitting the music stands. When he hit the bump gently, it sent her "can-over-teakettle."

Two or three weeks later Baruch was called into the offices of Young and Rubicam, the advertising agency, and told he was being replaced on "The Kate Smith Hour." He was taken completely off guard and asked what he could possibly have done wrong. He was simply told that the officials thought it was time for a replacement and that he would be moved to another Young and Rubicam program. What had happened was that Collins had reported the incident, inadvertent though it was, and demanded Baruch's removal.

According to the routine presented at the beginning of this chapter for that December 9, 1937, broadcast, the chorus presented "Every Day's a Holiday" in connection with the Christmas season. Smith's arrangement of the new hit "You're a Sweetheart" was precisely as she would record it three weeks later. Collins gave the introduction to the lively "You Can't Stop Me from Dreaming," pronouncing it "a Collins special." "Sleepy" Jim Crowley, football coach at Collins's alma mater, had been hired for the first ten weeks of that season, the football season. Gruen wristwatches were presented to all of the athletes selected. (Incidentally, one of those athletes was Byron "Wizzer" White, later a Supreme Court justice appointed by President Kennedy, and who retired in 1993.) "The Sunshine of Your Smile" was sung exactly as Smith would record it on her first album in 1941. "Bob White" was a swing sensation of the day.

Smith's introduction of the new segment, "Women of America," was emotional. Her heart was obviously in this project designed to improve the image of American women. She referred to that evening as "one of the most important of my life," as she was about to interview the First Lady. Roosevelt was in Washington, so the interview was done by cable or direct line. The sound quality was first rate, not like that of a telephone interview. This may well have been the first time an interview was done using that technology.

Now Eleanor Roosevelt and Kate Smith had a few things in common. Both were "First Ladies"—Roosevelt of the nation and Smith by now of radio. Both had radio programs (Roosevelt's was a commentary show called "My Day"). And both were being named in the top three in popularity polls of the most important and beloved women of the nation.

In the interview Eleanor Roosevelt talked about many things of special interest to women. It had to be an altogether fascinating interview at the time, as well as an historic one, heard by an audience of many millions. The interview contained these highlights:

KATE SMITH: Mrs. Roosevelt, what are you going to do after you leave the White House?

MRS. ROOSEVELT: [*Faint chuckle*] I haven't the faintest idea. I suppose, as has always happened before, something will turn up for me to do.

KATE SMITH: Why do you travel informally most of the time?

MRS. ROOSEVELT: What do you mean, "informally"?

KATE SMITH: Well, I was at the same theatre that you were one night and when the play ended you got up and walked up the aisle with everyone else, walked out into the street and hailed a taxicab.

MRS. ROOSEVELT: I like to be like everybody else and that is what I always used to do. . . . I like to shop, go to the theatre as a person, as an individual. Therefore, there's nothing strange in that. After all, I've only lived in the White House the last few years. I lived a good many years before and I hope to live a good many years after I leave as a private individual.

KATE SMITH: Do you supervise the housekeeping of the White House? Such things as the ordering of the meals, the hiring of the staff, buying new furniture, and things like that?

MRS. ROOSEVELT: Yes. The housekeeper, of course, brings me all the difficult problems. I have to look at new furniture. I have to know what is being spent, go over all the accounts. I have to go over the menus. It really is a supervisory job.

KATE SMITH: What is the oldest thing and what's the newest thing in the White House?

MRS. ROOSEVELT: I really don't know, unless it is some of the furniture, which goes back to Monroe's time. And the sword made for George Washington, which did not arrive in the White House until just a few years ago. The newest thing is perhaps the new coverings on the chairs in the Blue Room.

KATE SMITH: There are two ways of buying clothes: a planned wardrobe where you buy everything you need for a season, or just buying something that you like when you happen to see it. Which do you prefer?

MRS. ROOSEVELT: [*Chuckle*] It isn't a question of preference. I have to plan. I can give it just so much time, so I decide in the autumn what I'm going to need in the winter, and in the spring what I'm going to need until autumn. And then I'm finished.

KATE SMITH: What is your favorite material and color?

MRS. ROOSEVELT: I don't know about material, but color? Well, blue of every shade.

KATE SMITH: I thought that. I'm afraid I'll never get on the list of the ten best dressed women, but I have the usual weakness for clothes. What type of clothes do you like to wear, Mrs. Roosevelt?

MRS. ROOSEVELT: Oh, I like to wear chiffons, floaty things, and I also like sport clothes.

KATE SMITH: Do you have a special hairdresser who travels around with you?

MRS. ROOSEVELT: [*Chuckles*] No. Only my own two hands.

KATE SMITH: I'm in the world of entertainment and it is vastly different from your world, Mrs. Roosevelt. I pick up papers and magazines and discover things written about me by people I don't know. In a way I don't resent those things because I'm kinda thankful for them due to the fact that my profession is built on publicity. But I was wondering if these things happen to you and just how you feel about them.

MRS. ROOSEVELT: Of course they happen to me. After all, my life is much in the publicity field, too. Also, I get very critical and unflattering cartoons and articles. But after a time one becomes a little indifferent. Somehow you have to make up your mind what you want to do and then forget the other things.

KATE SMITH: We all know that your official home is the White House, and you do spend some time at Hyde Park. Just how many homes do you actually have?

MRS. ROOSEVELT: Well, I have a little apartment in New York, a sort of hideout which I tell very few people about and which I've tried to keep secret, where my secretary and I stay. We still have the cottage off the coast of Maine on an island called Campobello. The Hyde Park house, the big house, belongs to my mother-in-law. But I do have a little cottage there hidden in the woods.

KATE SMITH: Mrs. Roosevelt, how do you conserve your energy and distribute it so you can do all the things you have to do?

MRS. ROOSEVELT: Well, I don't know that I give it a great deal of thought. I simply try to eat sensibly and sleep when I have to and get some kind of exercise.

KATE SMITH: What is your greatest pleasure and relaxation?

MRS. ROOSEVELT: I like, for out-of-doors, riding and swimming, and for indoors, I like to read.

KATE SMITH: In your trips about the country do you find women taking an active interest in hospitals and institutions in their own cities?

MRS. ROOSEVELT: Oh yes indeed. I find them not only taking an active interest but an intelligent and human interest.

KATE SMITH: I think everyone is interested in Christmas plans now and I think it'd be nice if you'd tell me something of your plans. Do you have your Christmas tree on Christmas Eve and the exchange of presents?

MRS. ROOSEVELT: No, we have it on Christmas afternoon. The children come to luncheon and we have the Christmas tree after luncheon and exchange our presents then. Christmas Eve, of course, as you may know, is a busy day officially for us. The little children, of course, open their Christmas stockings early Christmas morning in their grandfather's room.

KATE SMITH: Will you tell us about the time you were shopping up here in a New York department store and you wanted to charge your purchase?

MRS. ROOSEVELT: [*Chuckling*] Oh, yes. I said, "Charge it to Mrs. F. D. Roosevelt, R double O S-E-V-E-L-T, the White House, Washington, D.C." The girl wrote it down very carefully and then asked, "Any room number, please?"

KATE SMITH: Well, thank you very, very much, Mrs. Roosevelt, and thanks, too, for this interesting chat. Once again radio has brought us a rare pleasure: the privilege of meeting the First Lady of the Land as if in the friendly intimacy of her own sitting room. Thank you, Mrs. Roosevelt, and good night.

MRS. ROOSEVELT: Good night, Kate, good night.

In the middle of this interview, Smith betrayed her unhappiness with the jibes and cartoons leveled at her by the press. She never learned to, as Eleanor Roosevelt put it, "become a little indifferent" and forget about such things. The fat jokes haunted her always.

In the format of "The Kate Smith Hour," the memory medley was a well-established feature, with the songs going back only four or five years of necessity, as she had been in radio only six years at the time. She would feature such medleys throughout her career, and they would always be enjoyed and appreciated by her audiences, whether for radio, TV, or personal appearances.

Another regular feature was the comedy spot. Smith and Collins gave Henry (Henny) Youngman his first break in radio. He was still going strong more than five decades later with his one-liners and his violin, occasionally caressing a few bars of "Smoke Gets in Your Eyes." Youngman told me he was playing at the Yacht Club in New York when Collins discovered him.

Youngman was a hot act and was praised by a columnist. Collins took in his show and signed him for the "Kate Smith Hour" at $250 weekly. Youngman, not a bashful person, said he was so hot on his first show that Collins let him go for ten minutes, making it necessary to abridge actor Franchot Tone's short play to a short-short play. He said Collins took twenty percent as his agent and later doubled his salary.

When I first talked with Youngman on the telephone, he was cold and abrupt, but the mere fact that he took the trouble to speak with me indicated a regard for Kate Smith. He asked me whether I had ever seen her when she was ill in Raleigh (in recent years). When I told him I had been there several times, he began to warm up and show his compassion for her plight. He told me something that was most interesting: he, Smith, and Jack Miller had a pact among themselves. He said he did not even think Ted Collins knew about it. The pact was that if anything ever happened to any of them—trouble or illness—the other two would come to their rescue. He said he tried to get to Smith in Raleigh, but her niece's husband would not let him near. He seemed genuinely sorry that he could not do anything to help her.

The Three Ambassadors were a talented trio of young men, not much over age twenty at this time, who hailed from California and were proud of it. They were Martin Sperzel, Jack Smith, and Marshall Hall. They had been with Smith for four years on the radio, and they accompanied her on several of her swing records for Decca and Victor. Jack Smith went on to fame as a vocalist (known for the smile in his voice) for Capitol records in the late forties, as the star of the Oxydol Show on the radio, and later as the host of television's "You Asked for It."

In October 1939, "The Kate Smith Hour" moved to Fridays at 8 P.M., where it remained for five highly successful seasons. By now Rudy Vallée had admitted defeat by the competition, and his enormously popular variety hour for a decade became a memory that same month. The peak of his career had come and gone, and he would be regarded largely as a has-been for the rest of his life.

ONE OF THE MOST MEMORABLE PATRIOTIC OCCASIONS in the Smith career—and the most publicized over the years—took place at the White House on Thursday, June 8, 1939. President Roosevelt had scheduled a state dinner for King George VI and Queen Elizabeth of England. Earlier that day there was a gala parade, complete with sixty baby tanks with ten "flying fortress" bombers soaring above. Roosevelt's motive in this was to make Americans more familiar with British royalty as a prelude to giving aid to England in the war that Roosevelt believed was sure to come.

Kate Smith, now a popular symbol of patriotism, was one of several singers invited to perform at "A Program of American Music" after the dinner. According to Ben Gross of the *New York Times*, "Kate Smith had impressed herself on the mass mind as the embodiment of the homey American virtues" to such an extent that, when the president asked which typically American performers the King and Queen wished to hear, they both mentioned Kate Smith first.

Others included on the program were opera singers Marian Anderson and Lawrence Tibbett and folk singer Alan Lomax. The program also included a choral group to sing Negro spirituals, a folksinging quartet, and folk dancers. The day had been stiflingly hot and the evening was sultry. As it happened, it was the night of "The Kate Smith Hour" and the broadcast had to be done twice: at 8:00 for Eastern, Central and Mountain time zones, and again at 11:00 for the Pacific zone.

When Smith was reminiscing, at the end of her tenure with CBS eight years later, she singled out this evening:

> I remember, too, how the Columbia folks put all their vast facilities on that evening [eight] years ago, when I was called to the White House to sing

for the King and Queen of England. . . . We had a "Kate Smith Hour" that
evening that was to be done in our Playhouse here in New York City . . .
the show had to go on. . . . But also, I had to sing my songs for our royal
visitors. . . . And so everybody pitched in with a will, and arranged what
then seemed to all of us a marvelous feat of engineering. . . . My show went
on in New York, with its audience . . . my orchestra performed on the
Playhouse stage, and as they played my accompaniment here . . . I, in
Washington, through the miracle of radio, was able to sing along with
them and do my part of our regular show . . . being on hand at the White
House, and, a few minutes later, singing for President and Mrs. Roosevelt
and their distinguished guests.

There was a morning rehearsal at the studios of WJSV, the CBS
affiliate in Washington. Then in the afternoon Smith rehearsed the songs
she would sing at the White House musicale with her pianist Tony Gale.
After the East Coast broadcast at 8 P.M., she returned to the hotel to dress.
On this unbearably hot night, she was thankful that the dress she had had
made expressly for the occasion was of black marquisette sheer, dotted with
hundreds of sparkling "rosebuds."

At 9:30 P.M. the phone rang. It was Mrs. Roosevelt telling Smith she
understood that she would have to leave in time for the 11:00 P.M. broadcast
to the West Coast. She said the dinner was running behind schedule, and
she would switch the order of entertainment so Smith would be first. The
thoughtful First Lady went on to assure Smith, "Don't worry. I'll have
everything in hand and I'll have a police escort and a White House car to
escort you to the studio."

Smith, Collins, and pianist Tony Gale were given the special privilege
of entering the White House by the front door. Nearly everyone else used
the east door. Smith later recalled, "I was so thrilled that I just could not
contain myself. When I got inside I met an old colored maid who smiled
and said, 'We're just as thrilled as you are, Miss Kate. We're looking forward to hearing you sing.' Well, that simple, homey greeting made me feel
I was among friends."

Eleanor Roosevelt arranged a private presentation to Their Majesties
for Smith, Collins, and Gale, as they would have to depart before the formal reception. At 10:35 P.M. an aide introduced Smith to the president,
who said, "How do you do, Kate Smith. It's good to see you." Turning to
the king, he said (to quote Smith herself from a *Radio Guide* magazine story
she wrote three weeks later), "Your Majesty, this is Kate Smith, one of our
greatest singers. Miss Smith is going to sing first in the recital tonight
because she has a broadcast at eleven o'clock." His Majesty said, "How do
you do, Miss Smith. I am anxiously waiting to hear you sing." Presenting
Smith to the queen, the president said, "Her Majesty," and Smith said,
"How do you do, Your Majesty." The queen replied, "It's charming to
meet you."

Proceedings were held up more when the queen's tiara became loose and she and her ladies-in-waiting went into an anteroom to adjust it. The musicale was held in the East Ballroom. The First Lady introduced Kate Smith, who sang "These Foolish Things Remind Me of You" (an English song she had introduced in this country in 1936), the Irish ballad "Macushla," and "When the Moon Comes Over the Mountain." The latter was requested by King George. Smith had told reporters that morning that she would also sing "Home on the Range" and "Ah, Sweet Mystery of Life," but these were not on the printed program.

Smith said that while she was singing she looked at the president and he gave her a subtle look of approval and encouragement. She said the king and queen appeared to be enjoying every moment of the evening's festivities, that the atmosphere was "regal, yet democratic." She was impressed with the homey atmosphere of the White House as compared to its stuffiness when she had been there before. (Smith's maternal grandfather was an interior decorator and had done some work at the White House.) They stepped out of the White House at eleven o'clock and were a few minutes late for the rebroadcast to two major cities west of the Mississippi: Salt Lake City over KSL and Los Angeles over KNX. This was one of the rare times when Smith deviated from the earlier broadcast, as she told these listeners of her thrilling command appearance.

A footnote is in order at this point. It has become a vital part of Kate Smith folklore that President Roosevelt is supposed to have said to King George, "This is Kate Smith. This is America." In fact it is so engraved inside the mausoleum where her remains lie in state. If this is true, Smith did not remember it when she wrote the details of the evening for *Radio Guide*'s July 7 issue.

The First Lady accepted Smith's invitation to be her radio guest the following Thursday, this time in person, not by cable. When Eleanor Roosevelt entered, she greeted everyone backstage, including the musicians. There was standing room only in the audience. Smith asked her how Their Majesties had enjoyed the evening, to which she replied, in her inimitable high-pitched voice, "The heat seemed to be too much for Their Majesties and two of my boys whisked them out onto the south portico for a breath of fresh air." Smith asked what they said after the party was over. "As soon as the king heard that you were to be one of our guests," she told Smith and the nation, "he asked, 'Will she sing her song, "When the Moon Comes Over the Mountain"?' and the president assured him that you would, for he himself had requested it. While the royal party was traveling through the Adirondacks at night, en route to Washington from Canada, some of the people saw the moon come over a mountain. They began to sing your song and the king asked them about it and about you."

Smith asked Roosevelt whether she always had to address the king and queen as "Your Majesties," to which Roosevelt replied, "As a matter of fact, after addressing them formally, you just address the king as sir and the queen as madam." Smith asked what impressed them most of all, and Roosevelt said, "Undoubtedly the welcome they received everywhere. They seemed particularly happy to find that the people of this country were interested in them, and so enthusiastic in their welcome, because they—the king and queen—felt that meant a real cementing of good will between the nations . . . and their great desire is to bring about a feeling that it is possible for nations to settle their differences without going to war about it."

Indubitably Eleanor Roosevelt was delivering some propaganda on behalf of her husband, whose prime concern was to strike a blow at America's isolationism. She did her job well.

THE FINAL SMITH-ROOSEVELT CONNECTION occurred on an extraordinarily sad day, Friday, April 13, 1945. President Roosevelt had died at Warm Springs, Georgia, the day before. Smith delivered this touching commentary on "Kate Smith Speaks":*

> During the past eighteen anguished hours, you have heard through your radios and read in your newspapers many eloquent tributes to Mr. Franklin Delano Roosevelt . . . guiding light of this great nation . . . known to all of us simply as Mr. Roosevelt . . . or Mr. President. Let this tribute of mine be simple . . . let it be little words straight from the heart at the passing of a friend . . . as well as a leader among men.
>
> For, in the beginning, there was no fanfare . . . no drum rolls . . . no oratory. There was just a little boy, growing, playing like other American boys, with abandon . . . skinning his nose, wearing holes through his shoes . . . planning to run away to sea. He always loved the sea and the sailing ships. His mind always reached out to far places and brave adventures. . . . Strangely, and in jest, destiny spoke to him when he was a lad of five. With his mother he was meeting for the first time a President of the United States . . . President Grover Cleveland . . . and the great statesman looked at the youngster, Franklin, and greeted him with these words: "I'll give you a wish to remember for the rest of your life, young fellow: Pray to God that He never lets you become president of the United States."
>
> The boy forgot those words as soon as he had heard them, but his mother carried them in her heart for the rest of her life . . . and Destiny must have been listening and smiling triumphantly then. . .
>
> It was in March, 1933, that he began his duties in the White House . . . and even then, long before the beating of the drums of war, he was weighed down with responsibilities. Remember those days? The banks were closed, there were breadlines; men and women shivered on street corners selling apples. . . Depression and want stalked across the land that was America. America, land of promise . . . land of plenty, almost without hope in those heartbreaking days of 1933. . . Apathetic, questioning, doubtful—Afraid! And the new president spoke and said, "The only thing we have to fear is fear itself. . . ."

*The many ellipses in the text are part of the original script.

There's no need to repeat the annals of his greatness when war did engulf us, or his magnificent leadership during those dark days when we were stunned and horrified by the suddenness of the lightning bolt in the Pacific.... All the world listened to him ... and leaned on him. Thus came the burden that proved too heavy to bear.... Work, and travel to the far corners of the earth ... worry, loneliness, problems, big tall thoughts in the stillness of the long night ... responsibilities of a magnitude few of us can understand became part and parcel of the life of this one man....

We all knew he must falter and someday fall; we all knew his physical health was growing weaker and weaker. And yet when we heard his cheerful and confident voice over the radio, when he imbued us with his courage, we forgot the iron braces, and the wheelchairs ... we forgot the strained look on the face of the man aged too soon by the responsibilities of war. He was a simple man. I think I remember him best as he was in those good old days before the war cast its blight on the world.... I remember him as he was that evening in the White House when the King and Queen were there.... I had been invited to sing some of his favorite songs and some of theirs. And there, even in the presence of royalty, he was outstanding in his graceful manners, his dignity, his genial informal courtesy, his magnetic personality that won admirers and friends for him even among those who disagreed with his political beliefs. Yes, I remember him best as he was on that evening when I stood there and sang simple American songs for the illustrious group gathered in that room.... And singing, I watched his face and saw him smile ... and when the songs were done, he applauded heartily and thanked me, saying he loved the old songs best. That evening is something pretty special to press between the memory pages of my heart, and though I saw him many times after that, they were serious times ... when there was no singing of old songs ... but only talk of war ... and bonds ... and meetings in far-flung corners of the earth.

And now he's gone ... a great soul has passed beyond the care and worry of this mortal world.... Let us pledge ourselves now to shoulder gloriously the burden he has had to lay down ... to follow his leadership ... to fight as he has fought ... to keep faith as he has kept faith through those dark days that lie far behind us now. Let that be our tribute to Franklin Delano Roosevelt, outstanding leader and great American gentleman. May he who died in the midst of war ... rest—in peace!

Throughout her career Smith was careful not to reveal a political party preference. But Franklin D. Roosevelt *was* her favorite president.

CHAPTER 7

"It's High Noon in New York"

Ted Collins had struck upon a new idea in the spring of 1938. "Kathryn," he declared, "we're going to start something new next week, something we haven't done before." Smith countered with, "Ted, you always have an itch for something new. Aren't things just fine as they stand?" Then Collins explained that it was important to move with the times, to keep one step ahead of the public so that audiences do not tire of you.

"This time, Kathryn, you're going to do a commentary program. No singing, just talking." Smith expressed her doubts and reluctance, reminding her manager that she was known as a singer, not as a speaker. But he reminded her that she had proven herself a competent interviewer of celebrities and of newcomers to the entertainment field and that she had spoken very effectively for various causes, such as appeals for disaster relief and for Christmas dolls for poor children.

Smith acceded to Collins's advice as usual, and "Kate Smith Speaks" made its debut at 3:30 P.M. Monday, April 4. It would be a quarter-hour program aimed primarily at homemakers. Smith knew there would be those critics who would suggest she stick to singing and cooking and leave the commentary to others. At first she was unsponsored, so there was nobody (except network officials) to tell her what or what not to say. She and Collins decided to have folksy heart-to-heart chats designed to furnish food for thought. Besides such benign topics as books, gardening, cooking, the movies, and fashions, Smith did quite a bit of editorializing.

Here, from the very first script, is the way Smith introduced her commentary series:

> Hello everybody. Today I'm tryin' somethin' new, that is, somethin' new for me. First of all, I'd like to have it pretty well understood between you and me just what this program is all about. In your newspapers in the radio

listing you'll see me listed as maybe, "Kate Smith, columnist." Well, it means just that. Yes, I've got some ideas about things, just as you have. But there's nobody who knows better than I do, that probably your ideas are just as good as mine and maybe lots better in some cases. In other words, I'm not gonna come here three days a week and tell you how you ought to comb your hair, or tell our Secretary of State how to run his business. How you comb your hair is your business, and on the other question I'm just one citizen with one vote—I'm no politician. Now what am I gonna talk about each Monday, Wednesday, and Friday afternoon?

Most of you know, I think, that I have a regular hour program on this network each Thursday evening. Because I've been on the air for many years, naturally a lot of folks write to me. Now they expect an answer, just the same as if they sat down and wrote to a good friend, and because I get more than a million letters each year, I've been a poor correspondent. No one can answer that many letters by mail. And that's where this program comes in.

This is your program. We're gonna talk over the things that are closest to your hearts, that interest you most deeply, whether it's how to make a lemon-chiffon pie or a discussion of Hindu philosophy.

We may, too, from time to time, if you ask for it, discuss some important subjects which affect the nation. When we do, I'll bring you the opinions of experts—and I'll give you both sides of every question so that you can draw your own conclusions. I may express an opinion also because I do feel strongly on certain subjects. But it must be understood that they're just my own thoughts and ideas. If you don't agree with them, I won't mind a bit.

Kate Smith the commentator denounced child labor, war, and discrimination against workers over age forty. She spoke of motherhood and the great women of history. Her most daring editorial in that three-month trial period was against the inclusion of sexual innuendos, revealing pictures, or other items that would bring shock or pain to young children in books intended for their use. (She did not actually use the word *sexual*: that would have been too shocking for 1938.) Although she, Collins, and the network feared angry reprisals, the response was overwhelmingly favorable. Again she was ahead of her time.

Smith derived much personal satisfaction from what she called her "speaks" programs. So, apparently, did the women (and others) who tuned into them. After a summer hiatus, during which she wrote her autobiography at her new summer home on Lake Placid, "Kate Smith Speaks" returned to the air with two significant changes. It had acquired a sponsor, Diamond Crystal Shaker Salt, a General Foods product. And the time slot had been moved to high noon in the eastern time zone, which allowed working people to tune in on their lunch hour. Many of us remember nostalgically such features of this program as

• the opening signature:
TED: It's high noon in New York and time for Kate Smith. Here she is.

KATE: Hello, everybody.
• Collins's news segment (before):
KATE: And now, Ted, what's new?
(after):
KATE: And in the news behind the news. . .
• Smith's wartime sign-off:
KATE: Thanks for list'nin' and remember, if you don't write, you're wrong.
• Collins's closing remark:
TED: Tune in again tomorrow when Kate Smith speaks.

Through May 1939, the program aired Tuesdays, Thursdays, and Saturdays, with Mary Margaret McBride in that time slot the other weekdays. From October 1939 until June 1951, "Kate Smith Speaks" was a popular fixture every weekday at high noon. No other network program could compete with it.

By 1940 the audience numbered ten million, making the show number one in daytime radio. Officials at CBS approached Collins about continuing it during the summer months. They were insistent. Collins and Smith were just as insistent that they would comply only if they could do it from Lake Placid. So a line was run all the way to Smith's Camp Sunshine on Buck Island in "the big lake," and a closet in her guest house was made over into a tiny broadcast studio. Bob "Believe It or Not" Ripley wrote it up as the world's smallest broadcast studio. Indeed it proved too small and later was moved to a corner of the large room above the big boathouse.

The main room upstairs in that boathouse was Smith's huge trophy room. The broadcast studio was in the back, a small room, about six by ten feet. At one end were Smith's records and transcriptions. At the other end a door opened under the eave of the roof. It was there that engineer Bob Ueker did his duties. He was obviously not a claustrophobiac.

Between 1939 and 1951 Kate Smith's routine for a typical weekday would have gone as follows. At 9 A.M. she rises. She dresses, plays a bit with her cocker spaniel Freckles, then at 10:15 she has breakfast. Promptly at 10:45 a sound engineer arrives to hook up the mike and check sound levels. Smith rereads the script for the day, noting words difficult to pronounce, making slashes where pauses should be, and checking the timing.

At 11:15 Collins arrives, and they make last-minute changes in the script. Collins has been up for several hours, preparing his news segment. At the Kated office two United Press teletype machines spill out the latest news from around the world. Collins has also perused several morning papers for items. There are scriptwriters to aid him in all of this, just as eight staff members have been gathering human interest topics for Smith's portions of the show.

At 11:55 Freckles is whisked into the bedroom, there to remain until 12:15. The mike sits on the table in the parlor, Collins to its left, Smith to its right. Their scripts are at hand. Precisely at 12:00 the program begins.

On one such typical day—Tuesday, April 24, 1945—the script read as follows:

TED: It's high noon in New York and time for Kate Smith.

KATE: Hello everybody! Lots of good wishes are being showered on the men who have assembled in San Francisco for the Great [United Nations] Conference which begins tomorrow, but probably no wish is more sincere than that of Louie Myers, who said to Mr. Stettinius one day last week, "When you go to California may the blessings of God be with you and the other delegates." Louie Myers quit the diplomatic corps last week, after 42 years in government service. He is the 72-year-old head messenger of the State Department who has been retired after long and faithful service. 33 of those 42 years were spent as a messenger and clerk in the Secretary of State's office, and nine in the departments of Labor and Commerce. Some thirty of his friends and associates crowded around him to say goodbye to Louie Myers. They gave him numerous gifts, including a Golden American eagle mounted on a wooden pedestal ... and Mr. Stettinius told him, "You have a right to feel pride in a career of devoted service to your government." That, I think, is the feeling of all of us toward a good and faithful servant ... Louie Myers has escorted numerous diplomats, watched countless diplomatic ceremonies, and has helped to serve state dinners, luncheons and teas held in the White House by six successive Presidents... Now he deserves a rest.

(First Commercial)

KATE: According to *Newsweek*, of all of the words in the English language, the one word which carries the most magic for the greatest number of women is *nylon*. At present, as we all know, nylons occupy the Number One place of things we can't buy. Even though women know this, it is a fact that thousands of dollars are being spent each year for bootleg nylons. Some of them are advertised as made in Mexico. Others are accompanied by elaborate explanations about government reject or fire salvage. Actually, most of these would-be nylons are plain, common garden-variety rayons treated with a chemical bath which imparts a special sheen of nylon—until the first washing. These counterfeits are usually stamped nylon and bear the forged names of reputable makers. Such makers are as eager as cheated customers to see the counterfeiters behind bars—where many already find themselves.

There are some stockings on the market—the black market—which actually do contain a small amount of nylon. ... The precious nylon for these was stolen, hijacked, or diverted in some furtive manner from wartime production. The black market nylon stockings are usually of shoddy workmanship and outrageously expensive, averaging as high as $10 a pair for stockings that probably won't give a week's wear. FBI and OPA agents are on the alert for nylon frauds. The next time you are offered a pair of fantastically-priced nylons, along with a salestalk about a warehouse clearance of Mexican imports, don't part with your hard-earned dollars. Instead, notify your local OPA or FBI office. Perhaps your tip will help the agents to uncover a serious leak of raw nylon from a parachute factory where the fabric is urgently needed to save lives of American flyers.

And now, Ted, what's new? [News]

(Second Commercial)

KATE: Often, in the past, I've talked with you about the products of my mailbag ... the letters, cheerful and gloomy ... approving, condemning ... friendly, chatty, and heartening ... that pour into my office every day of the week.

Today, though, I want to vary that procedure.... I want to tell you about *another* woman's mail.... And somehow I think this woman has received something of the same feeling from her mail that I so often do ... the feeling of a whole nation of friends, of warmth and interest, and understanding from all her fellow Americans.

This woman is the wife of a soldier. She's Mrs. Elva Gangwere of Allentown, Pennsylvania. Her husband has been overseas since January. It was just a few weeks ago—March 23, to be exact—that Mrs. Gangwere had the thrill of seeing a picture of her husband in print. It was a news picture sent back from the battlefront in Germany, at the time of the historic crossing of the Rhine. And the picture showed Private Gangwere keeping a lonely vigil. A literal "Watch on the Rhine."

The appearance of that picture in America's newspapers brought home to his wife the true spirit of warm-hearted America. For, from the moment it was published, she began receiving letters. From New Jersey and California; from Texas and Massachusetts, and places in between the letters poured in. Every one of them carried the same thought ... the friendly message of one American to another who carries the same burden. "Dear Mrs. Gangwere," they said, "We saw your husband's picture in our newspaper and we thought you might want the clipping. We knew we would want clippings if it were our boy. We know how you miss your husband, for we, too, miss our husbands.... We want you to know that other Americans share your loneliness." Yes, that's a composite of the hundreds of letters that poured into the home and heart of a soldier's wife in Allentown, Pennsylvania, and Elva Gangwere has drawn a lot of comfort from her mailbox in recent days.

Thanks for list'nin' ... and remember, if you don't write, you're wrong.

SMITH'S PLEA IN THAT CLOSING REMINDER is for the folks on the home front to write to those away in the service of their country. She first used that slogan on a "Spirit of '42" broadcast she did on May 17, 1942. She explained it two days later as follows:

This explanation is only intended now for every American who doesn't wear a uniform, and it's about every American who *does*. By that I mean Marine, Soldier, Sailor, Aviator, Coast Guard, Merchant Marine, and all of the men fighting for us away from home.... I tell you now, it is of great importance that you write to the boys—write every single day to your loved ones or your friends in the service. Tell them anything pleasant that is happening at home.... It may seem trivial to you, but I talked about this matter with over fifty different young men training in the Marine

Corps on Sunday afternoon and they all told me that when they get a letter from home, sometimes they read it as many as a dozen times. So please remember, everybody, the men who are ready to die for us, live on our letters and if you would like to adopt my words as a slogan to pass on to all of your friends, this is it—Remember, if you don't write, you're wrong.

Variety reviewed "Kate Smith Speaks" on October 11, 1939:

> This is the second year for the noontime chats (they are just that) of the CBS singer and her sidekick, Ted Collins. It's sentimental and philosophical, informal, unpredictable stuff. Ted Collins answers Miss Smith's question, "What's new?" by reading a couple of items from the United Press. And then they begin the "let's-talk-of-kings-and-cabbages" routine. Probably only Kate Smith could do this, or better, get a sponsor to trust her act. It is made sun-clear that the sponsor is Swansdown Flour and there is no reason why listener and advertiser won't be equally pleased.

I have in my collection a scant ten "Kate Smith Speaks" programs on tape. In one, dated August 28, 1946, Collins behaves in a strangely irritated manner, stumbling over his lines at times. In this program, done from the tiny studio at Kate Smith's Lake Placid home, Collins complains about returning from a fishing trip late the night before and getting lost because nobody had any lights on to guide him in the fog. He becomes quite testy and pokes fun at the summer folk who are not willing to spend "two cents a night and all ya hear about is they're [affected speech] going to the Riviera next spring or something." I asked Smith whether she remembered it, and she said she did indeed. She laughingly explained that Collins and "Uncle Hughie" had gone fishing and imbibed some alcoholic beverages. They arrived home around midnight, yelling and screaming and stumbling into the boathouse. Collins was apparently in the grip of a hangover "at high noon" the next day, but Smith knew how to handle him, and she survived the program. That quarter hour must have seemed like an hour.

Smith seldom missed a broadcast, but on Monday, December 9, 1940, she was away from the microphone. When she returned, she brought with her a case of laryngitis and opened her "Speaks" broadcast with these words:

> Hello everybody! This is not a bullfrog you hear, but me, with my old "Shadow," laryngitis, the bugaboo of all public speakers and singers.
> I feel somewhat like a truant this morning because yesterday instead of taking my usual place at the microphone, I was down home in Virginia. We often speak of radio and stage folks as being good troupers and sticking to their posts no matter what happens in their private lives, but I'm just old fashioned and sentimental enough to feel that family ties take precedence over everything else. So, when my only sister told me not long

ago that she had set the date for her wedding for Monday, December 9th, I made up my mind that nothing would stop me from being right on hand for the great occasion. The wedding yesterday was a quiet one . . . just the family and a few friends . . . a little laughter and a few tears. We threw rice and kissed the bride, and followed the traditions that make weddings something to remember through the years.

And before I forget it, thank you, Mr. C., for doing the program all by yourself—I'll do the same for you sometime.

Kate's sister Helena M. Smith married Lee Joseph Steene that day. He was a flyer and became a pilot in the Army Air Corps during the Second World War. After that he became a commercial pilot for Pan American Airlines. They had two daughters, Kathryn born in 1944 and Suzanne born in 1948. Joe Steene died in 1967.

In January 1943, Smith was away from the microphones for nearly two weeks. Friday, the 8th, had been an exceptionally busy day in a seemingly endless string of busy wartime days. She did both "Kate Smith Speaks" and "The Kate Smith Hour," then she suffered an acutely painful attack of some sort, recovering sufficiently to fulfill an engagement at the Stage Door Canteen on 44th Street. After going through with the repeat broadcast for the Pacific time zone (not without substantial pain) she was taken to a hospital, where her attack was diagnosed as gallstones. She remained in serious condition for over a week, was put on a low-fat diet, and released to return to the air at noon on Thursday the 21st. At this time she weighed perhaps the most ever. She later confided to a friend that when she stepped on the scales the indicator went all the way to 300 pounds. She did not know how much more than that she had weighed.

Collins, who had been filling in for Smith on the "Speaks" programs, announced her return with these words: "And now, ladies and gentlemen, I have with me here what I'd call the world's finest guest star. She needs no introduction. Here she is . . . Kate Smith." And Smith responded with these words:

Hello everybody! No words can ever express how glad I am to be with you all! Time is not truly measured in days or weeks, but in the thoughts that travel through the mind . . . and it seems years since that Friday of January 8th, when pain first took hold of me and left me puzzled and bewildered . . . and sort of ashamed that I could not hope to carry on as always. But I shan't talk much now about what's past and done with. Rather I'd like to speak of the combination of groups of people who have miraculously helped me to make a quick recovery from a serious illness. First and most important, I want to thank each and every one of you who sent me cards, letters, and messages. . . . They are a very real help in bringing back health, because behind them lie the thousands of shining thoughts that reach out and lift up . . . and supply needed strength. . . .

Now, thank God . . . and I say it reverently . . . I am myself again . . .

and if my voice is a little bit shaky . . . well . . . it's because it's my first day up . . . and I'm excited . . . and tremendously happy to be back. And now, Ted, tell us, What's new?

Although she suffered several more gall bladder attacks years later, Smith never had to have it removed. Once, around 1970, she had an excruciating attack while at Camp Sunshine at Lake Placid. She screamed with pain all the while she was being rushed across the lake to the hospital. She told me that bananas were her Waterloo, certain to provoke an attack.

"Kate Smith Speaks" was a noonday fixture at our house when my sister and I were growing up. My mother always had the little Arvin radio tuned to WPRO, the CBS radio station in Providence, and as we ate lunch Kate was truly like a fourth person at our table. We listened intently to every word she and Ted Collins spoke and shared every light-hearted moment with them, and it seemed they had many. One of these typical moments occurred in the summer of 1947:

> KATE: And while I'm on the subject of food, I see where a Chicago ice cream parlor is beginning to believe that people don't know a bargain when they see one. The ice cream man, Gerry Schemel, is offering a free sundae to any person who can eat two of his specialties . . . which he calls "monstrosities." And if you can eat *three*, they're all on the house. As far as I know, no one has won a free sundae.
>
> TED: Then he isn't taking much of a chance, is he?
>
> KATE: Here's the catch, Ted. . . The sundae weighs two pounds and contains . . . six large scoops of ice cream, two whole bananas, two large cookies, fresh fruit, chocolate and marshmallow syrup, two inches of whipped cream, a handful of chopped nuts, and two large Maraschino cherries. "Monstrosity" certainly is a good name for that concoction. But if *I* was in Chicago today, Gerry Schemel would be out of luck . . . because, from that description of those sundaes, plus the heat, I will guarantee you that I'd polish off three of them. I can taste them now. [*Laughing*]
>
> TED: And you know what, you are not kidding!
>
> KATE: I certainly am not, Ted! [*Chuckling*] I'll be back in a moment, but first our announcer.

Once, during a broadcast from the home of Smith's mother in Arlington, Virginia, the postman came during Collins's newscast, causing Freckles and Laddie (Mrs. Smith's dog) to bark. While Kate was rushing to quiet the dogs, she caught her foot in a telephone wire, pulling the phone to the floor. Through it all Collins kept his cool and completed the news segment.

Smith could rise up in righteous indignation over an injustice being done some or all of her fellow Americans. Take, for instance, this item from January 10, 1950:

Once again, yesterday, New Yorkers were shocked to see on the front pages of their papers, the pictures of six young boys, all teenagers except one, who is twenty, arrested for robbery, when two other teenaged members of their gang tipped off police. The list of their crimes is long and lurid. It is one of holdups, stabbing, stolen cars, double-crossing, and hijacking. All eight of these boys apparently were well schooled in the tactics of the dark underworld of gangsterism where law and order are jeered at, and moral responsibility is unknown.

You look at the picture, study the faces of these boys, and wonder what is happening to us. You wonder at what particular moment and for what hidden reason each lad was moved to take the first step toward a way of life that can only end in disaster and shame. The news story didn't touch on these phases of the matter.

Day after day, week after week, we hear the same sad story. Youthful gangs, holdups, murderous weapons, burglary, even death by violence, among teenagers in sweaters and blue jeans. And we see in our papers the sullen, disillusioned faces of young boys on the threshold of manhood—manhood which is already destined to be dissipated behind prison bars. There is a reason behind all this. And even the experts don't seem to agree completely as to what it is. Some blame juvenile delinquency on thriller-killer movies, on gangster radio and television programs, on so-called comic books and other questionable literature. And certainly there is reason to agree that they set a horrible example, and put many evil ideas into the minds of the young. Others are firm in their belief that the chief offenders are the parents. Two years ago Baker, Oregon, demonstrated in a small way how large a part parents do play in governing the actions of their children. They originated a plan whereby the parents, not the children, would be punished and judged responsible for conditions which led to the delinquency. Baker was being plagued by a teenage "club" known as the Panther Gang, whose purpose was stealing. After taking the boys into custody on numerous charges and gaining little by their conviction, it was decided to punish parents by fines up to $200 or 100 days in jail. The Panther Gang quickly broke up; delinquency rates dropped sharply—some said as much as 90%.

Perhaps this is a long step in the right direction. Environment and discipline can do much for impressionable youth. But there are more factors than movies, books, radio programs, plays, and parental guidance—or lack of it—in this alarming condition of criminal activity among the young. Perhaps the responsibility lies, not with any one group, but with society in general, and a growing disregard for the ideals and high moral standards which made our country great. It is a problem which must be solved, and solved soon—for today's children will be tomorrow's citizens.

As forceful as that timeless editorial was, it was not very controversial. "Kate Smith Speaks" did offer some controversial material, however, and this item from February 24, 1947, is a prime example:

Well, to law-abiding citizens it certainly was disturbing news when word came from Havana, Cuba, that Lucky Luciano . . . a notorious and distinctly unsavory racketeer . . . was doing business in that island republic. This man ... who for years was known as the "Vice King of Broadway" ... a dealer in the most loathsome types of crime ... had somehow made his way to Cuba.

He was prosecuted for his crime in 1936 by Governor Dewey, who was then District Attorney, and was sentenced to serve between thirty and fifty years in prison. Later he was released from prison and deported to Italy.

Lucky Luciano ... described by Governor Dewey as the most dangerous and important criminal in the country ... now lives in luxury in Havana.

His business? Reports say that he is masterminding gambling activities in the two places in that city where gambling is permitted by law. There ... at the Jockey Club and the National Casino, this evil, dangerous man rubs elbows, each night, with some of America's most famous celebrities.

How did he get there? Who is responsible for the issuance of a visa to this foul enemy of society? ... this dealer in white slavery?

Reports say that he has friends down there ... influential friends ... friends who are willing to swap protection for inside, expert knowledge of the underworld and how to make money outside the fringe of the law.

No one knows whether Lucky Luciano's visa is for temporary or permanent resident. If he is just there on a visit, then he must have signed a pledge not to work while there... But sometimes such things can be overlooked if one has political connections.

The people of New York don't need to be told what that would mean ... but perhaps the people of Cuba do.

Lucky Luciano, they say, is publicity shy and subdued now. And with good reason. For he knows now that the white glare of the spotlight might send him right back where he was sent before ... clear out of this hemisphere. Or ... if it's legally possible ... back to prison for a good long time.

In this editorial Smith had come a long way from describing how to make a lemon pie and reviewing flower shows. She was never afraid to speak her mind and to let the chips fall where they might. This time certain CBS officials who had not liked some of her other editorials were particularly annoyed by the one about Lucky Luciano.

Smith went to Chicago in May to receive the 1947 American Brotherhood Arts citation from the National Conference of Christians and Jews. Following the award luncheon, she called a press conference. In an uncharacteristically acid manner, she lashed out at CBS, saying, "You don't have freedom of speech on CBS. Every day I get orders that I must take this or that out of my script. Why, they wouldn't even let me talk about Lucky Luciano when he slipped out to Cuba. I've been in radio for quite a while and I've been fairly successful. I don't see why I should let anybody tell me how to run my program." She took the occasion to announce that she would be leaving CBS June 20 and switching to the Mutual Network. She said that the executives there had assured her they would not interfere.

Naturally, the press wanted a statement from Ted Collins. His only comment was, "If Miss Smith said that, she'll have to get out of it herself.

I think Miss Smith is leaving Columbia because she has a better contract."
That was an uncharacteristic comment from Kate Smith's mentor and the
president of the Kated Corporation. Officials at CBS refused to get into the
fray. They simply pointed to the fact that the contract with her sponsor,
General Foods, had not been renewed. The Mutual–Don Lee Network, in
need of big-name stars, had offered her a lucrative contract, involving
several sponsors.

Smith exited CBS with characteristic grace over the airwaves. She expressed her gratitude to the CBS officials "from Mr. William S. Paley,
friend all through the Columbia years, right straight down the line through
engineers, sound men, secretaries, typists, telephone operators, and all the
many other employees of the company. I have received help and cooperation and encouragement in my work, and I am grateful." She reminisced
at some length about her years at CBS and her affiliation with General
Foods. Ted Collins was conspicuously absent that day; he presumably was
not nearly as gracious about the parting. Smith did say, "Ted Collins
wasn't able to be with me on the program today, so I'd like to add that the
thanks and the appreciation, to Columbia and General Foods, are said on
his behalf, as well as my own." It is safe to assume that Collins did not ask
her to say that.

In an oblique way, Smith managed to plug her new network twice on
that broadcast. First she announced, "Ted and I are saying goodbye, not
to radio, which I guess will always claim us, but to this network. We will
be on the air every day when it's High Noon in New York as usual. And
you can find us at another spot on your dial." She got this remark in at the
end: "Yes, it's the end of a happy cycle today, and the beginning of a new
cycle, because don't forget, we'll be with you as usual next Monday, when
it's High Noon in New York—only we'll be on another network. Be sure
to join us . . . look for us on your dial!" CBS replaced Smith with something called "Wendy Warren and the News," a mishmash of soap opera and
news, but ten million listeners followed Kate Smith from Columbia to
Mutual. Smith greeted her listeners, old and new, with these words from
the script:

> Hello everybody! I hope you all had a very pleasant weekend, doing the
> things you most wanted to do . . . and finding time to get out into the fresh
> air and sunshine. As for me, I had a lovely, busy weekend and this morn-
> ing my heart is light in the thought that, along with many old friends who
> have been joining us at High Noon for many years . . . nine to be exact
> . . . we are welcoming today a large number of new friends . . . in cities
> and towns across the nation. For this program marks our first regular
> daytime broadcast on this network. For our old friends I'd like to say this:
> Though we are heard now at a new place on the dial . . . we're just the
> same people as always and we'll talk generally on a large variety of subjects
> just as we have in the past. . . We're still your neighbors. . . We've just

moved, that's all . . . to a house a little way down the block. For our new listeners, I want to say welcome. We hope you'll join us every day.

From time to time Smith found it necessary to defend herself against certain accusations. During World War II she was constantly urging Americans to sacrifice for the war effort. There were plenty who thought she was hypocritical: that she, with her fame and fortune, was living in the lap of luxury. On March 23, 1945, the script shows that she defended herself with this commentary:

> Do you mind now, if I talk for a moment about myself? Every now and then a letter comes to me that causes me unhappiness. Such a letter came last week; it was a bitter tirade. It made me yearn to clear away the false ideas of the writer . . . not because they were important, really, but because always with us there is the longing, the deep urge to be understood. "What do you know of hardships or sacrifices?" the letter asked. "You don't have to ride on streetcars or buses . . . or mill through crowds and do your shopping in a few odd moments from your job. . . You don't have to worry about looking for bargains." Those accusations set me to wondering. . . Do some of my listeners imagine that I sit in a gilded drawing room, while frenzied shopkeepers spread their fabulous wares at my feet? As a matter of fact, just the reverse is the case, and I'd be the loneliest, most unhappy person in the world if this were not so. Money and what some people refer to as "fame" can buy many things . . . but there is no coin of any realm that can purchase the things that have always been dear to me. I've always been a simple person. . . I love crowds and enjoy bargain basements . . . while a tour of the five-and-ten leaves me starry-eyed with amazement at the varieties of treasures that can be found there. Like most folks, I ride on buses and streetcars and sub-ways. . . I shop in all our stores without benefit of special escort or special favor. I have no chauffeur-driven car, waiting for me wherever I go. That luxury went out for me with Pearl Harbor . . . and I wouldn't want it any other way. I budget ration points like every other woman in America . . . and keep an eye on the dwindling quarter-of-a-pound of butter. I write letters to dear ones and friends overseas. . . I crochet afghans and do needlework and love it! I have no rosy dreams . . . to deny oneself nothing . . . to have no wish unfulfilled, nothing to plan for seems to me to make for a very unhappy existence.

It was an effective response. Smith was not extravagant in many ways. She did like elegant Lincoln automobiles, and her cook set a banquet table, to be sure. But a little later, when paper towels came into vogue, she often laid wet ones on the kitchen counter to dry so she could reuse them. She was raised with a "waste not, want not" philosophy. To this day the veteran New York cabbies tell of her legendary thrift when paying taxi fares. She supposedly never tipped them.

In February 1950, Smith found it necessary to defend herself against an entirely different accusation. Considering her well-known patriotic endeavors, it is hard to fathom this one. The closing segment of "Kate Smith Speaks" for February 7, 1950, concerns this episode, as reprinted from the script:

> KATE SMITH: Folks, have you heard the Fulton Lewis [news] program lately over this network? And did you hear a particular show . . . just last week?
>
> TED COLLINS: Kathryn, stop right there . . . don't say another word. I know the program you mean. The one in which Mr. Lewis mentioned a pressure group that has been trying to slander some of the most famous names in radio. This pressure group for which Mr. Lewis coined the nickname "Assassins Anonymous" apparently spends all its time victimizing well-known radio personalities. Its tactics are aimed at silencing the radio voices of a group of loyal and public-spirited Americans.
>
> KATE SMITH: Ted, I'm quite familiar with these well-developed smear tactics. As Mr. Lewis pointed out, my name is included on the list of those being attacked by the pressure group.
>
> TED COLLINS: Yes, I know. You are accused of being . . . and here I'm quoting . . . "a dangerous and vicious tool of Fascists' interests." Your accusers also charge you with endangering the freedom of American citizens. Can you tie that! It's hitting an all-time low in stupidity.
>
> KATE SMITH: Ted, I can only say that the group's accusation is too ridiculous even to be dignified by an answer.
>
> TED COLLINS: I agree with you there, Kathryn. However, I know that you do want to speak out against the shameful methods employed by that particular terror group . . . and its fellow travelers.
>
> KATE SMITH: I certainly do.
>
> TED COLLINS: As Mr. Lewis points out, this organization of evil-doers is trying to force off the air a few acknowledged patriotic commentators, one being Kate Smith. I hope you've noticed, too . . . that the underhanded scheme is not aimed at one network alone . . . but at leading commentators of all networks. Furthermore, the smear tactics of the pressure group would do credit to the best trained propagandists of the late Herr Hitler or Comrade Stalin. Now we have known about this deceitful scheme for some time . . . but until recently I hadn't realized how widespread it was. I still don't know the whole story, including the identity of the real backers of this un–American plot against leading radio commentators. I hope to know more soon.
>
> KATE SMITH: And when you do, Ted, I'm sure our listeners will be anxious to hear the truth about the group which seeks to destroy America with Fifth Column tactics. One thing is sure, even though I have been smeared by the Reds, I am not going to be silenced by any slanderous charges. My own conduct speaks louder than the venomous words of mudslinging pressure organizations, and I'm still on the air!

These attacks against Smith and others foreshadow the McCarthy era of smear tactics soon to come, although Senator McCarthy was out to get the Red Commies. Smith was outraged. She stood her ground, and her reputation survived and flourished. Would that the same were true for many other celebrities, whose careers were ruined by false and vicious finger-pointing.

In conclusion, let it be said that Kate Smith's reputation as one of the three most beloved and influential women of the world is due in no small part to her noontime commentaries. For the rest of her life, she looked back on "Kate Smith Speaks" fondly. It was what she liked to do best—because, she said, she could get close to her audience. She once declared that, given the choice of commenting or singing, she would opt for commenting. Fortunately, she never had to make that choice.

The final broadcast in the "Speaks" format took place June 15, 1951, although neither Smith nor Collins was aware of it. The script shows that the broadcast ended in a touching way:

> Just the other day I found myself thinking of the story I'd heard once about an old gentleman who had worked at the same job, for the same company, for sixty years. Finally, after three-score years of service, he decided to retire, and he talked—as people will—of how much he was going to enjoy doing nothing—and he certainly would never set foot in the office again. Two days later, there he was, back at the factory . . . "just to look around and see how things were going." That's the way I'll probably be this summer. Even though I haven't been at the job for sixty years . . . and I certainly am *not* retiring . . . far from it—I am still looking forward to my first vacation in fourteen years. Still, my life will seem very empty around this time every day, because I'll miss these talks with you. Fourteen years, day in and day out, you and I have met at mid-day to talk things over in a neighborly way. This association of ours has been far from a one-way proposition, you know. I have voiced my opinions over the air and you, in turn, have told me yours in countless letters, cards, even telegrams. Much as I love Lake Placid, and the idea of having the entire day, every day, all summer long, for relaxation and rest—I'm still going to miss talking with you folks. I hope you'll miss me too. . . .
>
> We'll be together again in the Fall, when we'll be able to share many more experiences together, but I couldn't let this whole summer go by without telling you how I feel. I hope you'll know now that I'll miss you this summer . . . and as far as the last fourteen years are concerned, I can only say a most heartfelt "Thanks for listenin'."

Collins had every "Kate Smith Speaks" script preserved in fourteen leather-bound volumes, which he presented to Smith. She kept them in a French Provincial bookcase in her living room, first in New York and later in Raleigh. Hers are in green Morocco, with Collins's news segments in red. When they returned in the fall of 1951—over a third network—the programs were not formally scripted. Rather, they used notes from which they more or less ad-libbed.

CHAPTER 8

Columbus of the Kilocycles

"The Kate Smith Hour" was a variety show. Besides music, there were segments devoted to drama and comedy. Many entertainers got their start on Smith's hour. It was an outstanding launching pad for comedians, for instance. The first comedian on the show was Henny Youngman, famous as the "king of one-liners," who did two stints with Smith and Collins. After several weeks performing solo, he added a character whom he called "Uncle Max." Max was played by the veteran comedian Charlie Cantor, who later joined Minerva Pious to form the team of "Charlie and Min." Pious and Cantor did hilarious Jewish comedy on Smith's hour in 1941.

Early in 1938 Youngman received an offer from Paramount Pictures, which he was not free to accept because of his contract with Kated, Inc., as resident comedian. Collins was willing to release him if he could come up with another comedy act. Enter Abbott and Costello. Bud Abbott and Lou Costello had come up through burlesque and vaudeville, but had been a team for only two years. Youngman told Collins to go see them on stage; Collins was not impressed. He feared that their stage routines would not adapt to the radio medium, as their comedy was too visual.

Young Sam Weisbord of the prestigious William Morris Agency was Abbott and Costello's agent. At a meeting in Collins's office, Weisbord assured him that they were a clean act, fit and proper for Smith's family-oriented show. He had brought along an impressive number of favorable reviews to show Collins, who caved in to Weisbord's enthusiasm and agreed to have Abbott and Costello replace Youngman for one week only, at a salary of $175 each. Although their initial radio routine elicited only a lukewarm reception, Collins liked them well enough to invite them back.

There was one problem: they sounded alike. So Lou Costello agreed to raise his voice to a falsetto, which made him sound like an adolescent. Abbott and Costello's routines grew on Collins, as well as on the studio and radio audiences. Smith loved them from the start. Youngman was released from his contract; Abbott and Costello were signed as regulars. Smith's ratings went up and Rudy Vallée's went down. Soon Collins raised the pair's weekly stipend to $375 apiece.

Now Abbott and Costello wanted to do their baseball routine, "Who's on First?" on the radio, but Collins did not care for it. The more he balked at it, the more determined Costello was to do it. To get his way he used a ploy. One week he told Collins they just could not come up with a suitable routine. Collins told them they had twenty-four hours to work one up. The next day, Wednesday, when Collins was firming up the show, he asked Abbott and Costello what they had decided on. When Costello insisted that they had come up blank, Collins replied, "Oh no, you don't! Do you still have that silly baseball thing?" They assured him that they did, and he shot back, "Use it." Costello pressed his luck and asked Collins if he was sure. He said he wanted it, and Costello got his way. It became probably the best-known comedy routine in history. A sample follows:

> ABBOTT: You know, strange as it may seem, they give baseball players peculiar names nowadays. On the St. Louis team, Who's on first, What's on second, I Don't Know is on third.
> COSTELLO: That's what I want to find out. I want you to tell me the names of the fellows on the St. Louis team.
> ABBOTT: I'm telling you. Who's on first, What's on second, I Don't Know is on third.
> COSTELLO: You know the fellows' names?
> ABBOTT: Yes.
> COSTELLO: Well, then, who's playing first?
> ABBOTT: Yes.
> COSTELLO: I mean the fellow's name on first base.
> ABBOTT: Who.
> COSTELLO: The fellow's name on first base for St. Louis.
> ABBOTT: Who.
> COSTELLO: The guy on first base.
> ABBOTT: Who is on first base.
> COSTELLO: What are you asking me for?
> ABBOTT: I'm not asking you, I'm telling you. Who is on first.
> COSTELLO: [*Exasperated by now*] I'm askin' you, who is on first?
> ABBOTT: That's the man's name.
> COSTELLO: That's whose name?
> ABBOTT: Yes.
> COSTELLO: Well, go ahead and tell me.
> ABBOTT: Who?
> COSTELLO: The guy on first.
> ABBOTT: Who.
> COSTELLO: The first baseman.
> ABBOTT: Who is on first.
> COSTELLO: [*Attempting to remain calm*] Have you got a baseman on first?
> ABBOTT: Certainly.
> COSTELLO: Well, all I'm trying to find out is what's the guy's name on first base?
> ABBOTT: Oh, no, no. What's on second base.

> COSTELLO: I'm not asking who's on second.
> ABBOTT: Who's on first.
> COSTELLO: That's what I'm tryin' to find out. . .

The studio audience roared at it. Pandemonium reigned. The radio listeners loved it; the switchboard lit up like a Christmas tree. The rest is history. They repeated it at World Series time, and it became by far their most famous routine.

In Abbott and Costello's radio routines, Ted Collins was often their fall guy, as in an early 1940 broadcast:

> ABBOTT: Costello, do you realize you've said hello to everybody on the program except Ted Collins? How did you come to miss him?
> COSTELLO: How did I come to miss him? He ducked! I'd have given him two black eyes if I hadn't been stopped.
> ABBOTT: Who stopped you?
> COSTELLO: Ted Collins.

On another show the pair went out for football. To Abbott's dismay, Costello got angry and quit the team with a parting shot:

> COSTELLO: I'll take my football with me, too. You can use Ted Collins.
> ABBOTT: Why should I use Mr. Collins for a football?
> COSTELLO: Because he's thick-skinned, tight-laced, and a bag of wind!

Lou Costello's daughter Chris wrote in her loving biography of her famous dad, *Lou's on First*, that Kate Smith was taken with Abbott and Costello from the outset. She took them aside and gave them advice about how they should dress and present themselves off the air. She said they would be famous now and should make a proper appearance in public. She even loaned them money to buy new clothes, without really expecting to be repaid. She bought them new cars, too: Packards.

When Abbott and Costello's routines were running overtime, Collins would come onstage and poke Costello gently in the ribs, whispering that they must wind it up so Smith could sing. Once one of her numbers had to be eliminated, but that never happened again. Abbott and Costello left "The Kate Smith Hour" in June 1940. By this time Kated was paying them $1,250 a week. Like Henny Youngman, they always remembered the kindness of Smith and Collins in giving them their start in the bigtime.

The fondly remembered situation comedy "The Aldrich Family" did not exactly originate on "The Kate Smith Hour." It evolved from a play written by Clifford Goldsmith called "What a Life!" which opened on Broadway in April 1938. Produced by the legendary George Abbott, it starred 21-year-old Ezra Stone as Henry Aldrich, with 18-year-old Eddie Bracken as Henry's sidekick George Bigelow.

The play became one of the major successes of that summer. with the result that the J. Walter Thompson advertising agency, which handled the

"Rudy Vallée Hour" on NBC, signed the cast for three sketches that August. Young and Rubicam, ad agency for "The Kate Smith Hour," signed them for the entire thirty-nine-week 1938-39 season, changing the title to "The Aldrich Family." After playing Henry's chum Dizzy a few times, Eddie Bracken went to Hollywood to begin his lengthy film career. Ezra Stone explained, "The advertising agencies were 'the powers that be' in those days in radio. Young and Rubicam [representing General Foods] were bidding against the J. Walter Thompson Agency, which represented Standard Brands [makers of Royal Puddings, Fleischmann's Yeast, etc., sponsors of the "Vallée Hour"]. Harry Ackerman was an executive in the radio department of Young and Rubicam. We were very lucky to have him direct us, as he was a top executive in the company." Bob Welch directed "The Kate Smith Hour," and it was he who came up with the Henry Aldrich signature:

> MRS. ALDRICH: Hen*ree*, Henry Aldrich!
> HENRY: Coming, mother.

"*What a Life!* ran two years on Broadway," Stone continued. "We'd hold the curtain for [the stage show] and we were always on the first half of 'The Kate Smith Hour.' As I recall, I was allowed to 'split' after our spot, but when we came back for the repeat broadcast she insisted that I join the entire cast for bows, because the stage door was stage left and Miss Smith's dressing room was stage left. She did her kisses and goodbyes and I thought I could scoot off without anyone knowing me. But this big arm nailed me to the wings: 'No one leaves the stage before me, Ezra.'"

When I asked Ezra Stone what impression he had of Smith, he told me that they had very little contact "because the show was rehearsed in elements and our spot was rehearsed separately. Usually she would be in the theatre but not involved with us in any way. I found her to be playing the *grand dame*, as I recall. I just had that feeling because she was larger than life, but a very graceful woman, and a very hearty woman. I can still hear her laugh, a wonderful laugh."

Stone recalled clearly seeing Smith in *Flying High* when he was in high school. He remembered that her graceful dancing stopped the show. He also recalled a later incident that made him wonder just how much education she had had. "I sat next to her at a table reading of a special script for the Community Chest or something," he told me. "She would lean over and point to certain words in the script while other actors were talking and whisper, 'How do you pronounce that?' They were usually three-syllable words. It kinda caught me up short. I couldn't believe that."

"The Aldrich Family" was so successful as a weekly eight-minute sitcom on "The Kate Smith Hour" that it became a spinoff with its own half-hour show the next season, also with General Foods as sponsor and Jack

Miller conducting the orchestra. They advertised Jell-O and their jingles, sung by Henry and his sidekick Homer Brown, are legendary: "Oh, the big red letters stand for the Jell-O family [repeated], That's Jell-O, yum-yum-yum, Jell-O Puddings, yum-yum-yum, Jell-O Tapioca Pudding, yum-yum-yum."

Homer Brown was Henry's whining pal. I was able to interview John Daley ("Jackie") Kelk, who played Homer for the entire thirteen-year run of "The Aldrich Family" on radio and television at the same time I spoke with Ezra Stone. The character of Homer was not added until 1940, so Jack Kelk was not on "The Kate Smith Hour" sketches. He was on her show later, in 1945, with a comedy act of his own, playing a sort of lovelorn wimp. Smith herself played straight-man for him. One of their routines occurred on the May 27, 1945, show:

> KATE: You know, the French say, "Cherchez la femme," meaning "Look for the woman." Well, we know a young man who took the French seriously and spends a great part of his time looking for the woman. If he ever finds her [*chuckle*] he'll probably gulp and run the other way. But after all, it's the spirit of the chase that counts. Well, you've asked for him back, so here he is, the lad who keeps lonely hearts columnists in business, Jackie Kelk.
>
> JACKIE: [*In a whiny voice, like Homer's*] Hello. Here I am again, 107 pounds of meat shortage.
>
> KATE: You know, Jackie, it's nice to have you with us again tonight, but where'd you get that big lump on your head?
>
> JACKIE: This? Oh, it's nothing, Miss Smith. This afternoon I visited the lady who lives next door and I played piggy-back with her baby.
>
> KATE: Well?
>
> JACKIE: I fell off. [*Laugh*] She also has a little boy about five years old. He's always running away from home. I ran away once, too.
>
> KATE: You did?
>
> JACKIE: Um-hum. I was gone for three days and my parents didn't find me.
>
> KATE: Why not?
>
> JACKIE: They didn't look. [*Laugh*]
>
> KATE: Jackie, I'm sure that your parents love you dearly. By the way, how are your folks?
>
> JACKIE: Oh, they're okay, thank you. My father had a little accident at the dairy where he works.
>
> KATE: Oh, really?
>
> JACKIE: Yeah. You see, there's a loose board in the floor. When he was walking in he stepped on it and it flew up and hit him in the stomach.
>
> KATE: That's terrible!
>
> JACKIE: It was even worse when he walked out. [*Laugh*]
>
> KATE: Well, tell me, Jackie, what's your mother been doing this week?
>
> JACKIE: Oh, my mother. She bought a new cookbook. It tells how to make the national dish of all the countries in the world.
>
> KATE: Oh, really?
>
> JACKIE: Sure. Wednesday we had Greek salad, Thursday we had Swedish

smorgasbord, Friday we had Mexican chili, and Saturday we had Hungarian goulash.
KATE: And what did you have today?
JACKIE: An American doctor. [*Laugh*]

Jack Kelk recalled that "she never wanted to rehearse. As a result, she ruined many jokes because she would just flub along and she spoiled an awful lot of comedy material which I paid for. But I enjoyed it. She was very jolly. She laughed herself out of it and it always worked out. It wasn't very comfortable for me, but it did work."

Ezra Stone offered several recollections when I asked him whether he had much to do with Ted Collins:

Well, as little as I could get away with. I didn't like Ted and he didn't like me. I don't know whether it's 'cause I caught him kissing Kathryn one night… Anyway, he had very little to do with me and our spot. I sorta had the feeling that he would have been much happier if "The Aldrich Family" were not a spot on "The Kate Smith Hour."

The classic contact I had with him in public was when AFRA [The American Federation of Radio Artists] and the agencies and networks would not negotiate with us for our first contract. After a union meeting we were all given strike buttons. I took a handful to hand to our cast. I put buttons on my lapel, etc. We were on the air doing our thing. As I was working stage left mike, and in the middle of a speech—as I recall, a rather complicated one—I see this cuff-linked hand come over my shoulder and pull the strike button off my lapel. It was Ted Collins with that big toothy grin of his. I did my line and I turned and showed him I had another button on the left collar of my sport shirt.

I naturally pressed Stone for details of the embrace between Smith and Collins, asking him whether it was just before the show went on the air. "I think so," he replied, "because I don't know what I was doing stage right, but I was crossing and I went behind a cyclorama that backed up Jack Miller's orchestra. It was a very narrow passage and very dark. They were wedged in there." When I suggested that it might have been only a good luck embrace, he opined, "Could have been, except for the tone of voice I got. You know, the startled kind of thing. I really don't know." I suggested that they did not appreciate seeing him, and he said, "That's right, yes. But they didn't appreciate seeing me for other reasons." Perhaps Ezra Stone and Henry Aldrich were kindred souls in real life.

A folk humor series called "Snow Village Sketches" replaced "The Aldrich Family" on "The Kate Smith Hour" in the fall of 1939. With Parker Fennelly and Arthur Allen cast as two New Hampshire rubes, "Snow Village" had aired under several titles off and on for a decade. Smith's prime time hour gave it a renewed popularity, and it continued as a spinoff until 1946.

Parker Fennelly was a master of the northern New England dialect, speaking in a few well-chosen words. In the "Snow Village" sketches, he played Hiram Neville to Arthur Allen's Dan'l Dickey. They were public officials in the mythical small town, likeable schemers in entertaining plots. Fennelly would later achieve greater fame as Titus Moody in the Allen's Alley sketches on the "Fred Allen Show." His classic greeting when Allen knocked on his door with his weekly survey question was, "Howdy, bub." Fennelly acted in many television plays in later years and also made into his nineties a long series of commercials for Pepperidge Farm baked goods, always cast as a Yankee bumpkin.

In the 1940-41 season, Willie Howard filled the comedy spot for a few weeks, followed by the team of Nan Rae and Maude Davis. Charlie Cantor, who played Henny Youngman's Uncle Max back in 1937, returned to "The Kate Smith Hour" on January 3, 1941, teamed with Minerva Pious as "Min and Charlie Potter." Later Minerva Pious lived next door to Titus Moody, as it were, along Allen's Alley, in the role of Pansy Nussbaum. Her brand of Yiddish humor was marvelous. She returned a couple of times during the war as a single with Collins playing straight man.

One of Smith's favorites was the comedian she said Ted Collins found under his Christmas tree in 1941, a comedian who made his debut on her show the next day. His real name was Olyn Landick, but he was much better known as "The Hackensack Gossip." Landick began impersonating female characters during his navy days in World War I. He played the part of a slovenly, gossipy housewife in a falsetto voice. Simply printing his comedy routine cannot begin to convey the humor, which lay in the homespun delivery. Landick's very first routine opened with these lines:

> [*Matter-of-factly*] I, uh, just run in from Hackensack. Had a few things I wanted to git and thought I might run in while I had a chance. 'Course they didn't want me to leave the house; you know how the young ones are—but I thought I'd run in. I was kinda nervous today. I was up at six o'clock this mornin'. I dunno why, I coulda laid there, I s'pose. But, uh, I got up and looked out. Then I went downstairs and started the oil burner—got that ta stinkin'. Then I got a little hash outa the ice box and threw that on the stove. I was gonna drop an egg in it but I missed and it went on the floor. . . .

The Hackensack Gossip proved popular enough to stay on the show for a year. A decade later he returned to Smith's television show several times.

Henny Youngman returned in January 1943 and went on tour with the show that spring, playing to howling military audiences, who loved his jokes. He recalled that when the troupe traveled across the nation by train, members of his family were not permitted in the same car, but had to travel separately by Collins's orders. Collins acted as Youngman's straight man; one example is found in a May 14 dialogue:

> HENNY: Good evening, dear boys. I'm Henny Youngman. I'm very glad to be here at the Great Lakes Naval Training Station. I love to visit these service camps. My brother's in the Army for three very good reasons. In the first place he's very patriotic. In the second place he loves his country. And in the third place, they came and took him. [*Laugh*] You know, my brother didn't join the navy. He said the pants are too tight. The navy's the only service force that has to shoot crap from the standing position. [*Laugh*]
>
> Say, Ted, you know, I was out at the Great Lakes rifle range this afternoon.
>
> TED: Did you hit anything?
>
> HENNY: Yes, Ted. How do ya stuff a lieutenant j.g.? [*Laugh*]
>
> Ah, but this is a great place. You know, I met a WAVE here this afternoon. You know what WAVEs are, they're women who go down to the sea in *slips*. [*Laugh*] A sailor met a WAVE on the street and he said, "Honey, I long for some old fashioned love." And she said, "Well, come over to the house tonight. I'll introduce you to my grandmother." [*Laugh*]
>
> You know, Ted, they have a nightclub here in town, Ted, strictly for sailors. They've got a room in the back where the sailors sit with the girls. There's a sign on the door which reads, IN CASE OF A BLACKOUT PLEASE TURN ON THE LIGHTS SO WE CAN FIND THE MAIN SWITCH. [*Good delayed laugh*]

October 22, 1943, marked the debut of a panel of "experts" who delivered a carload of belly-laughs in a segment of the program called "It Pays to Be Ignorant." Hosted by old-time vaudevillian Tom Howard, the dim-witted panelists consisted of Howard's old partner, George Shelton, along with Harry MacNaughton and Lulu McConnell. Howard would pose such deep questions as "In what room would you use a kitchen knife?" or "In the poem 'The Village Blacksmith,' what was the occupation of the man mentioned in the title?" or "How many shoes are there in a pair?" The panelists would ask all manner of irrelevant questions, spat with one another, and try to change the subject. MacNaughton, a Britisher, always opened with, "I have a poem, Mr. Howard." Miss McConnell was a salty old woman of considerable girth with a gravelly voice. She was the butt of many of the jokes and loved to wisecrack about "my old man." The February 18, 1944, program included this exchange:

> COLLINS: You know, it used to be that great men frequently were unappreciated until long after they died... Today, happily in our enlightened age, we're quicker to recognize greatness... So it is with pardonable pride that we bring you the renowned educator, Mr. Tom Howard, with his special group of experts who function under the name of "It Pays to Be Ignorant." Ladies and gentlemen, Mr. Tom Howard.

HOWARD: Thank you, Ted Collins, and good evening, ladies and gentlemen. Our board of experts tonight consists of three people. First we have the celebrated author, Mr. Harry MacNaughton, who has just written a book entitled *The Beekeeper's Guide or What to Do for the Hives*. [*Laugh*] Here he is, Mr. MacNaughton...

MacNAUGHTON: [*British accent*] I have a poem, Mr. Howard.

HOWARD: I see.

MacNAUGHTON: I have a lovely horse, to me he is a friend,
He has a lovely tail.

HOWARD: Well, finish it.

MacNAUGHTON: That's the end. [*Laugh*]

HOWARD: Marvelous.

MacNAUGHTON: His name is caboose.

HOWARD: I suppose he's always last on the track. I see what you mean. Well, next we have a woman who has so many chins she puts a bookmark between them so she'll know where to put her teeth in the morning—a woman who eats like a bird: a peck at a time. Miss Lulu McConnell.

McCONNELL: [*Loud voice of a salty old broad*] Mr. Howard—

HOWARD: Yes?

McCONNELL: You know, I was reading the most amazing thing in the paper the other day.

HOWARD: What was it, really?

McCONNELL: Well, it said last year over thirty thousand seals were used to make fur coats.

HOWARD: Well, what's so amazing about that?

McCONNELL: Isn't it a wonder what they can teach little animals to do? [*Laugh*]

HOWARD: I see your point there. Miss McConnell, if I didn't know you and someone described you to me, I wouldn't believe it. Next we have a man who went to boarding school because he wanted to learn to be a carpenter—a man who can't get life insurance because there's no way to prove he was dead—Mr. George Shelton...

SHELTON: [*Wise-guy Brooklyn accent*] Oh, there you are, Mr. Howard. I just saw ya.

HOWARD: I was there all the time.

SHELTON: Ya know, I feel like a pair of boxing gloves tonight, and just as punchy. Say, you know, a peculiar thing happened to me last night. I was scared to death.

HOWARD: You were scared? What'd ya do, pass a mirror by some chance?

SHELTON: No, no, no, not this time. Ya see, I was in the dark all alone. Suddenly I felt for my wallet and it was gone. Then I felt for my watch and *that* was gone. Then I felt for my coat, my hat, my shoes, my pants, and they were all gone.

HOWARD: Good heavens, where were you?

SHELTON: [*Matter-of-factly*] In bed. [*Laugh*]

It is time now for Howard to ask tonight's question, sent in by a listener, and it is "What President was born on Lincoln's birthday?" He asks MacNaughton if he is in a position to answer, and MacNaughton says his position is not very comfortable. He thinks McConnell should know the

answer and says to her, "That was back in your time." Then there are some
slurs about her age. Shelton thinks he ought to know that and says, "Now,
don't tell me." McConnell pipes up and says, "Don't worry, he won't; he
don't know himself." And so it goes, a hilarious script delivered expertly
by four veterans of vaudeville.

The skit spun off into a thirty-minute series of its own in 1944, lasting
for years and making the transition to television, using the same format.
Early in 1947 Lulu McConnell was ill and Kate Smith took her place on
the panel for a couple weeks. Although she got a bang out of it, it was rather
awkward for the regular cast members, as they had to avoid hurling insults
at the lady the public so revered and on whose program they got their big
break in radio.

Round-faced, heavy-set Harry Savoy began his tenure as Smith's resident comedian in April 1944. Savoy quit high school to go into vaudeville
as a blackface act. He was earning $275 a week by age 18. He later took
on a girl partner and soon they married. They played the circuits for a
decade. Savoy was stunned by his wife's untimely death, and he quit the
stage for a time. Eventually he returned to vaudeville, as he had three
children to support. Michael Todd cast him for a part in *Bring on the
Dames*. When war came, Savoy went on a nine-month USO tour. Ted Collins spotted him at a Philadelphia theatre and signed him for "The Kate
Smith Hour," even though he had no radio experience.

During that 1944-45 season, the last full-hour season, oldsters Pick
and Pat appeared with Smith several times. Pick Malone and Pat Padgette
were blackface comedians who were sometimes billed as "Molasses and
January." They were first heard on network radio in 1933. Two more comedy veterans destined to be giants of the television age appeared on "The
Kate Smith Hour": Milton Berle and Jackie Gleason. Ted introduced
Gleason's routine on January 14, 1945, as follows:

> COLLINS: You know, at one time or another we all feel that we're wasting
> our lives. Well, so does Jackie Gleason. At the moment he's in the office
> of a psychologist and he's trying to find what he really wants to do with
> his future. Now would he rather be a lawyer? Would he rather be an
> actor? Or would he rather be a pig [a reference to the current novelty,
> "Swinging on a Star"]? Anyway, here he is, Jackie Gleason: Mr. Gleason.
> PSYCHOLOGIST: Now, Mr. Gleason, if I'm going to advise you about
> your future, I'll have to know something about your background. I
> would say that your background is very egregious.
> GLEASON: That happens to be the way these pants fit. [*Laugh*]
> PSYCHOLOGIST: No, no, Mr. Gleason, I mean, tell me something about
> your childhood.
> GLEASON: [*To music*] Oh, I can see the peaceful dining room now, the
> chandelier all lighted up, the candles on the table all lighted up, and the
> old man sitting at the table. He was lit, too. [*Laugh*] It all comes back
> to me now.

FATHER: Jackie, my boy, when are you gonna amount to somethin'? When are you gonna spread your wings and crash through?

JACKIE: Aw, gimme some time, will ya? Didn't I just break outa reform school? [*Loud knocks at the door*] Hey, Pop, are ya makin' chopped liver?

FATHER: No.

JACKIE: Then there's somebody knockin' on the door.

FATHER: Open it, son.

JACKIE: Oh, it's Mom.

FATHER: Oh, come, my little pigeon, light o' my life, joy o' my heart.

MOTHER: Shaddup, you broken down old bum.

JACKIE: Now Mom, that's no way to talk to Pop. He's a very considerate man.

MOTHER: Whaddaya mean, considerate?

JACKIE: Didn't he open the winda last night before he threw ya outa it?

MOTHER: What was considerate about that?

JACKIE: He didn't wanna wake us kids.

That was the season during which the very talented comedienne-actress Shirley Booth played a lovelorn young lady named Dottie Mahoney for several weeks, with Smith playing straight to her. The versatile Booth even played the role of Homer Brown in an "Aldrich Family" skit. She is remembered as the man-hungry Miss Duffy on the "Duffy's Tavern" radio series. She was married to Ed "Archie" Gardner at that time. Later she starred on the TV sitcom "Hazel," as the outspoken maid of the Baxter residence. Shirley Booth was a consummate actress, whether in comedy or serious roles, her most famous play being *Come Back, Little Sheba*. Smith gave her quite an introduction on her first appearance, October 15, 1944:

SMITH: Our next guest is a young lady who has won for herself accolades, not only as a great dramatic actress, but also as a fine comedienne. It's my sincere pleasure to welcome to "The Kate Smith Hour" Miss Shirley Booth. Tonight Shirley creates for us the character of a Brooklyn girl, Dottie Mahoney, who may well become one of radio's comedy delights. And here is Shirley Booth as Dottie Mahoney to bring us "The Diary of Dottie Mahoney."

DOTTIE: [*In Brooklyn accent*] Thank you, Miss Smith. Gee, I can't believe I'm actually appearing on a radio program. Gee, this is the biggest thrill I've had since my Uncle Joe named his tugboat after me. Honest, I'm so excited I can hardly talk.

SMITH: The pleasure is ours, Dottie. The minute I heard that you were about to publish your diary, I said to myself, "Now there is something that our listeners would be interested in."

DOTTIE: Thank you very much. It's a true story to life: full of drama, pathos, human interest, and blots. You see, my fountain pen leaks. [*Laugh*]

SMITH: I'm sure it's a wonderful document, Dottie. Now will you let us hear a few excerpts from it?...

DOTTIE: I'll start at random: you know, from the beginning. "The Diary of Dottie Mahoney, 1741 Gawanis Avenue [*repeats for emphasis*]." [*Laughs*] The diary begins on May sixteenth.

Dear diary: Today I'm 27 years old. Papa says he knows a lotta girls of 27 who are already married. Mama says how come Papa knows so many girls who are 27? Personally I'm not interested in getting married, unless, of course, I happen to meet a man who measures up to my ideals. He must be tall, handsome, well educated, and interested in gettin' married. [*Laugh*] In the evening we had a little birthday party. Ant Catherine and Uncle Joe came over and Ant Catherine wanted to know why I didn't invite some boys up for the party. I told them I sent invitations to all the boys I know but he called up and said he'd rather play pool. [*Laugh*]

Others who occupied the Kate Smith comedy spot less often include Billy Gilbert, Judy Canova, Rags Ragland, Private Broderick Crawford, Ed "Archie" Gardner, Jerry Lester, Georgie Jessel, "Professor" Zero Mostel, Tommy Riggs and Betty Lou, Charlie Ruggles, Jay "Mr. District Attorney" Jostyn, Jan Murray, Johnny Burke, Harvey Stone, Pat O'Malley, Vera Vague, Jack "Baron Munchausen" Pearl, Al Bernie, Henry Morgan, and Pat O'Brien. Quite a roster indeed.

"WE HAD EVERYONE. ANYBODY WHO WAS ANYBODY WAS ON OUR SHOW!" exclaimed Smith in a radio interview as she reminisced about "The Kate Smith Hour." She was just about right. A frequent feature was a dramatic sketch or miniplay. It was often a radio adaptation of a scene from either a new Broadway play or Hollywood motion picture, as in the following examples:

Sept. 30, 1937:	*Camille*, with Tallulah Bankhead and Henry Fonda
Oct. 7, 1937:	Dennis King, Paul Lukas, Ruth Gordon, and Sam Jaffe in *A Doll's House*
Feb. 3, 1938:	*The Farewell Supper*, starring Miriam Hopkins
March 3, 1938:	Dorothy and Lillian Gish in *The Two Orphans*
March 24, 1938:	*Our Town* with Martha Scott, Frank and John Craven
Nov. 3, 1939:	Premiere from Hollywood of *Drums Along the Mohawk*, starring Claudette Colbert and Henry Fonda
Oct. 4, 1940:	Premiere of *The Great Rockne* from South Bend, Indiana (Notre Dame University) with Pat O'Brien, Ronald Reagan, Gale Page, and Donald Crisp
Oct. 11, 1940:	*Down Argentine Way*, with Don Ameche and Charlotte Greenwood
Nov. 15, 1940:	Premiere from Tucson of *Arizona*, starring Jean Arthur
Nov. 22, 1940:	Premiere of *Tin Pan Alley*, starring Alice Faye, John Payne, Betty Grable, and Jack Oakie
Dec. 6, 1940:	Ethel Waters in *Cabin in the Sky*
Jan. 17, 1941:	Charles Boyer in *Masquerade*

March 14, 1941:   Orson Welles in *Magnificent Failure*
March 28, 1941:   Bob Hope, Una Merkel, and Dorothy Lamour in
                  Road to Zanzibar
April 11, 1941:   Constance Moore, William Holden, Veronica Lake,
                  and Sterling Hayden in *I Wanted Wings*
Oct. 10, 1941:   Errol Flynn in *Heritage*
Sept. 25, 1942:   Fay Bainter and Edward Arnold in *The War Against
                  Mrs. Hadley*
Nov. 27, 1942:   Helen Menken in *Joan of Arc*
Oct. 15, 1943:   Mary Martin in *True to Life*
Oct. 29, 1943:   *The Iron Major*, starring Ralph Bellamy and Ruth
                  Warrick
Feb. 25, 1944:   Betty Hutton and Eddie Bracken in *The Snack Bar*
                  (about the Hollywood Canteen)
April 28, 1944:   Captain Burgess Meredith in *Land's End*
Oct. 1, 1944:   *The Woman's Way*, starring Helen Hayes
Oct. 29, 1944:   Mary Astor in *Farewell to Love*
Nov. 12, 1944:   Ingrid Bergman in *The Snow Goose*
Jan. 7, 1945:   *A Clock for Penny*, with child star Margaret O'Brien
Feb. 11, 1945:   Myrna Loy and Les Tremayne in *Compromise*
March 4, 1945:   Robert Walker in *Champagne Furlough*
May 6, 1945:   Olivia deHavilland in *The Little Things*
May 20, 1945:   *Sorry, Wrong Number* with Ida Lupino

Helen Hayes alluded to a particular guest appearance she made on "The Kate Smith Hour" in the Foreword. That was on February 23, 1939. Hayes asked to be on Smith's show, as she was a great fan of the Songbird. Permission was quickly and gladly granted. In their short role-reversing sketch, Miss Hayes sang a few bars of "When the Moon Comes Over the Mountain," and Smith recited a few lines from Shakespeare's "Quality of Mercy" speech. Smith referred to their few past meetings as "two ships that pass in the night: me the ocean liner and you the canoe." The audience howled.

Let us not forget Smith's own considerable acting skill as she narrated Charles Tazewell's *The Small One* each Christmas. It is the story of a boy, his aged donkey, and the first Christmas. The donkey is to be sold to a tannery for a single piece of silver because the boy's father feels it has outlived its usefulness. The lad attempts to save his faithful friend by selling him as a beast of burden, but people only laugh when they see the decrepit animal. Then the donkey is bought by Joseph and Mary on their way to Bethlehem to pay their tax. Pablo was played by child star George Ward, who told me that "The Kate Smith Hour" was his favorite program to be on, "a well oiled production." He said that Smith herself was rather distant, however. He gave me three original scripts that he had kept all these years.

On the occasion of the 1942 anniversary show, Smith and Collins starred in Tazewell's narrative patriotic drama, *Good Morning U.S.A.* It told of America at war, with Smith and Collins following the path of the sun westward, visiting cities and towns, hamlets and farms. On several occasions she narrated Norman Corwin's folk drama of everyday life in the U.S.A., *Between Americans.* And that June she presented Bernard Schoenfeld's *Little Johnny Appleseed,* based on legends surrounding Johnny Chapman, the American pioneer who almost frantically devoted his life to sowing apple seeds in unsettled areas as he trekked westward through Ohio in the 1880s. Smith recorded *Between Americans* and *Little Johnny Appleseed* in 78rpm albums. It is a pity she did not record *The Small One,* her best-known dramatization.

A long-anticipated chat with Smith's personal usher, Charles Callas, who worked at CBS from 1938 until 1943 and again for a year after he returned from military service, provided me with a highly personal glimpse of what went on at Columbia Playhouse No. 2 in those years of Smith's— and radio's—peak popularity. Callas was only 18 when he went to work as an usher in the spring of 1938. Throughout our chat he always referred to Kate as Miss Smith, explaining that she was a lady of class, and that he had great respect for her, keeping in touch through the years until her death. He, as I, had come to Lake Placid to pay final respects at services at the church and mausoleum.

Callas told me that although he ushered every weeknight, Thursday was special because it was Kate Smith's day. "The entire show was done with polish and professionalism," he related. He also had the highest regard for Ted Collins's self-taught handling of the show. A jovial man, Callas enjoyed recalling those halcyon days and telling amusing anecdotes. It was he who recalled Smith lifting Irving Berlin right off his feet after the show on which she introduced "God Bless America."

When I asked what Smith and Collins did between broadcasts, he replied, "Oh, they just sat around and talked—and ate. Well, actually she did quite a bit of eating. I hadn't been there long when Miss Smith sent me out to get a double malted. I wasn't sure what to get, but I didn't want to ask questions. So I ordered two chocolate malteds. I came back to her dressing room and quietly put them on the table. As I was walking down the corridor she shouted, 'Charlie.' I knew I had done something wrong and came running back. She asked why there were two. I looked at her sheepishly. Suddenly she began to grin and said, 'I know, 'cause I'm big and you thought I'd like two of 'em.' She laughed heartily and I was relieved."

I had just visited a lady downstate in the Catskills who—believe it or not—kept log books in longhand of the complete routine of nearly every "Kate Smith Hour" from 1940 on, both on radio and television, besides her many guest appearances. I had borrowed them to type, so I brought the first one in to show Callas, believing it would bring back memories, and it did.

He had a story to tell about nearly every guest celebrity. For instance, seeing one name, he commented, "Oh, Brian Aherne. Somebody told me he liked to make his exit out a side door, so I asked him if he'd like to be escorted out. He said he would and he gave me a two dollar tip. That doubled my pay for the night." Ushers were paid a dollar per show, and Smith did one at 8 and another at midnight.

Callas did not remember Cynthia Hoffman, keeper of the logs, but he did recall another ardent fan, Katherine Carruthers. He said she and her friend Helen never missed a show. The ushers called them the two angels, and they had reserved seats in the front row. He chuckled as he said, "I remember one night; I was standing by the stage when I saw Katherine making a motion with her arm. I thought she was waving, so I discreetly waved back. But she persisted and I could see that she was beckoning me. I crouched down and made my way to her seat. She whispered, 'There's a hand on my ankle.' And sure enough, a man's hairy hand had a firm grip on her ankle! You see, there was a pit underneath and the chief engineer was down there, dead drunk. I had him quietly removed and he was fired the next day. But imagine that girl's composure. Anyone else would have let out a scream." And that would have given the show an immortality rivalling that of the *War of the Worlds* episode on "Mercury Theatre" and the night an eagle got loose during "The Fred Allen Show," causing pandemonium.

When Callas saw Hollywood gossip columnist Louella Parsons's name, he told us that she was a nice lady, a great favorite of his. Whenever she came to New York, Collins would give her a two-minute spot on the show. Radio was not her medium, so Collins would give her a few reminders about speaking into a mike. Callas recalled that Parsons would answer him, "Yes, Mr. Collins," when he gave her a suggestion, or "No, Mr. Collins" and "Thank you, Mr. Collins." She was popular with both studio and listening audiences.

And then there was Tallulah Bankhead. We may rest assured that she did not sit around and chat between broadcasts. She disappeared from the theatre. Everyone knew she went to a nearby barroom and got herself tanked up. She was much looser on the repeat show. Callas recalled that after each broadcast Smith would bring all the guests out on the stage and reintroduce them to the audience, saying a few words about each. Each would take one step forward when called, bow to the applause, and step back.

Tallulah Bankhead took two steps forward when called, a bad omen. After Smith handed her a compliment about her performance following the midnight show, Bankhead announced that maybe they would like to hear a little story. "Well," Callas told us, "there was only one kind of story Tallulah liked to tell, so Miss Smith took hold of her firmly but politely, gave her a little push back, and said, 'I'm sorry but we don't have time for a story tonight.'" Bankhead, for those too young to remember, was a superb actress with a deep voice, with many successes on both Broadway and London stages. She is well remembered for calling everybody "Dahling." In the waning years of vintage radio, she hosted a weekly extravaganza called "The Big Show," designed to compete with television. There are a great many "Tallulah stories," as she became quite uninhibited when under the influence of alcohol, which was often.

It seems there was a cake (made with Swansdown flour and Calumet baking powder, naturally) to be won by someone in the audience after each show. Callas said the sponsor wanted it rigged so that an older woman from out of town would win. It was Callas' job to speak with several likely looking women as they waited in line before the show and to note where the lucky one was seated. The seat number was given to the announcer, who wrote it on his script. After the show Callas would escort the winner to the stage. Her picture would be taken with Smith, to be sent to her local newspaper. One evening a woman came up to Callas and inquired, "Young man, how is it that you always manage to be right near the person who has the winning ticket?" He had to think fast to squirm his way out of that one.

Callas said there were always four cakes: one for each of the two shows, one for the cast and crew, and one for Smith. One week her cake was missing, so she asked Callas where it was. He said, "It's downstairs where the party is." When she asked what party, he told her it was for her. She said nobody had invited her. Whereupon she tore into the stage manager whose duty it was to deliver her cake. Then she turned to Callas and remarked, "There. I guess I told him off!"

Smith and her top-notch variety program were honored by the *Philco Radio Hall of Fame* in December 1945. It was in reference to the many new talents discovered on her program that music maestro Paul Whiteman called her the "Columbus of the Kilocycles."

CHAPTER 9

"The Kate Smith Hour" Goes to War

No entertainer did more for the war effort on the home front than Kate Smith, who possessed an enormous amount of energy. She put every bit of it to work from December 7, 1941, until September 2, 1945. Her noonday chats were constantly giving moral support to those of us here at home. She sang more patriotic songs than any other singer, expanding her broadcast schedule to include Armed Forces Radio shows, public service messages, and bond drives. The cast of "The Kate Smith Hour" traveled some 52,000 miles on the North American continent to give entertainment to military bases and centers of war work. Her weekly salary for "The Kate Smith Hour" was $12,500, and for "Kate Smith Speaks" she received $5,000 a week.

A program from October of 1942 is illustrative of the war years. To the familiar strains of "Say It with Music," Ted Collins says:

America sings with Kate Smith . . . the newest and the best, the old and the remembered. Here's a letter from a camp on the West Coast. It's signed, "The boys from Georgia." "Dear Kate," it reads, "We'd sure appreciate it if you'd sing *to* the boys from Georgia *from* the boys from Georgia. Please tell them this: 'Hold the fort. We're 130 million strong behind them and we would give anything we could to be with them now. It's just our lot to be on this side for the present. But here's hoping.'" Yes, that's the message from the boys *from* Georgia *to* the boys from Georgia, the fellows somewhere overseas. Well, here's Kate's song for them ["We'll Meet Again"].

The second letter from our mailbag tonight is V-Mail, signed by a soldier who's thinking of a girl in Newton Centre, a girl named Leola, who's waiting for his return. All right, Spud Murphy, there's quite a stretch of blue water between New England and New Caledonia, but the wings of song travel far and they fly free to join hearts and hands across the long miles. So you listen and you'll know, you two, while Kate sings "How Deep Is the Ocean."

Kate's third song tonight is not for a sweetheart with blue eyes and fair hair. It's not for the love of a girl that this boy pines . . . it's for the love of the soil that is home. He's in Alaska now, but his heart is in a little island off Cape Cod . . . Nantucket is its name. Bill hasn't seen that sandy shore since the lilacs bloomed last May in the gardens along Main Street. But he can still smell the good salt air and he can hear the church bells ring. They're collecting scrap on Nantucket now, Bill, and they're working for the Red Cross. Those island steamers are still rounding Brant Point on schedule. The Old Guard at the Pacific Club is playing cribbage these cool fall nights . . . and they tell me that George Lake is still the champion. The moors are a sight to see now, Bill . . . they're purple and they're red and they're gold. It looks like a bumper crop of cranberries from the bogs this year. The Selectmen held Town Meeting last week. Folks are taking turns now manning the watchtower on Mill Hill. Cap'n Totten landed a fine lot of striped bass out at Green Point the other day . . . and the Nantucket High School football team played on home grounds last Saturday—and they won. Yes, the old island's carryin' on just as it has since those early whaling days. The little gray lady by the sea stands watch, Bill . . . and when the fog spins down at dusk and the victory is won, everybody in town will be at the wharf to greet you when you come sailing home. And you will, Bill, you and all those other island boys who are pitching in now. So good luck to every one of you! And here's a song now from Kate for every boy from Nantucket Island ["Ma, I Miss Your Apple Pie"].

Imagine the effect this account must have had on Bill up in Alaska. That is just the kind of word picture that inspired Smith's vast audience to pitch in 200 percent for the war effort. A medley from a spring 1942 script includes more vivid word pictures painted by Ted Collins:

Are you listening, Corporal Charlie Holmes, out there in Pearl Harbor, Hawaii? We understand that you're a Texas boy who enlisted with the Devil Dogs and that you saw Pearl Harbor before the war birds descended and you thought it was a mighty pretty town. Or so you wrote to a girl back home here. Charlie, that girl stopped in here and she's asked us to sing a song for you, and the lyrics will answer the question you asked her ["How Deep Is the Ocean"].

Having his first look at San Diego is a youngster named John Edwards. Johnny wrote us last week. He wasn't homesick—nothing like that. But he asks, "What is it like this spring in New York? What's new?" Oh, Johnny, we don't think for a moment that you're homesick! We know that you just want to keep in touch with things. Now let me see what I can think of . . . the tulips are out at St. Patrick's Cathedral . . . there's a sign on Broadway now that blows smoke rings. . . Oh, yes, the circus is at Madison Square Garden. . . The days are beginning to get warm, very warm . . . the sky today was blue. Oh, by the way, you know, the girls back here are busier than you've ever seen them before. The Yankees are still out in front, Johnny . . . and yuh, Brooklyn [the Dodgers] is, too. That's about all that's new that I can tell you at the minute, except that we'll try to keep the old town going until you get back. You know, we miss you and we miss all the other fellas like you that we used to see around. We hope it's not

too long until you'll all be back again. But in the meantime here's the song
you wanted Kate to sing ["My Gal Sal"].

In another memorable broadcast from that spring, Smith paid tribute
to another American patriot, George M. Cohan. She said that Cohan was
listening from his hospital bed, and she sang his greatest tunes with gusto:
"Give My Regards to Broadway," "You're a Grand Old Flag," "Mary's a
Grand Old Name," and the greatest song of the First World War, "Over
There." Cohan died a few months later.

Like Frank Sinatra and Tony Bennett, Kate Smith was a singer's
singer. She certainly had a way with a song. She could swing, sing country-
style, wax classical, or deliver a ballad—indeed her forté was the powerful
ballad. Jackie Gleason told her she loved "footballs," the symbols for a sus-
tained note. Wagnerian love songs were quintessential Smith. She could
really get into them emotionally, with that expressive, teary voice, her
famous glissando down an octave, the pregnant pauses, and that breathtaking final high note. She could have been an operatic diva par excellence,
but she preferred the popular ballads: songs like "When Your Lover Has
Gone," "Climb Ev'ry Mountain," "These Foolish Things," "What Kind
of Fool Am I?" "Love Is a Many Splendored Thing," "I Only Have Eyes
for You," and the like. Dramatic songs of love fulfilled, of unrequited love,
of separated lovers, or of love gone sour. The effect of her delivery was
greatly enhanced by television, for it then became possible for viewers to
see her histrionics as she sang before the cameras: the movement of hands
and arms, the facial expressions, and, as she approached the climax, the
planting of her feet, the set of her shoulders, the look down, then heaven-
ward, and the outstretched arms as she delivered that breathtaking final
note. So high, so loud, so long. The drumroll added to the drama, evoking
goose-pimples and threatening to break chandeliers.

Between 1936 and 1946 Kate Smith introduced more songs on the air
than any other singer, some six hundred or more. She was known along Tin
Pan Alley (28th Street between 5th and 6th avenues), where most of the
song publishers had their offices, as the number one hitmaker. As Collins
selected nearly all of her songs, the music publishers and their agents
courted him. He became the most powerful force in the lucrative pop music
business, as any song that made it to Smith's show was almost certain to
be a financial success, if not a hit.

Of course, it is true that she introduced many "misses" or "sleepers."
Collins's choice of songs was far from infallible. Seldom did Smith argue
with him about a song, although there were a few instances where they
disagreed sharply. One is said to be "The White Cliffs of Dover," which
he disliked intensely, while she loved it. She introduced and recorded it
over his protest—and it became a million-seller, as well as Number 1 on the

Hit Parade for seven weeks. Here is a list of ten Kate Smith hits and ten misses:

Hits	*Misses*
"The Woodpecker Song"	"Old Acquaintance"
"The Last Time I Saw Paris"	"Walking Arm in Arm with Jim"
"Once in a While"	"Say It Over Again"
"There Goes That Song Again"	"Spring Will Be So Sad"
"Don't Fence Me In"	"Question and Answer"
"I Threw a Kiss in the Ocean"	"Merry Christmas Everywhere"
"Wrap Your Troubles in Dreams"	"Heaven Watch the Philippines"
"How Are Things in Glocca Morra?"	"When the Roses Bloom Again"
"I'm Getting Sentimental Over You"	"An Old Fashioned Waltz"
"Comin' In on a Wing and a Prayer"	"Yarza Buncha Yacka Larry"

The fact that an artist introduced a song does not imply that he/she made a hit of it or even recorded it. "The Woodpecker Song," Smith's first red label Columbia record, did sell a million copies, and that in 1940. But the flip side was an excellent number, and very danceable: "I'm Stepping Out with a Memory Tonight," so who is to say which was the hit side? Records of "The Woodpecker Song" by the Andrews Sisters and by the Glenn Miller Orchestra sold very well too. Or consider "Don't Fence Me In." There is no doubt whatever that the Bing Crosby/Andrews Sisters record was the hit version. Smith's, done with Four Chicks and Chuck, was definitely an "also ran." An amusing list of some of the other songs Smith sang on the radio includes:

"I Get the Neck of the Chicken"	"The Honey Song"
"Tess's Torch Song"	"My Tumbledown Ranch in Arizona"
"Let's Tie the Old Forget-Me-Not"	"Two Little Fishes and Five Loaves of Bread"
"When the Crimson Snow of Russia Is White Again"	"How's Your Uncle?"
"I Hate Myself for Being So Mean"	"In a Little Blue Canoe with You"
"Timber"	"Come Out, Wherever You Are"
"What Are They Gonna Do with All the Jeeps?"	"They Gave Him a Gun to Play With"

Smith was very careful about the lyrics she sang, rejecting anything suggestive or offensive, anything that might compromise her all-American apple-pie image. This was not just an image, however; she really was that way. Although regular, down-to-earth, never putting on airs, she was always a lady. She may have uttered an occasional "damn" or "hell" in a very private moment of anger, but that was about the limit.

Although Smith advertised cigars, she never smoked anything. Her usual beverages were limited to water, tea, coffee, cola, and her favorite: the chocolate ice cream soda. There was an occasional exception, however. When I visited her at Lake Placid, we went to a church fair. The August day was hot and humid, a typical "dog day." I was taken aback when I glanced at her on the church lawn sipping a beer. I chided her a bit, remarking, "I don't believe it—Kate Smith drinking a beer!" She replied, "Well, it's so hot, Richard, and the beer does quench my thirst." And I'm sure she indulged in an infrequent cocktail or glass of wine. Over on the island we were discussing what she grew in her garden. She listed mint, quipping, "Now you notice I didn't say mint julep!"

Smith's selection of songs was influenced by her principles. She would never sing "Making Whoopee" or "Let's Do It" or "Moonlight Cocktail" (a pity, as it is such a lovely song) or "Rum and Coca Cola" or "The Beer Barrel Polka." In the early seventies she told me she had been rehearsing the Sammy Davis hit "The Candy Man" to do on a television guest spot, but that she was having trouble, as there were "too many words" to learn. I later learned that the song may have had a double meaning, that "candy" is a word used to denote a narcotic and that "the candy man" could be a drug dealer. Maybe it is just as well that she did not sing the song, cute though it is.

Over the years Smith sang her share of novelties, ditties with no lasting value that were just plain fun. When I read in her autobiography, *Upon My Lips a Song*, that she had sung "Mairzy Doats," I took careful note and determined to find that program. According to Cynthia Hoffman's carefully kept log, she never did sing it, though I tried to persuade her to when I visited her during her debilitating illness in the early eighties. I would succeed in eliciting perhaps a chorus of "God Bless America" or a few bars of "You're a Sweetheart," but when I coaxed her to sing "Mairzy Doats," she simply told me, "That's a terrible song." So much for my all-time favorite novelty song.

Smith and Collins enjoyed making production numbers out of certain songs. With the orchestra playing softly in the background, Collins would step to the mike and give a flowery buildup like the following examples:

December 19, 1941:

> This song is almost a hymn, a hymn to the shrine of St. Cecilia ... St. Cecilia, looking down on her village, noting the scarred buildings, the

silent clocks ... St. Cecilia, promising future miracles by the miracle of her own survival. I call this song a hymn because it is set to the measures of faith ["The Shrine of Saint Cecilia"].

February 20, 1942:

[*Piano tinkling the blues*] Well, you know that music, don't you? Sure you do. That music came out of St. Louis and Memphis and St. Joe. That's the music of Natchez and Mobile and the deep dark South. Now listen to the blues as soft and subtle and throbbing ... the blues, a wailing trumpet and a sobbing trombone, a melancholy clarinet ... the blues, the sigh of a lady feeling sad and low down and carrying a flaming torch. Now Kate Smith sings a song that everyone here has insisted on her singing, her own thrilling Columbia record arrangement of "Blues in the Night."

November 19, 1944:

[Thanksgiving show] We couldn't have a true plum pudding of entertainment without including for you the songs that have often been asked for. So here is a ballad ... it's rich, it's full, and it's beautiful, sung in that warm Kate Smith manner: "A Little on the Lonely Side."

November 23, 1945:

KATE: Ted, have you seen the motion picture *The Dolly Sisters?*
TED: I most certainly did, and, you know, I liked it.
KATE: Good music, don't you think?
TED: Oh, very, very good. You know, they certainly are going to make a big new hit out of that old favorite "I'm Always Chasing Rainbows."
KATE: That they are, that they are. But how about the new tune they've got, the one called "I Can't Begin to Tell You"?
TED: Oh, that's lovely, Kate. Let's do it now, huh?
KATE: All right. Mr. Miller, if you please?

December 8, 1946:

KATE: [Ted is listening from his hospital bed in an oxygen tent, having suffered a mild heart attack] You know, it's funny how different things can recall sentimental memories for different people... For one person it may be an old yellowing dance program... For another, perhaps an old baby shoe... For somebody else, maybe a photograph. I know that for me there are a lot of things that bring back sentimental memories ... memories of a time not long past, a time that was perhaps a little more gracious and a little less hurried... If the Four Chicks and Chuck will come out and join me now, I'd like to pay a musical tribute to the memory of "The Old Lamplighter."

On February 26, 1943, "The Kate Smith Hour" entourage was at Quantico Marine Base in Virginia. Collins had put together probably the biggest song production of wartime, complete with the Marine Choir. His lengthy, heart-rending buildup was spoken to the familiar strains of "Say It with Music":

America sings with Kate Smith. . . Yes, once again we bring to you that popular feature of our show. But tonight it's a special, a remarkable, a reverent occasion. For tonight America sings with Kate Smith and with the heart of a Marine.

[*Drum roll*] America, listen to a story . . . bend close, for I think it's important that you hear this story. This is the kind of story that doesn't happen every day, but when it comes into being it's the kind of a story that you know instantly belongs to the pregnant history of America's most creative moments.

A little over a year ago Paul Mills, a Marine private, was stationed here at Quantico, Virginia. There wasn't much about Paul Mills to distinguish him from his Marine fellows. He, they say, was singularly and sincerely intent upon the proposition that free men should offer their effort and their lives that the free spirit of mankind might be permitted to exist and grow. One morning, with his fellows, Paul Mills was put aboard a train heading west. And on another morning he waded through water up to his hips and found himself alone with his Maker and his cause on the beach of Guadalcanal. And then the mornings and noons and nights all became as one. Paul Mills was a breathing, fighting part of this kaleidoscopic nightmare.

But one day it was morning again, and there was rest for an hour—or maybe a day. Paul Mills, tired, sweating, bruised Marine private, began to think with great clarity on the deep union between himself and his comrades and the common exertion that was breaking the chains on man's spirit around the globe. And then and there, sitting dusty and worn in the steaming Pacific jungle, Marine private from Quantico Paul Mills wrote the greatest song to come out of this war. Paul's poem has just arrived in this country and has been put to music by Joseph Miro. Kate Smith will sing it for you now: Private Paul Mills' unforgettable "What Is a Marine?"

The cast and crew, sixty strong, of "The Kate Smith Hour" set out on a lengthy trip across the country and back that January, with Smith and Collins footing the bill for the added expenses, which averaged $6,000 a week. Its purpose was to entertain as many of the military and war workers as possible on the home front. Each week the program was broadcast "remote," starting with the installation at Sheepshead Bay, New York, then to the naval base at Lakehurst, New Jersey (where Smith sang "Here Comes the Navy," to the tune of "Roll Out the Barrel"); Atlantic City, New Jersey ("Song of the Bombardiers"); Manhattan Beach, New York; the Philadelphia Navy Yard, Quantico ("The Marines' Hymn"); Fort Meade, Maryland; the Rome Air Depot, New York (broadcast from a boxing ring in a hangar); Baltimore, and Toronto, Canada (Smith introduced Jimmy McHugh's "Comin' In on a Wing and a Prayer," dedicating it to the Royal Canadian Air Force, RCAF).

Next the troupe traveled to Fort Sheridan, Illinois (where they broadcast from a gymnasium), and then to the San Diego Marine Base, arriving there for the April 16 show. Smith's greeting on each of these shows was a hearty "Hello everybody! and Hiya fellas!" to which the well-rehearsed and enthusiastic audience answered in unison, "Hiya Kate!" Then to the anti-aircraft training center at Camp Haan, with the repeat broadcast done from a basketball gym at March Field. It was Good Friday, and she sang "Ave Maria," offering up an Easter prayer. The April 30 shows were done from the Army Ordnance Camp at Pomona and the Santa Anita Army Camp.

That week Smith filmed her cameo for *This Is the Army* and the troupe sailed to Catalina Island, where they were greeted by the Maritime Band playing "When the Moon Comes Over the Mountain" as they pulled into Avalon. There they entertained the men of the Merchant Marine stationed at the U.S. Maritime Service Training Station.

Smith enjoyed mingling with the servicemen after her shows. She gave out mail, played pool, ate chocolate cake, was shown how to assemble a machine gun, autographed all sorts of items, including torpedoes, sang with them, and looked at pictures of their best girls.

The most important part of each broadcast was what immediately followed it: a speech to the servicemen. Smith made them feel the love that went with them everywhere. Her speech went something like this: "After seeing all of you, I feel that the safety of this country is in good hands. I know that you'll all give a good account of yourselves whatever you're called upon to do. And when you leave, just know that the gratitude and love of the whole nation goes with you. With you, too, goes my own love and a prayer that God will keep you safe and return you to your homes and your loved ones."

The train departed eastward from California, traveling first to the Great Lakes Naval Training Base in Illinois, then back to Manhattan Beach on Long Island, and on to the SeaBees Base at Camp Endicott, Rhode Island, winding up at the Brooklyn Receiving Station for the final broadcast of the season. Comedian Henny Youngman went on the entire trip and scored big in the laugh department with topical jokes, Ted Collins acting as straight man.

Besides all of the patriotic songs Smith was singing, she was also singing the big love songs, and the war stimulated the writing of many fine ballads that have become standards. Just recall "Miss You" (actually composed in 1938), "You'll Never Know," "No Love—No Nothin'," "I Came Here to Talk for Joe," "Don't Get Around Much Anymore," "My Devotion," "Saturday Night (Is the Loneliest Night in the Week)," "Johnny Doughboy Found a Rose in Ireland," "As Time Goes By" (revived from 1931 in *Casablanca*), "Good Night, Wherever You Are," and "Long Ago (And Far Away)." In 1944 "I'll Be Seeing You" was revived in the picture of the same name. Written in 1938, it received a modicum of play with 1940 recordings by Dick Todd and by Tommy Dorsey's band with Frank Sinatra's swing vocal. But it was not until wartime that this gorgeous love song had its full impact. It occupied the top spot on "The Hit Parade" for ten weeks. Ted Collins called it "the greatest love song of this war," and it truly was.

THE LEGENDARY KATE SMITH WAR BOND MARATHONS are credited with a total sale of some $600 million, a staggering figure and a testimony to her power to persuade. Smith had long been a champion seller of various and sundry products she advertised: cigars, automobiles, coffee, cake flour, baking powder, shaker salt, cereal, Jell-O, and Postum. Her appeals on behalf of the Red Cross in time of flood or drought disasters yielded amazing results. When she appealed for Christmas dolls for needy little girls in 1935, the Kated offices were inundated with them. Her voice had that quality of sincerity that caused listeners to respond to her appeals or her salesmanship. Thus Smith was a natural choice to sell war bonds and stamps. Tuesday, October 6, 1942, was declared Kate Smith War Bond Day over New York's CBS flagship station, WABC. She was on the air at regular intervals for twenty-one hours, raising nearly $2 million.

The radio marathon was repeated on Washington, D.C., station WJSV in a twenty-four hour bond drive October 28–29. The 28th was officially designated Kate Smith Bond Day by the Treasury Department. Scores of high government officials dropped in at the station through the day and night. Ted Collins was appointed Radio Coordinator of Safety Education of the U.S. Department of Labor.

So successful were these two bond drives that Smith was asked to go nationwide during the Third War Bond Drive on September 21, 1943. This marathon lasted from 8 A.M. until 1 A.M. the next day, raising over $36 million for the war effort. It was such a selling phenomenon that Columbia University's Department of Psychology made an analysis of it. It was published in 1946 in a volume titled *Mass Persuasion: The Psychology of a War Bond Drive.*

During this marathon, Smith gave a one-minute appeal every fifteen minutes, being relieved occasionally by Collins. Writers were hired by the Kated Corporation in August, and a conference was held to decide just how to aim the appeal. It was aimed primarily at women: the housewives of America. Four hours into the historic marathon it was high noon in New York, and time for "Kate Smith Speaks." She opened that program with these words:

> Hello everybody! This is Kate Smith again... I say again because if you've been tuned in on Columbia before today, you'll know I've been on the air since eight o'clock this morning ... sixteen times on various programs ... at work on an assignment more important than any other job in the world! Yes, it's Columbia Broadcasting Kate Smith Bond Day today ... and until tomorrow morning if necessary, as long as my voice

holds out, I'm going to be telling America about Bonds . . . and asking America to help! But more about that later.

After Collins reported the news, Smith went on at some length about "a young man in khaki," his life in his home town, the pop tunes he liked to dance to, his love of country. And then, "He's lying on a battlefield now. Why should he be there? How can we repay him for even a tiny portion of his sacrifice? *Back the attack!* Buy bonds and more bonds." This appeal was sandwiched in between two afternoon soap operas:

> Hello everybody! This is Kate Smith again. There's just one story I'd like to tell you now, although I'll have many more to tell you before the day is over. But right now I'd like to tell you what a man said at a War Bond Rally up in Utica, New York. The quota they set out to raise in Utica was $15 million, and they had a meeting and lots of enthusiastic speakers. Then one man got up to talk and this is what he said: "You know, friends, when we buy War Bonds we're not buying guns and tanks and planes. What we're really doing is buying our boys back, bringing them home to us safe and sound again. I know there isn't a person listening to me who wouldn't give everything he has to buy his boy back. Why, you'd give the whole million dollars yourself to buy your boy back, if you had it, wouldn't you? I know I would. I'd be glad to. I'd give anything, all my money, my health, or my own life, to buy my boy back from war. But I'm afraid I can't do it—not any more. You see, I just received a telegram from Washington this morning. My boy isn't coming back."
>
> You know, I think that's one of the most tragic and yet inspiring stories I've ever heard. Because that's what War Bonds are to every one of us—a chance to buy our boys back. I'm sure that everyone within the sound of my voice wants his boy back home. So why don't you just pick up the telephone and call the War Bond number you'll hear over this station and *buy a war bond!* I'll be on the air as long as my voice holds out with many more stories. But for now, *won't you buy a bond?*

Quite obviously, Smith was tugging at the heartstrings. Her mention of being on the air "as long as my voice holds out" caused millions to stay tuned to see just how long it would hold out. Smith and Collins did it again February 1, 1944, this time extending it by two hours and appealing primarily to the male audience. Again the results were impressive and rewarding. In 1987 the Treasury Department inaugurated an annual Kate Smith Award in tribute to her magnificent record-breaking efforts in their wartime sales.

NOT ONLY DID "THE KATE SMITH HOUR" "go to war," but, of course, "Kate Smith Speaks" did too, as extracts from three of those scripts illustrate. The first dates from December 8, 1941, the day President Roosevelt declared war on Japan:

Hello everybody! This morning I speak to you with mixed emotions. . .
In sorrow for the transgression that has transformed us from a nation at
peace . . . to a nation at war . . . and yet in relief that we in America know
at long last exactly where we stand in this world conflict which we have
tried so earnestly to avoid. For many long months . . . months which seem
like centuries . . . we have seen the storm clouds gathering . . . we have
anxiously watched a darkening sky . . . hoping that the wind would
change and the weather would clear. Now that the lightning has struck
and the thunder has roared, we are no longer in doubt. All the small
differences, the petty problems that have occupied various separate groups
in the United States must recede into the background now. Republican
and Democrat, capital and labor, interventionist and isolationist . . . all
creeds and races who have enjoyed the good years of living in an America
at peace can forget their separate arguments. . . For out of the tragedy of
war the blessed spirit of unity is blossoming today. That is the bright spot
. . . the bit of blue sky in our picture today. Listening to my radio last night
and early this morning, it thrilled me, as it must have thrilled millions of
you, to realize how America has snapped into action. . . It has been said
in the past that we in America are soft . . . that we don't care . . . that we
have lost the spirit of our pioneers. . . Now the opportunity has come to
us to prove the fallacy of those ideas. We rise to the stature of giants in
times of crisis. . . We become aware again that might must never conquer
right. . . Our duty is clear . . . not to ask questions, but to obey orders . . .
not to obstruct, but to aid in every way possible the completion of the
business at hand . . . to place our faith in the President of the United
States and the able statesmen at his side. For it is truer today than ever
before in our history that it isn't life that matters . . . it's the courage we
put into it!

A pause for the news, then Smith's final message to the women:

Before I leave you, I'd like to add just another word, a word for the
millions of us women who are asking ourselves just exactly what *we* can
do. As time goes on, in every community of this country, our tasks will
be more specifically outlined. The work we can do with our hands will be
clearly set forth in the pattern of civilian defense. Meantime, while we
women know we cannot go forth and achieve glory and greatness such as
will be achieved by the men in our service . . . never forget that we are the
very backbone of this nation in keeping our morale at its highest pitch. We
can wipe fear from our consciousness, we can pray . . . and we can go
about our business of homemaking as usual. The most powerful weapon
in all the world still lies in the morale of its people. . . Britain has shown
us that. Let our watchword be forgetfulness of self . . . the will to sacrifice
. . . and the unswerving determination to go forward with faith . . . and
without fear. These are the ideals that brought America into being . . .
they are the ideals which will always keep her strong and free.

The next script comes from Thursday, June 8, 1944, two days after the
Allies invaded the Normandy beachhead. June 6 came to be remembered
as D-Day.

Hello everybody! This morning, the third day of the beginning of the end for our enemies ... the third day of full hearts and earnest prayers here at home, and superhuman courage and effort of our Invasion and Liberation troops... I'm thinking how good it is that as you and I stand and wait, there is work for our hands, something to keep us busy... How true it is that "Work brings its own relief; he who most idle is, has most of grief." There is a steadying influence in even the most simple tasks of washing dishes, making a bed. Yesterday, at the Red Cross Center on Fifth Avenue, here in New York City, every chair was filled ... every place at the long tables was occupied ... as women in white calmly and steadily went about the business of folding and turning and smoothing and rolling. Outside, in the sunshine and the breeze, thousands hurried up and down Fifth Avenue ... pausing now and then in reverence and admiration to look at the splendid parade of flags of the United Nations ... some of them displayed in store windows ... many waving proudly over the entrances. One big store had emptied all its showcases of merchandise and put in its place huge American flags. Another had a magnificent arrangement of sculpture ... winged victories, American eagles ... clean white plaster figures against the banners of red, white, and blue... Through the doors of the many churches along Fifth Avenue there was a steady stream of people ... and at the steps of the library at 42nd Street women in the uniform of our civilian defense services presided over War Bond booths. Soldiers and sailors in town briefly were not as gay and carefree as heretofore... In fact, there was little light laughter along the Avenue yesterday. The air was electric with the import of this hour... Faces were grim and filled with purpose... The day and the hour had struck ... and the echo rang, as it still rings now, in every American heart!

The last script comes from that happy Wednesday, August 15, 1945, after the Japanese surrender:

Hello everybody! Now, after years of agony, years of pain and heartbreak and endless waiting, we are at peace with the world and the world is at peace with us... The magic news that has transformed the entire world has brought forth from radios a steady stream of the events leading up to this moment of Victory and Peace ... millions of words have been spoken. I thank God that the fighting is over, that the enemy is vanquished. But this day, which will go down in history for those who come after us to read and to study, is only the beginning of the grave tasks that lie ahead. This chaotic world must be set in order, step by step ... millions must be fed and clothed ... other millions—the enemies who no longer feel the impact of our physical might—must be taught an entirely new way of life ... a philosophy which does not include aggression and cruelty and the absolute worship of a Hitler or a Hirohito. They must be taught that there is no super-race, that all men are equal ... and have an equal right to enjoy the fruits of this earth, and the tranquillity and decency to which the truly civilized subscribe. Surrender by Japan, for instance, does not necessarily mean that soldiers can get out of the Army within six months ... it does not mean that our responsibilities are over and that we will suddenly emerge into our pre-war status of a land of milk and honey. War extracts a high toll. . . We will be paying for war for many, many years. . . Only if we maintain the peace and improve the condition of all mankind, will war be worth the terrific price we have paid. We can't count on nylons for Christmas, or a sudden stoppage of food rationing, or an abundance of cars on the road, or a flood of the luxuries and conveniences we have missed since December 7th, 1941. And it seems to me, it is good that this is so. It's good that our mills and our factories will have to hum with peacetime projects to give industry a chance to catch up with consumer demand . . . for there will be millions of men and women who will need jobs. And so, on this blessed day of Victory when our joy runs high . . . it is not too soon to give serious thought to the heroes we applaud on this day, the Americans who won the war in the Pacific. . . What they need and will continue to need in the years to come . . . is jobs and security and homes, and a decent way of life for themselves and their families. Some of them will need education. . . Thousands of others, alas, will need expert care and hospitalization. Let us all . . . every individual, community, town, city, and state lend every effort to this accomplishment. . . It's glorious to have flags flying, and drums of peace beating instead of drums of war. . . It's wonderful to know the shooting is over . . . and Americans are going to come home, instead of going overseas. . . But it is not too soon on this day of thanksgiving and prayer to think about what we can do for them . . . they who have done so much for us. . . They need more than lip-service. . . Let us, who await their return so eagerly, see that they get every consideration, every facility, every aid, every job that it is possible to give them. . . Let's keep on doing First things *first*!

Thanks for list'nin', and remember, if you don't write, you're wrong (there are still many, many men far from home . . . looking for those letters from *you*!). Good-bye, folks.

It had indeed been a busy four years for Smith, and for Collins, whose duties had been increased substantially. Smith knew her work was important and she thrust her considerable energy into it. She was bound to feel a psychological letdown after the war ended, even though she was proud to have had a part in bringing her beloved homeland and its allies to victory.

A rare publicity photo from the six-week run of "Kate Smith Sings" on NBC,
which began on March 17, 1931.

Thanks for listening to my La Palina Cigar Program Kate Smith

Top: The Smith sisters in 1929: Helena, left, age 24; Kathryn, right, age 22; *bottom left:* Sponsor photo sent to listeners on request, 1931; *bottom right:* Smith about to spin her latest Columbia record, "My Mom," 1932 *(Paramount Pictures publicity photo).*

The Palace Theater's marquee during Smith's *Swanee Revue,* August 1932.

Movie still from the 1929 Vitaphone short subject "Kate Smith: Song Bird of the South."

Cliff "Ukulele Ike" Edwards, Ted Collins, Jack Miller, and Kate, from a 1932 Paramount Pictorial.

A promotion for A&P coffees, 1935.

Top: Smith meets her mentor, Ted Collins, in *Hello, Everybody* (1932); *left:* Kate dances the Charleston in amusement in a scene from *Hello Everybody* (1932); *right:* at the CBS mike in a 1934 publicity shot.

Top left: Baseball great Babe Ruth was a guest on the first "Kate Smith Bandwagon," September 17, 1936; *top right:* Smith sings a current hit from the first week of 1937 (*CBS publicity photo*); *bottom left:* Jimmy Durante visits the "A&P Bandwagon," January 21, 1937 (*CBS photo*); *right:* ice skating on Lake Placid, February 5, 1938 (*courtesy Boston University, Mugar Memorial Library, Dept. of Special Collections*).

Top left: A 1936 promotion for the American Red Cross; *top right:* Smith listens to a playback with headphones during a 1938 rehearsal (*CBS publicity photo*); *bottom left:* Kate and cast of "What a Life!" which became "The Aldrich Family": (pictured clockwise) Blaine Fillmore (Sam), Leah Penman (Alice), Ezra Stone (Henry), Smith, Betty Field (Mary), 1938 (*CBS publicity photo*); *above right:* Smith almost seems to be making eyes at Collins in this 1938 CBS publicity photo.

Ted, Irving Berlin, and Kate appear elated after Smith's introduction of "God Bless America" on November 11, 1938 in this publicity photo.

Collins and Smith on the "Kate Smith Speaks" radio show, 1940.

Smith in her classic speedboat on Lake Placid, July 1939 (*photo courtesy Boston University, Mugar Memorial Library, Dept. of Special Collections*).

"The Kate Smith Hour" premiered *Drums Along the Mohawk* in Hollywood, starring Henry Fonda and Claudette Colbert, on November 3, 1939.

BUY MORE BONDS

Opposite, clockwise from top left: Vacationing in the Blue Ridge Mountains, summer 1948; a Christmas 1945 publicity photo from CBS; a Mutual publicity shot; musical director Jack Miller discusses song arrangements with Kate for the first show of the 1941 season (*CBS publicity photo*); Smith was the leading celebrity war bond seller during World War II (*photo courtesy Boston University, Mugar Memorial Library, Dept. of Special Collections*).

Above: A scene from *This Is the Army* (1943).

Top left: Smith in a familiar pose on her afternoon television show, "The Kate Smith Hour," circa 1950 (*NBC publicity photo*); *top right:* a 1947 publicity photo; *bottom left:* Ed Sullivan welcomes Kate to his "Toast of the Town" television variety hour for the first time, December 4, 1955; *above:* Ted Collins at the radio microphone in a 1944 publicity photograph for CBS.

A 1943 shot at the Naval Training Station, Newport, Rhode Island (*official U.S. Navy photograph*).

Smith out for a drive in her postwar Buick convertible; Freckles is in the driver's seat.

Above: Kate often pretended to play the piano as she sang on television, as shown in this 1959 photo. She had many viewers fooled; *right:* showing a variety of Christmas toys on *The Kate Smith TV Hour,* 1954; *below:* host Bing Crosby joins Kate in a medley of winter songs on *Hollywood Palace,* December 24, 1966 (*ABC photo*).

Left: Smith and Andy Williams sing a medley of "home" songs, October 30, 1966, in one of Smith's four appearances on his show; *right:* a television duet with Dean Martin, 1967.

Smith and Tony Orlando on the *Tony Orlando and Dawn* show, January 29, 1975.

Top left: With Ted in Palm Beach, 1963; *top right:* with Rose Queen Anne Martin as Grand Marshal of the 1976 Tournament of Roses Parade (*NBC photo*); *above:* a 1957 portrait inscribed to the author in 1971; *right:* Smith shed a tear posing by a photo of Ted Collins in the trophy room at Camp Sunshine, July 1971 (*photo by author*).

CHAPTER 10

I Got a Right
to Sing the Blues

The end of the Second World War marked a turning point in the career of the First Lady of Radio. Like the popularity of the swing bands, Kate Smith's popularity appeared to take a sudden downturn. Had we heard "God Bless America" too many times? Could it be that she was so much a part of the war effort on the home front that now it was peacetime, the nation wanted to hear different voices? After all, Prime Minister Winston Churchill led England to victory over the Axis forces, yet he was soundly defeated for re-election after the war.

Everything seemed to change in that fall of 1945. There was a new president, Harry Truman. Two atomic bombs had been dropped on Japan that summer, so the potential for military destruction was greatly escalated. The atomic age had begun. Servicemen and women were returning from battle forever changed by their experiences. There was a record number of marriages, and the married couples needed housing. Thus there was a monumental housing shortage. The nation converted from a wartime to a peacetime economy; new cars were manufactured for the first time since 1941. Soon the newlyweds would be producing the baby boom. This was a time of record inflation and of the Cold War with the Soviet Union.

Kate Smith's radio hour was cut to twenty-five minutes and the title changed to "Kate Smith Sings." The format was also changed. It was now an all-music program, with the house band conducted by Jack Miller as always and a guest orchestra to play a tune each week. Perhaps even more important, there was no studio audience. It returned to Friday evenings, from 8:30 to 8:55 P.M. eastern time.

The lack of a studio audience removed the element of excitement and seemed to dampen Smith's enthusiasm. She was always at her best before a live audience. For the first broadcast in 1946, Collins made two changes. He brought back the studio audience, and he brought back minidramas with name actors. There were Boris Karloff, Brian Aherne, Joseph Cotten, Monte Woolley, Claudette Colbert, Linda Darnell, Pat O'Brien, Orson Welles, Walter Pidgeon, Lana Turner, Gene Kelly, Olivia de Havilland and Lucille Ball.

Guest stars also included the current heartthrob, Van Johnson. Young, blonde, with sparkling blue eyes, freckles, and a winning smile, he was having the same effect on teenyboppers as Frankie Sinatra. When Johnson appeared on Smith's March 1, 1946, show the reaction was reminiscent of what occurred when Sinatra graced the stage of New York's Paramount Theatre three years earlier. The bobby-soxers screamed and swooned. Van Johnson loved Smith and requested that she sing that popular novelty of the day, "Doctor, Lawyer, Indian Chief." She got a bang out of singing that number and gave it her all—which was considerable. There was pandemonium when she finished and dashing Van Johnson was on the stage.

"Kate Smith Sings" had regained enough popularity that CBS moved its time slot to Sunday from 6:30 to 7 P.M., opposite NBC's popular "Jack Benny Program." This happened in October 1946, and Benny did to Smith what Smith had done to Vallée seven years earlier. Such was the dog-eat-dog world of network radio. Smith was still using the harmonic quintet Four Chicks and Chuck to assist her in quite a few songs. The drama was replaced by comedy, with the likes of Harvey Stone, Milton Berle, Jack Pearl, Henry Morgan, Al Bernie, and the cast of "It Pays to Be Ignorant," all of whom had been on Smith's variety hour.

In her personal life, Smith was for the most part "on top of the world." (A columnist quipped that if she did that, the globe would collapse under her weight.) Her noontime chats were number one in the Crosley ratings and she was consistently named one of the three most important and influential women in the nation. Financially, she was well-heeled, being worth several millions of dollars; she drove a fancy Lincoln and lived in a luxury apartment at #20 Park Avenue. *Radio Guide* magazine described it, in a 1939 story as consisting of a living room, a small reception room, a bedroom, a tiny kitchen, and a bath. The writer noted that, although the decor was in excellent taste, it followed no particular style and had no pattern. The living room was described as having a fireplace; "the drapes are dark blue, faced with beige. There is a large phonograph, given her by Ted Collins, and a grand piano. The lamps are Chinese rose jade with beige silk shades. The couches are blue and beige. There is a custom-built secretary, done in antique green with flowers and birds painted on it." Her bedroom was done in green and rose, with a rose taupe broadloom carpet. The dressing table contained more than four hundred bottles of perfume, many unopened, her favorite being "Christmas Night." There was a large sofa in the bedroom, and she had a variety of china dogs and cats. The article described the kitchen as small and painted red and gray, with "lots of electrical gadgets."

Hal Schneider, her radio engineer in the early fifties, was totally taken with that apartment and described it forty years later:

> The elevator opened into her penthouse. If you turned to the left you would go into the most beautifully appointed living room you'd ever seen. She had gates like you would see in Heaven, gates that looked like a church: tapered wrought iron gates. Most beautiful paintings, many types of dolls, ladies' type of furniture. Her bedroom and her mother's were around the other side to the right of the main living room. There was a hallway, with a bath in the center.
>
> If you stepped out of the elevator and went to the right, there was a good-sized room that was used as a studio. To the right of that was the kitchen, and to the right of that was Hattie's quarters, her wonderful Negro maid.

Smith had her beloved and pampered cocker spaniel Freckles, given her in 1938 by actress friend Betty Garde. Her mother divided her time between Kathryn and Helene, now married and a mother and living in Connecticut.

The story surrounding the gift of Freckles is an interesting one. Garde was more or less a regular in the dramatic segment of "The Kate Smith Hour," often playing opposite actor Ray Collins. She was within a year of Smith's age and single at the time. One day as she walked past a pet shop, she spied two black cocker spaniels. She debated buying one of them, and by the time she decided to do so, the only one left was a male. As Garde was starring in the daytime serial (a.k.a. soap opera) "Mrs. Wiggs of the Cabbage Patch," she named the puppy "Mr. Wiggs."

Betty Garde was a great admirer of Smith's vocal talent. She had seen her in *Honeymoon Lane* and had been a regular listener to her quarter-hour shows in the early thirties. Garde told me:

> She was, like most heavy people, extremely light on her feet. When she was on radio, I listened to her because I thought, "This voice is so magnificent." So when I was hired for "The Kate Smith Hour," she wasn't a stranger to me. She never read a note of music in her life. It was God-given, this fantastic voice, and perfect pitch. I think I was on there for three years at least. We were friendly and at rehearsals we'd sit together out in the auditorium and I'd chat with her when she wasn't engaged in a song or when I wasn't in a sketch. But as far as any rapport, that never really happened. . . .
>
> I had "Wiggs" five years and in that time he was bred exactly twice. I used to take Wiggs to rehearsals at the theatre, Columbia Playhouse No. 2, which formerly was called the Avon Theatre. Kate fell in love with him. This was a most extraordinary thing. Kate used to pet Wiggs; he was a very gentle animal, very affectionate. She'd come out in the auditorium and

we'd sit with Wiggs. She said, "Oh, Betty, I would love to have one just like him, only I want him to be sort of a caramel color with freckles across his nose." I said, "Well, I don't know. I can't guarantee." I told her that he was going to have babies. That's the way you talked to Kate, because Kate was like a little girl as far as the facts of life were concerned. I never delved into it, but I got this picture of a very, very naïve, innocent, sweet, lovely soul.

"Well," I said, "there are going to be some puppies and we'll see what happens." Do you know that the mother had six puppies, five of which were coal-black, and the sixth was "Freckles" as ordered! The puppy was duly delivered as a gift from me. . . .

I sat up with her all night on two different occasions. He nearly died of distemper. We fed him brandy and gave him eyedrops. So there was a big bond there between us and Kate was eternally grateful. We got on a very friendly, chummy basis through the puppy, who turned out to be the monster of all time. Freckles grew large enough for her to cart him into her dressing room. He was there every week and nobody could come near the place. You never heard such a howl and a barking. He tried to attack me. He tried to attack everybody.

Everyone I interviewed who was associated with Smith's radio shows mentioned Sammy Schiff, whom Betty Garde referred to as "their gofer." André Baruch said he had a personality much like Collins, tough and all business, and Henny Youngman said he was a very important member of the team, Collins's right-hand man. Garde said Schiff would confide in her: "He told me, 'You know, Betty, you gave Kate the greatest gift that she ever had in her life.' She adored that dog. I've heard by the grapevine from Lake Placid that he was her world. And, of course, that was fine with Ted." (Smith had Freckles put to sleep on a Saturday in November 1953. His grave in Hartsdale Canine Cemetery in Westchester, New York, is marked by a sizable tombstone.)

Smith's maternal grandfather died January 23, 1946, at age 83. He died of pneumonia at his Virginia home, he and Granny Hanby having celebrated their sixty-first wedding anniversary New Year's Eve. Smith missed her broadcasts the next two days, opting to be with her family in their time of grief.

On the music scene things were changing. Many leaders of the swing bands reorganized, but they never regained their prewar popularity. The public was ready for something new and different. There was increased interest in smaller jazz combos, and something called "be-bop" emerged as a craze, sung by the likes of Ella Fitzgerald and Mel Torme. Whereas before the war there were only a handful of name pop singers (Bing Crosby, Alice Faye, Lanny Ross, Kate Smith, Barry Wood, and a few others), now there were many: Frank Sinatra, Dick Haymes, Andy Russell, Buddy Clark, Perry Como, Frankie Laine, Nat "King" Cole, Dinah Shore, Peggy Lee, Doris Day, Margaret Whiting, Ginny Simms, Jo Stafford, and others.

Most of Smith's records were lackluster now. Her voice tended to be weak and quavering on records, as opposed to the lusty, powerful, dynamic, Wagnerian voice that her fans loved. Music critic and discographer John MacAndrew called this her "Dinah Shore period," and she may have felt particularly threatened by the Tennessee Thrush's success with some of the same songs she was singing. Smith had the ability to imitate the singing styles of others, consciously or otherwise. Perhaps she was doing a Dinah Shore imitation now. At any rate, many found it annoying and disappointing. Then too, perhaps the knowledge that her ratings were on the wane and her records were not selling well contributed to her lack of enthusiasm.

It was not that Smith was not singing the best new tunes. Her songs included: "Till the End of Time," "If I Loved You," "It's Been a Long Long Time," "It Might as Well Be Spring," "I Can't Begin to Tell You," the melancholy "Autumn Serenade," the buoyant "Aren't You Glad You're You," "Seems Like Old Times," "Day by Day," the powerful "Symphony," "O! What It Seemed to Be," and the lovely "They Say It's Wonderful" from Irving Berlin's new hit musical, *Annie Get Your Gun*. Smith sang all of these during the 1945-46 radio season.

In her last season of live radio singing, Smith performed such top tunes as "To Each His Own," a big hit for singer/bandleader Eddy Howard; "The Whole World Is Singing My Song"; Berlin's poignant "You Keep Coming Back Like a Song," from the Crosby-Astaire musical *Blue Skies*; "The Old Lamplighter"; "Sooner or Later"; and Hoagy Carmichael's new novelty "Ole Buttermilk Sky." She tickled fans with "Zip-a-Dee-Doo-Dah" and "(That's What) Uncle Remus Said," from Walt Disney's *Song of the South*, and she caressed such lovely ballads as "For Sentimental Reasons," "Anniversary Song" (from *The Jolson Story*), "After Graduation Day," "Ask Anyone Who Knows," and "Midnight Masquerade."

Dorothy Lamour, the popular "sarong girl" of the Crosby-Hope "road" pictures, was a guest on the April 12, 1946, edition of "Kate Smith Sings," rendering her current hit, "Personality," with its rather risqué lyrics. On that same show was entertainment columnist Ed Sullivan, who had an award to present to Smith. Back in the early thirties he had, in his "Little Old New York" column, cast some slurs at her. That was long forgotten, as his comments obviously came from the heart:

> You know, ladies and gentlemen, I was just saying to Dorothy Lamour that it's seldom in this profession that a person comes along whose greatness as a performer is equalled by her greatness as a human being. Such a person is Kate Smith. So, Kate, in giving you this Ed Sullivan Award of *Modern Screen* magazine, I give it to you on these two counts: outstanding performance and outstanding citizenship. This silver plaque from *Modern Screen* reflects not only the warm respect of your own pro-

fession but the affection of a country your voice has charmed for fifteen years.

Sullivan was a fan, and the two of them were destined to have a significant association in television a decade hence, an association that would endure for many years, until Sullivan again said something uncomplimentary about her in his long-lasting column.

On Smith's December 8 show, she gave the world a grand standard when she introduced "How Are Things in Glocca Morra." There was a certain sadness in her voice as she spoke these words:

> For the past sixteen years on this program we have been accustomed to taking direction from a very able producer-director, one Mr. Ted Collins. In answer to many telegrams, letters, and phone calls as to where Ted is, I'm very sorry to say that he is, as he would say, "on the bench." However, he is here with us in spirit tonight, and particularly in regard to our next musical selection. You know, the men who conduct the activities at Tin Pan Alley will tell you that Ted Collins is the best picker of popular hit tunes in the radio business. [Chuckle] Being an Irishman, he very often comes up with an Irish tune that goes on to be a big favorite with folks who whistle and hum the nation's songs. Tonight he thinks he's discovered another hit. And you know, I sort of think so, too. We'll leave it up to you folks to judge. The title is "How Are Things in Glocca Morra," and here it is.

Collins had suffered a mild heart attack on Thanksgiving and was still in an oxygen tent as this show aired. Smith explained his absence from "Kate Smith Speaks" this way on December 2:

> It's high noon in New York and time for Kate Smith, as our own Ted Collins usually announces, but I'll have to be my own announcer for a while, so I'll just say this is Kate Smith. No doubt many of you have wondered why Ted was missing from this program on Thanksgiving Day, on Friday, and again last evening on our Sunday broadcast. During our sixteen years of broadcasting, Ted has always been right here on the job with me, except when urgent out-of-town business prevented. Now, however, I'm very, very sorry to have to tell you that it isn't business that's keeping him away from the microphone. It's because he isn't well. In fact, he hasn't been up to par for the last few weeks, but he kept on going. Now his physician has ordered him to take a complete rest, and you folks who know Ted Collins through his cheery voice every day at High Noon will realize that it's a hard prescription for him to take! I know all of you join me in hoping he'll be back with us soon... And I hope you'll add your fervent prayers to my own for his speedy and complete recovery to perfect health.
> Meantime, I'm going to carry on as usual, with the aid of various Columbia newscasters who will be glad to pinch-hit for Ted in bringing us the up-to-the-minute news each day. I'll never forget how Ted carried on

in my stead for several weeks four years back, when I was ill . . . and I only hope I'll be able to do as well as he did then. Anyway, he's going to be listening in, with a radio right beside his bed, so we better be good.

Collins did not return until February. He was 46 years old and would suffer another heart attack nine years later, and then a third. After this first attack, Smith carried on in fine style, introducing her own songs as well as her guests' in a manner that made Collins proud of her. But it was a troubled winter, for she loved Ted as a dear friend and depended on him for guidance and moral support. For a time this had to come from her daily visits to his bedside.

When Smith departed CBS in 1947 to sign with the less prestigious Mutual–Don Lee network, broadcasting from the studios of WOR in New York, "Kate Smith Sings" changed into a fifteen-minute Monday through Friday record show, with Smith and Collins introducing and spinning only Kate Smith records. The program was juxtaposed with "Kate Smith Speaks," sometimes preceding it, other times following it. Both went off the air together on June 15, 1951.

Smith also changed record companies in 1947. After all, Columbia Records was affiliated with the Columbia Broadcasting System. She was the first artist to sign with the brand new canary yellow MGM label. Her MGM records were less than memorable, consisting mostly of unexciting oldies. There were a few striking exceptions, however, done with that old verve that her admirers expected and loved. There was a thrilling rendition of the 1934 ballad "I Only Have Eyes for You," a Kate Smith standard recorded here for the first and only time. It was coupled with a lively "Please Don't Talk About Me When I'm Gone," the first recording of one of the songs she sang on her first CBS radio show in 1931.

These recordings included what was quite possibly her most vibrant rendition of "God Bless America." And she did record a few of the new popular songs, such as "Anniversary Song," "Ask Anyone Who Knows," "Dreams Are a Dime a Dozen," "Now Is the Hour," and "Far Away Places." She made three albums for MGM: "Songs of the Hills and Plains," "Songs of Stephen Foster," and a patriotic narration album of Norman Corwin's folk essay of Americana, "Between Americans." She had performed the latter on the radio, with appropriate sound effects and voices with authentic dialects of various parts of the country. The work attempted, cleverly and successfully, to analyze much that is unique about America and its people. The actors represented a wide variety of vocations and avocations, too. There was something with which everyone could identify. A fourth MGM album was "Little Johnny Appleseed," which was recorded for Columbia in 1940 and never released. MGM bought it.

Smith recorded many songs during her MGM tenure that either were never released or were bought later by National Records. Two dozen of them were released on three obscure ten-inch LP albums. Most were quite forgettable, the exceptions being a vibrant "Music, Maestro, Please," a powerful "Because" and "When Your Lover Has Gone," and a magnificent "Ave Maria." These are unfortunately the only Kate Smith recordings of any of these songs. "Music, Maestro, Please" has an interesting history. Written in 1938, it was recorded in a swing arrangement by Tommy Dorsey with the vocal by Edythe Wright. Frankie Laine revived it ten years later with an intimate cafe-style arrangement. Smith always sang it as one of the best of her powerful ballads.

Smith's career was definitely in the doldrums in 1949. Radio was taking a nosedive, what with television sweeping the country. Smith had not sung live on the radio for two years, and she had not had a real hit record for a few years. Groping for her niche in broadcasting in this time of transition, she did a weekly two-hour telephone talk-show over ABC radio. It was on Monday evenings from 9 to 11 and was called "Kate Smith Calling." The program contained occasional interviews with guest stars and a telephone giveaway, plus recorded music and comment by Smith and Collins. This was the era of audience participation shows with prizes to be won by listeners who correctly answered the questions asked. There was Ralph Edwards's Walking Man contest on "Truth or Consequences" and there was "Stop the Music." The latter ran opposite humorist Fred Allen, who countered by offering to double what any of his listeners would have won had they been called by "Stop the Music." Eventually Allen's clever and funny show was forced off the air.

Critics were saying that Smith would never survive in the visual medium of television because of her bulk. Was this to be the end of her career? Hardly.

CHAPTER 11

Kate's OK for TV

Enter the television age, as well as the second half of the Twentieth Century. In almost every neighborhood there was at least one family with a television set. In ours it was the folks next door. Their rich uncle bought them a very large DuMont with a 12½-inch screen. We lived fifty miles from Boston, the nearest city with television stations, so the picture, even with an elaborate outdoor antenna, was snowy at best. We were often invited on Tuesdays to watch "The Texaco Star Theatre," starring Milton Berle. That was preceded by Roberta Quinlan's musical show (remember "Carpets from the looms of Mohawk" with the drums beating?), followed by John Cameron Swayze's fifteen-minute news broadcast. Everything we watched was exciting—and live.

By 1950 prices of television sets were coming down and they were selling like hotcakes. That is the year we—and four million others—purchased a television set. And that is the year television really came into its own, with "Your Show of Shows," "Big Town," "Your Hit Parade," "The Lux Video Theatre," "Robert Montgomery Presents," "What's My Line?", Groucho Marx's "You Bet Your Life," "Beat the Clock," "Life Begins at 80," and the afternoon "Kate Smith Hour."

There was an air of excitement and expectation that summer of 1950 at Camp Sunshine on Lake Placid, where Smith and Collins were making plans for a daytime television series. Collins had grown tired—and irritated—of reading the columns of critics suggesting that Kate Smith would not succeed in the new medium, that her weight would make her appear awkward and detract from viewers' appreciation of her singing. Kated, Inc., negotiated a sweet five-year contract with NBC (they were still on the outs with CBS, and ABC was not yet into television) for a daily, Monday–Friday hour-long variety show. It would be called "The Kate Smith Hour" (like old times on the radio) and would begin on September 25 at 4 P.M. EDT. To be sure, they both had misgivings at the start. After all, they were "green" at the new medium and somewhat unsure of just how well Kate would come across on it. Smith later admitted, "I was a little afraid of it. After all, I'm a large woman and I knew the screen would make me look even larger. I didn't know how the public would react."

The announcement came in late June. Columnist Jack O'Brian's reaction was that "it will bring the wonderful Kate Smith back in all her personality-packed glory." Said Sid Shalit, "one of the hottest deals in video history . . . the first of the great radio names to step into TV on a lavish daily scale . . . would bring back Kate as a singer, a move that would immeasurably brighten the TV picture."

Jack Miller would conduct the orchestra as usual. The programs would be divided into quarter-hour segments, each with a different sponsor. And there was no shortage of sponsors waiting for the opportunity. There was early talk of a Saturday evening Kate Smith Hour, to be similar to her prime time radio hour. That was eventually scrapped, to be revived a year later. Collins kept inquirers in the dark as to details of the program as he and Smith summered on Buck Island as usual, she at Camp Sunshine, he next door at the more modern house he had built after the war. He didn't finalize the arrangements until September 23.

Smith and Collins would divide the hosting duties, and there would be singing and dancing groups. John Butler was signed as choreographer. Directors were young Greg Garrison (later producer of the "Dean Martin Show") and Alan Newman. Former vocalist Barry Wood was hired as co-producer with Collins, and Lyn Duddy directed the chorus.

From the outset that old bounce was back. There would be no more lackluster deliveries. Smith seemed to love the new medium and the audiences loved her. It was 1931 all over again, this time with pictures. For good luck, and not to break with tradition, her first number on the first program was "Dream a Little Dream of Me," the first song she sang on her CBS radio premiere. She ended with "God Bless America," another surefire hit. In between she rendered "Tea for Two." Collins was there to read some news items. It must have been a great feeling for Smith to know that her fans had not forgotten her and to have her old confidence back after several years of floundering.

The initial telecasts were well received. Columnist Nick Kenny called it "a show that would do justice to evening or night viewing, most of the time . . . Kate's program is considerably stronger than the regular run of daytime television fare. . . . Ted Collins adds a masculine touch that is welcome by way of balance and relief." Sid Shalit commented, "The series is a happy blend of songs, shopping and makeup tips, comedy, news, and ballet. But the standout feature is Kate, who comes out of retirement as a singer. She still warbles with the best of them. On the non-singing side, Kate presides over the program with authority, hosting the proceedings in sincere and impressive manner. . . . Ted Collins emerges as a free-swinging editorializer and his sizzling style promises to make for provocative listening. However, shorter editorials would punch up the Collins spot immeasurably." *TV-Radio Mirror* writer Mary Temple asserted this about Smith's television image: "So much had been said about her size that viewers were surprised to see how trim she was, how gracefully and lightly she moved about, how little conscious they were of her weight after the first few moments of watching. If Kate herself had any moments of doubt, they were now proved unnecessary."

On several occasions Smith sang a little song from *Top Banana* that seemed to sum up "The Kate Smith Hour" nicely.

> You're OK for TV, that's easy to see,
> You're OK for TV and OK with me.
> You're my favorite program, my big song and dance,
> My hour of charm, my voice of romance.
> I'd like to predict you're the hit of my set,
> The prettiest picture that I'll ever get.
> If I may T-ell you, I tell you it's L-U-V,
> Which means that you're OK with me.*

Many of us recall "The Kate Smith Hour" with a feeling of nostalgia since we grew up watching her in those halcyon days of TV.

June Bundy, reporting for *Variety*, the "Bible of Show Biz," reviewed the tenth show, which aired on Friday, October 6:

> Entertainmentwise, the show is one of NBC's all-purpose specials, complete with music, guest stars, ballet, news, household hints and situation comedy. "Ethel and Albert" is so good that it's probably only a matter of time before a sponsor snaps 'em up for a TV show of their own.... The real charm of the program is best realized when Miss Smith starts warbling. Wisely eschewing elaborate production backing, she delivers her numbers attired in a smart but simple afternoon frock, standing in front of a plain drop. The gal is in wonderful voice—rich and clear, and her personality conveys more warmth on video than it does on radio.... Miss Smith, who televises amazingly youthfully, is relaxed and happy in front of the cameras, albeit a bit too coy at times on her emcee chores. Ted Collins is just so much excess baggage on this show.... Collins' heavily personalized news commentary slows down the pace of the program.... The video version of "Ethel and Albert" alone is enough to insure the success of the program. Scripter Peg Lynch is one of the best situation comedy writers in the business.

"Ethel and Albert" occupied a segment on each Friday's hour for two seasons. Originating as a local radio sketch in the late thirties, it went on network radio in 1944. Not only did Peg Lynch create all of the sketches and write all the scripts, she acted the part of Ethel to Alan Bunce's Albert. Her skits were from real life, amusing incidents we can all identify with and laugh at. She was—and still is—a comedy genius.

Every sketch was a masterpiece of hilarity, based on something that could happen to any of us under the right circumstances. Lynch as Ethel, had a frantic way of acting, as if everything were a calamity, a matter of life or death. Albert was constantly exasperated at her behavior and her outlandish ideas. The segment was a smashing success, with nobody enjoying it more than Kate Smith.

I had the pleasure of visiting Peg Lynch and her husband of many years at their lovely, secluded home in the Berkshire Hills of western Massachusetts. When I asked Lynch (who is just as amusing in real life as when acting the role of Ethel) how well she knew Smith on the show, she surprised me by saying she did not know her well at all. She said Collins seemed to protect her and isolate her from the rest of the cast, but she did not consider her at all snooty. Everyone liked Kate, according to Lynch, but nobody got to know her well. Whenever there would be a cast party, she would not be there. Lynch never even had her picture taken with Smith, although she said she was always gracious and remembered special occasions, such as Christmas, birthdays, and the birth of a baby. She felt that Smith missed all the fun connected with the show, thanks to Collins's sheltering her.

Peg Lynch did not have kind words about Ted Collins. When she learned that she was pregnant sometime in the fall of '51, she informed him that she would not be able to finish out the season. His reply was "Nonsense, you'll make it just fine." She did remain, but was quite large by May. Lynch said Collins had a big ego and loved to clown around with the band and the cast, telling corny jokes in preference to properly rehearsing. He would throw off the timing so that when they were on the air they would sometimes have to speed things up to complete the segment on time. She also said that everyone in the cast—except Smith—knew Collins was having an affair with the fashions director.

Peg Lynch and I watched a videotape of two "Ethel and Albert" skits from "The Kate Smith Hour." Lynch had never watched a kinescope of the show and had no idea of how the sketches were showcased because Smith was on one side of the stage at the Hudson Theatre and they were nowhere near her. She was fascinated to see Kate Smith's introductions and enjoyed the skits every bit as much as did the rest of us, although she did not recall either one.

Variety's prediction came true and "Ethel and Albert" became a thirty-minute spin-off for the 1952-53 season. Later it was revived on radio. But Peg Lynch is a largely underrated and unheralded talent as a writer of situation comedy; "Ethel and Albert" ranks with "Vic and Sade," "Easy Aces," and "The Aldrich Family" as one of the funniest and cleverest sitcoms in broadcast history.

Kate Smith's TV "Hour" opened with a paper moon sailing over a cardboard sky with a mountain. She sang a few bars of "When the Moon Comes Over the Mountain," followed by applause, then "Thank you, thank you very, very much. Hello everybody and welcome once again to our show." Then she went into a swing tune, something like "One Dozen Roses," "I Talk to the Trees," "Aren't You Glad You're You," or "'S Wonderful." Then she would introduce a commercial.

Smith had a sweet, captivating smile and a hearty, contagious laugh, which she often used after a little novelty number. From the beginning in radio, Collins had advised her to act naturally, to be herself. It was one of the big secrets of her success and longevity. She was often described by phrases like "just folks," "everybody's next door neighbor," and "America's favorite aunt." Her trademarks of informality included the dropping of *g*'s from words ending in *-ing*, such as in her sign-off, "Thanks for list'nin'." She could speak into a microphone or talk to a television camera as one might speak to a friend over the telephone or the back fence. She was not awed by that little red camera light staring back at her. She would wink at it, right through it, and into our homes.

Smith loved live television, with its sometimes unexpected happenings. When she and I were once discussing its merits, she asked me, "Did you see the show one day when I was singing and I flipped my head around when I was laughin' and my earring flew off my ear?" When I said I did not recall it, she continued, "Well, that was a beautiful earring and it bounced across the floor right off the stage, right out into the audience. And I hate to tell you, I never saw the earring again. . . . It happened several times, but the one good earring I lost, the others I didn't. I got them back and so I just popped them on my ear again and went on with the show." I said I thought spontaneity was the great thing about live television, and she replied: "You said it. Whatever happened happened right then and there and the audience saw it and that was it. There was no retaping, no redoing. They saw it just as it was happening. I used to love it, personally."

Fred Rogers, of the long-running PBS children's program "Mister Rogers' Neighborhood," was a floor manager for Smith's show in those days. He recounted an incident in which she "was singing a song in front of a flat that looked like a farmhouse. I thought she was finished and so I cued the people—in those days you just raised the flat—and so the farmhouse started to go up, which made Miss Smith look like she was going into the ground. But we quickly stopped it, so it was sort of in mid-air."

Gabe Meinhardt, now of Port Charlotte, Florida, was a member of the Jack Allison Singers on the daytime TV hour. He had the utmost respect for Kate Smith's singing ability and love for her as a human being. He recalled an amusing happening. One afternoon, as four o'clock was rapidly approaching, Kate had not arrived at the studio. Collins was sitting in the control room, visibly fuming. The show opened, the chorus readied itself to accompany her on "Blues in the Night," and—at the very last second— in she strode, just in time to sing:

> My mama done tole me,
> I can't see the cue cards.

That, of course, broke everyone up. She had not had time to put on her contact lenses. During an impromptu commercial break she put them on and they redid the number. That was television at its liveliest. (Her taxi had gotten stuck in traffic.)

Smith was quoted in a February 1951 *TV-Radio Mirror* story:

> I just love it when a stranger comes up to me and talks to me as if she had known me all her life. I feel as if I belong to all those people on the other side of the screen. People ask me if I don't mind being a "public figure," if I don't get annoyed by autograph hunters. Truth is I love it. When they stop bothering me, that's the time I'll start to worry. I owe them everything. If it weren't for my public, where would I be?

To be sure, television was more complicated and demanding than radio. One had to think of hair styles and dresses, camera angles and stage sets. Smith tended to be conservative, never wearing short dresses ("My audience wouldn't be comfortable if I wore a dress that showed my knees"), avoiding a short haircut ("My audience wouldn't expect anything so different from me"), and never wearing loud colors (for the studio audience), although she did select many jewel tones herself: strong blues, deep greens, wines. To quote *TV-Radio Mirror* again,

> Many had failed to realize how pretty she is, how her light brown hair ripples around her face, how expressively she uses her hands, how feminine she is in her dress. One of her co-workers commented, "A lot of Kate Smith's charm lies in her infectious laughter. We feel it flowing from her to us and to the audience. Her sense of fun is contagious because it is so natural, so unforced. You never think of it as part of her act, because it isn't."

The financial magazine *Sponsor* put it this way in 1951:

> Not since Al Jolson swept back into the hearts of all America on the crest of *The Jolson Story* tidal wave and his own irrepressible personality has any performer made such a sensational "comeback" as has Kate Smith on her NBC-TV hour.... But now ... has television brought, not only Kate Smith's voice, but her full ingratiating personality into millions of American homes. That she is welcomed by those who remember her as well

as by the younger set, many of whom are seeing her and hearing her for the first time, is evidenced by a top daytime 26 point rating and commercial billings amounting to more than $7 million a year.

Did Smith's and Collins's enthusiasm for the show, cast and crew last for the four seasons of the show, or did it become old and fade? For the answer we turn to a May 1954 *TV Mirror* story:

> They say of some show business performers that, even if success doesn't go to their heads, it often goes to the heads of the folks who surround them—the people who work with and for them. In Kate's case, and in Ted's, not even this is true. You never saw a cast and crew who work harder and put on less airs. Kate herself, although the years have made her a famous and fabulous performer, is still a sort of plain, wholesome housewife type at heart. . . . Both she and Ted are available to anyone who needs them or has legitimate business with them. They are quick to remember those who work with them when there is sickness and trouble, quick to remember small kindnesses and to praise and reward.

Not satisfied to merely resuscitate the golden oldies, Smith sang many hits of the day, for which the orchestra had ready-made arrangements. She sang "It's a Lovely Day Today," "The Best Thing for You Would Be Me," "Orange Colored Sky," "Hello Young Lovers," "Be My Life's Companion," "Too Young," "We Kiss in a Shadow," "Because of You," Johnny Ray's "Cry," "The Morningside of the Mountain," "Anywhere I Wander," Kay Starr's "Wheel of Fortune," Joni James's "Why Don't You Believe Me," Jo Stafford's "Shrimp Boats," "Mockin' Bird Hill," "You Belong to Me," Patti Page's "Tennessee Waltz," "I Have Dreamed," Mario Lanza's "Be My Love," Les Paul and Mary Ford's "Vaya Con Dios," Eddy Howard's "Be Anything" and "(It's No) Sin," Eddie Fisher's and Eddy Arnold's "Anytime," "Auf Wiedersehn, Sweetheart," Rosemary Clooney's "Half as Much," Teresa Brewer's "Till I Waltz Again with You," Nat King Cole's "Pretend," Frank Sinatra's "Young at Heart," Kitty Kallen's "Little Things Mean a Lot," Perry Como's "Wanted," "Three Coins in the Fountain," and many more. Smith believed in moving with the times, unlike some of the other legendary singers, who kept to singing a handful of their standards.

To be sure, there were the "America Sings with Kate Smith" segments, in which she often sat at a grand piano, pretending to be playing as she sang. Most of these medleys consisted of oldies, though even then she mixed in some new tunes. At times she would read requests; other times she would weave in the language of love between selections. Her quarter-hour "get-togethers with the band" were especially enjoyable, as they were more informal and the orchestra was visible. She would speak to them and kid with them at times, too.

Consider Smith's musical guests. The list reads like a Who's Who of Twentieth Century vocalists: Louis Armstrong (at the top of many such lists), Andy Russell, Lauritz Melchior, Jack Leonard (who preceded Sinatra with Tommy Dorsey's band), Tony Bennett, Helen Kane, singer-songwriter Joe Howard, Benny Fields, Patrice Munsel, Lanny Ross, country singer Jimmy Wakely, Donald Novis, the Merry Macs, Wee Bonnie Baker, Tommy Edwards, Harry Belafonte, Cliff Edwards, Private Eddie Fisher, Phil Regan, Leontyne Price, the Ink Spots, Al Martino, Ezio Pinza (three times), Jean Sablon, Rusty Draper, soprano Margaret Truman, and Nat King Cole.

The show did not neglect the name bands, either. The roster included: Frankie Carle, Richard Himber, Charlie Spivak, Tommy Tucker, Eddie Heywood, Art Mooney, Nat Brandwynne, Shep Fields, Count Basie, Duke Ellington, Russ Morgan, Jimmy Dorsey, Tex Beneke, Ted Lewis, Freddy Martin (with vocalist Merv Griffin), and Ralph Flanagan.

The McGuire Sisters made their debut on "The Kate Smith Hour," appearing for several weeks in the fall of 1952. She also featured the DeCastro Sisters and the five DeMarco Sisters, late of the Fred Allen radio show. There were male vocalists who were more or less part of the company, such as Vinnie deCampo, Jeff Clark (a "Hit Parade" singer), and Danny Sutton. There was resident pianist Evalyn Tyner, whom Smith called "the queen of the 88."

"The Kate Smith Hour" was, as in radio days, a variety show. There were countless dancers: tap, ballroom, and soft-shoe. There were jugglers, acrobats, and ventriloquists galore. And there were comedians, including such notables as Phil ("Sergeant Bilko") Silvers, Olyn ("the Hackensack Gossip") Landick, Georgie Price, George Kirby, Jack Carter, and Wally ("Mr. Peepers") Cox.

Although this was a daytime show with a somewhat limited budget, there were name actors in quarter-hour dramas, such as Luise Rainer, Molly Picon, Douglas Fairbanks, Jr., Ella Raines, Eva Gabor (several times), Martha Scott, Paul Lukas, John Forsythe, David Niven, Chester Morris, Audrey Hepburn, Arthur Treacher (later Merv Griffin's British sidekick), Sir Cedric Hardwicke, Constance Bennett, Basil ("Sherlock Holmes") Rathbone, John Carradine, Paul Douglas, Charles Coburn, and Shirley Booth.

Ted Collins conducted in-depth interviews with newsmakers throughout the four-year run of the show. His segment was dubbed the "Cracker Barrel Session." He pulled few punches, and his interviews were often lively. The historic value of the kinescopes of these shows is obvious from this roster: Dr. Ralph Bunche, Harold Stassen, Drew Pearson, Earl Warren, Senator Joseph McCarthy, Cecil B. DeMille, Sherman Adams, Senators John O. Pastore and Everett Dirksen, John F. Kennedy (three times:

twice as congressman and once as senator), John Foster Dulles, Hubert Humphrey, Sam Yorty, Henry Cabot Lodge, Senator Leverett Saltonstall, Ezra Taft Benson, Governor G. Mennen Williams, Eugene McCarthy, Claire Boothe Luce, Senator Paul Douglas, Werner von Braun, W. Averill Harriman, Estes Kefauver, Justice William O. Douglas, Governor Thomas E. Dewey, Representative Walter Judd, Jacob Javits, Senator Henry Jackson, Walter Reuther, Krishna Menon, Senator Wayne Morse, Barry Goldwater, Attorney Roy Cohn, and Senator Warren Magnuson.

There was ex-boxer Sugar Ray Robinson, who tap-danced. Smith interviewed Hollywood reporter Hedda Hopper. Hal LeRoy tap-danced and did the old soft-shoe. The Great Ballantine, legendary magician, appeared twice. Talented ventriloquist Paul Winchell was on with his dummy Jerry Mahoney. Remember Señor Wences, the amusing ventriloquist from "The Ed Sullivan Show"? He entertained on Smith's show too.

Then there were the special features. There was "The House in the Garden," described as a family serial. There was Collins's international forum with college students from home and abroad. There was lovable Charlie Ruggles as a general storekeeper in "The World of Mr. Sweeney," which, like "Ethel and Albert," became a series of its own. Yet another popular feature was Dorothy Daye's fashion shows. Since women in the viewing audience far outnumbered men, these were received with great interest.

Then there was the popular children's feature, "Annabelle Story-Telling Time." It began with Smith singing children's songs and introducing a puppet act or a magician. Soon she added an Annabelle "prayer for the week." At first she told the stories; later the "Storytime Princess" told them. Smith wrote a children's book in 1951 called *Stories of Annabelle.*

This was the era of the Korean War, so occasionally films of wounded soldiers in Korean or Japanese hospitals were shown and the injured GI's got to speak to their folks at home. These were touching segments that were very much appreciated by relatives and friends.

It was also the McCarthy era, and Collins did not shy away from the issue, but interviewed attorney Roy Cohn and even Senator McCarthy himself. Between May 22 and June 17, 1954, the program was often partially preempted by the fascinating Army-McCarthy hearings.

A very unusual event took place on the Tuesday, February 5, 1952, telecast. Twelve minutes into the show, after a Prell shampoo commercial, the camera focused on a dead serious Smith, seated at her desk. She spoke these words:

> Ever since late Sunday evening I've been receiving many, many telegrams and letters, and we've received quite a lot of telephone calls at our office about something which was said about me by Mr. Red Skelton on his television program of last Sunday evening. Now I want to be per-

fectly truthful and perfectly frank with you. I didn't hear what Mr. Skelton had to say because I don't watch his program. However, from what I have learned, he is supposed to have used what is known in the theatrical business as a switch on a very obscene joke and saw fit to make me the brunt of it. I'm very thankful to those of you who have become a bit irritated and annoyed by such bad manners. But I assure you that anything Mr. Skelton says or does is of no concern to me. I sincerely think that this man has a tremendous amount of talent and I only wish that he would use it to do some good. However, he certainly has the right to conduct himself as he sees fit. Again, I repeat, he is the master of his own salvation. Anyway, thanks a lot to all of you wonderful people for your great interest in my behalf. I appreciate your concern. As I said before, don't let it worry you. It doesn't worry me. Thank you a lot and so much for Mr. Skelton.

So much for Mr. Skelton indeed! That was a strong statement, especially her assertion that "he is the master of his own salvation." Several of us who visited Smith on the occasion of her 75th birthday were viewing a few kinescopes that her nieces had had shipped there from storage when we came upon the one with that scathing editorial. Frankly, we were stunned and mystified as to what she was referring to. The mystery was solved when I had occasion to interview her radio engineer at the time, Hal Schneider. He remembered the incident well.

It seems that Skelton had altered an old risqué joke that went something like this. The fat lady in a circus married a midget. Everyone predicted the marriage wouldn't last. Someone saw them five years later, and they were just as happy as the day they were wed. The midget was asked, "She's so huge and you're so small, how can you possibly get along together?" To which the midget replied, "Well, I'm happy because I run up and down her back and I've got acres and acres of ass and it's all mine."

In his switch, Skelton made Kate Smith the fat lady and changed the word *ass* to *back*. It was a joke familiar to many. "Ted really gave it to Skelton the next day" in his radio editorial, the engineer related. Ted apparently apprised Kate of what was said when he came to the theatre that morning. She was so deeply hurt that she cried all day long. They had all they could do to prepare her to go on the air that day. Collins was just as upset, as he had promised Smith years ago that she would never be hurt like that again. By Tuesday she had recovered to the point where anger had replaced hurt, so she delivered her own editorial, in cool and dignified fashion. Did Smith and Skelton patch things up later? Perhaps so, as Skelton endorsed her cookbook six years later with a kind remark on the flyleaf.

Quite possibly Smith's favorite guest was the old songwriter and song and dance man Joe Howard. Some of Howard's songs went back to the Gay Nineties. A Hollywood version of the early part of his life was told in the 1947 picture, *I Wonder Who's Kissing Her Now*, which took its title from one of his best-known songs. We chanced to show a kinescope with one of his appearances at that 75th birthday celebration. Smith was ill and not very responsive at that time, but when she saw that film, her eyes sparkled and she smiled broadly. She even answered a few of our questions about Howard; it was evident that he had been a special favorite.

A nimble man with a twinkle in his eye, Joe Howard was a delight to watch as he performed some of his best known tunes: "Hello My Baby," "Honeymoon," "On a Saturday Night," "Be Sweet to Me Kid," "Goodbye My Lady Love," and "The Handicap," the latter a production number complete with horse bettors and spectators with field glasses. Dressed in his best bib-and-tucker, with top hat, bow tie, and walking stick, Howard was a consummate and lovable showman. In her introduction, Smith referred to his boyhood in such Wild West towns as Dodge City and Tombstone. She said he was known in those days as "Master Joseph, the boy soprano" and she could hear him chuckling offstage. When he stepped out, he said he was "glad to be home again with Miss Kay and Mr. Collins." It was a standout feature, with the audience joining in the singing.

Television as an entertainment medium was little more than two years old when Kate Smith entered it in 1950. Very little had been done with daytime TV, so she was a true pioneer, as she had been in the early days of network radio. During the four-year run of "The Kate Smith Hour," the medium reached a precocious adolescence. Smith took notice of the fact that by the 1953-54 season her audience had become much more sophisticated and discriminating:

> People who had some basic knowledge of fine drama and good music and clever comedy now want more and more of these. Others, whose opportunities for learning have been limited, have now been exposed to the best through the medium of television, and their education is being rapidly accomplished. Even folks who thought they didn't like longhair music or ballet are learning to understand a little more of what these are all about. . . . It seems to be a case of the more they see, the better they demand. This is all to the good. A few years ago we were all pioneers in television and any program was fun to watch, as long as it had a picture and sound. Now the novelty has worn off, the medium has grown up to adult stature, and each viewer wants some programs geared to his own particular taste. This is why Ted fills our shows with such a variety of good things—music, drama, comedy, and serious discussion.

A brief financial report may be of interest at this point. In the first twenty years of her radio career, Kate Smith was said to have grossed some $30 million. In *Sponsor*, a journal devoted to the business end of the entertainment media, a May 1951 article stated that in two decades she had done 7,612 radio broadcasts, for which advertisers had paid $29 million, not including the cost of time. In 1950-51 alone her TV program brought in over $6.5 million, was aired over sixty-three stations, and reached an audience of some ten million viewers per week, about twice as many as any other daytime program. Her appeal was chalked up to two attributes: her patriotism and the fact that "she has the common touch."

By the fourth and last season, 1953-54, competition was much keener and many of "The Kate Smith Hour"s were unsponsored or partially sponsored. That season opened with a memorable show. The Kateds, the Showtimers, and a camera crew had been brought to Lake Placid to film a highly unusual and very entertaining half hour. The show opens with Ted Collins joking with resident comedian Joey Faye about Kate's being late to the theatre. The scene shifts to Smith and all the gang, standing on the dock at Camp Sunshine, singing "Ridin' High." (Actually they were backstage singing to the silent film being shown.) Next we see them in Kate's speedboat going across the lake, singing "It's a Big, Wide, Wonderful World." Collins and Joey Faye clown around a bit more as they wait, then we see the gang singing as they board a southbound bus. In the next segment they are all suddenly in the studio singing "It's Been a Grand and Glorious Summer." This clever idea was reviewed in *Variety*:

> With all the new daytime plans NBC-TV has in the works (largely the result of last spring's affiliate uprising), Kate Smith's one-hour variety segment still stands as the bulwark of the entire structure. Program has been moved ahead an hour to 3 P.M. to serve as a pivotal point for the new shows coming before and after the segment and also to shorten the existing gap between morning and afternoon network service. Time change hasn't affected the program in any way: it's still a lavishly laid out production that's got something for every hausfrau.
>
> Program teed off with six participating sponsors (15 minutes each) so that the first half hour is sustaining. That sustaining half hour gave producer Ted Collins an opportunity to try for some fancy effects on the opening show. What Collins did was to stage a hoked-up stall, with Miss Smith and the rest of the cast "missing" and "on their way from Lake Placid." Purpose of this, which ran most of the half hour, was to provide a vehicle for comedian Joey Faye, who did a harried stage manager routine, and to experiment with some film clips and a live street scene.
>
> Aside from the fact that Collins and Faye stretched things a bit thin, it made for a good opening. Clips had Miss Smith and the cast singing and dancing a couple of numbers in country settings, and the switch being that there was no sound track on the film—they sang the songs live from back stage. As a further means of integration, cast piled into a bus previously shown in one of the clips and drove down 44th Street to the door of the Hudson Theatre, where a camera picked them up live entering the house. It all made for an interesting session highlighted by Faye's antics, Collins' personable emceeing and especially some socko singing by Miss Smith and the ensemble. . . .
>
> High spots of the show continue to be the songs. . . . Miss Smith can still belt a number in top notch style, and she's backed by a versatile and effective ensemble and a very competent orchestra under Jack Miller. Renditions of "Ridin' High" and "Big, Wide, Wonderful World" were tops.

Although the Kated Corporation had a five-year contract with NBC, the show ended after four seasons on June 18, 1954. Both Smith and Collins were exhausted. Collins, in fact, was absent from a number of programs toward the end, presumably because of fatigue and cardiovascular problems. Then there was the difficulty in procuring sponsors and the likelihood that the show had run its course. Smith's last production number was "Ridin' High," and she was still doing exactly that.

A POSTSCRIPT IS IN ORDER REGARDING FOUR YEARS of kinescopes of "The Kate Smith Hour," as well as a season's worth of kinescopes from the prime time "Kate Smith Evening Hour" of 1951-52. A kinescope is a 16-millimeter film record of a television show. Kinescopes are of mediocre quality, compared to ordinary 16-mm movies. They are to early television shows what 16-inch transcriptions (huge records) were to early radio shows. Both were later replaced by tapes (audiotape for radio shows, videotape for TV shows). Hal Schneider revealed that he would bring the kinescopes from the previous day's show to Smith's apartment, where, after doing the midday radio hour, they would watch them critically. They were eventually taken to Camp Sunshine at Lake Placid, where they were stored under an eave of the large boathouse. (She told me that the sheer weight of them, some 2,200 pounds, had caused the boathouse to tilt slightly.) The eave had been lined with tin to preserve the 16-mm film from deterioration. In later years Smith and Sal Gelosi, her bodyguard, would sometimes retreat on rainy days to her large trophy room upstairs in that boathouse to watch the kinescopes. Most of them are now in the custody of the Department of Special Collections, housed at Mugar Memorial Library of Boston University, where Smith arranged for the memorabilia of her career to repose. The kinescopes, like the rest of her memorabilia, are available for viewing by appointment. Other items in the collection include scrapbooks of press clippings, professional pictures, records (both commercial and aircheck discs of individual songs), and miscellaneous items. I have made good use of these materials in researching this biography.

CHAPTER 12

From Limelight to Sunshine

A typical Wednesday's work for Kate Smith began with preparation for a full hour of live radio, broadcast from noon until 1 P.M. Rehearsal for a full hour of live television followed, then she was on the air from 4 to 5 P.M. After a quick bite to eat, she made final preparations for another hour of live television from 8 to 9 P.M. (Ted Collins wisely eschewed the Tuesday and Wednesday daytime hours, as he was working on "The Kate Smith Evening Hour" those days.)

That was Smith's routine every Wednesday for the thirty-nine week season of 1951-52. It required experience, confidence, and stamina, all in large measure. NBC was deriving plenty of mileage from the woman who was now known as the First Lady of Television and Radio. She had spent nearly two hundred hours under the klieg lights already.

NBC scheduled "The Kate Smith Evening Hour" opposite the popular "Arthur Godfrey and His Friends" on CBS. Smith, like Godfrey, had a folksy manner, although she was a much classier individual. Being pitted against Godfrey in 1951 was as much of a challenge as being up against "Amos 'n' Andy" in 1931. The team of Smith and Collins gave it "the old college try."

The evening hour resembled the daytime hour in most ways, the principal difference being that the budget allowed for more name guests and the show was divided into two half-hour segments rather than four fifteen-minute units. Sponsors were B. T. Babbitt (Bab-O cleanser) and Norge (mostly refrigerators) on alternate weeks, with the Reynolds Aluminum Company (Reynolds Wrap, etc.) and Congoleum-Nairn (floor covering and polish) in between. The show was done at the huge RCA Convention Center, a former ice rink and an imposing theatre with four balconies. Peg Lynch said it was awfully frightening to go on that stage.

Variety reviewed the initial program (September 19) favorably:

> [The] race for viewers [with the Godfrey show] should be a hot one but, if Miss Smith can retain the quality of her preem [hep for premiere] entry,

she may win it. . . . Miss Smith's show, particularly because of her long-time radio rep, should snag distaff viewers, as well as the males and the bulk of Godfrey's audience traditionally has comprised mostly femmes. This display, of course, spotlights the usual type variety acts featured on NBC's big hour revues but, where they concentrate mainly on comedy, Miss Smith has branched out into more serious stuff for a deserving payoff. [NBC] has given her producers Ted Collins and Barry Wood, a hefty budget to play with, which led to the pacting of such names as Paul Lukas, William Bendix, and Kay Thompson and the Williams Bros. on the preem. . . . As for Miss Smith herself, she displayed those solid pipes to maximum advantage with three numbers (opening with "Blues in the Night"), in two of which she received the full production treatment—complete with lush-looking sets, a ballet and vocal chorus. If possible, some attempt should be made to integrate her into the production jobs, as it looked slightly incongruous to have her just stand in the middle of a group of whirling terpers while she gave out with the vocals. Show-backing by Harry Sosnik's orch. was tops. She and Collins, her longtime personal manager, co-emceed adequately, although they were too prone to term everything "wonderful"—from their guest artists to their sponsors' products.

Consider some of the guests. For thespians they had Miriam Hopkins, William Gaxton, Herbert Marshall, Douglas Fairbanks, Jr., Dolores Del-Rio, Lilli Palmer and Rex Harrison, Charles Laughton, Gloria Swanson (imitating Charlie Chaplin), Dick Powell, Fred Allen (in a dramatic play), Kirk Douglas, Akim Tamiroff, Broderick Crawford, Richard Greene, and Richard Carlson.

Tallulah Bankhead's name is notably missing from this roster. It seems that she was to be a guest and was rehearsing her segment of the show. Kate was watching as Tallulah made her stage entrance and thought it should be made differently. Apparently the irascible Bankhead was presuming to direct her part of the show. At any rate, Kate passed her complaint along to the director and he related it to Tallulah, who flew into one of her legendary rages. She is supposed to have shouted, for all present to hear, "I'm not taking my directions from that fat tub of shit. I was on the stage twenty years before her goddamn moon came over the mountain!" With that she stormed out of the theatre, not to reappear ever, if Smith had her way—and she did.

In addition to the regular "Ethel and Albert" segment, the evening hour employed such comic talents as Ed Wynn, Olson and Johnson, Jack Pearl, Jack Carter, Jackie Gleason, Victor Borge, Myron Cohen, Herb Shriner, Jan Murray, Phil Foster, and old standby Henny Youngman. Milton Berle, riding high on Tuesday nights, did a stint with Smith, returning her guest appearance on his "Texaco Star Theatre." On that program Uncle Miltie kidded her about allowing him to do the commercials when he was on her radio show. Berle did a funny skit with Arnold Stang. When he attempted to sing, Collins took his arm and began to pull him off the stage, reminding him that they *had* a first-rate singing guest, one Ezio Pinza, costar of *South Pacific*. Pinza joined Smith in a Western setting, both wearing ten-gallon hats, for an entertaining duet to "Don't Fence Me In."

Smith and Collins did not spare the expense when it came to musical guests, either. They engaged Tommy Dorsey and his orchestra, Ralph Flanagan's big Glenn Miller–style band, the popular vocal quartet the Four Aces, Xavier Cugat and his rhumba orchestra, the Three Suns, and Benny Goodman and his orchestra, among others. It was Tommy Dorsey's TV debut.

Josephine Baker, the talented, voluptuous, controversial black dancer-chanteuse who spent most of her adult life in France, also made her TV debut. Smith narrated "The Small One" on the Christmas show, with puppets. The all-star Second Annual *Look* TV Awards show took place on January 9. On March 5 Dorothy Daye staged a fabulous fashion show, featuring expensive jewels, furs, and gowns. The show of March 12 was done from the deck of the aircraft carrier *Wasp* at the Brooklyn Receiving Station.

On the March 26 show the stars of the "Grand Ole Opry" made their national TV debut, led by Roy Acuff and featuring young and peppery June Carter (with Mother Maybelle), as well as Hank Williams, who sang his composition "Hey, Good Lookin'" in what is said to be his only television appearance. He died the following New Year's Eve. The grand finale that night was a memorable production from the Broadway revival of *Of Thee I Sing*, with Smith singing and dancing with verve to the title tune.

Many of the acts came right from Smith's daytime hour, which may have been a ratings mistake. Besides "Ethel and Albert" there were actors, singers, and acrobats from the popular Broadway show *Top Banana*, the singing DeCastro Sisters, a juggler, Joe Howard, precision dancers, old-time singer Benny Fields, pianist Evalyn Tyner, and would-be pianist Kate Smith, who went through the motions at the Steinway while she sang. She sang the same songs, too. She opened the show three times with "It's a Great Feeling" (from the 1949 Doris Day picture) and thrice with "Be My Life's Companion." Perhaps, in hindsight, if Ted Collins and Barry Wood had made more of a deliberate effort to make this prime time hour different and special, the ratings would have been higher. As it turned out, Arthur "Buy 'em by the carton" Godfrey usually topped Kate Smith in the polls, and her show ended with that one season. After all, Godfrey was more spontaneous, unpredictable, and controversial.

BOTH SMITH AND COLLINS CONTINUED to spend summers at their homes on Lake Placid. NBC radio, like CBS before it, wanted them to do their midday show during the summer, and they agreed to do it in 1952.

This required that engineer Hal Schneider, his wife, and two children spend the summer at Lake Placid, also. Schneider reminisced at some length when I interviewed him at his home near Cooperstown in 1990.

The Schneiders looked for a house to rent in the village of Lake Placid, but, Hal said, "When [the owners] found out I was working for Kate Smith, the rent would suddenly double. I didn't like that, even though NBC was paying." So they found a reasonably priced rental ten miles west at Saranac Lake. Smith and her mother would often drive over to visit them for an afternoon. Smith and Mrs. Schneider would walk along Main Street and admire dresses in the store windows. If Smith saw something she really liked, she would ask Mrs. Schneider to order it for her, as merchants would inflate the price if she purchased it herself.

One day Smith surprised the Schneiders by driving up to the house with her mother and two friends. She went in first, and Hal's wife whispered to her, "What shall I do? We don't have enough glasses for everyone for iced tea." Kate told her not to worry, that she would drink it out of a jelly jar if need be. It was that kind of down-to-earth attitude that endeared her to the Schneiders.

The Kate Smith radio hour was aired from noon to 1 P.M., from her broadcast studio off the large trophy room. Schneider moved his engineering apparatus out into the main room, while Smith and Collins sat at a small table behind the soundproof glass with a microphone.

The show was done live only on Tuesdays and Fridays, with the Wednesday and Thursday shows being "fed" to New York on Tuesday, where they were taped. Monday's show was fed on Wednesday and taped. This allowed Smith and Collins more freedom during their summer vacation. This show went off the air in 1952 because radio was slipping and they were preoccupied with the daily television hours. There is, after all, a limit to anyone's stamina.

While Smith and Collins took a lengthy vacation from the whirlwind world of show business in 1954, the media reported that Smith had retired. When she reappeared as a guest on the Dorsey Brothers' "Stage Show" the following March, she was making a comeback, according to the press.

In their original verbal agreement, Collins told Smith, "You do the singing and I'll fight the battles." Well, he was wearying of fighting the battles, especially with his weak heart. He desperately needed a long rest, and she did too. For the first time ever they were able to totally relax at Lake Placid without concerning themselves at all with the upcoming TV season.

KATE SMITH'S COZY ISLAND PARADISE was her favorite spot in all the world, her heaven on earth. She discovered Lake Placid in 1932 when her doctor ordered her to take time off to recuperate from a nasty case of bronchitis. She fell in love with the laconic village, the lakes and mountains, and the clean, crisp air. After she recuperated she vowed to return, and return she did, staying at the exclusive Lake Placid Club for four summers. In 1936 she began looking for a piece of land of her own, falling in love with a "shack," as she termed it, on about an acre of waterfront. It was on Buck Island in Lake Placid, "the big lake." She said it was nothing but a shell when she bought it, but she could see the possibilities if she had it rebuilt, as every room had a view of the lake.

The property was owned by a Methodist minister from Flatbush in Brooklyn, a Reverend Norton. He named it Camp Sunset; Smith changed the name to Camp Sunshine. She told me:

> He believed in having a view of the lake no matter where you were in the house. I had never seen this before. I noticed that, even in the old building . . . you could see the great possibilities, what could be done with it, and that's why I really bought the property—plus the fact of southern exposure. We have the sunrise in the east . . . and we have the sun all day long . . . not only that, but the same thing happens with that big beautiful moon when it comes up over those mountains!

Smith had to have the building jacked up, as it sat on the ground, rising and falling with the seasons (fall frost and spring melt); she also had a foundation and cellar built. She had a new outside of quarter-logs, new floors, a new roof, and everything painted inside and out. It is a striking two-story house, with an open piazza on the first floor facing the lake and a closed screened-and-windowed porch above.

The house has a quaint, homey thirties feel and look about it. The main door from the piazza opens to the dining room, with built-in window benches and an alcove with a fieldstone fireplace. In the middle is the rock maple dining set. To the left is the white kitchen with stainless steel countertops. Smith had a 1936 General Electric double-door refrigerator. Off the kitchen is a room with a washer and freezer. To the right of the dining room was the bedroom used by Smith's mother for many years.

Upstairs, directly over the dining room, is the spacious living room, with closed-in porch to the front and another fireplace to the rear. There are also three bedrooms.

Smith had four other main buildings constructed, including two boathouses. The smaller one, to the left of the main house, contains an inside and an outside boat slip. There is a sitting room on the first floor, built right over the water. Upstairs there is a guest bedroom done in knotty pine. The large boathouse is a sight to behold. Besides containing three indoor boat slips, there is her "big, luscious, spacious" trophy room, fifty-five feet square, with a lovely view of the lake. At the rear is a large fieldstone fireplace, and to the right of it the tiny broadcast studio.

Partly hidden by the large boathouse is a guest cottage, also done in knotty pine. It consists basically of one large all-purpose room, a bath, and a closet which was converted into the original tiny broadcast studio in 1940. To the rear of the main house is a small cottage with two bedrooms and bath: the maid's and cook's quarters.

Smith penned a description of her new summer home in the Foreword of *Living in a Great Big Way* in the summer of 1938 that conveys perfectly how she felt about her retreat:

> As I write this, here in my sitting room at Lake Placid, I am serene. Life, so far, has been good to me. It is that moment of twilight when the world seems poised, motionless—entirely without sound or movement. The pine trees, green sentinels of the deep woods, fill the air with their aromatic sweetness. Not a twig stirs. There is no slightest ripple on the lake. It lies level, blue, and still within these peaceful country hills. Then, as swiftly as it came, the breathless moment of silence is gone. A robin outside my window sings gaily as he goes about the business of getting his supper. A breeze stirs the rope on the flagpole, its fitful flap-flap a pleasant sound to my ears. There is the slap of water against the rowboat moored at the edge of the lake. There is a happy sound of laughter, as a canoe slides lazily along under the shadow of the trees. From far across the water the thin, clear notes of a bugle summon its party homeward.
>
> The sheltering walls of my old house cast friendly shadows. On the hearth, bright flames leap and dance, for August evenings are cool up here in the mountains. Nearby are my books, my plants, the fluffy roll of wool I'm knitting into a bright shawl. Rubbing her velvety body against my ankle, Mittsy, my little gray kitten, purrs with a contentment that parallels my own.
>
> Soon, the splendor of the setting sun will slip down behind the hills. The wavering path of gold across the lake will fade. Sky and water will be painted with scarlet, orange, and pink, deepening finally into dusky purple, sapphire, and smoky gray. We have seen many such sunsets, Mittsy and I, in the past few months. Never two alike, but always stealing like a benediction into our consciousness, to remind us that ours is a good world, a beautiful world.
>
> Money, fame, excitement, and activity—all these material things of life may be important. But they fit into this picture only as a dim background. What have they of value compared to this magic of deep woods, and splendor of descending sun? This, then, is our answer, whispered through the twilight: there is no success like peace of mind, and the contentment that comes with a little house in the country—a garden sweet with growing things—a hearth fire gleaming bright.

Ted Collins bought a piece of land to the south of Camp Sunshine—on the right when approaching by boat. He had a more modern home built of quarter-logs after the war, in 1946.

Over the years, Smith entertained a great many people at Camp Sunshine, including, of course, family members. Fred Ditmars, her uncle by marriage, loved to visit and to fish with Collins. Her mother spent the entire summer there, and so did her Granny Hanby after her husband died. Sister Helena and her two daughters also visited each summer. Suzanne (Steene) Andron, Smith's younger niece, recalled those summers for us:

> Aunt Kathryn loved to drive her big mahogany boats on Lake Placid. I can picture her smiling face as she raced across the lake's surface, for she had only two speeds: idle and full open. How she loved those boats. On hot summer afternoons we would go on family picnics: to Old Forge or Ausable Chasm, there to play in the water, eat, rest, and be together.

SMITH'S RETURN TO TELEVISION TOOK PLACE March 12, 1955, on Tommy and Jimmy Dorsey's Saturday night musical series "Stage Show." She sang a medley of standards, including a powerful rendition of "When Your Lover Has Gone," looking youthful and radiant after a nine-month respite. "Stage Show" occupied Jackie Gleason's time slot while Gleason was ill. She was so well received that the Dorseys asked her back May 7. On that show she sang the 1951 Perry Como hit "If," receiving a deafening round of bravas, whistles, and applause.

There was a definite connection with Jackie Gleason and his shows over the years, doubtless because of Gleason's friendship with Ted Collins. They were drinking buddies, and Collins got Gleason on Smith's radio show several times. Kate emceed for Gleason on his TV show when he was ill in 1957. Gleason's producer, Jack Philbin, produced her 1960 TV series. Kate Smith guest-starred with Gleason for the last time on December 30, 1967.

CHAPTER 13

The Man in Kate's Life

In the 1874 Daphne duMaurier novel, hypnotist Svengali develops in an artist's model named Trilby a wonderful singing voice. Ted Collins was often called Kate Smith's Svengali, and in a way he was. To be sure she already had the voice, but Collins molded her image and career. She became dependent upon him for professional advice, and he became her dearest friend.

The "burning" question, of course, is this: Were Kate Smith and Ted Collins lovers? This question was asked many times during their thirty-four year association. So often was it asked that, in fact, the Kated office printed a letter of denial to send to inquiring folks. A few weeks after Smith died, one of the scandal sheets published an amusing story. The headline indicated, in a "now it can be told" fashion, that Smith and Collins had long been in love but were never able to marry. It stated that the two of them rented a summer cottage at Rockaway Beach on Long Island each year from 1934 through 1945. They were never seen outside the cottage. Smith was referred to as a very gracious lady who never failed to pay the rent ahead of time.

This fable is so patently absurd that there should be no need even to address it. The fact is that the Collins family lived not very far east of Rockaway Beach and Smith was occasionally invited to have dinner with them. In fact, this is where Collins was headed that fateful evening in 1930 when he missed his train and decided to take in *Flying High* while waiting for a later train. As Kate became better acquainted with Ted and Jeanette, she spent more time at their home, being invited for an occasional weekend. Neponset is about a forty-minute ride from Manhattan. Soon Smith bought a small boat to use on the pond near the Collins home.

In point of fact, Smith spent what vacation she had during the summers of 1934–37 at the Lake Placid Club, and every summer thereafter at her own Camp Sunshine at Lake Placid. The Collins family rented a place on the mainland, visiting her camp frequently. Members of Smith's family were usually also at her Lake Placid home. Furthermore, Smith had little to do with paying bills of any sort, leaving most of them to her accountants, so that part of the story was also implausible. During the radio season when Kate invited Ted to dinner at her Park Avenue apartment, her mother was often there and the cook was always present, in case they needed a chaperone.

The question of a Smith-Collins romance followed Kate's entire career and was often the first question asked of any of us who were her friends. Generally the asker had his or her mind made up that the answer was yes, regardless of what we might assert to the contrary. That still happens. A 1936 *Radio Stars* magazine story asked the question, "Wedding Bells for Kate Smith?" Another story was titled "Why Kate Smith Never Married." A third read "Untold Story of Kate Smith–Ted Collins."

It is worth exploring the Songbird's relationship with men in general. As a girl she preferred to play with boys. She had few if any beaux in high school, however, as she was becoming quite chubby. When on the New York stage, she was occasionally invited to dinner by men who had bets on how much she would eat. Her rude treatment by comedian Bert Lahr left a lasting impression upon her. Then there was the bitter episode with producer George White when she asked to be excused from *Flying High* to go to the bedside of her dying father.

When Smith became a radio star, there were men lurking everywhere who would use her if Collins would allow it: men who wanted her to sing their songs or give them money or steal her personal property. After she became Queen of the Air, she was often flattered by men who complimented her on her singing or her dress or her hairdo. While those compliments pleased her, she never got beyond being wary of men's attentions. I saw the same reluctance when I visited her many years later. At Camp Sunshine she brought out a number of glossy photos. When I asked her to autograph one for me, she asserted (erroneously, though perhaps she thought it was true) that she had never signed an autograph for a man before. That indicated that she was beginning to trust me as a loyal friend without ulterior motives.

Smith explained her relationship with Collins in answer to the eternal question asked her on "The Mike Douglas Show" in 1974:

> Ted? Oh, so many people thought that because of our close association. We formed our company in 1930; Ted was the president, I was the vice president. He was the producer, I was the artist. And he was my confidant. I went to him for everything because I lost my father in 1930, so I had no Dad to go to when things came up. So I took everything to Ted. He had to shoulder everything. I was very close to his family. Ted was married when I met him. He had a lovely daughter, he [later] had two grandchildren, and I was kinda adopted into their family.... But Ted and I? No, there was never any romance between Ted and I.

That same week Smith declared that the most common question she was asked in interviews was "Why didn't you ever get married?" She offered this explanation for remaining single:

> I felt that, to my way of thinking—only me, now—that two careers cannot be carried on perfectly. One of them would have to suffer. If I married, I would want to devote all of my time and efforts to my husband, to making him a home, raising a family, and being with him. And that would mean giving up my career to do that. Now again, on the other side, I'd hate to give up something that I've worked forty-three years to secure, and that is my career. I'm really married to my career and to all the wonderful people that have been with me all these years.

A year later on "The NBC Tomorrow Show," host Tom Snyder asked her why she had not married. She said she had been asked by six gentlemen, all Washington, D.C., area businessmen, and that she had turned each of them down because she simply felt that she could not both pursue a career and properly raise a family.

Although Kate Smith and her mother were always close, there is reason to believe that she was not nearly as close to her father. In her second autobiography she related the scene when he slapped her face because she insisted on being a singer, not a nurse. Though he later apologized, that incident left an indelible impression on the teenager.

By the time her older sister Helena married in 1940, Kate's career was going so well and consuming so much of her time that she had become reconciled to not marrying. She said she became acutely aware of this during Helena's wedding reception, when she realized she was not jealous of her sister at all. After that, Charlotte Smith moved to New York and lived with her famous daughter.

What kind of man was Ted Collins? I asked veteran comedian Henny Youngman this question. Henny had known Collins since 1935. When he was the resident comedian on Kate's radio hour, Collins often acted as his straight man. One would think they were good buddies. Youngman said that Collins was a very astute businessman and gave him good advice about his career. He said, however, that both Smith and Collins were cold and rather distant; he was never invited to either of their homes. During the war, when the troupe traveled across the country by train, doing shows from military bases, Collins would not allow Henny's family to be on the same train. He himself did eat meals with Smith and Collins on the train, however. He said they had their little clique and he was an outsider.

In an attempt to learn as much as possible about the Collins marriage, I interviewed one of Smith's caretakers at Camp Sunshine, as well as the widow of another. Branchford James Cook was her second caretaker, serving from roughly 1940 to the middle fifties. Now over ninety, with all of his faculties intact, he was happy to talk with me about his recollections of those days. He succeeded one Johnny Moorhead, an Irishman with a temper who was fired after an altercation with one of Smith's guests.

Cook told me, "Miss Smith was a wonderful person, very common, and very generous to the Lake Placid community." He recalled fondly that she always called him "Beejie" and would shout to him on Main Street in the village. One day he approached her and told her she had a run that went all the way up her stocking. She said she didn't care. She was regular and put on no airs. Collins was, on the other hand, "immoral, miserable to get along with." Cook recalled warmly that Smith's mother and grandmother were often at the camp and liked to sit on the porch. He considered them nice ladies who could be quite amusing. One day Mrs. Smith called to him as he was mowing the lawn. He stopped the mower and came over to the porch, where she invited him to sit and rest a spell. She gave him some advice, allegedly saying, "You watch out for that Mr. Collins. He'd like to have you fired." Cook said neither Mrs. Smith nor her mother had any use for Collins.

The Cooks had a black cocker spaniel that they would bring to the island. It liked to curl up in Lottie Smith's lap. One day as Beejie was repairing the dock, he supposedly heard Mrs. Smith suddenly shout an oath at the dog. He laughed at the recollection. The dog had nipped her nose. He said Miss Smith doted on the dog and at the slightest whim she would take it to the veterinarian, perhaps to get its nails clipped or something else of a minor nature. He confirmed Betty Garde's observation that her own cocker, Freckles, was a monster, totally undisciplined. Freckles also liked to bite. One day on the boat he bit Beejie, and he gave him a good slap. He made sure Miss Smith did not see him, however.

In 1955 Cook suffered a severe heart attack while working at Camp Sunshine. Collins threatened not to pay him for the remainder of the season. When Cook had recovered sufficiently, he wrote Collins a long letter telling him exactly what he thought of him. He remembers writing, "I hope you don't die at Lake Placid [he did], for if you do, they'll have to hire pallbearers, as there aren't six men in town who have any use for you." Collins paid him.

Cook took great pride in the appearance of Camp Sunshine, working from dawn to sunset on the lawns, gardens, docks, and buildings. Each spring he set out about a thousand flowering plants and sowed a sizable vegetable garden. Mrs. Cook, who in fact served as cook, would "put up" some of the vegetables so that Smith could take them back to the city in the fall. He said Smith also puttered some in the gardens. Cook remembered having lunch in the kitchen one day when Smith came in. She told him she owed everything to Collins. His instant reply was, "Oh no you don't. You owe it to your own voice." She did not appreciate his remark.

Cook told me, "One day Miss Smith came up to me in the garden and said she would like to speak seriously to me for ten minutes. I got up and she explained that there was trouble between Mr. and Mrs. Collins and that it was likely to be publicized and to get nasty. She said that I might be subpoenaed. I told her they wouldn't learn anything from me, as I minded my business and didn't know anything of her or the Collinses' business." He was not subpoenaed and the case never went to court. Jeanette refused to give Ted a divorce.

Cook remembered Jeanette Collins as "a very nice lady, a pretty lady." He never heard a bad word about her. Ted, on the other hand, had a bad reputation. He was known as a womanizer and a drunk. Cook said, "Collins would go fishing about three times a week. He'd come back about midnight drunk, bumping into the dock and cursing."

Mrs. Glenna Durkin, whose late husband was Collins's caretaker from 1946 until his death in 1960, recalled, "Miss Smith was never allowed to set foot on the Collins property as long as Mrs. Collins was there. Just as soon as they split up, she was over there all the time." She believes the separation took place in 1955 and that Jeanette Collins did not come up to the camp that summer at all. That was the summer that gossip columnist Walter Winchell reported the scandal to the world. Both Cook and Durkin recalled the "other woman" as Dorothy Daye, the same woman who produced the fashion shows on Smith's television hour. That this affair had been going on for several years is confirmed by Peg Lynch, who said she and the rest of the cast and crew knew by 1951.

The charming and salty Beejie Cook also clearly remembered another incident: "One summer after the separation Collins brought a gal up to the island. She stayed at Miss Smith's camp. The next summer he rented a place on West Lake." He added that Smith found out about it and would take one of the smaller boats with a fishing pole and go over to the shore at West Lake and spy on them. Cook said that word had gotten around town that Doris Day was going to visit Kate Smith and that when she arrived, all manner of small boaters with spy glasses gathered to catch a glimpse of Doris. Actually it was Dorothy Daye, not Doris Day.

Cook said that Collins did much of his drinking and womanizing at a night spot in nearby Saranac Lake. Jeanette Collins was very religious and would get out their motorboat on Sundays, rain, wind, or fair weather, to go to Mass while Ted slept.

André Baruch also had definite opinions about Ted Collins. He believed Collins had an ability to find talent and a great business acumen, but guarded Smith jealously, keeping one and all away from her. After the "bumping" incident related in Chapter 6 and Baruch's subsequent transfer, he heard nothing from Collins for many years, not until sometime in the fifties when Smith was going to do a television special. Collins referred to him as "old buddy" and asked him to do the announcing chore once again. Baruch decided there was no point in holding a grudge, asked about salary, and agreed to do it. When he appeared at the studio for rehearsal, he was greeted like the old friend he was by both Kate and Ted. From that time on, he and his wife Bea kept in touch with Kate.

Not long after that TV special, in the summer of 1957, the Baruchs journeyed to Lake Placid to visit their child at camp. While there, they decided to pay Smith a visit at her camp. They rented a boat and drove across the lake to her dock. She immediately admired André's new mocassins and asked to try them on. They fit her perfectly and she asked him to buy her a pair and have them shipped up from New York, which he did.

Collins was there that day, and he kept badgering Baruch to go water skiing. Baruch said he did not feel in the mood, but when Collins would not take no for an answer, he reluctantly agreed. Collins used Smith's ChrisCraft speedboat, Sunshine I, and got going quite fast with Baruch holding on behind. Suddenly Collins took a sharp turn, leaving Baruch stranded in the middle of the lake. Baruch explained, "Lake Placid is a 'bottomless' lake with very cold spots. I could have gotten a leg cramp and drowned. I made it to shore, but that's the kind of son of a bitch Collins was." He said Collins lost a lot of money on sports teams he owned, notably the New York Titans.

Ted Collins was a person who was either liked or disliked intensely. His old fishing friend, Hal Gillen, described how he happened to meet Ted. He and his wife Fran lived in New Jersey but summered at Saranac Lake. Gillen was leisurely boating up the river into Middle Saranac Lake when he came upon two fishermen anchored by an old stump. A "How ya doin'?" was quickly answered with, "If you think you're gonna do any better, tie up here and sweat it out with us. They're here all right, but the only bites we're getting is mosquito bites." Gillen accepted the invitation and the cold beer offered by Collins and his friend and guide Otis King. Gillen said, "That chance meeting was the start of a beautiful and warm friendship that lasted until Ted went fishing in the streams of eternity."

That was the mid-fifties and Smith and Collins had a fishing camp near the Gillens' camp, "a place where they could lunch and entertain friends after a day in the sun." Gillen said Collins was a great story teller. "His tales of his show business experiences, told with his inimitable dry wit and humor, were fabulous and could hold one spellbound for hours.... Ted was good company, whether fishing or just relaxing and chatting. In my book of memories, he was a great, gentle and kind man and I was privileged to be able to call him friend."

A typical Collins joke was this one. He had just crashed his big Lyman speedboat into a rock. His seat cushions and fishing gear flew up onto the bank, but he just sat there and grinned, quipping, "That rock reminds me, the French Navy just captured the Rock of Gibraltar and renamed it—De Gaulle Stone." Some loved his corny jokes, while others, forced to listen to them as a captive audience, gritted their teeth, laughing on the outside but seething on the inside. I refer to members of the cast, crew, and band back in New York City. Collins fancied himself a comedian; some thought otherwise.

Sanford Becker, chief accountant for the Kated Corporation from the outset, described Collins as a man of great perception and said, "He displayed rare judgment and insight." He recounted Collins's investments in such sports teams as the Kate Smith Celtics (basketball), the Boston Bulldogs (football), and the New York Yanks (not the Yankees). In actuality, Collins lost millions in some of these investments, which showed poor judgment. Becker added, "Whatever he went into, he devoted his full energies, which were many. Even when it came to a hassle with the income tax authorities, he was untiring and backed us up through the United States Tax Court where we won our case after years of perseverance. . . . A true and loyal friend, one who will always be missed by those who knew him well."

Actress Betty Garde, on the other hand, bristled at the mention of Ted Collins's name in our interview and explained her opinion of him:

> About the fourth or fifth time I went down to Kate's apartment on lower Park Avenue, she had a rather sad look on her face and she said, "Betty, you're not to come here any more." And I said, "Oh, okay, I'll see you at the theatre." I suspected what it was. Ted evidently didn't want her to escape from his realm in the form of friendships, be they casual or what. That is the truth and it was sad.
>
> Kate was so unsophisticated I couldn't talk shop with her the way I could with fellow actors. She was an entity apart. She wasn't show business. Whether it was Ted's prevention or whether she just didn't care for that end of our business, the fraternity sort of thing that you always have. . . She was really not of our world. . . It wasn't a curt dismissal. She was very sad about it, as a matter of fact.

I asked the inevitable question, "Do you believe they were in love?" Her answer came swiftly:

> She was terribly in love with Ted. My friends would say, "They're an item" and I would say, "I would swear on a stack of Bibles that is not the case." In the first place, I think Ted was too shrewd to let anything like that happen. Everybody thought I was nutty and protecting. Everybody knew he was married and I also knew that he had a mistress and that Kate found out and was furious, but not for the reasons that most people would think. He kept it platonic. His feelings for her were strictly business, because he was as cold as ice and as hard as nails.

Garde also told me of two incidents that took place in connection with a soap opera she conceived called "My Son and I" in 1939. She had sold the rights to Collins for $1.50 to make it legal, a big mistake, she realized later. The day came to audition candidates for the role of the son. Garde described that scene:

> I did what I felt was a very fair thing. I knew all of the four kids who were lined up for the audition. Ted and Kate wanted to come; fine. So we're all three in the control room. I lay down on the floor so I could hear and not see. I said, "Don't announce their names." I picked a young actor named Billy Redfield. Ted, who could see all these boys, picked the handsomest, the one who would probably get a movie contract that Ted could finagle. He was a charming boy, Kingsley Colton, but he was not the actor that William Redfield was.
>
> All during that audition Kate could not keep her hands off Ted. She was like a child playing with a puppy. She'd rub his knee and rub his neck. You'd say, "Well, we know what goes on at home," but I still say no. Now if that isn't love, I don't know what it is. I think if he'd told her to go jump in the lake, she'd have gone and jumped in the lake.

But Garde firmly believed it was unrequited love. Her description brings to mind Ezra Stone's inadvertent intrusion on a private embrace between Smith and Collins.

Betty Garde recounted another incident with Collins. She had to go to the Kated offices to consult with him about "My Son and I." This is how she described the scenario:

> He had a big mahogany desk and he had a cigar in his mouth and he put his feet up on the desk and said (pointing to Kate's office), "You know, that girl, I could let her go like that (he snapped his fingers) because we never had a contract and we never will." I said, "You son of a bitch!" Of course that rolled right off him. He thought that was very funny. I thought, "Where would you be if it weren't for her?" You see, that was his first stroke of luck, pouncing on this girl in *Flying High*. Nobody had ever heard of Ted Collins.

Returning to her analysis of Kate Smith, Garde continued: "She was a very, very naïve lady. Everybody loved her at Lake Placid because she was permitted to be warm and friendly. I never felt that she was a cold person, not by any means, but I don't think her life was ever completely fulfilled because of this bizarre arrangement." It was indeed much like the Trilby-Svengali relationship. Smith had a blind spot when it came to Ted's faults.

Lyn Duddy, the noted arranger, pianist, and chorus director on Smith's early fifties television shows, knew Collins for over a decade. When I asked him for his opinion of the man, his instant reply was, "A bastard.

He was very difficult to do business with. He never paid me a penny for what I did [in connection with her 1963 Carnegie Hall concert]." After Collins died, Smith asked Duddy to come to Lake Placid and bring his body back to New York. She rode back with him. At one point she commented, "You can say what you want about Ted, but he was always good to his star."

And then there was Kathryn's sister, Helena, who wrote a story in the Ted Collins memorial issue of our club magazine. The story was titled "'Uncle Ted' — The Lovable Magician," and it painted a very warm and happy picture of those long-ago summers at Lake Placid. She described Collins as "an extraordinarily warm and compassionate human being," adding that "kindness and understanding motivated his every action."

As if this is not enough sweetness and light, we have a favorable report from sound engineer Hal Schneider, who said he liked and respected Collins. He spoke of his duties on the shows and said he often went to Camp Sunshine on other than workdays to copy some of Smith's records on acetates for broadcast, so as not to wear out her originals. One day Collins looked at him at work and said, "You know, Hal, we've known each other a long time. Every engineer I ever worked with always asked for a fee. You have never asked for a fee in the years that I've known you. Why not?" Schneider replied, "Because I don't require a fee. I consider you my friend. If I make a mistake, that little bit of money you're gonna give me each week allows you to tell me how stupid I am. I don't need that; I think we're friends." He said, "You know, that's a different attitude than I've heard for a good many years." "But," Schneider remembered, "every Christmas Kate would send a big box loaded with champagne, hams, and God knows what else." Schneider knew that Collins was not well liked in the business, but he felt he was fair. He laid down his rules and expected people to obey them. Schneider considered him a reasonable boss.

Hal Schneider also reminisced about Collins's liking for exotic food. There was a very expensive restaurant in New York City where he would dine on, for example, breast of alligator or thigh of elephant.

In Schneider's opinion, Collins did not like to exploit Smith in any way. "In fact," he exclaimed, "Ted took good care of her; he was just great." He recalled a cocktail party at which there was an embarrassing incident. Although both Kate and Ted disliked these parties, they could not avoid them all. Schneider would go along with a recorder in case they wanted to interview anyone for their show, although he did not think they ever did. Schneider described the incident in question:

> Kate had been talking with quite a few people, but just now she was alone over on the side nursing a colorless drink. Ted made a grab for the glass she was holding. Some people said he knocked it out of her hand; in reality

he didn't. He said, "I don't ever want you doing that again." She asked what she had done and he retorted, "You had a cocktail glass in your hand." She said, "But I only had ginger ale in it." To which Ted answered, "I don't care. It looks like you have a cocktail. Kate Smith doesn't carry a cocktail around."

So there we have it: two distinct sides to the man Kate Smith called "my wonderful friend." Some loved him. Some respected him. Others despised him. In the business world he was tough, cold, and demanding. With friends he was warm, witty, and charming. His primary concern for half of his life was the welfare of the star he created. Like all of us, he had his strengths and weaknesses. Kate Smith did succeed because of her marvelous voice, but also because of Collins's wise guidance. He was guilty, however, of preventing her from having many close friends and many good times, which is regrettable.

CHAPTER 14

As Long as He Needs Me

In the autumn of 1955 Ted Collins signed an important contract with Ed Sullivan Productions for Kate Smith to make five appearances on Sullivan's "Toast of the Town" variety show during that season. It seemed that the entire nation tuned in to CBS-TV from 8 to 9 on Sunday evenings. Sullivan was genuinely thrilled to have Smith on his "really big shew" for the first time December 4. He introduced her with these words: "Ladies and gentlemen, it is with a tremendous sense of privilege that we present for the first time on our show the woman with the most remarkable voice that God ever gave anybody in show business. Here is Kate Smith."

Smith walked briskly onstage, looking youthful and vibrant. She was impeccably coiffured, with the teardrop earrings she preferred, a sparkling necklace, and an attractive three-tiered pleated gown. Her program was hardly original, as she sang the same three numbers she had sung on the Dorsey Brothers' "Stage Show" that March: "Just One of Those Things," "When Your Lover Has Gone," and "I've Got the World on a String." Afterwards she took her bows, walked over to Sullivan and gave him a kiss, and then left. He remarked, "I always wanted her on our show. She is the greatest!" Collins had signed her for four more guest spots between January and June 1956, but disaster struck suddenly and unexpectedly.

It happened Saturday, January 14. Collins suffered a very severe coronary thrombosis. Dr. Garlan, physician to both of them, called Smith to tell her the bad news. She wanted to go to the hospital immediately, but the doctor begged her to stay home, as Ted was under heavy sedation in an oxygen tent. She felt numbness, fear, grief. Her mother was with her to comfort her, if that were possible. Collins's thrombosis had occurred in his apartment in the late afternoon. Dr. Garlan had promised to keep Smith posted on his progress, and it seemed an eternity until the phone rang again just before 9 P.M. Collins's condition was stable, but he was by no means "out of the woods."

The next morning Dr. Garlan said it would be all right for Smith to come to the hospital to see Ted. She was warned that he looked poorly, but she was shocked when she peered down at his small, gray form in that oxygen tent. After she stopped sobbing, she went directly to the Chapel of Our Lady of New York at St. Patrick's Cathedral to pray. She promised God and herself that she would not sing again until Ted recovered. Each day she divided her time between his bedside and St. Patrick's, praying morning and afternoon. (Smith was not Catholic, though she often attended Mass.)

Smith and Collins's secretary had decided for the time being not to make a statement to the press. But Smith was scheduled to appear on Ed Sullivan's show January 29 and would have to cancel. The media would want to know the reason, so a press release was made on the 24th.

It was touch and go with Collins for several weeks. He had a history of heart trouble, having suffered his first episode late in 1946. Dr. Garlan spoke sternly to him when he was eventually able to be discharged. He was to get a great deal of rest and was not to smoke. Both orders were hard for Collins to follow, but he knew his survival depended on his obeying them. Smith's prayers and those of many others had been answered and she could fulfill her contract with Sullivan Productions.

Collins had had ideas of a television spectacular to commemorate the twenty-fifth anniversary of Smith's start in radio. Now that was out of the question. There was not enough time, and Collins was under doctor's orders not to undertake anything that ambitious. The occasion was marked in her April 29 appearance on "Toast of the Town." Sullivan was away in Japan, and actress Eve ("Our Miss Brooks") Arden was guest hostess. Smith opened with "'S Wonderful," sung as a "thank you" to her loyal fans. Then she spoke briefly, alluding to Collins's heart attack only as "unforeseen circumstances," saying she was to have sung the 1955 Academy Award–winning song "Love Is a Many Splendored Thing" in January but would sing it now. Her rendition, with a dancing couple in the background, was splendid; the song would become one of her standards in the years ahead.

Smith ended with a rousing "Fine and Dandy," after which Arden presented her with a bouquet of American Beauty roses and a message from Ed Sullivan. Smith thanked everyone for being loyal to her for twenty-five years. She paid tribute to Collins, who was "in the control room as always," the camera went to Collins, who nodded and smiled. At the end she introduced conductor Jack Miller, who took a bow. Things were apparently back to normal. Smith also did the Sullivan show on May 27 and June 24. Then followed another long and restful summer at Lake Placid, just what the doctor had ordered for further mending of Collins's heart.

Smith's television schedule was light during the 1956-57 season, with three guest spots with Ed Sullivan and two stints as guest hostess on "The Jackie Gleason Show" when the Great One was ill. Her season's highlight was a special "Kate Smith Hour" on April 28 to celebrate her twenty-sixth anniversary. Sponsored by Youngstown Kitchens, it was done from the ABC Television Center at 7 West 66th Street. It was a star-studded show, with ventriloquist Edgar Bergen (who brought along Charlie McCarthy and Mortimer Snerd), comedy by Ed Wynn, Boris Karloff, Benny Goodman and his orchestra, and lovable Gertrude ("Molly Goldberg") Berg. The studio held an audience of only two hundred.

Smith opened with a personalized rock song titled "Hello Everybody!" She also sang "I've Got the World on a String," "It's All Right with Me," "Mr. Wonderful," and closed with "(I'll Go My Way) By Myself." The Billy Williams Quartet joined her for a familiar rendition of "After I Say I'm Sorry." Highlight of the Benny Goodman segment was an oh-so-smooth rendering of "Memories of You." Karloff recited "September Song." Smith and "Molly Goldberg" chatted as apartment dwellers gossiping. It was a superb variety hour and a fitting observance of a quarter century of broadcasting.

SMITH HAD PLENTY OF LEISURE TIME during these years. The question was what to do with it. She used some of it to pursue her hobbies. These included photography, a special interest since the early thirties. She owned the best in both still and motion picture equipment, and she used her cameras often. In the early days she took movies of Minnie Klinge and her daughter Kathy, some in color. She knew enough to pan slowly and to hold the camera steady. She would ask the camera shop to rush their processing so that she could set up her 16mm projector and show the films before her guests went home. The February 1938 issue of *Popular Photography* featured an article titled "Camera-Mad Kate Smith." She had an impressive array of special lenses and filters, as well as a custom-made viewfinder for her movie camera. She would take candid shots at radio rehearsals and develop them in her kitchen, which doubled as a darkroom.

Smith was a collector. A specialty was Hummel figurines, 142 of them. She also collected authentic early American antiques to help furnish Camp Sunshine. One of her favorite pastimes was driving through the Adirondack countryside searching for bargains in antique glassware, Dresden china, and porcelain miniatures painted on ivory. She explained the art of unearthing treasures this way: "You have to know and like the country people to get them to take you to the top of their barns and show you their really old pieces, and especially to get them to part with their heirlooms they have treasured for years. They want to know who is going to have their things."

According to Smith, she could have stocked a fine antiques shop with her collection, and she sometimes yearned to open a store of her own. She enjoyed occasionally helping out at the Lavender Shop, a fine gift shop at 7 Main Street in Lake Placid that was owned by her friend Flora Donvan.

About 1970 she seriously contemplated buying a house on the mainland and working at the shop. When Donvan was seriously ill, Smith ran the shop and, as area residents fondly recall, that even included sweeping the sidewalk. She went to wholesale suppliers in New York City to purchase replacement gift items. She loved waiting on customers, and the pleasure was certainly mutual.

Smith's collection of Moon and Star glass was considered one of the finest and most complete. She also had a collection of some three hundred perfumes, though she used only a few herself. In her Camp Sunshine kitchen was an extensive collection of glass pitchers. Then there were the fans, the kind one cools one's face with. Her fan collection included one used by diva Jenny Lind in her first concert, as well as one bought by Napoleon for Josephine. Later she sold most of her antique glassware and some of the furniture, realizing that it was taking up too much space. She kept the Dresden china, but all of the Hummel figurines were sold in 1978.

Certain active sports appealed to Smith. For a heavy person, she was amazingly agile and was quite adept at tennis and golf. She was a pretty good ice skater and loved the thrills of bobsledding. She also loved to swim in Lake Placid, right off her dock. She would often swim across a narrow spot in the lake to a camp on the mainland and back, but Collins warned her that it was dangerous because of passing speedboats. Of course, she had her own 1938 ChrisCraft speedboat, one of the fastest on the lake.

Smith was a great sports fan, aided and abetted by Collins. She enjoyed watching hockey, football, baseball, and basketball, and she was loud and vigorous in her support, cheering, booing, and yelling from the grandstands. She had more than a sporting interest in some of the teams, as she and Ted owned several in the thirties and forties. In a radio interview she recalled these enterprises:

> We owned, in the National Football League [NFL], the New York Yanks professional football team. We were there seven years. Then we sold the franchise to Dallas. Dallas dropped it and they became the Baltimore Colts. In the 1930s we owned the championship Celtics basketball team, which consisted of Joe Lapchek, who later became the coach of St. John's University in New York, and Dutch Stennert and Doug Banks. On our football team we had a couple of sensational quarterbacks, George Rattiman and Bobby Lane. I'm a professional football nut, but even ahead of that I am crazy about ice hockey.

Smith's favorite indoor pastimes were talking and playing cards. She could sit on the porch at Camp Sunshine in an old-fashioned rocker and engage in small talk by the hour. She enjoyed penny-ante card games; that was the extent of her gambling. She often played penny-ante poker with her women friends. When I visited, we played an interesting and rather complicated game called contract rummy.

TELEVISION APPEARANCES FOR SMITH in the late fifties were few and often far between, in deference to Collins's need to take it easy. She made a couple more appearances on Ed Sullivan's "Toast of the Town," and she did a guest spot on "The Big Record," which starred Patti Page.

In 1958 she appeared twice on "The Perry Como Show." On the March 1 show she sang Sinatra's current hit "All the Way" and Perry's hit from 1951, "If." Then they harmonized in a medley of moon songs, beginning with Kate's "Moon Song" from *Hello Everybody!* Next came "It's Only a Paper Moon," "Wabash Moon," and "When the Moon Comes Over the Mountain." It was a superb blending of voices. As Kate exited to thunderous applause, Como remarked, "Terrific thrill, singing with a lady like that. I'll tell you that!"

On her return engagement in December, Smith sang "Love Is a Many Splendored Thing," which caused Como to quip about her breaking a chandelier with the high note. Then he asked her to do "a bouquet of all the wonderful songs you introduced on radio." They agreed to do a handful of them: "Home" (1931), "Stars Fell on Alabama" (1934), "These Foolish Things" (1936), "I'm Thru with Love" (1931), and "I've Got the World on a String" (1932). Guest Andy Williams joined them for the finale, which consisted of the new Christmas hit "Jingle Bell Rock," plus "Nevertheless" and "Give Me the Simple Life."

Kate returned to her favorite medium, radio, for almost exactly the calendar year 1958 (January 6, 1958, through January 2, 1959). She was back on the Mutual network with a Monday–Friday disk-jockey/commentary program, often with Collins present. It was called simply "The Kate Smith Show" and was aired from 10:05–10:30 A.M. Eastern time from WOR, New York. The programs were pretaped, with Smith's and Collins's spoken parts done separately and spliced to the music and public service spots by the engineers. I later acquired a number of the reels of tape, and the splices are evident.

There could be no news segment, and the topics of conversation, while timely, were not "of the hour." They were mostly of the "in the news behind the news" variety. There was the familiar light-hearted banter between Smith and Collins. The show usually began and ended with a Kate Smith record, with a recorded guest artist in between. There were editorials, delivered with just as much forcefulness and meaning as on the old "Kate Smith Speaks" broadcasts.

Here is an ecological story with a timeless message:

> Last summer, while I was enjoying my vacation up at Lake Placid, a friend of mine told me, with a great deal of pride, about her brand new house. So I drove over to look at it one day, and I must say it was lovely. She had boasted about how everything was "automatic." All you had to do was press a button and everything worked beautifully and

effortlessly, to do the work that our mothers and fathers had to do by hand.

I thought then that we're very proud of the way we have overcome Nature with air conditioning machines, color TV sets, airplanes, and cars that get better and better. But I've noticed that Nature usually wins. Now just the other day I had a letter from my friend with a long tale of woe. A heavy snowstorm had knocked down a power line and not one single thing in the house worked except the fireplace, which was old fashioned. So for a couple of days my friend had been doing her cooking over the open fire, the way her ancestors had done when upper New York State was first settled.

You know, it's strange but every once in a while Nature has a way of slapping us down whenever we get just a little bit too proud of ourselves. And if you want a perfect example of that, just notice the way traffic gets tied up the next time there's a light snow. Cars start skidding and stalling, the tires slip so much on the light covering of snow that even a modest little hill can tie up a hundred cars and the next thing you know, folks are wondering if it wouldn't be better if we went back to the old horse and sleigh for the winter months.

Could it be Mother Nature's way of showing us that she isn't beaten yet? Well, I say it could be. If you want any more dramatic proof of this, I can point to the headlines in the newspapers just a few years back and show where Mother Nature took a violent hand in things. There was the case of the Flying Enterprise. Do you remember that? I don't know how much larger it was than Mr. Columbus's flagship, the Nina, and certainly it was far stronger and more powerful, but the wind and the sea defeated it and sank it.

And there's the tale of one of the world's most modern trains. Do you recall the "City of San Francisco"? It certainly was far faster, far more luxurious, and far more elegant than the creaky old covered wagons which carried settlers across the country years ago. And yet heavy snow in the high Sierras stalled this modern means of transportation, just as it must have stalled the old prairie schooners back in the 19th century.

Fortunately, in both these cases no one was hurt. I think it was just Nature's way of saying, "Looka here, let's have a little respect around here." Just her way of kinda showing that, as wonderful as modern science is, Mother Nature is still the boss!

The program was almost a revival of "Kate Smith Speaks," as Smith talked of all sorts of things, such as why statehood for Alaska was being delayed (it would join the Union the next year), Ten Commandments for parents and their children, water shortages, how greeting card makers get their ideas, pensions for ex-presidents, whether men or women are better drivers (Collins got his two cents' worth in on that subject), plastic eyelashes in various colors, a new development to reduce the cost of steak, men going to beauty salons, J. Edgar Hoover's comments about the courts, teenage jurors, the cathedral building of St. John the Divine in New York, Paris fashion shows, the motion picture *Bridge Over the River Kwai*, the Miami

Seaquarium, kids going to fresh air camp, phony charities, a man who caught a fish with his car, the ingenuity of handicapped persons, Mrs. Minnie Guggenheimer's stadium concerts, small-town motels coming to the big city, and whether men would land on the moon.

On the last show in this series, January 2, 1959, Smith announced that she had several television commitments and that continuing with the radio show would be too much. She said she had enjoyed it and that she might return to it at some future date, but she never did. Four days later on "The Eddie Fisher Show," she sang her old chestnut "When Your Lover Has Gone." Then, going from the sublime to the ridiculous, she and Fisher joined in a duet of a zany rock song. America's first lady of television was moving with the times.

This was followed by two spots on "The Tennessee Ernie Ford Ford Show" (Mr. Ford was sponsored by the 1959 Ford automobile). Smith was right at home with ole pea-pickin' Ern. They were a couple of pros and knew just where they were going. On the January 15 show she sang two standards, then harmonized with Ford on "You're Just in Love." She was invited back the very next week for a western barbecue. She rendered a lovely "Gold Mine in the Sky," and she and Ford sang harmony to "Hey, Good Lookin'." Ford was obviously pleased to have Smith on his show, as evidenced by his first introduction:

> I don't remember if I ever told you what a kick it's been for me doing this every week for the past couple of years. It's been work, but I'm not complainin'. It beats plowin' and coop scrapin', I'll tell ya. But it's been fun because every week I get to meet the most wonderful people in the entertainment business. Our guest tonight is the queen of them all. She's America's most beloved personality and her visit is a real honor. Here she is, Miss Kate Smith.

Smith reciprocated at the end of the program, saying that she had never enjoyed working with anyone as much as she had with Ernie Ford.

That April, Smith appeared on the Garry Moore variety show. Moore introduced her by showing a page from *Variety* with a multitude of people named Smith, along with her picture and the caption, "There's Only One Smith—Kate." Each week Moore featured That Wonderful Year, and this week the year was 1931. Kate sang a medley of four top hits from that year, including her theme song, "Who Cares?" "As Time Goes By," and the lovely "Home."

Also in April, Smith was interviewed by Hollywood columnist Hedda Hopper, who asked whether she would consider a series of her own again. Smith's firm reply was:

> Never, although we've been offered many. We'll never go through that again. We only work now when we feel like it. After twenty-eight years we

can take life easier. That four years of steady grueling schedules shot my blood pressure up until I had hypertension. My doctor warned me he wouldn't be responsible for what happened if I didn't ease up. He said I was heading for a stroke. But we have contracts. . . . Once in a while we'll do an hour's musical like we did before. . . . We whipped up an hour show in two weeks. Ted knows where to put his hands on a production staff. But if you haven't had that experience you can get into a mess with those Spectaculars.

Kate Smith cohosted a spectacular in October called "The Startime Show," along with Polly Bergen. The show traced the evolution of pop music by decades, from the teens through the fifties. She also recorded five albums, all in one week, for the small Tops record company that fall.

Early in December Smith played a role in a musical fantasy called *Once Upon a Christmastime* with Claude Rains, Patty Duke, Margaret Hamilton, and old friend Charlie Ruggles. The story was about Vermont villagers wanting to welcome the town's orphans into their homes for Christmas. Stern Miss Scugg (Margaret Hamilton), who runs the orphanage, will not let the children out. Smith sang two Christmas carols and a song titled "Christmas Spirit."

Smith made a third appearance on Tennessee Ernie Ford's program that month, singing "White Christmas" and doing a hilarious kitchen skit with Ford in which he demonstrated how to make "pig taters" with her help. He nearly gored her with a bitstock drill.

Smith should have been singing "I'll Never Say 'Never Again' Again" that fall, because Collins was negotiating for a weekly series.

CHAPTER 15

Upon My Lips a Song

May I offer thanks, dear Lord
For the gifts with which I'm graced,
Especially for having placed
Upon my lips a song.
My life has been a symphony of melody and harmony.
I raise my voice and sing to Thee
For having been so good to me.*

"Now here's the star of our show, Miss Kate Smith!" With that pronouncement, the First Lady of Television was back on the air with a new weekly musical series. It was Monday, January 25, 1960, at 7:30 P.M. EST. It was Ted Collins who initiated the deal. He worked out the essentials, and then informed his artist. Smith was surprised and hesitant, because of his health. He assured her that Dr. Garlan had okayed it as long as he had help producing the series. Collins had asked Jack Philbin to be the producer; he would be executive producer. Philbin would procure the guests, line up the sponsors, and perform all the time-consuming tasks that Collins had seen to in the past.

Smith then was ecstatic. It was what she had longed to do all along, deep down inside. She began to think of all the preparations that had to be made. There were gowns that would have to be fitted (she had lost quite a bit of weight), music to be chosen, guest artists—so many things. Once again she was busy—and in her glory. And she was back on the network that gave her her first success: CBS.

For several years both Smith and Collins had had plenty of time to watch television, and Collins was especially critical of many of the programs. There were too many "horse operas" in his opinion, and he was incensed at the trend toward violence. He did not appreciate rock music and thought the soap operas were insipid. Collins felt there was an audience

*"Upon My Lips a Song" by Jackie Gleason. Lyrics reprinted with permission of the Gleason Family Partnership.

161

clamoring for a return to sensible, beautiful mainstream popular music. Smith gleefully agreed with her old-fashioned mentor. CBS was receptive, though not for prime time, and Whitehall Pharmaceuticals and the Boyle-Midway Division of American Home Products Corporation shared sponsorship. The bandleader would be young, creative Neal Hefti, as Jack Miller had retired. A twenty-five piece orchestra was assembled. Hefti, who would conduct on eleven of the nineteen shows, had had his own orchestra for eight years, having previously played trumpet with the legendary big bands of Woody Herman, Harry James, Charlie Spivak, and Horace Heidt.

CBS announced "The Kate Smith Show" on December 29. It would be pretaped, Smith's only series not to be broadcast live. Those were the very early days of videotape. It was two-inch tape in contrast to the half-inch tape so popular for home videocassette recorders today. It would be a half-hour show, taped before a live audience but with audience reaction augmented. In other words, the network reserved the right to enhance the applause. This was stopped after the second show. It was out of character for Smith, whose trade mark was sincerity.

The premiere show was taped in mid–January. After a few bars of a rousing swing arrangement of "When the Moon Comes Over the Mountain," the announcer proclaimed with enthusiasm, "And now the star of our show, Kate Smith!" Kate began to sing Ethel Merman's current hit from *Gypsy*, "Everything's Coming Up Roses," when suddenly a critical light bulb went out. A friend who was in the audience told me Smith lost her composure and shouted to someone to replace that light. She then stepped forward and apologized to the audience, explaining that she had been rehearsing all day long and that her feet were killing her. The light was replaced and taping started over. Just imagine what might have happened had the show been done live.

Actually, at the beginning of a TV spectacular that Smith did in 1959, the cue card man was "asleep at the switch." The band began to play her opening number, "I Cry More," but the words were not there. Smith finally had to say, "Jimmy, could we have the first card for the first song, please?" while the orchestra vamped. It had to be an embarrassing moment for Smith, and we can imagine what transpired between Collins and poor Jimmy after the show. That was always a contingency of live television.

Most of the 1960 shows followed this format:

> Opening swing tune by Smith
> Commercial
> Selection by guest(s)
> Commercial
> Memory medley by Smith
> Commercial
> Return of guest(s) or second guest

Commercial
Ballad by Smith
Closing

After the opening rouser of the premiere broadcast, Smith greeted her audience with these words:

> Hello everybody! It's grand to be with you all again, particularly because I'm a seller of songs from way back. Why, I've sung songs on some fifteen thousand radio programs and over twelve hundred hours of television. And I want to tell you something: I've enjoyed every minute of it! We've come back to bring you music, the best music that we can possibly find. And in spite of what you may have heard, Tin Pan Alley is still there to give us the songs of the great composers. Oh, we'll have guests on our show, young people who perhaps haven't made their mark and who need that extra little push, and, of course, you'll see others who have already become your favorites. I will tell you this: you won't see any who-dun-its or private eyes or listen to any sob stories. I'll guarantee you one thing: there's gonna be no cowboy dash across our stage firin' a six-shooter!

Smith then introduced her guests, the Barbara Carroll trio. Her memory medley was introduced to the strains of "Memories of You" and consisted of "Dream a Little Dream of Me" (her first song on her CBS radio show in 1931, sung again as a good luck token), "Stars Fell on Alabama," "(You) You're Driving Me Crazy," "The Last Time I Saw Paris," "(Our) Love Is Here to Stay," and "I've Got the World on a String."

Ted Collins had found the task of engaging guests very taxing. He commented, "Booking guests has become an almost impossible job. You go to the talent agencies and they offer you the same tired seven names, none of whom wants money for a performance, but a swap-appearance deal." Now this task would fall to Jack Philbin, Jackie Gleason's producer.

All of the guests were from the field of music, naturally. There were pianists Seymour Bernstein, Eddie Heywood, Joe Bushkin, Cedric (Skitch) Henderson, and the aforementioned Barbara Carroll. There were harmonica virtuosos John Sebastian and Richard Hayman, classical guitarists Sabicus and Carlos Montoya, harpist Robert Maxwell, and the Irving Fields Trio. There were the June Taylor Dancers from the Gleason show, as well as a dancing duo called Augie and Margo. There were vocal groups: the Four Aces (alas, lead singer Al Alberts had departed in 1958), the Brothers Four (whose big hit that year was "Greenfields"), and the Axidentals.

Arthur Tracy, the Street Singer of the thirties, was nicely showcased in an especially nostalgic show, and Philbin engaged the Great One to conduct his own orchestra on one show, with Smith singing Gleason compositions such as his theme song "Melancholy Serenade" and a lovely brand new number called "All Are Wondrous Things." Smith called Gleason's attention to a Joyce Kilmer poem that contained the phrase "upon my lips a song," and he composed a song with that title just for her. There were the Fort Dix Chorus and the John LaSalle Quartet, featuring Marlene verPlanck. Yet another show was given over to the Latin music of Xavier Cugat, with Cugie and his band very much in evidence. Smith sang "Nightingale," "My Shawl," "Take It Easy," "Granada," and other songs.

Two shows were given over to popular composers, Jimmy McHugh and Jule Styne. Smith opened the McHugh show with his "I Feel a Song Comin' On" and closed with "Comin' In on a Wing and a Prayer," which she had introduced in 1943. She opened the Jule Styne program with "Just in Time," ended with "Time After Time," and sang a Styne songfest in between. In each case the composer played a couple of his hits on the piano.

Maestro Hefti left after the April 25 show "to tour the country with his own five-piece jazz ensemble," according to the official press release. Maybe. Or maybe Hefti preferred a brand of music more progressive and jazz-oriented than the Songbird's commercial pop style. Bill Stegmeyer was hired to conduct for the remainder of the series. Stegmeyer had begun his career as a clarinetist with Glenn Miller's legendary band and Bob Crosby's jazz ensemble. He had served as musical arranger on Smith's NBC-TV shows in the fifties and had replaced Jack Miller on a few of her MGM 78s before that.

When Kated, Inc., signed for this series it was to run twenty-six weeks, with the last six being reruns. At this point in their lives, Collins and Smith were unwilling to give up any part of their Lake Placid summer for anything. And Smith's mother had suffered a stroke at age 80, so Kathryn wanted to give her the summer at Camp Sunshine to recuperate. She might not have many more summers, and she loved Lake Placid as much as her daughter did. The summer of 1961 would in fact be her last.

The entertainment press is always on hand for a premiere, watching with a jaundiced eye. What did they think of the latest "Kate Smith Show"? There were forty-seven reviews from coast to coast, all but one favorable. The *New York World Telegram* was particularly enthusiastic:

> Miss Kate Smith, who burst upon the small screen with full-throated rapture last night, is setting television back ten years—which happens to be what television needs right now.... Last evening, tuned to CBS and comfortable Kate, we felt Time turning gently backward in flight. Back to the days when a popular song had a melody rather than a decibel count.
> Miss Smith comes on in one of her plain, dark Madame Chairman gowns, throws back her head and SINGS. Sings with the easy competence

of one who has been performing professionally for thirty years. No rock 'n' roll, no hillbilly dirges, no hound-dawg laments. . . . Old admirers of Kate doubtless noted that she looked extremely well. Somewhat slimmer, and in consequence looking a good bit younger, she still sings in that clear, robust style. And she still has the sense to eschew all songs that call for interpolated dramatic readings ("How Did He Look?") or a sudden wild seizure of the "cutes" (any song introduced by Betty Hutton). . . .

The popularity polls failed to support the forty-seven favorable reviews, so after its contracted 26-week run, "The Kate Smith Show" was not renewed. Some have chalked it up to the earliness of the hour, at least in part. The results might have been different had it been put into a prime time slot.

Some of the swing tunes Smith sang to get her shows into high gear were "I Know That You Know," "Too Close for Comfort," "Who Cares?" "Just One of Those Things," "This Can't Be Love," "'S Wonderful," and "You." For many viewers the highlight of each show was the nostalgic memory medley, with a timely spoken introduction by Smith. (Collins was unseen in this series, restricting his presence to the control room.) Take the medley for the third program, for instance: "P.S. I Love You," "Georgia on My Mind," "Moonlight Saving Time," "What Is This Thing Called Love?" "A Little Bit Independent," and a full treatment of "Please Don't Talk About Me When I'm Gone." My favorite medley was this one: "Little Old Lady," "It's a Lonesome Old Town" (Ben Bernie's theme song), "Smile, Darn You, Smile" (a Fred Allen theme), "I'll Always Be in Love with You," "Home (When Shadows Fall)," and "Three Little Words."

As for climactic ballads, Smith chose "Climb Ev'ry Mountain" (from *The Sound of Music*), "Strange Music" (from *Song of Norway*), "I Only Have Eyes for You" (which she introduced in 1934), "The Music of Home" (from the current musical *Greenwillow*), "I Hear a Rhapsody," Mario Lanza's magnificent hit "Be My Love," and "Upon My Lips a Song." Smith delivered each in her legendary powerful Wagnerian style. Her voice was at its peak: rich, rangy, and mellow.

THAT MUSICAL COMPOSITION JACKIE GLEASON WROTE for Smith was indeed inspired by the poem "Love's Lantern" (ca. 1913), by soldier-poet Joyce Kilmer. The poem contains these lines:

> Because the road was steep and long
> And through a dark and lonely land,
> God set upon my lips a song,
> And put a lantern in my hand.

The phrase "upon my lips a song" gave Smith not only a song title but also an appropriate title for the biography she was writing at the time of the

television series. It was a revealing book in some ways, as any autobiography worth reading ought to be. It opened with the dramatic story of
Collins's heart attack in 1956. She wrote of the lonely and painful times
before he had discovered her, of her start in radio and the Kated company.
One chapter recaptures the excitement and dedication of her radio war
bond marathons.

Smith wrote at some length about the life of a single woman, beginning
by recounting a long conversation held with her mother after Helena's wedding. She assured her Momsie that a spinster could lead a happy life and
that hers was so busy and full that she seldom thought of marriage. She
stated her opinion that not all women are suited for married life, but that
some are career-oriented. She emphasized her belief that as single women
grow older it is important that they associate with younger people, and that
is how she maintained her youthful zest. And she addressed one of her principal problems during Ted's long convalescence: not having enough con-
structive activities. She wrote of our nation's increasingly pleasure-oriented
society, extolling the old-fashioned work ethic, as she often had on her
commentary programs.

In one of the most important sections of *Upon My Lips a Song*, Smith
discusses how she learned and sang her songs. She stated that while she was
capable of singing in a variety of styles, she believed in sticking close to the
way the composer intended the song to be sung. In learning a new song,
she first listened to someone play it on the piano. In later years her pianist
was often Lyn Duddy, whom she had known since he directed the chorus
on her earlier TV series. She would go to Duddy's apartment (in the same
building) and rehearse for an upcoming album, television guest spot, or live
concert. That is why rehearsals with an orchestra were minimal. She had
done her homework and was well prepared.

Alternatively, Smith would sometimes play a record of a new song over
and over, studying the lyrics, the rhythm, and the musical arrangement.
Then she would make suggestions as to how *she* would like to sing it. She
stressed the impact of a song's lyrics. After reading them carefully to get the
message, she would practice certain words to get the proper enunciation,
believing that each word should be sung clearly.

In the book she addressed her God-given gifts of perfect pitch and
perfect rhythm. People having perfect pitch can detect the slightest discord
in a musical instrument, and on more than one occasion this caused friction
between her and her orchestra members. She would insist that a certain instrument had played a clinker until the error was rectified. She never har-
bored a grudge against an errant player; it was simply that she could not
tolerate the slightest discord, in the same way that many of us cannot
tolerate a fingernail running across a chalkboard. Some call perfect pitch
a curse rather than a blessing.

In rehearsing with Jack Miller's orchestra, Smith insisted that her accompaniment be exactly as she wanted it. In this regard she was a perfectionist, as any singer ought to be. A 1942 *Saturday Evening Post* story related a revealing anecdote from the rehearsal of a song in which her voice was to be completely unaccompanied for a trick closing phrase. Smith was certain she detected a sour saxophone note and ordered a repeat, then another, until the phrase was repeated seven times. Finally the bandleader protested that no sour note had been played. "Kate scowled, and, turning from the mike toward the band, hands on hips: 'I . . . say . . . somebody . . . blew . . . a . . . sax . . . note,' she pontificated. There was an embarrassed silence. The bandleader looked blankly at the musicians, and they at him. Miss Smith stood her ground. "Finally [Miller] said with a defeatist sigh, 'Okay, whoever blew that sax note, let him hereafter lay off.'"

Smith's greatest musical flaw may well have been her timing. She sometimes came in on the orchestra too soon, necessitating a quick adjustment by the musicians or a double take on her start. This may have been the result of inadequate rehearsal with the orchestra.

Another flaw was Smith's mastery of memorizing the lyrics. She was spoiled by radio, where she always had the lyrics in front of her if she needed them. Even on television she sometimes had cue cards to rely on. But occasionally she would muff the words to a song, sometimes to humorous effect.

Smith seldom sang "Just in Time" or "What Kind of Fool Am I?" correctly, and she murdered "Wrap Your Troubles in Dreams" at Carnegie Hall, even with the lyrics on the music stand. She once admitted, "When we miss the lyrics, we just pick up and go on and nobody knows the difference." Maybe it bothered her privately, but she was not about to confess to a group of fans. Several of us held our collective breaths as she sang "More" on Howard Cosell's "Saturday Night Live" ABC-TV variety hour in October 1975. We knew she was singing the wrong line near the end and wondered how she would recover. Somehow she did, and rather smoothly, too, with no one but us longtime fans seeming to realize her fluff.

In her autobiography, *Upon My Lips a Song*, Smith revealed a secret about her hair, writing that although it was really blond (I would rather say auburn), she darkened it for television because it came across as grayish. She remarked that she did not dislike rock-'n'-roll music so long as the words were not offensive and the sound not too raucous. She admitted, however, that she would not sing rock-'n'-roll on TV because her audience would not want her to. This was Collins's conservative thinking, and it was substantially correct.

The reader should not depend on *Upon My Lips a Song* for reliable data, as it contains a modicum of factual errors. Take, for example, Charlotte Smith's age. In the book Kate gives it as about 70 at the time of Collins's heart attack in 1956. Her mother was actually 76, as Kate knew very well. Mrs. Smith resembled her famous daughter in build, being stocky, although she was several inches shorter. Like Kate, she had a very attractive face. Helena told me that when her mother became ill with her stroke, Kathryn brought her to stay with Helena, even though she was teaching and still raising her family. I know of no professional activities of any kind for Kate in 1961, so perhaps she devoted her time to her mother, despite what Helena told me. Mrs. Smith died in February 1962 at age 82. It was a very sad time, naturally, for Kate, as she and Momsie had always been very close, especially since her mother had come to New York to live with her.

Smith returned to "The Ed Sullivan Show" on January 21, 1962, after a hiatus of four seasons. Sullivan made up for lost time by showcasing her in a nostalgic set, complete with an old radio mike and a large projected picture of her radio orchestra in the thirties. They reminisced a bit about her radio programs and some of the band members and guests who went on to greater fame. Sullivan then asked Smith to sing a medley of songs she introduced on the radio, and she obliged with "When the Moon Comes Over the Mountain," "Did You Ever See a Dream Walking?" "Just One of Those Things," "The Last Time I Saw Paris," "Now Is the Hour," "Thinking of You," "Comin' In on a Wing and a Prayer," and "God Bless America." The latter was dedicated to astronaut John H. Glenn. Smith appeared to have a lump in her throat as she stood beside Sullivan while the audience applauded with spirit. Was she moved by the audience reaction to her return to TV after an absence? Or was she thinking that this might well be the last time her mother would see her on television? I have seen a picture of her mother at this time. Her resemblance to Kathryn's appearance in her last years is uncanny: a tiny, frail body with eyes staring into space, unsmiling and so sad.

Kate Smith returned to the Sullivan show that June for its fourteenth anniversary. Ed sat in the audience while a cavalcade of stars paid tribute to his many illustrious guests over the years. Smith's duty was to honor Oscar Hammerstein II; she sang "Climb Ev'ry Mountain." A couple years later, when casting for the film version of *The Sound of Music*, was being done, she was seriously considered for the role of Mother Superior. It is said that Rodgers and Hammerstein rejected her because they felt her fame would detract from her credibility in the role; audiences would be thinking, "That's Kate Smith," not the Mother Superior. The role was ultimately given to actress Peggy Wood, famous for her role as the Swedish mother in *I Remember Mama*. That was unfortunate for Smith, because the role suited her perfectly and would have been an important one because of the immortality the picture has achieved.

CHAPTER 16

Carnegie Hall: This Is All I Ask

Kate Smith looked younger than springtime when she made a pre-taped midsummer appearance on "The Ed Sullivan Show" in 1963. She was, at age 56, in the prime of her life. Her hair, the pleated gown, the multitudes of flowers in the set, the songs she sang, and the way she sang them represented perfection. It was also rare that at least one of the three numbers was not a jump tune.

Smith opened with "I Wish You Love," ended with a tried and true Smith standard (and a favorite of Sullivan's), "When Your Lover Has Gone," and in between was a stupendous, thrilling, glass-breaking rendition of the hit ballad from the 1947 motion picture *Road to Rio*. In the movie Bing Crosby sang it sweetly; now Smith lifted "But Beautiful" to the heights. When her left teardrop earring broke loose midway through the song, she caught it and threw it to a stagehand, never missing a beat. At the climax came a prime candidate for her highest note ever.

Smith guest-starred four times with Ed Sullivan that year. She was never more elaborately showcased than on October 6, when a wartime Stage Door Canteen set had been fashioned for her medley: a stage, a door-way, and a number of round tables at which sat servicemen with their dates. Sullivan introduced her with these words: "Armistice Day will be celebrated in just a few weeks and I'm thinking that Army, Marine, Navy, and Air Force veterans who passed through the Port of New York will never forget the Stage Door Canteen. So tonight we re-create the Stage Door Canteen and present, seemingly on West 44th Street, in a medley of World War II vintage songs, Miss Kate Smith."

Smith entered, youthfully radiant, mingling and chatting with the GI's and their girlfriends. When the band began to play, she made haste to the small stage, singing "Don't Sit Under the Apple Tree." She asked a British soldier to listen carefully to "The White Cliffs of Dover"; it was the only time she ended it on a lovely high note. Then she went over to the table of an airman and his date, dedicating "Comin' in on a Wing and a Prayer" to him. She finished with a rousing "God Bless America." It was the closest thing to reliving the moment. Now, twenty years later, Smith looked lovelier and sang even better than during the war, despite a bad cold. She stopped the show with wild applause, after which Sullivan acknowledged the twenty-fifth anniversary of the anthem. As Smith left the stage, he announced, almost as an afterthought, "Incidentally, on November second, for all of you around the country, on November second at Carnegie Hall here in New York, Kate Smith is going to make a gala personal appearance."

That is how we heard about the grand evening that Kate Smith would later regard as the high point of her career. "You can't top the tops," she remarked. Ted Collins realized that he was not in robust health and could not afford the risk of yet another heart attack, so he decided to break in someone to help manage Smith's career. The man he chose was Raymond Katz of Durgom-Katz Associates in Los Angeles. That was in 1962, and for the next two years they worked together. Katz played an active part in arranging for the concert at Carnegie Hall. This included press releases and television spots. Smith appeared on the prime time "Jack Paar Show" the night before, so a last-minute plug was given.

I found a precious little typewritten note that Smith had sent to Minerva ("Aunt Minnie") Klinge some weeks before Carnegie Hall. It was stuck inside one of her diaries from the thirties. It is incomplete, so we can only guess how the last sentence ended:

> To give you a brief resumé of how it came about. . . When we were here to do the Sullivan shows in May, some VIPS of the R.C.A. VICTOR CO. contacted Mr. Collins to discuss my making an LP album for them. Well, Ted didn't show much interest at the time and we went on up to Placid. They kept getting in touch with him up there and finally came up, via plane, to talk at greater length with him about it. The outcome was this Concert at the Hall, with R.C.A. Victor paying to put all of their recording equipment into Carnegie that night and taking the entire performance down just as it is being done and then they'll put out the ALBUM after that. I have never done a Concert of this type and everyone concerned over it thought it would be a good thing, for there seems to be many people who want to hear an evening of just my singing, and that's exactly what it will be. Ted hired Skitch Henderson as my conductor for the evening and Victor is giving me a 40-piece orchestra to accompany me. Mr. Henderson is an outstanding musician-composer-pianist-conductor and I know the whole "background" will be in very competent hands, as far as the music is concerned. And with Ted handling everything else . . . I feel we'll have a fine evening of music. Of course with me being the only performer, I will have two 50-minute sessions on stage with two overtures (of 8 minutes each) and a 15-minute intermission, thus we will fill the evening. I can't begin to tell . . .

She probably said, "I can't begin to tell you how thrilled and excited I am," or words to that effect.

I called Carnegie Hall the morning after Sullivan's announcement and purchased three of the best seats in the house at $5.50 each. I went with my parents, and if they were not Kate Smith fans before, they certainly were won over by the time we left the legendary concert hall at 11:30 P.M.

We arrived half an hour early for the scheduled 8:30 P.M. performance, hoping to possibly catch a glimpse of Kate and Ted arriving. No luck. The Hall was impressive: its large size, carpeted aisles, several balconies, box seats. We sat beside an elderly lady who was alone and excited to be seeing her Kate. I recall seeing Van Johnson and his wife walking down the aisle to their seats. On reading the program notes, I discovered that the entire concert was to be recorded, which made it all the more exciting.

Promptly at 8:30 the curtains parted and a magnificent concert orchestra conducted by Skitch Henderson played the overture. Several legendary musicians were in this orchestra: Doe Severinsen on trumpet, Al Klink (who played with Glenn Miller) on alto sax, guitarist Tony Mottola, and Buddy Morrow on trombone. We listened impatiently, all eyes glued to stage right (our left), anticipating the magic moment when the lady we had come to see and hear would make her entry. The orchestra commenced her familiar theme song, the spotlight shone on the left entrance, and Smith, radiant in a gorgeous royal blue gown, moved quickly and gracefully to center stage.

Smith bowed to the wildly applauding audience and picking up the microphone, went into her opener, "I've Got the World on a String," à la Sinatra's arrangement. Surely she had the assembled audience on a string. After twenty minutes or so, I heard the familiar introduction to my all-time favorite, "I'll Be Seeing You." The audience sighed audibly in unison. And that must be the sweetest sound a singer can hear.

After "I'll Be Seeing You," Smith greeted the audience warmly, saying, "I just want to take a moment before going into the next song to say hello to each and every one of you and to tell you how happy I am that you were able to be here and that you put yourself out and came here to be with us at Carnegie Hall this evening." She recalled that she had appeared in 1933 at the Palace Theatre for sixteen consecutive weeks (actually the year was 1931 and the duration was eleven weeks) and joked that it had taken her thirty years to get from 47th and 7th (the Palace) to 57th and 7th (Carnegie Hall), blaming it on the traffic. She sang practically nonstop for a full hour before she announced, after a spine-tingling "What Kind of Fool Am I?" that it was time for intermission.

During intermission I made my way to the front of the theatre, then through the doorway at the left, where I had seen quite a few others go. I had hopes of getting to say a few words to Smith, whom I had never seen in person. At least I did see Ted Collins for the one and only time. He was at the door leading to the dressing rooms, sort of standing guard and admitting a few close friends. I thought he looked quite well and dapper. He was obviously very proud of his protégée this evening.

The program for the evening went as follows: "Three Little Words," "If I Had You," "(I'll Go My Way) By Myself" [the first three songs constituted the overture, played by the orchestra], "I've Got the World on a String," "Say It Isn't So," "All of Me," "Please," "Don't Blame Me," "Fine and Dandy," "Carolina Moon," "I'll Be Seeing You," "Wrap Your Troubles in Dreams," "I'm in the Mood for Love," "But Not for Me," "When Your Lover Has Gone," "My Coloring Book," "Blue Moon," "Stars Fell on Alabama," "Who Cares?," "Moon River," "What Kind of Fool Am I?," [intermission], "Just in Time," "Moonlight in Vermont," "I Left My Heart in San Francisco," "Back Home Again in Indiana," "Tenderly," "Come Rain or Come Shine," "As Long as He Needs Me," "I Can't Give You Anything But Love," "How Deep Is the Ocean," "Margie," "This Is All I Ask," "God Bless America," and "When the Moon Comes Over the Mountain." For an encore she performed "Now Is the Hour."

When Smith returned for the second half of the show, she had changed into the full black gown on the album cover. As is evident from the program of songs, carefully chosen by Collins, with perhaps some input from Ray Katz, there was a nice mix of old and new. It was especially exciting to hear the new songs, some performed for the first time. I refer to such numbers as "My Coloring Book," "I Left My Heart in San Francisco," and "This Is All I Ask." Of all of the new songs, the 1958 Gordon Jenkins composition "This Is All I Ask" is surely the one that left the greatest impression on me. She stood bathed in the spotlight, singing these meaningful lyrics:

> As I approach the prime of my life
> I find I have the time of my life
> Learning to enjoy at my leisure
> All the simple pleasures.
> And so I happily concede—
> This is all I ask, this is all I need...
> ...And let the music stay
> As long as there's a song to sing,
> And I will stay younger—
> Yes, I will stay younger than Spring.*

There was some spontaneous humor when Skitch Henderson nearly tripped over a cord. Smith interjected a few little jokes, laughing heartily when, for instance, she quipped about her size. She said that research had revealed that the female of the species was composed of 92 percent water and then asked, "Now don't you think I've done a wonderful job with the other eight?"

Smith made a little production number out of "Blue Moon," telling of the lyrics having been changed three times and singing each version. The rhyming in the second one was atrocious, provoking a hearty laugh from the audience.

The standing ovation following "God Bless America" was fully expected by all, though nonetheless thrilling. On the album a male voice is heard speaking over the applause, saying, "Ladies and gentlemen, we are witnessing a standing ovation here at Carnegie Hall. This audience is on its feet in tribute to a great artist, Miss Kate Smith." Once when Kathryn and I were reminiscing about Carnegie Hall, I asked about this comment. She explained that one of the engineers for RCA Victor was so overcome with emotion that he could not keep himself from picking up a mike and saying that. She was quite obviously flattered. Still later I learned that it just was not so. Someone at RCA had invented that little story to flatter her. Actually RCA added it during the production of the album, because the applause was so prolonged.

Although RCA did record the entire concert, they did a great deal of editing for the finished album. And they took liberties with the sequence, placing "Who Cares?" at the beginning, for example. The album is, nevertheless, one of the finest of all live concert recordings. It quickly sold over a million copies and is still available in cassette form.

Midway through the second half, Smith made mention of Collins as she told the audience that the album would be out in only one week. (Actually it was out in three weeks, which is still remarkable.) At the mention of Ted Collins, the audience began to clamor for him to come out on stage. Smith said she planned to bring him out, but the clamor made her say, "All right, we'll bring him out right now." She called repeatedly for him to no avail. A friend who was in a balcony told me she could see Ted offstage, but he steadfastly refused to come out. Was he bashful? Decidedly not. Was he fearful that the excitement of the moment might provoke a heart attack? Possibly. I rather think it was because he did not want to take away one bit of the limelight from his star. It was her night to shine, not his. She paid him a fine tribute:

> He's a wonderful person, Ted is. I owe all of my success to Ted because he's the one who gave me my first break in records. Then he put me in radio in 1931. We formed a partnership in business on a handshake and we have been together these thirty-three years—with nothing more than a handshake; no arguments, nothing. We get along beautifully and, God bless him, he's a wonderful person.

Smith was somewhat overcome with emotion at the outpouring of affection following "God Bless America," so that as she began to sing her perennial theme song, one could hear a lump in her throat at one point. It almost sounds like a sour note, but it is the result of emotion. Following "When the Moon Comes Over the Mountain" all sorts of floral pieces were brought out and placed from one end of the stage to the other, and it is a very large stage. She said her good night to the audience, but we wanted more. She said she had completed her repertoire, but when someone shouted "Now Is the Hour," she turned to Skitch and asked him whether he knew it. He did, of course, and she proceeded to sing the song with a special set of lyrics, possibly written by Lyn Duddy for the concert. It was the perfect ending to a perfect evening, whether rehearsed or truly spontaneous. She told us that she hoped "it will be just the beginning of many more such meetings for us."

My friend Bill Freeh, Jr., told me that some time after the concert ended, Smith was greeted by many fans who waited for her outside the hall. Bill, age 15, was one of them. He said that despite the cold and windy night, she autographed their programs on the roof of her Lincoln for over an hour.

Several years later, when I was preparing an article about Smith's Carnegie Hall concert for her "friends club" journal, I inquired of her whether any pictures had been taken there. She told me there were none, but indeed many were taken by RCA. I was able to acquire several contact sheets, perhaps two hundred shots in all. One of them was used for the artist's portrait for her second RCA album, "The Sweetest Sounds." The artist took the liberty of changing the blue gown to green.

In an interview a few months after Carnegie Hall, Smith remarked:

> The Carnegie concert was my first concert—and the most rewarding of my career. I had four generations in that hall—kids, teenagers, even people in wheelchairs. Before I went on, when I was standing in the wings, I was sort of wondering how everything would go. But when they played the opening bars of "When the Moon Comes Over the Mountain" and I heard the applause break out, I knew it was going to be all right. I thought, "These are my friends." I could have gone on singing all night. I don't think my voice ever sounded better. I don't want to do another. You can't top the tops.

Reviewer John S. Wilson of the *New York Times* offered this praise:

> Miss Smith ran through what amounted to a hit parade of the 1920s, Thirties, and Forties, sprinkled with a few recent popular successes. Her voice has lost none of its robust resonance. Her delivery was easy and effortless, her tone mellow and smooth, and she can still belt out a powerhouse climax. She quickly established a folksy rapport with her audience, and it was this, more than the rather elementary interpretative touches she

brought to her songs, that helped to sustain her program. In most cases she sang only a single chorus of each song, frequently reading the lyrics from a music stand at her side. Her audience, which almost filled Carnegie Hall, was enthusiastically responsive.

A *Variety* reviewer (Nov. 4, 1963) was also complimentary:

[Her fans] gave the rotund warbler a resounding ovation before she belted a note. And they gave her a double encore before intermission. Backed by a mammoth orchestra under the baton of bearded Skitch Henderson, and aided on some numbers by a chorus of 20 boys and girls, Miss Smith ran through scores of melodic standards, rousing the highly prejudiced audience mostly with her straightway belting in the more stirring tempos. She read the lyrics most of the way, booting a line here and there to no one's dismay. . . . Miss Smith handled the new as the old in her pleasing voice range and firm, big, round tones.

A year later a reviewer for *Audio* magazine said it this way:

Anyone old enough to tune a radio set in the Thirties will be astounded to hear how fresh and rich the Kate Smith voice sounds today in this stereo recording made during a Carnegie Hall appearance. Receivers of that day and 78 rpm discs could not hide the fact that Kate Smith was one of the show business greats. This RCA disc reveals in full detail the amazing vocal technique that took her to the top. With the help of an orchestra under the direction of Skitch Henderson and a chorus under Will Irwin, Miss Smith delivers a smartly-paced program. . . . It would be asking too much to expect today's swinging generation to dig Kate Smith in her entirety. It is, however, worthy of note that this recording marks one of the very rare occasions when a great voice of the past has been captured in such a state of preservation on a modern recording.

Composer Lyn Duddy said he wrote the entire show (meaning, presumably, the spoken portions, as well as the original lyrics of "Now Is the Hour") and selected all of the songs. He told me it was Ray Katz who made it possible and that he (Duddy) never received a penny from Ted Collins for his work. Duddy also volunteered that Smith would sometimes not be in the mood to rehearse seriously. At these times pianist-conductor Jerry Bresler would play some of her oldies and she would sing them. Smith preferred her older, tried and true numbers, Duddy said. Once he told her, "Let's do current material. You haven't learned a song since 'Always'!" It was an exaggeration, but it snapped her into an awareness of the need to incorporate some new songs into her performances. Duddy said, "We put a gun to her head. She rejected seven top new hit ballads." She analyzed lyrics carefully, looking for anything that would detract from her apple pie, squeaky-clean image. One she did not like at first was "The Summer Knows," from *Summer of '42*, because of the line "She sheds her clothes."

Smith was persuaded to include it in a medley for her 1973 TV special, however.

Kate Smith may have said in 1964 that she did not want to do another concert at Carnegie Hall, but by 1970 she was ready for a return visit. She told me that negotiations for a second concert were in the early stages. She sounded enthusiastic and hopeful, but they fell through. It just was not to be. And anyway, "You can't top the tops."

CHAPTER 17

If Ever I Would Leave You

Little did Kate Smith know what troubles lay ahead following that triumphant evening at Carnegie Hall. To begin with, just twenty days later the entire nation was stunned by the assassination of President Kennedy. The British Broadcasting Company (BBC) produced a tribute program on which was heard a touching ballad composed by Herbert Kretzmer and David Lee called "In the Summer of His Years." RCA Victor called Kate Smith in to record it as a single, coupled with her live Carnegie Hall rendition of "God Bless America." It was rushed into production. Sung in a minor key to a slow march tempo, the lyrics told of the events that Friday in Dallas, ending with words of hope as "his soul goes marching on."

The fateful year of 1964 began innocuously enough for Smith when she made yet another Sunday night guest appearance with Ed Sullivan. Sullivan's rather cool introduction was limited to "Ladies and gentlemen, the thrilling voice of Miss Kate Smith." It seemed to indicate a tempering of his enthusiasm for her. Maybe something had happened in connection with the Carnegie Hall concert that he did not like. He had helped promote it and had written the liner notes on the live album, and he is shown in a photograph with Smith on the back cover. She would appear only twice more on his show. Wearing the same blue gown she wore at Carnegie Hall, she sang as one of her selections the poignant and powerful "This Is All I Ask."

Ray Katz, who was now working with Collins, began to mold Smith into a more youthful, less matronly, appearance. Color TV was coming in big and he convinced her that she ought to wear brighter colors and sing more of the currently popular tunes, along with the standards. She was booked at Miami's posh Fontainebleu Hotel for nine days in February at $4,000 a day. It was Smith's first nightclub engagement in thirty years and she had serious moral reservations about playing in such venues. The 29-piece orchestra was conducted by Jerry Bresler, with Lyn Duddy as pianist. This Smith-Duddy-Bresler association would continue for twelve years.

After dress rehearsal on opening day, Monday, February 17, Smith slipped and fell on the marble floor of the hotel lobby, fracturing her right ankle in several places. She went on with the show, with the ankle in a cast. She regarded it as a warning from the Almighty about playing nightclubs, however, and said she would not play them again. A few days after the engagement ended, she made her debut on ABC-TV's popular Saturday night vaudeville show, "Hollywood Palace." Host Efrem Zimbalist, Jr., quipped about her having "fractured the audience" with her singing voice, how nice it was to have her "in the cast," and he wished her a safe "trip" home. It was amusing and she took it in good spirit.

Kated had a two-year contract with RCA for two albums and two singles a year. Smith was scheduled to record her second album in March, but she caught a severe cold that settled in her throat and bronchial tubes. It was so severe that she had to be hospitalized for a week, so "The Sweetest Sounds" was recorded in April. It contained contemporary and recent popular tunes, two of which Smith had done at Carnegie Hall, although they had not been included in that album: "My Coloring Book" and "I Left My Heart in San Francisco." In May she made a narration album for *Guideposts* magazine with Dr. Norman Vincent Peale. Titled "Guideposts to Freedom," it contained inspiring stories of patriotism and faith.

Following her recovery from illness and the RCA recording sessions, Smith and Collins went to the sunny clime of Palm Beach, Florida, so she could fully recuperate. It was from that locale that she wrote her first letter to me. I had written her in care of "The Ed Sullivan Show" to tell her how much I had enjoyed her Carnegie Hall concert and to inquire about keeping posted on her coming professional activities. I was elated at receiving a personal reply. Miss Smith was impressed that I was collecting her records and sent me a copy of the Guideposts album, which she said would be hard to find.

Smith told me that she and Collins would be going to Lake Placid May 19th to begin to open both Camp Sunshine and Camp Rocky Hill, Ted's summer home, for the season. Twelve days later tragedy struck.

Smith had driven Collins to the office of Dr. George Hart on the morning of May 27 for a routine cold shot. He also performed an EKG, and it was just after that that Collins collapsed and died of a heart attack. The nurse ran to Kathryn, screaming, "Quick, Miss Smith! Something's happened to Mr. Collins." As she ran into the office she saw Ted on the floor. A rescue truck had been summoned, and firemen were administering oxygen as the physician worked over him in a vain effort. After a few minutes Dr. Hart looked up at Smith sadly. She cried, "Please, Doctor, don't tell me Ted is gone." His voice choking, the doctor replied, "I'm sorry, Kathryn. It's all over." Her beloved friend, business partner, and adviser for nearly thirty-four years was dead at the age of 64 of a massive coronary thrombosis. She knelt beside his limp body and prayed, weeping.

Lyn Duddy drove from New York City to take Collins's body back. Smith made the long, sad journey with him. He tried to console her as they talked about Collins. Her statement that, despite his faults, "he cared about his star," seemed to sum it up for her. André and Bea (Wain) Baruch recalled a pitched battle over Collins's casket. Smith did not think the casket Jeanette Collins had picked out was good enough. They had quite an argument, with Smith ultimately prevailing. The casket was exchanged for a much more costly and elaborate model.

Young Bill Freeh, attended Collins' wake. Mrs. Collins and the family were there in the afternoon, while Smith was there in the evening. Freeh said that Smith was devastated. She remained in a state of shock for several days. A requiem Mass was celebrated at St. Vincent Ferrer Church. Smith was consoled by Father Albert G. Salmon, pastor of St. Agnes Church at Lake Placid. Several close friends watched over her, including Flora Donvan, proprietor of the Lavender Shop in Lake Placid, and a friend of many years. Gradually she became resigned to her loss as God's will. Years later she said she knew exactly what caused Collins' death. "He was a dedicated coffee drinker, 15 to 20 cups a day, and a four-pack smoker. He turned a deaf ear to the doctor's plea for less stimulation. Had he listened, he might still be with us today." Now her mother and her best friend were gone, and she and her sister were not close. Whom could she turn to? She decided to return to Palm Beach and stay with her trusted friend Elsie Elwell.

What next? Smith had been in seclusion at the Elwells' home for less than a week when, on June 8, she fell through a plate glass shower door, severing a main artery. She lost a great deal of blood and was rushed to Good Samaritan Hospital, where it took twenty-five stitches to stop the bleeding in her left arm and close her wounds. Some would believe it was a suicide attempt in her despondency, but I feel sure that she was in a dazed condition and failed to realize that the shower door was there. She remained hospitalized for eight days and thus had plenty of time to dwell on the tragic events of the past few months. She had decided she would not— could not—sing without Collins to guide her. She pondered what God might be trying to tell her, and on the fifth day she made a decision to rededicate her faith.

It was not that Kate Smith had been a nonbeliever or agnostic. Hadn't she attended Presbyterian Sunday School as a child? And hadn't she attended church services, both Protestant and Catholic, many, many times over the years? Indeed her own father had been a Catholic. She was betwixt and between, and now she decided to formally embrace the Roman Catholic faith. She did the requisite reading and was given the proper instructions, attending convert classes in Lake Worth, Florida (which adjoins

Palm Beach). Her instructor was Father Sean O'Sullivan of Sacred Heart Church.

Smith wrote a letter in longhand to Billy Freeh that December. In it she said:

> I'm almost ashamed of myself for not writing you before this, for you were faithful in writing me, so please forgive me. Somehow I haven't felt too much like writing anyone. The shocks I've had this past year have kinda taken "the wind out of my sails." First a kidney stone attack (Thanksgiving Day last year), then breaking my foot in two places and a leg cast for 8 weeks. Then bronchitis, then the great "shocker," Mr. Collins' death—after that my bad accident in Palm Beach, cutting my arm so badly. And then 3 weeks ago my dear friend down here, Mrs. Elwell's husband, had a heart attack.

Freeh next heard from Smith the following May. He was nearing the end of his junior year in high school, and she congratulated him on "being picked as Business Manager of the School's yearbook. Again, the best of luck and happiness in everything you do, particularly in your exams. . . . It doesn't seem possible that my Ted Collins will be gone 1 year the 27th of this month. Yet, to me, it seems years and years since I last heard his dear voice and laughter. God have mercy on his soul."

In September there was a long, upbeat letter to "dear friend Billy" from Smith. She reported in great detail her conversion to Catholicism, saying that she called Father Salmon, then at a church in Glenfield, some 125 miles from Lake Placid, and drove there with three friends. He questioned her for three hours, then proclaimed, "Kathryn, as far as I am concerned you are ready for Baptism and I shall make the arrangements." She told Bill Freeh, "I was so happy and excited I could hardly speak. You see, it was Father Salmon who gave Mr. Collins the Last Rites of the Church in the doctor's office after he passed away. So I have felt very close to Father." The date was set for July 23, with Flora Donvan as sponsor and godmother. In August, Smith was confirmed at the bishop's private chapel in Ogdensburg. Donvan acted as proxy for her other sponsor, Collins's sister, Mary Hubbard of Burbank, California.

Smith made a second big decision late that summer of '64. She decided that Collins would have wanted her to go on singing, so she told Ray Katz, her new manager, and he in turn contacted Andy Wiswell at RCA in New York. Together they finalized her third album, on which she and Collins had worked that spring. It would be titled "Kate Smith: A Touch of Magic." The touch of magic was, of course, that of Svengali Ted Collins. Smith would write liner notes about Collins, and there would be a portrait of him on the back cover. The notes began, "To know Ted Collins was to love him" and ended with "I'm grateful that God gave me the courage and strength to do this one last thing for Ted, the finest person I ever knew." Smith recorded the album with a heavy heart on three successive evenings in late September. She was impressed with the "excitingly imaginative arranger," Peter Matz, who had also arranged and conducted on her previous album, linking the songs by giving a little hint of the next one at the very end of the previous one, a clever touch.

Smith had turned the corner; things were beginning to look brighter. She was signed for a guest appearance on Jack Paar's prime time show Christmas night. Paar's introduction was touching: "I wanted to send all of you a present tonight, but I wasn't sure of your home address. So I brought *her* here tonight. Her voice has been gift-wrapped for as long as I can remember. This is her first appearance on television in a year. Welcome back, Kate Smith." Smith stepped quickly to the mike and sang "Make Someone Happy." The audience clamored for more, so she sang "More." It was a very emotional moment. Under Katz's management, she was wearing more colorful gowns and fancier hairdos, often with false hair, although her own hair always showed in the front.

In January, Smith returned to "The Hollywood Palace," this time as hostess for the hour. She opened with a lively number from her "A Touch of Magic" album, "Danke Schoen," a big hit for young Wayne Newton when his voice was still high-pitched. Smith had fun with the nation's newest heartthrob, Trini Lopez, joining him in a chorus of his hit tune, "Lemon Tree." She ended the show with two more numbers from the new album, then a rousing "God Bless America." Yes, Kate Smith was back, rebounding with characteristic resilience and vitality.

Smith's next album was destined to be a million-seller. A fine selection of inspirational songs, it was titled "How Great Thou Art." Its success prompted RCA to produce two more religious Kate Smith albums. Her faith is evident in the manner in which she sings: a mixture of religious fervor and "the peace that surpasseth all understanding."

WHICH BRINGS US TO THE DEAN MARTIN ERA, so to speak. Smith first joined Dino on his show on Veterans' Day, 1965. Producer Greg Garrison showcased her nicely, and Smith and Martin enjoyed a very evident chemistry on the tube. She appeared with Martin seven times between then and 1970, and each time his ratings shot upward. On the first, and again on the last, show they did a medley of each other's hits. Smith sang "That's Amore," "Volare," and "King of the Road," while Martin rendered "I'll Be Seeing You" and "The Last Time I Saw Paris." They joined in a duet of the novelty arrangement of "When the Moon Comes Over the Mountain."

Smith and Martin even danced together on three of the shows, and very gracefully, too. They did some cute medleys of oldies, choosing children's songs, a Gay Nineties group, and an "I've Heard That Song

Before" medley. The Gay nineties set was an old-time vaudeville show, complete with dancing girls, featuring the hilarious Lucille Ball as the bird in the gilded cage with the bass voice. That broke Kate up.

Smith insisted that Martin never drank during rehearsals and that he was a perfectionist about his shows, in contrast to the image he projected. He was always thoughtful of her, having American Beauty roses delivered to her hotel room and, after the show, thanking her and wishing her a safe flight back east. She loved the fact that he always had peanut butter and crackers in her dressing room. Indeed Martin—or perhaps producer Greg Garrison—knew what Smith liked.

Everything was rosy between Smith and Martin until that brass firepole came between them. In the 1971-72 season all of Martin's guests appeared on stage by sliding down a firepole. I was visiting at Camp Sunshine when a call came through from Katz regarding an upcoming guest spot with Martin. Smith had insisted on being exempt from making that kind of entrance, but Garrison informed Katz that *all* guests would be required to do it. Smith was outraged and told us about it at the dock as we were leaving. "No woman over 55 should be asked to do such a thing," she exclaimed, with such volume that she could be heard on the mainland. She thought it was an ungrateful way for Garrison, who had "cut his teeth directing my show" twenty years before, to treat her. She never returned to Martin's show. By then it was on the skids anyway.

A rather amazing thing happened whenever Smith appeared on television. Although she had been a household name for thirty-five years, her name still attracted a larger than usual audience. In other words, the ratings of the shows went up. That is undoutbedly why Martin had her back seven times. The same thing happened for ABC's "Hollywood Palace." Smith was again the mistress of ceremonies January 8, 1966. She was at ease on that sort of show, not only in singing her songs but also in introducing the varied acts and even getting into some of them to "ham it up" a bit. Her third and last stint as hostess was March 19, 1967. She and country singing star Jimmy Dean (now perhaps better known for his sausage) had flown to L.A. on the same plane and had played cards en route. After Dean had sung his new recording, Smith joined him for a chorus (again in swing) of her theme song. They joked about the gin rummy games, and their voices blended rather nicely.

On that show Smith sang a medley of songs she had introduced on the radio from her new "Kate Smith Anniversary Album." RCA had the idea of putting together eight medleys of three songs each to commemorate her thirty-fifth anniversary in broadcasting. Again talented Peter Matz did the arranging, skillfully interweaving the songs. The team of Matz and Katz were doing right well by Smith. RCA even numbered the album LPM/LSP-3535.

Smith did another medley from that album on her last ever appearance on the "Ed Sullivan Show." It was May 15, 1966, and the set was reminiscent of the radio days, with the orchestra fronted by a floor mike and Smith approaching the mike as she would have at Columbia Playhouse No. 2. She opened with her theme song, then a gently swinging "Seems Like Old Times," and for the grand finale the lovely and powerful "All the Things You Are." What a way to go! Between January 1964 and May 1966, there was one other memorable "Sullivan Show" appearance, in October 1965, when she sang "The Lord's Prayer" like an angel, with a lovely stained glass window as her only prop.

Later I asked Smith why she was not appearing with Ed Sullivan any more. She told me that after she appeared on, say, "The Andy Williams Show" or "The Dean Martin Show," folks would tell her how much they enjoyed her on "The Ed Sullivan Show." That story really did not wash, but she would not tell me the true story, as she did not know me well then and may have feared that I would print it in our club journal.

It may have been Smith's appearances on "The NBC Tonight Show," hosted by Johnny Carson, that came between her and Sullivan. In April 1966 she was promoting her new anniversary album, to be released on her May 1 birthday. In December she was promoting her new "Kate Smith Christmas Album," as Carson's guests usually did. Sullivan was still writing his "Little Old New York" column, and he saw fit to accuse her of being blatantly commercial on "The Tonight Show." She took offense and that is probably what terminated their friendship.

Seven years later these two show biz giants would meet again briefly, in, of all places, Las Vegas. It was the occasion of the third annual American Guild of Variety Artists (AGVA) awards, and Smith was to receive the coveted Entertainer of the Year Award. They were civil to each other on stage, but the warmth of the past was replaced by a chill to equal the rare Vegas cold wave.

In April 1966, America's songbird was invited to travel to London to host an NBC-TV "London Palladium Show." It was NBC's exciting answer to ABC's "Hollywood Palace" shows. Smith agreed to do it; it would be her first, and only, overseas journey. She was quoted in an interview: "I just never had any desire to go overseas before. I'm very much in love with my country. But this was the third time this year I was asked to go to London and I began to think, 'Kate, maybe you should go. Maybe that is what you are supposed to do.'" She also told reporter Margaret Bancroft that retirement was out of the question for her. "If the Lord will spare me," she said, "I'll keep on going. I'm just so grateful to know that after 35 years I'm still in demand. It makes me very, very thankful."

Smith did not travel to Europe alone. Since Collins had died, there was no man in her life, save for manager Katz, who was headquartered across the continent in Los Angeles. She needed a chauffeur-bodyguard and valet, so she hired a six-foot-tall ex-Marine Sergeant named Salvatore Gelosi, who weighed 210 pounds and packed a .38. Gelosi was an ideal choice for the position. He had been an admirer for many years and held her in high esteem. One day in Sparks, Nevada, when several of us were seated in a restaurant booth, I asked how Gelosi and Smith had met. He told me that it was at the bank. She had an appointment there, and he was at the next desk. He recognized her and asked to be introduced. He said she replied rather brusquely, "How do you do, Mr. Gelosi?" and went on with her business. When he chided her about it, she replied, "Well, after all, Sal, I didn't know you at all. What was I supposed to say?" He was big and strong and intelligent, wise to the ways of the world. He was not a person to be trod on. Smith had received some threatening letters from a couple of weirdos, so one of Gelosi's first duties was to silence them. He was good at that.

"The London Palladium Show" was a triumph. Smith tackled the hosting chore with great gusto. After riding onto the stage in a Rolls-Royce, she told the large audience how thrilled she was to finally be in London. She rocked with England's heartthrob Tom Jones, and she touched the audience at the end when she reminded them of their king and queen's visit to America in 1939 and of her entertaining them at the White House. She had just sung the big English hit "What Kind of Fool Am I?" composed by native son Anthony Newley, and she ended with "A Nightingale Sang in Berkeley Square," which she introduced in the United States in 1940.

Smith was interviewed in London by Virginia Ironside, who headlined her column, "Here at last . . . Kate Smith, the 16-stone mother image." (A stone is a British weight unit equal to fourteen pounds, so 16 stones would equal 224 pounds.) Ironside wrote, "For four days the 16 st. singer who is to America what Vera Lynn is to England, is recording and hosting a television show in between raving about our Beefeaters, Bobbies, and dear little taxicabs and what she calls Piccadilly Circle." Smith said she was delighted to get a message from the Queen Mother and that it was almost thirty years since she had met her. Both she and the Queen Mother were disappointed that they would not be able to get together, as Smith had to leave for Rome.

Francis Cardinal Spellman arranged a private audience for Smith with Pope Paul VI. Sal Gelosi told me that the only time he had ever seen Smith in awe of anyone was when she met with the Pope. Gelosi warned her not to tell him any religious jokes, as she loved to do with the priests at St. Patrick's Cathedral in New York. He said he thought she almost regarded the Pope as if he were the Lord Himself.

An incident occurred in Rome that jarred Smith emotionally and left a lasting impact. She, Gelosi, and Katz hired a car with an English-speaking Italian chauffeur and drove to Observation Hill. Smith related the incident in *TV Picture Life*:

> It was a clear April day and we could see the seven hills of Rome from where we stood. I took my camera. There is a lovely long area with a railing along it. You can see everything from there. I was taking pictures and was unaware of somebody standing on my left. Suddenly Giuseppe, our chauffeur, who was on my right, came around in back of me and stepped between the man and me. Then Sal said, "Let's go for a Cappucino." We went up to the counter of the little restaurant and Sal and Giuseppe were both on my right once more. The same man entered and stepped up on my left side again. Giuseppe took me by the arm and walked me to our car. From inside the car I saw Sal come out of the door with the man. They walked over to a car parked off by itself. By that hour, there were only three or four people besides ourselves up there. I couldn't see what was going on at the car but after a few minutes it backed up, turned and drove away.
>
> As it drove past, I saw two more men in the car, besides the driver. They had never gotten out of the car at all. I said to Giuseppe, "What's going on here?" There was no reply. Sal returned to us and I said to him, "What was that all about?" He said, "Never mind." Sal looked at me and I could see that his face was very severe. "Those men knew who you are and you were pegged for a kidnapping." "You're kidding!" I said. "No," Sal said, "They knew you were an American singer and supposed to be well-fixed. They knew when you arrived here and were following you, but they didn't know I was with you."

"What did you say," Smith asked Sal, who replied, "I said, 'You've got the wrong person. Nothing is going to happen to this lady.'" When Smith insisted, "What did you really say to them?" Gelosi would not tell her. He just said again, "You have nothing to worry about." But Smith was terribly frightened because she had never known the feeling of anyone wanting to do her bodily harm. She said, philosophically, "I feel no bitterness toward anyone. I feel sorry for people who are mean and nasty."

So much for Rome, city of contrasts: from a papal audience to an attempted kidnapping. From Rome, Smith, Gelosi, and Katz flew to Paris. Smith had sung "I Love Paris," but that was before she went there. She found the people unfriendly. When WOR's Joe Franklin asked her how she enjoyed her trip abroad, this was her reply:

> I was gone from my country three weeks and I was never so glad to see the shores when I saw the East Coast from the air coming in. I hadn't begun to realize how marvelous it was to be an American and to have the privileges that we have, to have the freedoms that we have. Why, people in those other countries don't have anything. They don't have the great amounts of food and everything, the plenty we have here. And I really, literally, got down on my knees and thanked God that I was back in the United States. You've got to go away from here, really, and see what the other countries are going through, the people there, to realize how thrilled

and how happy and how thankful to God you should be to be an American—the want, the degradation, the no homes, they have nothing over there. There's just two classes: extremely poor, "poor as church mice," as they say, or extreme wealth. There's just no in-between in those countries.

Smith said a bit more about her trip overseas on the "Tonight Show" that December. She said, "I will say this; after I got over there I was glad that I had gone to see what was there, because it made me appreciate just that much more what I have right here in my home sweet home."

The standout song in "The Kate Smith Christmas Album" was "Christmas Eve in My Home Town." Smith related quite a story about the song and her reaction to it. She was discussing what to include in the album with producer Andy Wiswell, she said, when she spied a little 45 rpm record on his desk with that title. When Wiswell played it for her, she fell in love with it. She borrowed the disc and took it to her home in Arlington, Virginia, where she played it a number of times in order to master the melody.

The song was written in 1951 by two ex–GI's, Stan Zabka and Don Upton. Wiswell was happy to include it in her album. It was selected by Armed Forces Radio and Television (AFRTS) to be played at all United States military bases throughout the world. (The war in Vietnam was on by now.) Smith taped messages to go with it for every base, aircraft carrier, and battleship around the world. When she was Bing Crosby's special guest on the Christmas Eve edition of "ABC Hollywood Palace" she sang it again, with Bing introducing it as "her big new Christmas hit."

Yes, Smith was now living in Arlington, Virginia, next door to her hometown of Washington, D.C. She was very lonely and confused after losing Ted Collins. Perhaps she had too many memories in New York, so she rented an apartment in Arlington. Then she realized that most of her old friends were not there anymore. Furthermore, she was so busy with her career and taking vacations at Palm Beach winters and at Lake Placid summers that she spent only a total of twelve weeks in Arlington. She told me she did not really know why she had taken the apartment. She maintained a penthouse apartment at the Sheraton Hotel on 42nd Street in New York at the same time. So she gave up the Arlington apartment and went back to the Big Apple, where she had her eye on a luxury apartment building under construction on the East Side near the United Nations building.

At this time negotiations were under way for two Kate Smith firsts: an acting stint in "The Man from U.N.C.L.E." television series (which fell through) and a recording session with Arthur Fiedler and the Boston Pops Orchestra. It was maestro Fiedler's idea, and it would mark the first time that a vocalist had recorded with the hundred-piece orchestra. It would take a strong voice to be heard over that orchestra, and Smith had that voice. The album would be released on RCA's Red Seal label, reserved for classical music. The recording sessions had to be postponed, however, because Smith was stricken with another of her severe sore throats.

The long-delayed sessions took place at Boston's Symphony Hall June 8 and 9, 1967. They were attended by Smith's invited guests, Brother Gerald Fath and Father John Fabian Cunningham of Providence College. The former wrote about the occasion for the magazine of the Kate Smith U.S.A. Friends Club, which I edited. He gave his manuscript to Smith to approve and pass on to me. It read, in part:

> As Miss Smith entered the hall, great applause greeted the Star. Kathryn thanked the orchestra and gave a short introductory speech expressing her sincere gratitude to work with the "Pops." ... Arthur Fiedler then entered, assumed his position on the podium, and raised his baton. It was quite a scene, two perfectionists sharing one stage. We were impressed with Kathryn's sense of humor; she danced, conducted, and gave a few pointers to the first violinist during the preliminaries.
>
> A more serious tone was created as the recording progressed. It might appear that cutting a record is a very simple job since there is no audience with which to concern oneself. On the contrary, if Miss Smith weren't satisfied with the recording, another "take" would be in order. As many as five recuts might take place before Miss Smith and Mr. Fiedler were both pleased.
>
> On the first day side one, containing six songs, was completed, and on the next day, the other side, with six more songs. Due to union regulations, two songs would be cut and then there would be a break so that both star and orchestra could relax. During this time we would go upstairs to the engineer's control room and listen to the final product with Kathryn and Mr. Fiedler.

I was amused when I received Brother Gerald's slightly edited story from Kathryn. In the sentence beginning "Everyone was impressed with Miss Smith's sense of humor," she had carefully blacked out "except for Mr. Fiedler." Fiedler was not known for his sense of humor, except in public. In fact, though a superb and revered showman and a consummate musician, he could be downright crotchety to work with. Lyn Duddy, with whom Smith rehearsed these songs, told me that she had to put Fiedler in his place a couple times. When Fiedler began playing the piano as they went over the songs, she began to put on her coat. He asked her where she was going, and she said, "I can't play the piano at all and I play better than you." At another point she reminded the maestro, "Mr. Fiedler, I'm *not* the girl singer with the Boston Pops Orchestra!" Nevertheless he was a legend in his own time, beloved by Bostonians until his death at age 84 in 1979.

At one point Smith, with her perfect pitch, detected a sour note in the orchestra. Fiedler denied it, but a careful listen to each section identified the instrument. To his credit, Fiedler removed the white conductor's scarf from his neck and placed it on Smith's, a touching and amusing moment of truth.

A careful auditioning of that album will reveal that Smith's voice still was not quite up to par after her severe throat infection. Reviewer Frank Stephenson of the *Boston Herald-American* had this to say about the album:

> This is the first time we can recall that the exuberant Pops has taken a back seat to anyone, but in the background they are with Fiedler playing second fiddle.... Even one hundred of the best men are no match for the erstwhile Songbird of the South. The program is unsaturated schmaltz, sure to be loved by the largest of audiences.... And it's all great!

In a July 1966 letter to Billy Freeh, Smith mentioned her plans to be on Roger Miller's and Milton Berle's shows that fall. In her next letter she commented, "I have decided NOT to appear with Roger Miller or Milton Berle, at this writing, for they have very low budgets for guests, so I'm not interested. As Ted always said, and I continue in his stead, if they want me, they have to pay my price, RIGHT? Right."

In yet another letter to Freeh, Smith made an amusing statement, in view of the fact that she often sat at a grand piano on her early television shows and pretended to be playing as she sang. She was very convincing. On a few occasions her hands were actually shown on the keys. Freeh had told her that he was taking piano lessons. Her comment was, "So . . . you're taking piano lessons, well good for you, and just think, you'll be real good in a year. I'm for that, for I always wished that I could play one, just so that I could put down on those keys the musical ideas and thoughts that come into my head and I have a difficult time, sometimes, explaining to arrangers exactly what I want them to play. Who knows . . . maybe someday I'll decide to take lessons also. Good luck." This proves that she was not really playing the grand piano when she appeared to be, on earlier television programs.

Smith also had a correspondence with young Chuck D'Imperio of Albany, New York. He first met her when he was 18 while his family was en route to the Expo '67 at Montreal, deliberately passing through Lake Placid. A friend had told him that his favorite singer lived there, so they stopped at the Lavender Shop. D'Imperio recognized Smith's voice at the back of the store. She was seated at a desk doing some paperwork for her friend Flora Donvan. D'Imperio introduced himself, a tall, strapping young man, telling her how glad he was to meet her. Smith was flattered to have yet another teenage fan at that point in her career.

D'Imperio recalled, "The minute she touched my hand I was at ease. She boomed out in her friendly, warm manner, 'You came eighty miles out of your way to meet me? Well, God bless you. I'm happy to meet you.'" He had brought along his album covers, and she graciously signed each and every one. She even gave him two of her albums that she said were collectors' items.

Smith had a soft spot for D'Imperio from that time on. He visited her several times and was always greeted with open arms. He was in the nation's capital on Honor America Day, July 4, 1970. After Smith had sung "God Bless America" in front of the Lincoln Memorial (which miraculously seemed to unite both the patriots and the rebels gathered), she walked through the memorial and down the back stairs alone, to her waiting limousine, driven by Gelosi. D'Imperio came running, and she recognized him. She called him and told him to hop in. They drove around to the pool and watched the fireworks together.

In a letter to D'Imperio in 1972, Smith gave him, a budding tenor, some sage advice about show business: "You keep at it, Chuck, and someday you can be a big star. But remember, the most important thing is to be true to yourself and be sincere. Then, no matter how successful you become, you will always remain happy and as pleasant as you are now. Fame is a funny thing. It can be a curse if you let *it* handle *you*. Be careful, it's quite a responsibility."

CHAPTER 18

Sing, Sing a Song

Kate Smith did not sing around the house much. She confined most of her vocalizing to professional appearances and church. Although she never had her own television series after 1960, she did have many opportunities to sing before audiences in the years to follow. These years were a time for live concerts, TV guest spots, and recordings.

Smith guest-starred on "The Andy Williams Show" four times. She delivered her first thrilling rendition of "What Kind of Fool Am I?" in January 1963. Williams was an ideal host, relaxed and soft-spoken. He and Smith rendered a light-hearted medley of moon songs, then they sang a pretty waltz, "'Til Tomorrow."

October 30, 1966, was a standout "Andy Williams Show," with three legendary singers: Kate Smith, Bing Crosby, and Ernie Ford. To open the show, each in turn stepped to a standing mike and sang a few bars of his/her theme song. After Smith sang "Who Can I Turn To?" Williams joined her in a long medley of "home songs," tunes like "Back in Your Own Back Yard," "Way Back Home," "Carolina in the Morning," "Back Home Again in Indiana," the mod "I Know a Place," "Chicago," "I Left My Heart in San Francisco," and "Home Sweet Home." It was a delightful segment.

Smith was supposed to be Williams' guest again on October 4, 1969, but during one of the final rehearsals she suffered agonizing pain in the small of her back and was rushed to a hospital. X-rays revealed five large kidney stones, so an operation was mandatory. As she was experiencing heart fibrillation, surgery was risky. She said afterwards, "I died on the operating table." Her heart did stop beating momentarily. Williams announced on the show what had happened, as the media had heralded her as a guest and he knew many would be concerned as to her whereabouts. She made that postponed appearance on January 17, singing a new ballad called "Where Do I Go?" Then she met up with the Andy Williams bear, who was always after a cookie.

Williams' shows were becoming sillier, as he attempted to move with the times. As a party raged all about her, Smith was singing "The Party's Over" in a zany skit. Her last spot with Williams was that November 7, highlighted by her singing the powerful and inspiring "Anyone Can Move a Mountain." Williams's show, like Dean Martin's, was by now headed for oblivion.

Jack Paar is best remembered as the emotional, unpredictable host of NBC's "Tonight Show" before Johnny Carson. Few remember his prime time show, although Smith was his guest three times. The first was April 26, 1963, on which occasion she sang "Call Me Irresponsible," the Academy Award winner from *Papa's Delicate Condition*. Paar said of her afterwards, "When a nightingale heard her, he hung his head in shame." On November 1, the day before her Carnegie Hall triumph, she returned to Paar's show, singing "As Long as He Needs Me." Paar approached her after the song, took her hand and said, "Kate, if a rainbow could sing, it would sound like you." Then there was the Christmas 1964 appearance, with his touching introduction mentioned in the previous chapter. Paar certainly had a way with words.

"The Kraft Music Hall" had a long history, beginning on radio in 1934 with Paul Whiteman and his orchestra. Bing Crosby was host for a decade. Al Jolson succeeded Crosby, and then the preeminent variety hour moved to television, where Perry Como became the relaxed host for several seasons. After that there were a variety of hosts. Smith appeared twice: with Roy Rogers and Dale Evans in a salute to America in October 1968 and with Johnny Cash the next April. On the first show she sang Cole Porter's "Don't Fence Me In," which she had introduced in 1944, and took part in a medley of presidential campaign songs, singing those of Taft and FDR. She sang "If Ever I Would Leave You" on the April 1969 show, after which Cash commented, "Oh, Kate, there just isn't anybody that can make those words come to life the way you do." Smith and Cash sang a duet to "I'm So Lonesome I Could Cry," with Smith exhibiting the tear in her voice. She could sing a country tune quite competently.

The final chapter in the Kate Smith-Jackie Gleason story occurred when she was a guest on Gleason's December 30, 1967, show, along with Milton Berle. As Smith watched the pretaped show in her East Side apartment, she became furious when, after her first song, "The Impossible Dream," she faded out of the picture in favor of Berle's and Gleason's lengthy comedy routine. Her second song was to have been "What Makes It Happen?" and that is what she was asking. That was the end of her friendship with Gleason.

The next show was called "The Beautiful Phyllis Diller Show" on NBC, an obvious reference to Diller's self-admitted lack of ravishing beauty, which was in actuality her one gag. *Variety* suggested that the show was "put together with scotch tape, certainly not by any knowledgeable production execs or writers." Smith's songs were nothing new: "Just in Time" and "More." In one comedy routine she and Glen Campbell are stuck in an elevator and she smashes his guitar. The date was October 20, 1968, and she had just recorded Campbell's hit song "Gentle on My Mind" for her "Songs of the Now Generation" album.

By the time Smith appeared on "The Jonathan Winters Show" that November, there was a musicians' strike. Ray Katz had a tape of her "Gentle on My Mind" recording flown to Los Angeles so she could lip-sync it. Zany Jonathan Winters, a natural wit if ever there was one, appeared in the character of the Late Maynard Tetlinger, with Smith singing oldies to him. They were amusing and relaxed together. Later Smith sang "Bless This House," as it was Thanksgiving eve, *a cappella*.

"The Smothers Brothers Comedy Hour" was popular in the late sixties. Dick and Tom Smothers were not above some cutting political humor, which eventually got them into hot water with CBS officials. But with America's First Lady of Song they were charming. Smith took a shine to Tommy, who acted the part of a mischievous young man. She appeared with the brothers three times: 1967, 1968, and 1975. On the first show, after singing "The Splendor of You," bedecked in a two-piece gold gown with fur collar (both the song and the gown from her new "Kate Smith Here and Now!" LP), she gave Tommy a lesson on how to project his voice, using "You'll Never Walk Alone" in a very funny skit.

There was a hilarious "Sergeant Pepper's Lonely Hearts Club" segment on that show, a takeoff on a Beatles routine. Smith was dressed in a royal blue suit with bonnet, marching with the rest of the cast, including comedian Pat Paulsen (who was running a gag campaign for president) as a hopeless alcoholic. Smith looked more like a Salvation Army worker, trying to show Tommy Smothers the evils of drinking. It was a scream.

Another routine planned for the show never materialized. When Tom Smothers told a new young writer named Einstein that he wanted a short routine for himself and Smith, Einstein "came up with what I thought was very funny. It was just a thirty-second thing, Kate as Oliver Hardy and Tom as Stan Laurel, and he did a great Stan Laurel." On the first day of rehearsal, Einstein remembered, "Everyone was at the table and it got to this spot. Kate Smith said, 'Who wrote this?' I said I did. She stood up. 'I'm not doing the show,' she said, and walked out." Tom Smothers added, "She said, 'Boys, I'm not going to play this. I've been working very hard at losing weight, and I'm not going to play an overweight man. I'm adamant.'" Smothers concluded the story by averring, "She was a very good sport. So we put her into something more comfortable, which was a uniform like the Salvation Army with an Army hat on, which was a little more feminine. But she had a good time." Years later he salvaged the Laurel and Hardy routine and did it with Dom deLuise as Hardy.

On the 1968 show Smith sang the lovely ballad "Yesterday I Heard the Rain," dressed in a striking ecru gown with sequins and a mink collar. Then Tom Smothers joined her for a cute song-and-dance duet to Mason Williams' novelty, "Cinderella Rockefella." *Variety*'s complimentary review stated that Smith's "honesty and open acceptance fit the hour's groove with a warmth and ease not at all surprising . . . she is so unquestioning as to her own thing that one is bound to take her seriously, with quite pleasant consequences." When Tommy described composer-singer Mason Williams as "kinda weird," Kate ad-libbed "You should know," which brought the house down.

Between the taping of "The Smothers Brothers Comedy Hour" and "The Jonathan Winters Show," there was a period of five days. Sal Gelosi rented a car, and he and Smith took a sightseeing trip, visiting Yosemite National Park, Lake Tahoe, the coastal Redwood Highway, and the Hearst Castle. Upon their return to the Sportsmen's Lodge in Hollywood, where Smith usually stayed, she phoned me. I had never heard her in such high spirits. She got a bigger kick out of traveling than taping the shows. How she raved about the Hearst mansion, which she also had seen in the forties; she sounded like an excited schoolgirl. Some would have sworn she was "high," but it was a natural high: fresh air and beautiful country.

Tom and Dick Smothers returned with another successful TV series for the 1974-75 season, this time on NBC-TV. They asked Smith back, as she was terrific for the ratings and they enjoyed her. She gave new meaning to "I Have Dreamed," from *The King and I* and then did a delightful song-and-dance vaudeville number, "Me and My Baby," eventually joined by Tommy Smothers. They had the choreography down pat, and it stopped the show. Kathryn was 67 years old at the time.

Another popular TV series was "Rowan and Martin's Laugh-In"; it appealed especially to the anti-establishment contingent of the younger generation, consisting largely of topical takeoffs and slapstick comedy. The show was composed of literally scores of short jokes and sight gags. Rowan and Martin invited just about anyone who was anyone to be on the show, including such "squares" as Billy Graham and Kate Smith. In her most memorable skit, Smith was dressed as one of Casanova's women, accompanied by four doddering musicians and standing on a balcony. It was December 30, 1968.

ABC's answer to "Laugh-In" was "What's It All About World?" or so they thought. The host was Dean Jones, and the date was March 6, 1969. Jones comes on stage at the beginning, to scant applause. He tells the audience he is surprised, as he had been told the applause would be greater than usual that night. Then he remembers he forgot something, returns with Kate Smith, and the applause is tremendous. Smith tells him that she likes "being on shows that are new and smart. And yours is really terrific! After all, it has a freshness to it. It has no violence and that's what I love about it." She tells him she enjoys satire, that it reminds her of her old radio shows. Jones asks, "Kate, do you mean that in all these years the world hasn't gotten any better?" She replies, "No, the *jokes* haven't gotten any better." She also says, "I don't get upset about some of the things I read about in the newspapers. I have a philosophy and I think it's best expressed by an old Gershwin song." She sings the 1931 tune "Who Cares?" with new lyrics, "Who cares what outer space brings us" and "Who cares how history rates me, as long as your kiss intoxicates me."

Lovable Jimmy Durante was long a favorite of Smith's, so she was happy to accept an invitation to take an acting part on the Thanksgiving 1969 edition of the show with the unlikely title "Jimmy Durante Presents the Lennon Sisters" on ABC-TV. Smith was not long out of the hospital after her operation for kidney stones, so this was a tour-de-force for her. The entire hour is a comic play that is a takeoff on the story of the Pilgrims. Durante is a latter-day John Alden to Smith's Priscilla Mullins. He meets her aboard ship (the *Mayflower*?) as he retrieves her handkerchief. The scene includes this dialogue:

> JIMMY: Tell me, where are you headed for, Miss?
> KATE: I'm heading for America.
> JIMMY: What a coincidence. So am I.
> KATE: Is is true that one can make a fortune there?
> JIMMY: Does the moon come over the mountain? [*Laughter*] Once we get there stick with me. We'll make a bundle. Then after we're rich we'll get on a boat and take a trip to Europe. [*Laughter*]

Durante plans to open a tavern in America and will name it for the maiden he has just met, Hermione Staffington Whistleham Shropsdale (Smith). She describes his schnozz as "your little button nose," which prompts him to turn to the audience and quip, "You know, folks, they say that love is blind. And she just proved it." Smith sings "Just in Time" to Durante. After they arrive in America, Smith (as Hermione) sees how beautiful the land is and is inspired to sing "America the Beautiful." It may be the only time she ever sang that anthem on the air.

When Durante's tavern is completed, Smith exclaims, "Oh, Jimmy, this is magnificent. The decor is exquisite." He responds, "Yeah, but tell me somethin', how do ya like the looks of the jernt?" She says, "Lovely, I adore all the furniture." Durante's next line is, "Ya know, I did it all by myself. I call it Early American." As the finale the entire cast, including, besides the "lovely little Lennon Sisters," comedian Louis Nye and football star Roosevelt Grier, join to sing "Bless This House."

Smith told me about the making of this show. She said the whole play was shot in one long, grueling day. Sal Gelosi told me that the great Jimmy Durante was one of the few true friends Smith had in show business. How well we remember how, at the end of each performance, he would tip his felt hat and say good night to the audience, then, as he walked away and replaced his hat, would add, "and good night, Mrs. Calabash, wherever you are." Some class.

Smith made two memorable guest appearances on "The Jim Nabors Hour"; they were memorable because she played Tarzan's mother in side-splitting sketches on both. Two naturally talented singers, Smith and Nabors worked well together. Nabors spent several seasons as country bumpkin Gomer Pyle on the "Andy Griffith Show," and then on his own show, before his singing ability came to the fore. He showcased Smith nicely, featuring his special guest more or less throughout the shows, rather than in a single segment. On the first she wore a becoming powder blue silk gown and sang "Who Can I Turn To?" Nabors had given her a glowing introduction: "Ladies and gentlemen, if this country ever sets up a Hall of Fame for singers, our guest tonight would be the first one they'd call: the wonderful Miss Kate Smith." Later they sang another medley of moon songs, their voices blending nicely. But it is the Tarzan scene that is the most memorable.

Nabors plays Tarzan, sidekick Frank Sutton is Tarzan's father, and yes, Kate Smith is his mother. Smith gets to give Sutton some healthy whacks. The slapstick humor is largely in remarks about Tarzan's long hair, the generation gap, the new morality, and the double meaning of *grass*. Smith fights a losing battle to keep from breaking up laughing. It was all done in good taste, but some of her stalwart older fans thought it was degrading. She explained to me that a guest is hired to do whatever is asked, what will bring the greatest audience for the sponsors' products. Besides, she enjoyed the comedy. For the finale the entire cast joined in a group of George M. Cohan songs, dressed in red, white, and blue, with Smith rendering "Mary's a Grand Old Name" and "You're a Grand Old Flag," the latter with Nabors joining in.

A year later, October 1, 1970, to be precise, Smith returned to "The Jim Nabors Hour," wearing a yellow and orange gown and singing "If He Walked Into My Life" from *Mame* in a beautiful living room setting, complete with mirrored entrance. She and Nabors sang a pleasant country-style duet to "I Knew I Was Fallin' for You."

In this year's Tarzan skit, Tarzan's parents go to the jungle to visit their son in his tree house. Smith says, "Oh, my baby, it's been so long since I've seen ya." Tarzan replies, "Yes, it's been many, many moons." Smith asks, "When are you gonna come home?" to which Tarzan answers, "When the moon comes over the mountain." Tarzan's parents discover that he is married, to Jane, of course. Tarzan's father makes a few suggestive remarks about the beautiful Jane, to which Mama Kate responds, "You just wait 'til I get you home!" They then discover that Tarzan and Jane have two children, one theirs and one adopted. One is played by Ronnie Schell and the other is a monkey. Tarzan's parents ask to take their real grandchild home, only to learn that it is the monkey.

This show's finale was a Spirit of '76 patriotic medley, in which Smith sings "Hail Columbia" and "America" ("My Country, 'Tis of Thee").

Just after the first of the new year of 1971, Lawrence Welk called Smith and asked her to be on a special "Lawrence Welk Show" saluting Irving Berlin and his music. ABC-TV had decided to move Welk out of prime time to the 7:30–8:30 spot on Saturday nights, and the Champagne Music Man responded by choosing a popular theme and inviting a popular special guest—something he seldom did. Smith was happy to oblige. Welk offered to make it easy, she told me afterwards, by having her fly the round trip in a day and letting her lip-sync her songs. She turned him down flatly on both scores. She related to me, "Mr. Welk is a very nice, kind gentleman, but a bit of a skinflint. He wanted to save money by not having to put up my entourage in a hotel. I said 'Nothing doing,' as it would be too stressful." Smith much preferred to sing her songs with a live microphone. They were "Say It Isn't So" and, naturally, "God Bless America." She said she offered to sing a third one, one she had introduced twenty years before on television, "For the Very First Time," but he limited her to two selections. She was quite svelte at this time, attired in a gorgeous lavender gown with chinchilla collar as she sang her anthem, with a huge flag as a background.

Smith's next TV appearance was four weeks later, February 20, on "The Pearl Bailey Show." Lovable Pearlie Mae Bailey gave Smith her usual warm introduction, and she sang "More" once more. Later in the program Bailey again introduced her guest, saying, "When you hear about Miss Kate Smith you think of a Fourth of July finale. . . . We like new songs, but there's nothing like the wonderful old songs, too, the beauties. Listen to Miss Smith sing this one." Kate sallies forth, singing "When You Wore a Tulip." Guests George Kirby and Phil Harris, and lastly Bailey herself, join in the nostalgic medley. The camera closes in on Bailey and Smith as the former observes, "You are so divinely happy. Are you always happy?" Smith replies, "I sure am. Anybody has to be around you, Pearl. I'm not kiddin'. You're somethin' else." Bailey asks Smith to sing the last few bars of "God Bless America" and she obliges.

Ray Katz Enterprises also managed such performers as the Osmonds, Mac Davis, and Sonny and Cher, so it was easy for Katz to arrange to have Smith make guest appearances on their shows. She was a surefire ratings booster, even if their styles and personalities did not always mesh well. In "The Sonny and Cher Show," for example, Smith did a guest spot on January 17, 1972, and she was not even introduced. She simply appeared, sang "If He Walked Into My Life," and faded. My friend Gerald Jancik, who attended the taping of that show, told me she had to do the song three times before the final taping. First the cue cards were being turned too fast. Another time an extraneous noise in the studio ruined the take. He said Smith always made the sign of the cross before she sang. According to Jancik, the laughter and applause were added later, as there was no audience at the taping. He had a special invitation as a member of her "Friends" club.

There was an inane comedy skit with Smith dressed as a waitress, complete with apron, while Sonny and Cher were seated at a table ordering various and sundry items. Three years later she did a guest spot on the just plain "Cher Show." This time she appeared out of an egg, again sans introduction by the hostess. Cher is a bored bird who wants to leave Mama Kate's nest. Kate sang, appropriately, "What Kind of Fool Am I?" Late in the show she was upstaged for the first time since Bert Lahr upstaged her in 1930. Cher, Tina Turner, and Kate Smith were doing a medley of Beatles hits, and it was not long before Cher and Tina left Kate alone, with no choice but to watch them in embarrassment.

In November 1975 Smith joined Donny and Marie Osmond on their special, along with comedians Bob Hope and Paul Lynde. She sang with the teenage Osmond siblings in a medley of rock-'n'-roll songs, saying, "You know me, I'll attempt anything." (I doubt that would have been Collins's advice.) Then she sang an uncharacteristically slow version of "God Bless America." She was outfitted in an off-white plumed gown, and the rendition was very sweet.

The next February Smith made a return visit with the Osmonds, this time joining them for an entertaining medley of each other's hits. They sang her novelty hits "Rose O'Day" and "The Woodpecker Song," while she did Marie's "Paper Roses" and Donny's "Puppy Love." In a "fifties" segment Smith is viewed cavorting around a 1950s juke box singing rock-'n'-roll again.

It was time for country singer Mac Davis to be the beneficiary of a Kate Smith guest appearance. It was on April Fool's Day, and Smith actually sang a disco version of "Baby Face."

KATE SMITH MADE TWO TELEVISION SPECIALS, one in 1969 and one in 1973. Both were syndicated, produced by Columbia Screen Gems in Hollywood. The first, simply titled "The Kate Smith Show," was, from most viewpoints, one of the finest things she had done. She looked slender and sang beautifully, even if she was now beginning to eschew the high notes. Her guests were the Charlie Byrd Trio, a fine jazz combo, and the Kids Next Door, a group of sixteen young men and women who sang and danced up a storm. It was a varied and lively program: "Who Cares?";

"More"; "Gentle on My Mind"; "Mister Clown"; "Love Is a Many Splen-
dored Thing"; "By the Time I Get to Phoenix" (with Charlie Byrd);
"Daydream"; "Mame" (performed with Kids Next Door); a medley of "I'll
Be Seeing You," "Fine and Dandy," "How Deep Is the Ocean," "The Last
Time I Saw Paris," and "Please Don't Talk About Me When I'm Gone";
"Didn't We?"; "Yesterday"; "God Bless America"; and finally "When the
Moon Comes Over the Mountain."

The only detracting element was that the orchestra was prerecorded.
This meant that Smith had to listen carefully to the orchestra and had no
flexibility to sustain any notes or deviate in any way.

I had the good fortune to hear one of the Kids Next Door twenty years
later, as he related his recollections and impressions to a convention of
Friends of Kate Smith. He is Victor Henderson Vail, and he was eighteen
when he performed with Smith. He said he knew little about Kate Smith
then, except that he had heard jokes about her size and knew she was a big-
name entertainer of the past. Vail was astonished when into the rehearsal
room walked this older woman who really was not large at all—"a bit
plump, maybe"—and not as tall as he had been led to believe. She looked
like an ordinary older woman, not a bit like a star. Vail found her gracious
and pleasant to work with, though he did not recall that she ever spoke
directly to him.

Vail told us of her unhappiness with the prerecorded orchestra and
said that she had to listen intently to get her singing cues—she was
somewhat hard of hearing—which made her rather tense during the recording. She had to do "Mister Clown" three times, as she missed a cue the first
time and she lost an earring midway through the second take. That meant
the real live clown had to do his thing thrice, too: a very cute number from
her "Now Generation" album.

Vail said he was very impressed with the transformation from Kathryn
to Kate. She went into the dressing room at 2 P.M. on the day of the taping
looking like an ordinary 61-year-old woman. Five hours later she emerged
looking totally different. "She was beautiful and looked every bit as lovely
as any Star." He said every one of the Kids Next Door stood amazed at her
radiance.

The thing that most impressed Victor Vail took place just as Smith was
going into her first number. The songs were not taped in the order of the
final production, so her first number was "Love Is a Many Splendored
Thing." She wore a wine red sequined gown. Turning away, she said a brief
prayer, then crossed herself before going into the song. Two decades later
Vail remembered this clearly. "It just burned into me that this lady, after
all of her years in show business, still had this great faith and was not
jaded."

The long medley near the end of the show was cleverly propped. As she stood by a long, narrow table, Smith asked, "Are you folks anything like me? You know, I'm not a great one for looking back. As a matter of fact, I live for today and hope for tomorrow. Of course, my world has always consisted mainly of music, so I compare the times with the songs. And I thank those good songs for some awfully good times. Here's one that I've always enjoyed singing ['I'll Be Seeing You']." Then an old time radio microphone appears and she reminisces a bit about singing songs like "Fine and Dandy" into those mikes. Next she approaches a display of what seems to be her gold records, and says, as she points up to one, "This one in particular I'm really close to." Then she sings "How Deep Is the Ocean" (which she never recorded).

Pointing upward to another gold record, Smith reminds the audience that "it was brought to me by its composer, Mr. Jerome Kern. He wrote it with Oscar Hammerstein and I'm happy to have had the honor of introducing this song ['The Last Time I Saw Paris']." We next see a replica of the first television camera. "I'm proud that I was in front of a camera like that. I appeared on the very first [CBS] telecast. That day you didn't see a very fine picture as you do today. All you saw were a lot of little lines and faint images... I think it was in the year around 1934 or 1935 [it was 1931]." She did sing "Please Don't Talk About Me When I'm Gone" on that telecast. Then we see "a present-day television camera, the kind we're using right here on our show." And she sings two more songs she recently recorded, Jim Webb's "Didn't We?" and "a song that was written by two of the Beatles, Paul McCarthy and John Lennon ["Yesterday"]. Her mispronouncing (or misreading?) of Paul's last name speaks volumes about her knowledge of the Beatles.

Smith told me she made a mistake when she signed the contract for this special, as she accepted a flat fee, rather than opting for residuals for each time it was broadcast. Four years later she was wiser for the experience when she made "Kate Smith: Remembrances and Rock." This time the show was replete with guests. There was comedian Dom deLuise, the Supremes sang two numbers, Florence Henderson sang and danced, and the Dueling Banjos (Eric Weisberg and Steve Mandel) played. In between, Smith had a chance to sing with the Kids Next Door, "Sing," "Make Your Own Kind of Music" and, by herself, two medleys. Her "new music medley" consisted of "Up, Up and Away," "Day by Day" from *Godspell,* "The Summer Knows" from *Summer of '42,* Neil Diamond's "Song Sung Blue," and "Didn't We?" The memory medley included "Embraceable You," "Walkin' My Baby Back Home," "Once in a While," and "I've Got the World on a String." She did also sing a new song with odd lyrics called "Summer Me (Winter Me)," composed by Michel Legrand.

AT THE CLOSE OF KATE SMITH'S CARNEGIE HALL concert, she said she hoped it was only the first of many more to come. She did give quite a few more concerts over the next dozen years. The first was at the Theatre-in-the-Round at West Covina, California. Then there was LaRonde at Miami's Fontainbleu Hotel. In the spring of 1968 she went on a short concert tour in several southern states, playing in Nashville and Knoxville, Tennessee; Atlanta, Georgia; Jacksonville, Florida; and Greensboro, North Carolina. Her conductor was Mitchell Ayres, who was long associated with Perry Como and was the conductor on the "Hollywood Palace" shows. For comedy she had Pat Paulsen of "The Smothers Brothers Comedy Hour," and she took along a group of Kids Next Door (there were several such groups).

The first concert was Friday, the Ides of March, at the Nashville Municipal Auditorium. My friend William Byrge (who later played the character role of Bobby in the *Ernest* movies) was thrilled to attend, and later, to write about it for our club magazine. Some of Smith's oldies were "The Last Time I Saw Paris," "Tenderly," and "I'm Getting Sentimental Over You," while for recent numbers she sang "Strangers in the Night," "The Impossible Dream," and the inevitable "More." Toward the end she sang two hymns, "How Great Thou Art" and "May the Good Lord Bless and Keep You." Byrge said that in his excitement he found himself stepping into the aisle at the end and walking toward the stage, from which Smith was descending. He spoke briefly to her, thanking her for all the years of enjoyment she had brought. She smiled sweetly and said to him, "God bless you." At one point during the concert, she unexpectedly brought down the house when she said that the governor had made her an honorary citizen of Texas instead of Tennessee.

Our report on the Knoxville concert the next evening came from member Dave Bryan, who said she opened with "Fine and Dandy," then sang "On a Clear Day." Her first gown was a stunning pink covered with sequins; she wore matching pink pendant earrings. When she returned after the Kids Next Door segment, she was dressed in a deep purple sequined gown. Her songs included "Who Can I Turn To?" and "You're Nobody 'Til Somebody Loves You." A brief intermission was followed by yet another gown, this time olive green. She thrilled the audience with "Love Is a Many Splendored Thing," then an intimate "Call Me Irresponsible." Bryan called "I Left My Heart in San Francisco" "a real show stopper." After Paul Paulsen's routine she came out with yet a fourth gown, the gold one with the mink collar. Her medley of standards included "It Had to Be You," "Stars Fell on Alabama," and "These Foolish Things." She belted out a fantastic "I Gotta Right to Sing the Blues" with "all the punch imaginable."

We also had a fan reporter at the Atlanta concert which was held at the brand new Civic Center. Anna Mae Cone said Smith received three standing ovations and could have kept the audience much longer. Nashville entertainment columnist Bonnie Lucy described the performance in these terms in *The Nashville Banner* (March 17, 1968):

> A marvelous lady with a fabulous voice proved . . . that it's never too late to begin a new segment in an already established career. Miss Kate Smith, the charmingly big lady with the flowing big voice, enhanced herself even deeper into the hearts of her Nashville fans Friday. . . . The fast-paced show . . . was delightfully down-to-earth. . . . As the last glorious note died away, her entranced audience broke forth into exploding applause, which then became a standing ovation and two curtain calls for the fantastic Miss Kate Smith.

Knoxville's Don Ferguson reported that Smith's audience numbered three thousand and that each of her gowns was more beautiful than the others. "Then at the end she sang 'When the Moon Comes Over the Mountain,' he said. "You can imagine what it was like if you are old enough to remember, and love, Kate Smith. It was great." On March 23, Bob Tate reported in his column, "The Spectator," in the *Jacksonville Journal*:

> It's always nice to meet a memory—and find that it's as alive and warm and vibrant as you've always thought it to be. . . . What a pleasure to hear a woman who really knows how to deliver a song. When she sings— whether softly or belting out—you can clearly hear every syllable of every word, and you get the full sense of what the composer was trying to say. In her 37 years in show business, Kate Smith has introduced more than 600 songs which have become standards—and she sang 26 of them last night during what was only the fourth live concert she has ever given. I hope it's far from the last one she'll give here.
>
> [The audience] didn't mind a bit that she was handicapped by a cold, and they liked it that she never held back in spite of the fact that a cough and the heat on the stage obviously were making her uncomfortable. Many singers would have tried to fake a little or take some musical short-cuts, but not Kate. They were also indulgent about her nostalgic patter between songs, which sometimes was overlong. And when she closed with "God Bless America"—the song she sang all during the dark days of World War II—I don't think there was a dry eye in the place. You know what? That audience got to its feet and sang that song with her. For these were mostly older people who remember when it wasn't considered square or sloppy or gross to have pride in your country and when patriotism and love of the flag were things you didn't consciously have to think about— they were just a part of your nature and you were glad of it.
>
> It's a shame more of the "modern" generation couldn't have been there to see and hear it, but I suppose they wouldn't have understood. So God bless you, Kate Smith—and come back to see us.

Smith called me upon her return to New York to convey her enthusiasm at the way she had been received. She did have to cancel a planned concert in Charlotte, North Carolina, however, as all they had was a high school band to accompany her. According to musicians' union regulations, aside from a few sidemen an artist is allowed to select, most of the orchestra members must be local. Apparently there was a scarcity of them in the Charlotte area.

On Saturday, March 13, 1971, Smith gave a concert in Toledo, Ohio, accompanied by the Toledo Symphony, no less. It was given at the Masonic Auditorium and was a Shriner's benefit for widows of Masons and for orphan children. She gave a similar concert in Wichita, Kansas, for the benefit of families of college students killed in two separate airplane crashes. She sent me all of her notes from the Toledo concert, including the lyrics, the jokes, and the asides.

Incidentally, Smith received (and accepted) an engraved invitation from President and Mrs. Nixon to attend a state dinner for President Josip Tito of Yugoslavia on October 28, 1971.

SMITH VOWED NEVER TO PLAY ANOTHER NIGHTCLUB after she fractured her ankle at Miami's Fontainebleu Hotel in 1964. After her resounding successes with the aforementioned concerts, she began having second thoughts, although she did have personal and religious convictions against playing nightclubs and gambling casinos. She had been asked time and again during the 1950s and 1960s by the leading Las Vegas clubs. Jim Thompson, entertainment director at John Ascuaga's Nugget Hotel in Sparks, Nevada, had been trying to engage her for four years when she finally consented to give it a try in 1972, but only after much soul-searching.

Smith explained her decision in this way: "Before I said 'yes' I talked to church leaders and several close friends. All of them said it was all right. They pointed out that Andy Williams (a Quaker), Jack Benny (a Jew) and so many other singers and entertainers played casinos. They also told me that gambling is legal in Nevada, just like horse race betting in New York, and that the profits from Nevada casinos do much good for the state." She went on to explain, "I have to perform. There aren't enough television specials and concerts to keep me busy."

Ray Katz signed a contract for two shows daily for two weeks in the posh Circus Room of the largest casino hall in the Reno area, June 28–July 12. I was determined to go there, so I flew to Reno with my friend Lois over the long Fourth of July weekend. Like any fan magazine editor worth his or her salt, I was armed with camera and notebook. We had made reservations for the midnight show on the evening we arrived. Sal Gelosi saw to it that we four, Lois and I, Patricia Castledine and her mother, had the best seats in the house, front and center, just two seats from the stage.

Long before midnight Gelosi escorted us backstage, where Smith stood in her dressing room, getting ready for the "cocktail show," as it is called. She greeted us warmly as always, glad to see her "friends from back east." She showed us the key to the city of Sparks given her by the mayor. Then she told us about her strep throat, which nearly caused her to miss the opening night shows.

After a rugged schedule back in New York, of having gowns altered (again she had lost eighty pounds), rehearsing with Duddy and Bresler, consulting with Katz about the orchestra and the Kids Next Door and other details that had to be arranged ahead of time, the Kate Smith entourage had flown to Reno on June 24. The group included Emma Johnson, her maid; Donna, her hairdresser; musicians Bresler and Duddy, and the ever-present bodyguard and "gofer," Sal Gelosi.

The drama preceding the show's opening began Sunday morning. Smith awoke with a nasty sore throat and ached from head to toe. Barely able to swallow, she thought, "How will I ever open Wednesday night if I feel like this?" She called a local physician, who examined her throat and began a series of huge doses of penicillin. She began to treat her throat herself too. As she put it to us, "I've been taking care of this throat of mine ever since I was a youngster and I kinda know what it needs." She gargled and swabbed faithfully and she spent most of Sunday in bed, even missing Mass, and stayed in bed all of Monday.

When Smith awoke Tuesday she felt even worse, if that was possible. That day she was to meet with John Ascuaga and other officials of the club. She asked herself, "How can I do this feeling as I do?" Sal and Emma encouraged her to do her best, and somehow she went through with the meeting. She ached so and had such a fever that she did not even remember what she said to them. Later she phoned her physicians in New York and Los Angeles, and they confirmed that her treatment was correct and that she should continue along those lines. That night she prayed and prayed. As she related it to us, "I took my problem to the Man from Galilee."

When Smith awoke Wednesday morning, she had improved so dramatically that she was able to open on schedule. And what an opening performance, according to Gelosi. Smith said she had some fears about that first performance in the strange atmosphere, but that the applause which greeted her at the first dinner show allayed all her fears. When she described the audiences to us, tears came to her eyes.

Naturally enough, the two seventy-minute shows each evening were a strain on Smith's strength and voice. She had to conserve her voice before, between, and after the shows, not an easy task for a woman who enjoyed talking. It became Gelosi's reluctant duty to cut her conversations short. The program listed Sam Donahue and His Orchestra playing "Roses of Picardy," "I Can't Give You Anything But Love," and "Blue Moon"; then an elephant act; then Smith singing "Just in Time," "On a Clear Day," "More," and "Who Cares?" After a performance by the Kids Next Door, she was to return with "By the Time I Get to Phoenix," "Didn't We?," "It Had to Be You," "I Left My Heart in San Francisco," "What Are You Doing the Rest of Your Life?," "What Kind of Fool Am I?," "God Bless America," and "When the Moon Comes Over the Mountain."

On the day we arrived, Smith was visibly tired after the midnight show. Although she was still having daily penicillin shots, her throat still hurt some. She told us she was thankful for the amplification system because her voice was weaker than usual. She would explain to her audiences, "Now if my voice isn't quite as strong as it usually is, it's because I'm having a bout with a bug that I picked up the day after I arrived here. So please bear with me." They chuckled in sympathy, but they were never disappointed.

When Smith's time on stage came, the thirty-piece orchestra led by Jerry Bresler went into the opening bars of her theme song. Smith entered from stage right, attired in a lime green gown, looking slim and moving quickly and gracefully. Following the first two numbers, she greeted the audience, telling them it was "so nice of them to come" to see her and that it was her first nightclub engagement. (She must have forgotten the Central Park Casino in '32 and the Fontainebleu in '64.) As she sang "Who Cares?" she danced across the stage, mike in hand. Then some chitchat about the generation gap. "We had our fun and pranks, too," she reminded the audience. She introduced twelve Kids Next Door and made her exit.

The well-oiled routine of the Kids Next Door included a clever and entertaining segment on trends in pop singing and dancing styles of the last fifty years. Especially amusing were takeoffs on Carmen Miranda and the Andrews Sisters. When Smith returned, she was wearing a striking red gown. She sang a medley of "now" songs, followed by the anticipated "God Bless America," accompanied by the Kids Next Door. After she received the customary standing ovation, she thanked the audience for receiving her show so well and said if they liked it to tell their friends and "if not, then tell me."

How did the critics like her show? A writer in the July 12, 1972, issue of *Variety* had this to say:

> Miss Smith has always seemed matronly and the apparition of the comfortable American mom of the '30s materilizing on stage in a pink glow 40 years later is somehow breathtaking, as if Glenn Miller should stroll out. Actually she is only 63—the portly warmth of her early years seems to have preserved her and the famed voice in suspended animation. She's looking good this stand, coiffed and made up to perfection and lighted and costumed becomingly. Voice, delivery, and mannerisms are of another era but they are less antique than classic and the confident expression of songs with full expansive gestures before a standing mike is warm and forceful rather than mummified. As for the legendary Smith voice, the famed organlike chords and ready upper registers are still there, but her straightforward melodic expansiveness is ill-adapted to chord changes of

much contemporary music. . . . Her adventurous spirit in trying modern material when she could easily bask in certain audience warmth and cadaverous "nostalgia" is praiseworthy, but she's no Ella Fitzgerald and material should be carefully chosen.

An entertainment writer for the *San Francisco Chronicle* was more enthusiastic on July 1:

> We sat there enthralled as we listened to the wonderful, wonderful Kate Smith. . . . It was one of the thrills of a life-time to listen to this star . . . this great performer unabashedly in love with the U.S.A. sang her heart out despite a cold and the crowd went wild. . . . She's the greatest star in the skies.

At a pre-opening press conference Smith was asked, since this was supposedly her nightclub debut, whether she was scared. Her unhesitating reply was, "No, I'm not scared of anything." She did have a few butterflies as she waited in the wings for that first dinner show. After that it was all downhill. She told the audiences how much she liked Nevada on this, her first visit. The unvarnished truth is that she hardly dared venture out of the hotel, as the combination of heat, dry air, and high altitude bothered her terribly. Was she ever glad to get back to the Adirondacks.

On the occasion of the thirtieth anniversary of Japan's surprise attack on Pearl Harbor, Hawaii, Smith was invited to be the special guest of the Pearl Harbor Survivors at the site of the attack. It was a very moving experience. She, of course, sang "God Bless America" during ceremonies at the memorial. In 1972 she accepted the group's invitation to be with them in New Orleans, where she ended up in Touro Hospital. "I woke up on a Tuesday," she replied. "I could hardly breathe. It took me two hours to get my clothes on. Finally, a friend [Sal Gelosi] came to see me and I urged him to get me to a doctor as quickly as possible. We immediately went to Touro, where my condition was diagnosed as pleurisy. I had trouble in my left lung. I was put into intensive care for five days." Smith phoned me from her hospital bed to assure me that she was going to be fine. She said her trouble was a blood clot.

In February 1974 Smith returned to New Orleans to take part in the Mardi Gras festivities. She was an honored guest at the ball of the Krewe of Naides. As the band played "God Bless America," the lieutenant governor escorted her to the king and queen of the ball. She looked like a queen herself, wearing a flowered gown and carrying a large bouquet of mixed flowers. This was a week before Shrove Tuesday (Mardi Gras itself). Smith was entertained for five days, attending the Krewe of Alphus ball Thursday and dining at the elegant and famous Antoine's Restaurant on Friday. On Saturday she walked some in the French Quarter and then was taken to see Lake Pontchartrain, where she said she greatly preferred her "much prettier and nicer" Lake Placid.

CHAPTER 19

The Way We Were

I'll always remember the first time Kate Smith called me. It was February 1968. She had learned that I was to be the editor of the journals and newsletters of her newly formed fan club, the Kate Smith U.S.A. Friends Club. I was stunned to be actually talking to my favorite star and was scarcely able to utter a few words. So she did all the talking. She told me of her recent recording session and her coming concert tour in the South. In later years we joked about my being at a loss for words. When an article in *TV Guide* later that year titled "The God Bless America Girl at 59" made reference to the club, I was quoted as revealing, "I know my heart skipped a beat." And so it did. That conversation, largely one-sided, lasted for ten precious minutes. We would have many, many more as she would tell me of her professional activities and discuss club business.

Kate Smith was very much involved with her club. She wanted us to make mention of folks who might be ill, she would give the names and addresses of people she would like to be in the club, and she had a special interest in two regular features: the spiritual message following her personal letters, and the food column. She was impressed enough with the contents of the first issue of *Our Kate* in the spring of 1968 that she offered to help finance future issues, so that they might be printed by offset rather than mimeographed. That also allowed us to include photographs, a decided improvement. She took a great interest in the club and its publications through thirteen issues, ending in 1975.

I had been corresponding with Smith for nearly seven years by mail and three years by phone when I was given the opportunity to meet her in person. She was to make three television commercials for Chase & Sanborn instant coffee in January 1971, and the J. Walter Thompson advertising agency was looking for some props to use in a scene simulating her trophy room at Lake Placid. As it was winter, they were unable to get to her real trophy room, so she told them of my collection of her memorabilia. They contacted me, and I loaned them some sheet music and glossy photographs to use. They in turn asked me whether I had ever met her. When I said I had not, they invited me to attend the taping session on January 7.

I flew to New York from Providence at 7 A.M. on a glorious winter morning, armed with camera, portable tape recorder, and Smith's two autobiographies. I took a taxi to Eastern Video, where I met my friend James Robert Parish, author of numerous books about Hollywood and its movie stars. I had been given permission to bring Parish, who had done numerous favors for me and was also eager to meet his favorite singer.

We had not been in the studio long when Miss Smith emerged from her dressing room wearing her favorite smock, accompanied by bodyguard Sal Gelosi, to take a coffee-and-doughnut break. Gelosi introduced her, and we introduced ourselves and shook hands. She excused herself temporarily, quipping, "You know me and my sweets." Within a few minutes she was back to explain what would take place that day. There were many technicians getting things ready. The studio was a maze of cables, cameras, and microphones on booms. I could see the trophy room set, complete with a large wicker chair just like hers, with my photographs and sheet music framed on the walls.

Smith said she would be quite busy but would talk with us whenever there was a break in the procedures. And that she did, all through the long and grueling day. Shortly after 10 o'clock, almost on schedule, the taping began. The first thirty-second commercial was filmed against the trophy room background, with Smith seated at a desk looking through a scrapbook. On the desk was a jar of Chase & Sanborn instant coffee and a cup and saucer. Her script read:

> Hello everybody, I'm Kate Smith. You know, my forty years of show business have given me many happy memories, like being introduced to the King and Queen of England, selling U.S. bonds in 1943 . . . I've made lots of friends. And [*placing her hand on the jar of coffee*] perky Chase & Sanborn is one of them.

The shooting stopped, the timekeeper stated the number of seconds that it took, a hasty conference was held, a suggestion or two were made, such as speaking a bit faster or slower, and placing her hand on the coffee jar a bit sooner or later. It was all very exacting. Each take was numbered, notes were taken on it, those that might be usable were checked, and we moved on the next take.

Cue cards were used and the nearsighted Songbird wore contact lenses to read them. These eventually became troublesome because the heat from the klieg lights dried the fluid so that they irritated her eyes unbearably. Whenever there was a wait between takes, she put on sunglasses to rest her eyes. Also, because of the way the heat affected her fine hair, she wore a hairpiece for the session, just as she usually did on television, especially in later years. She explained that the front of the hair always was her own.

During the breaks Smith chatted with us about the benefit performance at Wichita, Kansas, the previous November 28, after two separate plane crashes killed a number of students at Wichita State and Marshall universities; about her plans for spring; and about her foolhardiness in renting an apartment in Arlington, Virginia, after Ted Collins died. She reminisced about the members of her band in the early days of radio and was thrilled with winter pictures I had brought to show her of Lake Placid for an article Pat Castledine had written for our club journal.

From time to time I had a chance to converse with Sal Gelosi, who kept an eagle eye out for Smith's well-being at all times, doing whatever little thing he could to make the effort a bit less arduous for her. He spoke of her stamina, patience, and wit and told of a number of instances where she would put herself out for an ordinary person while shunning celebrity parties. Gelosi marveled at her professionalism, that she could come into any situation and work under any conditions with apparent ease, charm, and ready wit. I observed that they seemed to understand each other rather as I imagined she and Collins had in years past.

After the lunch hour the trophy room set was dismantled, and a portion of the studio where six replicas of war bonds hung on invisible wires served as the background for the second commercial. Smith had exchanged the light lavender dress of the morning for a light green one. In this commercial she told of her "My America" contest, pointing to a replica of the Declaration of Independence, which was to be sent to all entrants in the contest free of charge.

Smith remained cool, calm, and collected through most of the dozens of retakes. The precision, the repetition, the split-second timing, and the coordination required to make the end result acceptable were enough to try anyone's patience; yet she was always ready with a smile or a wink or a quip whenever she sensed things were getting tense. The crew marveled at what a good sport and grand lady she was to work with. I observed about 4 o'clock, after she had made numerous retakes to perfect the timing, that there were tears in her eyes. She was becoming exhausted, understandably so.

By 5 o'clock everybody was obviously getting weary. There was only one brief scene left to be shot, and Smith did not have to speak in this one. All she had to do was to sit at a table with several 1943 vintage telephones and a SILENCE: ON THE AIR sign behind her, pretending to be taking orders for bonds from erstwhile listeners to her marathon radio bond drive. She would pick up the phone and say, for my amusement, "Oh, hi, Mom. What? You'd like to buy a $25 bond? Okay, I'll turn you over to a secretary. See you tonight." Then, turning to another phone, she would exclaim,

"What's that? Ten thousand dollars? Oh, that's wonderful. God bless you. Thank you so very much." She told us that when she was actually conducting a bond drive from Washington, her mother did call her. She also recalled the "Kate Smith Hour" she did from Washington by remote broadcast in 1939, saying that it was the only time it had ever been done.

By six o'clock the day's work was over and a full ninety seconds of commercials were "on ice" after sixty-three takes. For that day's work, plus posing for some pictures and taping five radio commercials, Smith was paid $50,000.

A call from the dressing room, "Richard!," beckoned me. It was Smith asking me to bring in the tape recorder so we could do an interview for the club members. That I did and everyone left us alone, Sal Gelosi closing the door behind him to keep out all extraneous noise. She finished combing her hair, happy to remove the hairpiece, removed her contact lenses, and breathed a sigh of relief. There we sat, side by side, I with a card containing questions, with the microphone resting on the dresser. I had it aimed slightly toward her, but she suggested I point it toward myself, as her voice was sure to boom out. She told me she was singing some songs with the pianist just for fun, including her theme song. She said, "You know, Richard, I never did record the verse to it":

> All by myself at twilight
> Watching the day depart,
> And with the fading twilight
> Happiness fills my heart.*

I could not resist the urge to correct her, so I gently reminded her that she had recorded it four times. She seemed genuinely surprised and said, "Oh, you know more about those things than I do."

We made our introductory remarks, then Smith asked me to rewind the tape and play it back to be sure it was recording. She had undoubtedly done this before, only to have the tape come out blank. It sounded just fine. We went on for half an hour, talking about high points in her career, about some of her important songs, about how it felt to have been a celebrity for forty years, about her staying awake until the wee hours of the morning that day, and about our club and its members. Toward the end Gelosi tiptoed in, sat down, and listened. It still amazes me that she had the energy and the desire to do that for me and for the club after ten hours of nerve-wracking work.

*"When the Moon Comes Over the Mountain." Howard Johnson, Kate Smith & Harry Woods. Copyright 1931 (Renewed 1959) Metro-Goldwyn-Mayer Inc. Rights throughout the world controlled by Robbins Music Corporation. All rights of Robbins Music Corporation assigned to EMI Catalogue Partnership. All rights administered by EMI Robbins Catalog. International copyright secured. Made in U.S.A. All rights reserved.

My first meeting with Smith ended with Sal Gelosi's kind offer to drive me to LaGuardia Airport in her new 1971 Lincoln Continental (license plates 1-KS) to catch the 8 o'clock flight home to Providence. We four got into the car, Gelosi at the wheel and Smith beside him, with her maid Emma Johnson and me in the spacious back seat. Gelosi let Smith out at her apartment on East 57th Street, where we parted with a handshake and wave of the hand. En route to the airport, Gelosi spoke of how physically exhausting such sessions were and said that recording sessions were even more demanding. He reiterated Smith's professionalism, using as an illustration the fact that she did not have to practically swallow the mike as so many singers with small voices do on television.

Smith invited me to visit her at Lake Placid that summer. We recorded another interview, and I took pictures and wrote a feature story for the fall issue of *Our Kate*. I flew from Boston to Albany and met Pat Castledine, our club president. We drove to Lake Placid, where we went for a ride in her motorboat, which was docked at Holiday Harbor. As we walked toward the dock we met a white Volkswagen with a black top and the license plate KES-1, just being driven out from its reserved parking space. The moment Smith spied us she alighted from the car, walked over the greet us, and explained that Father Salmon was in town and wanted to visit with her at his hotel. She asked us to phone her in the morning, then she, Sal Gelosi, his wife Nancy, and their son Ross left for town.

We admired Smith's classic speedboat before we embarked on a tour of the lake. I had my first look at Camp Sunshine, situated on the shore of Buck Island a scant ten minutes from the harbor. All five of the buildings, painted white with green trim, looked immaculate, and the grounds were well manicured, a tribute to Smith's caretaker, John Viscome, who lived in town. It was his job to open the camp in the spring, care for the buildings, grounds, and boats each day during the summer, close the camp in the autumn, and check it monthly during the winter.

Saturday morning we made a telephone call to Camp Sunshine at ten o'clock, to be sure our hostess had arisen for the day. Smith told us she would have Gelosi meet us with *Sunshine I*, her 24-foot 1938 Chris Craft speedboat with 6-cylinder inboard engine, at 1:30 P.M. Gelosi met us as planned and gave us another tour of the "big lake." *Sunshine I* had a mahogany hull which was kept shiny and spotless. In the cabin was seating for five, with the driver seated at the steering wheel at the front right. In the stern was contoured leather seating for four or so additional passengers. This boat reminded me of an antique automobile, maintained like new with loving care. There was a nautical wheel and a gear shift on the floor. (In 1980 when Camp Sunshine was purchased by Robert E. Grant for about $115,000—a steal—he told me he did not even know that the boat went with it. He had the speedboat appraised at $35,000.)

Gelosi's guided tour, which Smith had suggested, was followed by a docking inside the large boathouse. We were escorted upstairs to the trophy room of America's First Lady of Song. The knotty-pine paneled walls of this awesome room with a view were comfortably filled with awards, plaques, citations, and photographs spanning a lengthy show business career. Here and there were a few assorted tables and chairs. In a dormer on the east end was a "one-armed bandit," a nickel slot machine from Las Vegas. Under the east eave were the 2,200 pounds of television kinescopes in cartons.

We had not been there many minutes when we heard footsteps slowly making their way up the stairs. It was Smith come to greet us and guide our tour in person. She showed us the famous broadcast studio described in Chapter 7. We next toured the guest house, where the original closet broadcast studio had been located; in the heyday of radio it served as a rumpus room for visiting sponsors and advertising agents.

By now it was 3 P.M., so we moved quickly to the main house, entering by way of the full-length front porch, complete with several old-fashioned rockers. The dining room table was set for luncheon. Prepared by Smith and her cook, Alberta, it consisted of shrimp salad, Swiss cheese, ham sandwiches, potato salad, cottage cheese, olives and pickles, and lettuce and tomatoes from the garden. We sipped iced tea flavored with garden mint. For dessert we enjoyed mace-chiffon-butter cake. Pat Castledine and I were given the seats of honor, facing the lake. Smith sat at her customary place, the end nearest the kitchen. She had a buzzer on the floor so she could ring for Alberta whenever anything was needed.

After our delicious repast, eaten leisurely with good conversation, Smith suggested I set up the portable tape recorder I had brought so we could do an informal interview right at the dinner table. We (mostly Kathryn) talked for nearly ninety minutes, she giving us an extensive word tour of what she called, laughingly, the "Sunshine compound." She spoke of the upcoming TV season and the scarcity of musical-variety shows and of all that goes into preparing to give a live concert.

After our taping session (it was now six o'clock on July 31), we all went outside for a tour of the grounds and some pictures before the sun set. There were numerous lovely flower gardens and a small vegetable garden. As we observed the vegetable patch, our hostess threw peapods at us, urging us to eat the raw peas. I was taking pictures and asked Gelosi to photograph Kathryn and me standing on the lawn. I took several of her by the flower beds.

There were flagstone walkways around Camp Sunshine. The water's edge was lined with birch, spruce, and cedar trees, and a tiny brook meandered from the woods in back to the lake below. A large flagpole by the big boathouse displayed the American flag. It was easy to visualize the picturesque tourboat going by, the captain announcing, "We're now passing Camp Sunshine, home of famous singer Kate Smith, and there she is waving to us."

We went back inside and talked for a long while, as the sun set and the moon came over the mountain. We looked at many old 8×10 glossies (some of which are in this book), mostly from the war years, especially looking for some of Ted Collins for the coming memorial issue of *Our Kate*. It was ten o'clock when Gelosi took us to the mainland.

Early Sunday afternoon we drove to St. Agnes Church, which was holding its annual bazaar. We met Smith and the Gelosis there, tried our hand at various games, and generally enjoyed the warm, humid midsummer afternoon. After 5 P.M. we all returned to Camp Sunshine, some in *Sunshine I* and the rest of us in Pat's boat. This time Edna Castledine, Pat's mother, and their collie, Cindy, went along. I taped some of Smith's transcriptions while she gave Edna the tour of the compound. About nine o'clock we thought we'd better leave, as it had been a busy day for our hostess. The next day we tried water-skiing, then went back to Camp Sunshine to thank Miss Smith and say our goodbyes.

I next saw Miss Smith at John Ascuaga's Nugget Hotel in Nevada the following July, and again at the Arie Crown Theatre in Chicago on Mother's Day, 1973, where she gave two concerts. By this time I was calling her Kathryn. In August 1974 I was with her at the Allentown Fair in Pennsylvania, where we discussed my return visit to Camp Sunshine. We agreed that August 18 and 19 would be the best time. This time I drove, again meeting Pat Castledine in Albany. We arrived at Holiday Harbor at 8:15 P.M. that Friday, and Pat immediately telephoned Kathryn. Within a few minutes she and John Viscome pulled into her reserved slip in *Sunshine I*. She was standing and waving, and she looked in the pink of condition. When I told her so, she said she was feeling better than she had in a very long time.

Saturday forenoon Pat Castledine and I cruised around the lake until the rains came. At 1 P.M. we pulled into Smith's large boathouse, and I unloaded my recording equipment. This time I came equipped to properly record anything and everything in that broadcast studio, with Smith's blessing. We enjoyed small talk in the dining room for an hour or so, during which time a terrific rain and wind storm battered the area. Later the sun came out and at 2:30 Kathryn said, "Well, Richard, you have your work to do up in the broadcast studio so you go along and do your taping." She wanted to be sure it was warm enough up there and that I had enough light. I taped three hours' worth of music that day and another three hours' worth on Sunday.

Smith told me she would ring her loud railroad bell, which stood beside the front porch, when dinner was ready that Saturday afternoon. As

I had headphones on, I did not hear it, so she sent Pat to fetch me. Kate and her cook had prepared a memorable hot meal for us. First came the appetizer, a large cantaloupe slice with raspberry sherbert. Then the main course, roast-fried chicken: delicious legs, wings, and breasts cooked with a covering of rice crispies. There were fresh string beans, garden salad, and "butter-and-sugar" corn on the cob. Kathryn offered us a choice of beverage, but we chose her own "London Fog," half milk and half cola, a refreshing summer drink. She had recommended the combination on the "Mike Douglas Show" that season when she prepared the "mixed drink." For dessert Bertie Jones had baked a butter cake with powdered sugar covering.

I returned to the broadcast studio the next day to complete my taping. When I saw the churchgoers emerging from the main house, I went down to greet them. I asked Smith whether she recalled a song she sang in 1947 called "Love and the Weather." She did not, but I thought it was outstanding. (She had introduced it on the air for composer Irving Berlin.) She asked whether I had come across the record with Ted Collins singing "Wabash Moon." I did remember it, though I did not tape it, not knowing who the vocalist was. She said Collins had arranged a recording session for a young man who did not show up. Rather than pay the musicians and technicians for nothing, Collins made his recording debut that day, singing in a falsetto voice. Kathryn gave an imitation of what he sounded like, saying as she laughed, "It was so funny. At one point his natural low voice came through. Now that's a real collector's item."

Smith's cook and maid had Sunday afternoon off, so the four of us went to McDonald's in town, but not before enjoying another "London Fog," snacking on leftover cake, and playing cards. While we were in the kitchen, Kathryn spied another cake Bertie Jones had made to take to her friends in the village. This was a yellow cake with white frosting. She took her finger and tasted the frosting from around the edge, smoothing it out so Jones would not know. At McDonald's, Kathryn ordered for all of us, but when I insisted that it was my treat, she allowed me to pay. We sat at a corner table, and nobody paid any mind to us, apparently oblivious of the celebrity in their midst. That suited her just fine.

KATE SMITH WAS ADDICTED TO FOOD, and particularly to high-calorie foods. Her downfall was always chocolate; she might well have been called a "chocoholic." It may sound amusing, but it eventually took its toll on her health.

Kathryn Elizabeth Smith began to gain weight significantly at age thirteen. The gain came quickly and it has been blamed on a suddenly underactive thyroid gland, although she denied any thyroid problem. She simply liked to eat in quantity. It never affected her agility; she always danced gracefully and her legs remained slender. Over the years her weight went up and down markedly. When she decided to diet seriously, she possessed willpower and the pounds would slowly melt away.

Too often, however, the temptation to devour not one but several cream-filled doughnuts, slices of chocolate layer cake, or frozen custard ice cream cones was simply too much. Yes, Smith loved her sweets. She was not much for vegetables, except for sweet potatoes, and she did not like many meats. She did enjoy lamb, steak, and chicken, however.

During World War II the Kate Smith radio troupe broadcast from military camps coast to coast. Smith's reputation for loving sweets preceded her, naturally, so she was presented with huge chocolate cakes and a variety of other high-calorie treats wherever she went. They were tempting and, after all, she was there to make the G.I.'s happy, so down the hatch went the cakes and up the scale went her weight. It is little wonder she had an attack of gallstones after about a year. At that time when Smith stepped on the scales the pointer went all the way to the right, so she knew she weighed over 300 pounds. Years later, when we were looking at all those wartime glossies, Smith pointed at herself and remarked in disgust, "Look how fat I was then." Then she tore several photographs into little pieces. Back then her physician put her on a strict low-fat diet, warning her that if she did not stick to it religiously she would have another gallstone attack and surgery would be necessary. It never was, and she did slim down noticeably for a while. As she became thinner she became much more attractive.

Camp Sunshine caretaker "Beejie" Cook told a couple of amusing anecdotes about Miss Smith's eating habits there. He and Mrs. Cook stayed in the guest cottage, from which they had a good view of the laundry room of the main house, where there was a large freezer. Each evening around 8 o'clock Smith would turn on the light and quietly open the freezer, removing a gallon container of ice cream. She would stand there with a spoon in her hand and consume a pint or more, thinking nobody was watching her. Her cook often made doughnuts for breakfast, and it was not uncommon for Smith to down a half dozen at one sitting. If she saw Ted Collins coming down the path from his house, she would hide the sweets and tell him she was sorry, but there was nothing left but toast and coffee. He was onto her game, of course, but would grin and say, "Oh, that's okay with me."

By the middle fifties, Smith had put back much of the weight she had lost over a decade before. As a result of this, plus the stress of four years of daily television shows, her blood pressure had become alarmingly high. She was placed on a 1000-Calorie diet which, out of fear for her life, she followed faithfully. By Christmas 1959 she was, for Kate Smith, almost sylphlike. She had lost eighty-five pounds over a three-year period.

In the midst of that long period of reducing, she actually wrote a cookbook. During her tenure with General Foods, three smaller (48-page) soft-cover cookbooks had been offered to listeners, but this was a hard-cover book, *The Kate Smith "Company's Comin'" Cookbook*, published by Prentice-Hall in 1958. The project helped occupy her spare time. The book contains "three hundred sumptuous recipes for the hostess to delight her guests." On her Mutual radio broadcasts that year, Smith would mention the book from time to time, asking listeners to send in recipes for one particular chapter. In the foreword she admits that she had been interested in "good food" and not much concerned with its vitamin, mineral, or caloric content, but rather, in cooking for her guests. The truth is that she did not do very much cooking over the years. She always employed a cook, both at home in New York and at Camp Sunshine. Occasionally she did try her hand at something intriguing or an old family recipe.

In a 1960 article in *Today's Health*, Smith gave some advice on dieting based on her considerable experience. She related that she had never taken any drug to curb her appetite, and stated that the important thing is to diet sensibly and systematically. She found it possible to limit herself to 1000 Calories per day and not go hungry. She firmly advised anyone needing to reduce to get a physician's advice, as everyone is different. Once again she denied that she had a glandular problem; she simply liked sweets. She admitted that the first six weeks on a diet are awful: "I was unhappy; I was short-tempered; I was hard to be around. But that finally passed." She described a typical day's meals:

> BREAKFAST: A poached egg, fresh fruit, toasted whole wheat or gluten bread, tea or caffeine-free coffee
> LUNCH: Cottage cheese, a fruit salad or leafy salad, skim milk or buttermilk
> DINNER: Green vegetables, lean meat: lamb or fowl; no duck, goose, or pork (too much fat)

Smith added that she sometimes ate two meals a day and drank a glass of milk or tomato juice before bedtime. She confessed: "Sometimes I get so hungry for some cake or pie that I can't stand it. So I eat some—but that's all I eat that day. The next day I go right back on the diet." In a 1975 *Lady's Circle* article, she had this advice for heavy women: "Wear a good foundation to smooth out the lumps and bumps around the stomach—the most popular place for those extra pounds to settle. Without support, there's strain on the back muscles, which brings on backaches. When you feel like eating, do something energetic."

Smith kept a fairly trim figure until after Ted Collins died in 1964. With each television appearance in '65 and '66, however, it was apparent that she was regaining her rotund figure. By 1968 her blood pressure was astronomical and her diabetic condition was diagnosed. She told me the bad news on the phone, saying she was not surprised, as diabetes was on both sides of her family tree. Again she was put on a strict diet and again she lost weight dramatically. By the time of her 1969 TV special, she looked half the size she was a few years before on those last two "Ed Sullivan Shows." In 1979 when Smith's apartment was being emptied, candy was found stashed in various out-of-the-way places. This addiction to sweets would eventually be her undoing.

CHAPTER 20

Seems Like Old Times
or
Good Luck Charm
for a Hockey Team?

Ted Collins would have been proud of Kate Smith. After forty-seven years in the limelight, she was still in demand. Hosting "The Tonight Show," Mother's Day concerts in Chicago, a second television special, three weeks at the largest dinner hall in the Reno area, and best of all, an association with a champion hockey team. Indeed it did seem almost like old times.

With all these engagements in the works for the spring and summer of 1973, Ray Katz deemed it essential that Smith gave them the proper publicity. What better way than to plug them on Johnny Carson's "Tonight Show"? He signed her as guest host for Monday, April 2. It was not Smith's finest hour-and-a-half. She seemed strangely ill-at-ease, not at all her customary relaxed self. Maybe she was trying too hard. Maybe it had been too long since she had done this sort of thing. After all, she was nearly 66 years old now. Those who knew her well were aware that she suffered from heart fibrillations, hypertension, and diabetes and was also experiencing eye trouble. In fact, she wore glasses on TV for the first time on this occasion. They were causing a problem with the picture, so she was asked to exchange them for her tinted glasses during the first commercial break. That may have further shaken her.

Smith entered the stage in a blue-and-white cocktail-length dress, with a young-looking and becoming auburn hairdo. She sang "Just in Time" and "On a Clear Day," then was joined by conductor "Doc" Severinsen, who was assuming duties as "second banana" for the evening. Doc got his start back in 1951 on "The Kate Smith Hour" on TV and played trumpet in the 46-piece orchestra at her Carnegie Hall concert, so they did a bit of reminiscing. Then Smith introduced the first guest of the evening, veteran comedian Jan Murray. He remarked of having early aspirations of making it to "The Kate Smith Hour" on radio, but said he never got there. (Actually, he did. How could he forget that?)

Next came actress Jean Stapleton, at that time a sensation as "Edith Bunker" on television's "All in the Family." She was charming in her first "Tonight Show" appearance, and it was clear that she and Smith liked each other. Smith kept calling her "Edith." The third guest was comedian/actor/game-show-regular Charles Nelson Reilly, who brought along a very old Kate Smith record. It was her 1931 Clarion recording of "Shine On, Harvest Moon" and "I Apologize," a rarity indeed. Reilly had either boned up on Smith's career or remembered some of the earlier highlights. He was fun and there were some good-natured laughs.

An embarrassing moment came when Smith took a sip of a drink that was on the coffee table. She had said earlier that the hot chocolate was delicious; now she was calling it tea. Reilly called her on it, with no malice intended. He asked her, "Now, which is it, hot chocolate or tea, Kate?" She was obviously chagrined and replied, "Well, it is tea, but what difference does it make, really? It's a hot drink and it's good."

The show was about an hour old, with thirty minutes or so to go. Smith sang a medley of oldies: "Don't Blame Me," "It Had to Be You," and "My Melancholy Baby." Then she sang the recent Michel Legrand ballad "What Are You Doing the Rest of Your Life?" She started it off-key, a rarity for her. Perhaps she was anticipating her final guest. And who was it? It was sometime-actor, sometime-singer George Maharis, costar of TV's "Route 66."

Smith had been provided with cards containing questions to ask the guests; she had used them throughout the program, and rather awkwardly, too. She had some facts about Maharis' childhood, including his large number of siblings. When she inquired about his father, that gave him an opening for a crude reply. She quickly changed the subject, but went from the proverbial frying pan into the fire.

The next question concerned a centerfold Maharis had done. He implied that it was X-rated and that her knowledge about such things was nil. He said it was a "centerspread," not a centerfold. Smith admitted that she did not know what a centerspread was and did not care to know. She gave a plug to her coming concerts in Chicago when Maharis referred to a play he had recently done there. When he described the sleazy hotel he stayed at, where he had to do his own sweaty laundry, Smith said her experience there had been quite the contrary and said she did not know what kind of hotel he stayed at. Maharis asked her where she was going to stay, but she would not tell. She also said she did not sweat or perspire (she did).

Maharis was interrupted just in time when he began to remark that Smith was a great singer but a lousy emcee. She knew what was coming and cut to a commercial. She nearly missed the famous final note of "God Bless America," no doubt unnerved by the Maharis interview in particular and the shaky show in general.

Sal Gelosi told me that he came very close to breaking Maharis's jaw after the show. Smith either was not fully aware of just how bad that segment was, or else she was not owning up to it. *Boston Globe* columnist William Buchanan had this to say the next day: "Poor Kate Smith seemed terribly dated when she subbed for Johnny Carson. She had to read virtually every word of dialogue from 'hello' to 'goodbye.' And she was really thrown by the frankness of some of the guests. That kind of honest talk was unknown in the days when she had a daily afternoon show."

How DID KATE SMITH RELATE TO OTHER WOMEN? This is an intriguing question to explore. She was a domineering woman and could intimidate others who were afraid to stand up to her. She doubtless intimidated Jeanette Collins in the early years. Jeanette was her chief competitor for Ted's attention, albeit in a different and ostensibly noncompeting role as his wife. The same thing happened much later with Nancy Gelosi, her bodyguard's wife.

It had become the expected thing for Sal, Nancy, and their youngest son Ross Gelosi to spend the summer at Camp Sunshine, looking out for Smith's welfare and giving her company. If it were not for them, in fact, she would no longer have been able to vacation there, given her medical problems and advancing age. It is often said that two women cannot live peaceably under the same roof for a long period of time. It was especially true for two strong-willed women such as Kathryn Smith and Nancy Gelosi. Smith had the distinct advantage of being a celebrity, owner of the property, and Sal's employer. Nancy was, in a sense, just so much excess baggage, to be tolerated and indulged to a point. She could not help feeling Smith's scorn. Sometimes they even had words. In truth, I am told they occasionally had knock-down-drag-out verbal battles. Often the tension could almost be cut with a knife.

Nancy Gelosi suffered in silence for several summers. Inevitably, relations worsened with time, so that by 1974 Nancy refused to go to the lake at all. In that summer of my return visit, Smith was able to be there only because Pat and Edna Castledine worked out their days off to be there with her. It was a tremendous sacrifice for them, as they both worked in the Albany area, over two hours away from Lake Placid. Edna's day off was Wednesday, so she would drive up there late Tuesday and return early

Thursday morning. Pat had weekends off, so she could be there from Friday evening until early Monday morning. That way Smith was alone only a couple days a week. If she had a problem in the night during those two days, the cook and maid were right next door, and caretaker John Viscome was around days.

Strangely, Smith did not seem to appreciate fully what Pat and her mom were doing for her. During the weekend I was there, she seemed to derive satisfaction from criticizing them and putting them down. A couple of times I heard minor arguments between Kathryn and Edna in which I knew Edna was right, but Kathryn asserted herself and Edna gave in to her. I took Edna aside and told her I did not think I could do that, and she simply said, "What's the use?" After all, they were the free guests of a beloved star, weren't they? They enjoyed just being in her company and were willing to pay that sociological price: being lower than Smith in the pecking order.

An important part of Smith's life at Lake Placid was her old and dear friendship with Flora Donvan, a charming and well-bred little lady weighing all of eight-five pounds. Donvan lived upstairs over her Lavender Shop, and she had a guest room reserved for her famous godchild. She even placed a star on the door, as is done in show biz for a star's dressing room. That tickled Smith. When she came to "Placid" during the months when her camp was closed, she always had a place to stay.

In April 1967 Flora Donvan was hospitalized for major surgery. Smith took over the running of the shop, and she got plenty of press coverage for it. It served to further enhance her image as the girl next door. A few years later, for no apparent reason that Smith knew of, suddenly Donvan began giving her the cold shoulder. Smith was very fond of Donvan and thought the feeling was mutual. To suddenly be turned away hurt her deeply. Was Donvan jealous of Pat and Edna Castledine? Was she becoming senile? Had Smith said or done something to offend the dear lady? She never was able to solve the mystery, and the estrangement lasted until Donvan's death in 1974 at age 87.

Over the years Kate Smith did not have many close friends of either gender, perhaps in part because Ted Collins discouraged her from forming strong friendships. She shunned other celebrities, preferring to associate with ordinary folks and she was suspicious of the motives of those who tried to get close to her. Could they be trusted or were they using her because of who she was? In the thirties she had Minerva Klinge and her secretary, Jane Tompkins. There were several good friends in Palm Beach. In the forties and later there was Major Edith Aynes of the Army Nurse Corps. There were, to be sure, others. Ted Collins was certainly her best male friend. Later Sal Gelosi more or less took Ted's place in her mind. She often called Sal "Ted," and Sal always corrected her. In our journals we had a "Guest Personality" column. Smith had Pat Castledine tell me never to feature

Dinah Shore in that column. Why? Maybe because she and Dinah Shore
were rivals as the most popular female pop singers in the forties and she was
jealous of Shore.

On May 13, 1973, Mother's Day, Smith gave two well-received concerts at the new Arie Crown Theatre in Chicago's McCormick Place. Pat
and Edna Castledine and I attended the afternoon performance, again having front and center seats. I had my camera loaded with black-and-white
film and with the zoom lens, so I was able to get some excellent close-up
pictures for our magazine. Smith was glamorous in her light pink gown
with pleated sleeves, large white pendant earrings, and a matching white
string of beads across the front of her hair. Jerry Bresler conducted the orchestra, and she had eight Kids Next Door to accompany her on a few
selections.

Smith's repertoire included a "new kind of music" medley, with "Up,
Up and Away," "The Summer Knows," "Day by Day," "Song Sung
Blue," and "Didn't We?" just as on her recent television special. Later she
sang a delightful memory medley: "Embraceable You," "Once in a
While," "On the Sunny Side of the Street," "The Very Thought of You,"
"Don't Take Your Love from Me," and a rousing "I've Got the World on
a String." I gasped inaudibly when her string of beads broke, and they
began to fall on the floor. A little later her right earring fell off. Undaunted
by these events, she picked up the earring and passed it to Bresler.

After the show we visited with Smith in her dressing room. She was
tired, and we felt for her, knowing she had another long show ahead of her
that evening. Besides her other medical problems, she was experiencing an
eye infection and had not slept well. In fact, she was so exhausted by the
end of the second show that she forgot some of the words to "God Bless
America."

Ten days after the Chicago concerts Smith returned to the stage of the
Circus Room at John Ascuaga's Nugget Hotel in Sparks, Nevada, for a
three-week engagement. Her show was much like that of the previous year,
although she did sing a few different songs. There was a swing arrangement
of "Somebody Else Is Taking My Place," an intimate rendition of the Tony
Bennett hit "The Good Life" (accompanied only by Jerry Bresler at the
piano), and "What Are You Doing the Rest of Your Life?" A review in
Variety said:

> Kate Smith emits a radiance few femmes can match. Distinctive soaring
> contralto sounds better this year than last at the Nugget and audience rap-
> port appears to grow.... Kate Smith is no antique. She attempts songs
> that chirps 30 years her junior wouldn't touch and although results aren't
> always up to her standards, her game, adventurous spirit carries the mo-
> ment. "Love Is a Many Splendored Thing" allows full use of powerful,

resonant pipes and "I Have Dreamed" with tuneful, straightforward melody lines is the kind of song Smith delivers peerlessly.

Very early in the new year of 1974 Smith flew to Las Vegas to accept a very special and coveted award. It was the Golden Award of the American Guild of Variety Artists (AGVA), and she would be only the fourth to receive it. She was preceded by Jimmy Durante, Jack Benny, and Duke Ellington. As luck would have it, Las Vegas had just experienced a rare snowstorm, and Smith caught acute laryngitis soon after her arrival. She went on with the show, which was taped January 6 at Caesar's Palace with Ed Sullivan as master of ceremonies. Sullivan introduced her with this speech:

> Tonight we add to this illustrious list of superstars a great singing lady who has been entertaining America for nearly half a century. You know, it would actually take an hour to list all the show business records this great performer has set. She is one of the top selling recording artists of all time. In 1932 she played eighteen consecutive weeks* at the Palace on New York's Broadway. She was one of radio's first major stars. She introduced the daytime talk show to television. Her bigtime variety shows set new trends in both radio and TV. Ladies and gentlemen, the Songbird of the South, Miss Kate Smith.

Smith entered to enthusiastic applause and sang "Sing" and then "God Bless America," accompanied by the Kids Next Door, but it was evident that something was wrong with her voice. She received a standing ovation, then stepped to the podium. After Ed Sullivan gave her the Entertainer of the Year Award, she said, with a great deal of vocal straining:

> Thank you [bowing], thank you very, very much. You know, folks, you who are watching our show this evening, we've had quite a bit of snow [eight inches] out here in Las Vegas, and with it I lost my voice. But we did the best we could tonight under the conditions. And I want to say, in the few days I've been here, this is the first time I have ever been in Las Vegas and I've been received so beautifully by all the wonderful people here that I'm going to be looking forward to coming back again very soon.

Smith made no speech extolling her achievements or thanking all those responsible for her success, perhaps in order to save her voice. In fact, she seemed to take the award rather lightly, even though it was quite an honor, coming from her fellow artists. She probably would have been more impressed if it had come from a vote of the public. She never did go back, either to Vegas or to Sparks-Reno.

That spring saw the release of the last Kate Smith record, except for a

The year was in fact 1931, and it was 11 weeks.

multitude of reissues. After a hiatus of five years, she made a 45 rpm single in November 1973 in Philadelphia. On a catchy new tune called "Smile, Smile, Smile," she was joined by Dr. John, a jazz pianist out of New Orleans, an unlikely pairing if ever there was one. Born Mac Rebinak and also known as the Night Tripper, Dr. John became associated with psychedelic music in the sixties. Atlantic Records producer Joel Dorn added some members of Count Basie's band and a handful of banjo-pickers from the Philadelphia Mummers Marching Band.

Smith was amazed that her part was completed in only 45 minutes. "I sang only with a rhythm section, a few background singers, and Dr. John on piano," she said. The rest was dubbed in later for a pleasing effect, but Smith hardly recognized the finished product. It was a far cry from that first recording session in 1926 across the river in Camden. The flip side was a slow soft-rock ballad titled "A Perfect Love." The record received considerable air play, reaching the Easy Listening charts and remaining there for a number of weeks, but it was almost impossible to find it in a record store. Smith sent me a box of records to sell to our club members.

ALL OF WHICH BRINGS US TO THE UNLIKELY association between an aging Songbird and a rising young professional hockey team. The Philadelphia Flyers' management was disturbed that the crowds at their home games were not being properly respectful when the national anthem was played. Vice President Lou Scheinfeld suggested that they try using Smith's record of "God Bless America," which was done with good results. This was in December 1969, and they began to notice that the team usually won when that record was played. It was sparking the Flyers to victory, so it seemed. In the 1972-73 season they won 34, lost 3, and tied 1 when "God Bless America" was played, so the record was used at games they really needed to win on home ice. Scheinfeld now suggested that Kate Smith be brought to the Spectrum in person, but when manager Katz was contacted, he said he thought it was beneath her stature as an artist.

Now Smith's Uncle Fred Ditmars, a Philadelphia native, had been sending his niece newspaper clippings relating how successful she was as a good luck charm for the Flyers. When Katz mentioned the offer to her, she responded in the affirmative.

On October 11, 1973, Flyers fans were given a surprise as the team opened its season. A limousine had brought Smith from New York to the Spectrum. She met with team officials, had dinner at the clubhouse, and at 8 P.M. a red carpet was rolled out on the ice. Smith strolled out to deafening applause to render her anthem in person. The 17,007 fans whistled and clapped for nearly five minutes. Doug Favell, goalie for the Toronto Maple Leafs, said, "I knew our goose was cooked." Smith was paid $5,000, and the Flyers won the game. The score was Philadelphia 2, Toronto 0.

Announcer Gene Hart wondered how Smith's voice would hold up to her 1939 record after more than three decades. "But Kate put the final touch on her glorious night with a rendition that brought chills and another standing ovation of three minutes. It fully met the ultimate definition of the word *triumph*," he wrote in a 1992 story.

It turned out to be a banner season for the pugnacious Flyers. They defeated the New York Rangers 4 games to 3 in the semifinals, and then the Boston Bruins gave them an exciting contest in the Stanley Cup finals. By Sunday, May 12, the Flyers had won three games to the Bruins' two. It was a "must win" for Boston. The Flyers had secretly brought back their talisman. At 1:57 P.M. a portable organ was wheeled onto the ice. Then the fans began to chant, "We want Kate, we want Kate!" Then came the red carpet, followed by the "God Bless America" lady. She sang her song, and the crowd went wild. Even the Bruins skated over to shake her hand in sportsmanlike fashion. Well, the Flyers won, 1 to 0, clinching the Stanley Cup for the first time since the team was formed in 1967. Such banners as "Kate for MVP" and "C'mon Kate—Light Our Flyers" were flying those days.

It was arranged that Smith would cohost "The Mike Douglas Show" the week of May 13–17. That syndicated talk-variety show on the Westinghouse Network would be taped, to be televised several weeks later. A truly exceptional event occurred on Monday. All Philadelphia went wild after their hockey team's victory. The whole city closed down and held a colossal parade. Kate Smith was one of the most visible participants, riding in a fire engine and sounding the siren from time to time with her foot. At points along the parade route, the fire engine would stop for a rendition of "God Bless America." It was one of the most exciting moments of Smith's life, she told Mike Douglas afterwards on the show, which that day in Philadelphia was done live. She exclaimed, "That was the greatest ovation I ever received as a performer, and I was just thrilled, thrilled, thrilled!"

That was quite a "Mike Douglas Show." A videotape of Smith singing at the Spectrum was shown, as well as footage of some of the most exciting moments of the game, with Smith rooting as fervently as anyone in the crowd. The Amazing Kreskin was on the show to discuss the psychological impact of Smith's singing on the motivation of the team to win. Smith said she thought it gave them just a little extra something that made the difference, not that there was anything mysterious about it. Another guest that day was singer Tony Orlando. He paid Smith some glowing compliments, and it marked the start of a friendship that would lead to five guest spots on his popular television series.

On Mike Douglas' Tuesday show, Smith sang "Smile, Smile, Smile" to a receptive audience; Douglas predicted it would be a hit. Smith explained the origin of her theme song, and she made a "London Fog," half milk and half cola. Douglas managed, in the course of that week, to bring out almost every facet of Smith's life and career, even persuading her to tell about Bert Lahr's bad manners toward her during the run of *Flying High* (see Chapter 1). On Thursday she answered questions from the audience; one person asked whether she planned to sing "When the Moon Comes Over the Mountain" before the week was over. She said she would if time permitted, and Douglas said, "Sing it right now." It was a poignant moment.

On the Friday show Douglas made this statement to Smith: "You know, there are certain standard questions that people ask of you when you're in this business. What is the most asked question of you, Kathryn?" Her instant reply was, "I know exactly what you mean without your ever saying what it is: 'Why didn't I ever get married?'" Douglas seemed genuinely surprised, responding, "That's the one?" And Kate said, "That's the one. Every interview, every time anyone talks to me, people always come up to me and say, 'You know, Kate, I always wondered why you never got married.' That is the first thing they say and it's the leading question in every interview." Douglas, not wanting the opportunity to pass, asked, "What do you say?" And she gave the reply quoted in Chapter 13. Douglas then ventured this observation: "Many people thought you were married to Ted Collins," to which she responded again as quoted in Chapter 13, categorically denying any romance there.

Changing the subject completely, Douglas asked Smith about the fire engine ride she had Monday. She described it in jubilant detail. Philadelphia fire chief Rizzo (brother of the mayor) appeared, presenting her with a helmet and an honorary chief certificate. Douglas remarked to Smith, "The kid in you came out when you were describing that." "What do you mean, 'the kid'?" she replied, "I'm a kid anyhow. Oh, I'll never be anything but a kid. Age? It's all in the mind." How true, especially for Kate. She was in a sense admitting her naïveté and her dependence upon others to take care of most of the serious business in her life.

It was an outstanding week in the life of Kate Smith, that week in Philly. The entire city of Brotherly Love, it seemed, was in love with her and what she apparently did for their champion Flyers. It really did seem like old times for her, being so in the limelight, in the newspapers and magazines from coast to coast, and doing a TV variety show every afternoon, if only for a week. By week's end she was physically exhausted but emotionally exhilarated.

Goalie Bernie Parent was on one of the shows, and he gave Smith a lesson in how to score a goal. The Flyers referred to her as their "rabbit's foot," their "secret ice weapon," their "good luck charm." And she remained just that for the 1974-75 season. The magic happened all over again on May 14, 1975, when this time a green carpet was rolled out and she sang her patriotic anthem to help the Flyers keep the Stanley Cup by defeating the New York Islanders. When quizzed on how she felt about it, she told reporters, "I've been honored by presidents and welcomed by kings, but the tremendous ovation and response by the fans here beat anything else I've ever experienced. I've never been touched like this before in my life. It made me bawl." The reporter quipped that it had had the same effect on the defeated Islanders.

Yes, Ted Collins would have been proud, and in his element. He was always a sports-minded person, despite heavy financial losses from owning losing teams. He did own the champion Kate Smith Celtics basketball team in the thirties, however. The Flyers were another winning team, and Smith was winning much free publicity and a tremendous revival of popularity in what would be the last two years of her career. The team even nominated her, unofficially, as Most Valuable Player. They had thousands of red lapel pins made proclaiming WE LOVE KATE. Yet another generation had discovered her too. On May 22, 1987, nearly a year after Smith's death, the Flyers played a videotape of her good luck anthem from 1975 to open a critical game against the Edmonton Oilers, again for the Stanley Cup—and they won. To this day ceremonies at the Spectrum are concluded with Gene Hart simply announcing, "Would you now stand and join in the singing of ⌣*ur Song.*"

ONE DAY EARLY IN 1974 SMITH PICKED UP her pen to write a check and found she could write only in a very shaky fashion. She could not seem to grip the pen properly with her right hand because two fingers refused to work normally. It was a slight stroke. With practice her handwriting improved, but her beautiful penmanship never completely returned. That summer she confided to me that growing old was no fun.

Kate Smith's success with the Flyers spurred her on, and her career was in full swing those last two seasons. She began 1975 with two standout guest spots, one with the Smothers Brothers, now on NBC, and the other on the new "Tony Orlando and Dawn Show" on CBS. Smith and Orlando seemed to have a special rapport, despite the obvious age difference. It was somewhat reminiscent of her rapport with Dean Martin a few years earlier. Although Orlando was thirty years her junior, they had a chemistry and the audiences loved them together. Proof of that is found in the show's ratings, which reached a peak every time Smith appeared.

On that initial show, January 29, 1975, Smith opened with one of her big ballads, "Love Is a Many Splendored Thing," which evoked an unusual (for television) standing ovation. Then she and Orlando led into a remarkably funny and entertaining duet. Smith said she would have to put her glasses on, as the lyrics had been carded and she did not know all the words. Orlando asked if he could take off his tie, telling the audience, "We're gonna get funky now." The song was the Jim Croce hit "Bad, Bad Leroy Brown." Once again "they killed 'em," just as Smith had done every night in *Honeymoon Lane.* Indeed she moved with the times, at least to a degree.

The barrage of letters and the rating report demanded Smith's return, so return she did on March 19, singing "As Long as He Needs Me" and receiving another "standing O." This time she and Orlando did a rock-'n'-roll medley, in which Smith sang two Elvis Presley hits, "Heartbreak Hotel" and "Hound Dog." Again the ratings soared, and she was signed for October 1, the opening show of the next season. This time she was dressed in a very becoming black sequined gown with a large diamond brooch and sang Helen Reddy's hit, "You and Me Against the World." Then followed a group of "friends" songs, including "You've Gotta Have Friends" and "You've Got a Friend." She did have a friend in Orlando, who called upon her whenever his show needed a boost in the ratings.

In the wee small hours of June 19, 1975, Smith was Tom Snyder's guest for the full hour on the NBC "Tomorrow Show." When asked by Snyder why she had never married, she stated that six businessmen from the Washington, D.C., area had asked for her hand in marriage but that she had put her career first. She brought along the newest journal from the Kate Smith USA Friends Club and told about the club, holding up the magazine for all to see. Bill Freeh happened to be in the building, having completed his day's work as an NBC sound engineer, so he waited for the show to end at 2 A.M. and attempted to gain entrance to the studio to visit his friend Kate. Gelosi tried to exclude him, but he presented his identification. Smith greeted him with pleasant surprise and open arms.

I vividly recall Smith's fourth appearance on "The Tony Orlando and Dawn Show." It was December 10, 1975, and Smith never looked more radiant or sang more beautifully. Orlando introduced her as "Kathryn the Great, the Queen of Song, the Queen of Show Business." And he introduced her big song simply by saying, "I would love to share a beautiful song with a beautiful woman, Miss Kate Smith." A blue spotlight shone on her as she gave a rendition of "The Way We Were" that put Barbra Streisand's lovely one to shame. Within less than a year, her voice would be effectively stilled.

CHAPTER 21

I'll Be Seeing You

I'll be seeing you in all the old familiar places
That this heart of mine embraces,
All day long.
In that small café, the park across the way,
The children's carousel, the chestnut trees,
The wishing well.*

America's Songbird was going great guns as our Bicentennial commenced. It was the fiftieth calendar year of her career and she was still thankful to the Almighty to be in demand. And in demand she was! Just two days before New Year's, *Boston Globe* music critic Richard Dyer devoted his column to her, titling it "Kate—everybody's favorite auntie":

> Don't laugh. This column is going to be about Kate Smith. Not that there isn't some reason to laugh. Nothing ages faster, dates more radically, than a popular singing style. Kate Smith may put on a sequined dress and shimmy a bit when she turns up on TV these days—surprisingly she's turned out to be everybody's favorite foxy old auntie rather than everybody's favorite white-haired grandmother—but basically she sings the same way she sang nearly fifty years ago. A style that once had some freshness in it is now an institution."
>
> Unlike jazz singers who alter and sometimes improve their material, Kate Smith sings pretty straight. She imposes few variations on the melody and only one conspicuous vocal geegaw, an octave-sweeping portamento. Her rhythm is sometimes criticized as "square" by the young who, as listeners to rock singers, should know. Actually, her sense of rhythm is subtly pliant. . . .
>
> Kate Smith has never been particularly associated with "class" material—i.e., theatre songs; her repertory of more than 2,200 songs contains more junk, probably, than anyone else's. Yet, despite all this, Kate

Smith is worth listening to. First, of course, as a historical phenomenon. Next year will see the 50th anniversary of her first recording—a span that is probably almost unmatched. Her popularity has been immense—her lifetime earnings, the clips say, exceed $35 million. The statistics of her career are overwhelming—more than 10,300 radio shows, more than 1,000 television appearances.

Then there is the appeal of her personality: the directness of her singing reflects it. Kate Smith is about the only performer who can address the public as "folks" without making you think she's putting you on. Her humor is so natural, so corny, that you know that some writer isn't engineering her personality.... And there is the central fact that she has arguably the best voice of any female popular singer; the only competition is Vaughn deLeath, Bessie Smith, Sarah Vaughan, maybe Jane Froman. The voice has size, fullness, range, quality, beauty. Although she says she can't read music and has never had a singing lesson in her life, Kate Smith can scale her sound down to a velvety ballad intimacy and belt out the loudest climaxes of anyone. She can sing with a lovely feminine contralto quality, yet also carry a full chest registration an octave higher than any opera singer in her right mind would ever attempt. Fifty years after it all started, Kate Smith still sounds good, which shows she's doing something right.

Smith initiated the nation's 200th anniversary celebration with a bang as grand marshal of the Tournament of Roses Parade in Pasadena, the most prestigious parade in the land. It was evident from the television coverage that she was in her glory, riding in the back seat of a famous yellow 1929 Rolls Royce touring car, waving and throwing kisses to the spectators. Beside her were a plethora of American Beauty roses, and riding in the front seat, in all *his* glory, was bodyguard Gelosi.

Smith was only the third female grand marshal, preceded by actress Mary Pickford in 1933 and child star Shirley Temple in 1939. When she was interviewed by one of the three networks and reminded of that fact, she beamed: "I'm very thrilled about it because, when you think that the Tournament of Roses has been going on for eighty-seven years and there's only been three women, it's time now that they get a few more women in as their grand marshals." When the interviewer said that sounded women's libbish, Smith snapped back, "No, it isn't, but I feel the amount of men have been so many and so few women, I think they should have more women. As for women's lib, forget it!"

Smith was also called upon to sing both the national anthem and "God Bless America" at the Rose Bowl game that afternoon, a first for a grand marshal.

A few weeks later Smith was on the road again with more concerts in the southland. On two evenings early in March she appeared at the Van Wezel Auditorium in Sarasota, Florida. Her avid fan Dorothy Mull finally got to see and meet her idol, having written to Smith in advance. Smith recognized Mull's name from her letters and from our club's roster. Gelosi was instructed to get three of the best seats in the house for Mull and her friends. They sat in the third row left. Mull came prepared; she had written a note to Gelosi to be given him by an usher. In it she said she would love to go backstage to see Smith. Lo and behold, ten minutes later the usher appeared with Gelosi. As she went to shake his hand, he picked her up, carried her through the crowd and up onto the stage, put her diminutive body down and escorted her to Smith's dressing room. Smith greeted her warmly, and they chatted like old friends. It was yet another fan's dream come true.

There were half a dozen more television guest appearances. Smith did "The Tony Orlando and Dawn Show" for the fifth time, Donny and Marie Osmond's show again, and "The Mac Davis show." The latter two were under Ray Katz's management. She was a singing guest on "The Women of the Year Awards" hosted by Barbara Walters. On that show she looked radiantly mature and delivered a thrilling rendition of "I Have Dreamed" from *The King and I*. All guests and honorees gathered together at the end to sing "God Bless America," with Smith standing beside First Lady Betty Ford.

Smith played "The Hollywood Squares" game show a few times, then went to Oklahoma City to be featured in a two-hour, star-studded bicentennial special called "The Stars and Stripes Show." Her grand finale, preceded by a brief impassioned patriotic speech, was—what else?—"God Bless America." That show was taped June 17 and televised June 30, just four days before the nation's bicentennial. It was to be Kate Smith's final television performance, and an altogether appropriate one it was. She came in like the proverbial lioness on the Broadway stage in 1926, and she went out like the same lioness on the Oklahoma City stage half a century later. Kate Smith was not much like a lamb.

SO MUCH FOR THE GOOD TIMES. Actually, Kate Smith was fighting several health battles at the outset of that bicentennial year. She suffered from high blood pressure, and occasional heart fibrillation (rapid heartbeat) and had a difficult case of diabetes. In addition, she had experienced a slight stroke affecting two fingers of her right hand and also suffered from arthritis, as a look at her rather gnarled hands would reveal.

Sometime in 1974 Smith had begun experiencing vaginal bleeding, a cancer signal. At first she ignored it, hoping it might go away. After cervical cancer was diagnosed, she had radiation treatments, with attendant gastrointestinal upsets and the loss of her hair, so that she took to wearing a hairpiece even around the apartment. The treatments worked and the cancer was cured. But her face was noticeably puffy in television appearances during those latter months.

In the summer of 1976 all of Smith's ailments caught up with her. She was not feeling well enough to go to Lake Placid. Instead she moped around her apartment, resting and sleeping a great deal. Her heart was fibrillating alarmingly, and her blood sugar was so out of control that she was taking nearly 400 units of insulin at a shot. Her physician felt that the great lady ought to be allowed to eat all the sweets she wanted, so he administered massive doses of insulin. And she was taking forty-two pills (of various kinds) every day. She was forced to cancel scheduled performances at the Canadian National Exhibition on August 23 and the Nebraska State Fair on September 3. Officially the reason given was "a severe throat infection."

On a Friday evening in late August, Smith was taken ill. She began behaving strangely, fading in and out of consciousness. Sal Gelosi stayed with her until Pat Castledine arrived for a weekend. Smith had gone into insulin shock exactly a week before this. Castledine was there then too, fortunately, sleeping in the guest room as usual when for some reason she awoke to utter silence. She sat up and listened intently, unable to hear the slightest sound from Smith's room—not even her breathing. She tiptoed in and found Smith lying with her eyes open but not responding. Unable to rouse her to consciousness, Castledine called her physician, who lived in the same building. He administered glucose and Smith regained consciousness.

Not long after Gelosi left on this second occasion, Castledine found Smith becoming unresponsive just as before. Again she phoned the doctor, and again he gave Smith glucose. This time she did not respond. An ambulance was called and she was rushed to Boulevard Hospital. There her throat was suctioned and a large mass of thick phlegm was removed. More glucose was administered and eventually she began to regain consciousness. It was widely reported by the press that she went into a diabetic coma. Quite the opposite was true: it was insulin shock.

After several weeks at this hospital, Smith's physician had her transferred to Terrace Heights Hospital, where she continued to slowly recuperate. Upon her release in early October, Gelosi took her to the Uihlein Mercy Center at Lake Placid for a two-week period of convalescence. She had participated in the ceremonies when the center opened a few years earlier and was a major donor. While there, Gelosi had Smith admitted, under an alias, to deGrosbriand Hospital in Burlington, Vermont, where she underwent an extensive battery of tests, including a brain wave, to discover the extent of damage done. Gelosi brought her home to her East Side apartment late in October.

Autumn turned to winter and winter to spring, but Smith just was not herself. In late winter the Gelosis took her to Florida, where she continued her slow recovery. Nancy Gelosi put her on a strict sugarless diet. One day, when they were dining out in Palm Beach, who should spy her but her old radio announcer André Baruch. He came over to their table and unobtrusively inquired of Gelosi whether he thought Smith could be a guest on a telephone–talk show he and wife Bea Wain were doing. Gelosi told Baruch that she could go on for five minutes only, as she was still having some trouble remembering and speaking. It was agreed, but she stayed on for two hours. Smith was remarkably alert and answered callers' questions with great delight. Apparently the old "show biz bug" called forth a supply of adrenaline that cleared her mind. Sal Gelosi attributed it to Nancy's diet regimen. At any rate, by the time they returned to New York, Smith was doing pretty well. Although she was having trouble walking and her mind was not as keen as before, she had improved decidedly and was looking forward to getting back in the public eye.

Nancy Gelosi agreed to go to Lake Placid for the customary summer vacation. That August Lou Dumont, a professor at Keene State College in New Hampshire, called to ask about taping an interview. He had a grant to produce a series for National Public Radio called "First Ladies of Radio." Sal Gelosi gave permission and the taping took place in the cheerful Camp Sunshine dining room, just as mine had six summers before. It was evident that Kathryn's speech was a bit slow and that her memory was not up to par. She did remember Oscar Shaw from *Flying High* in 1930, but could not recall all of the lyrics to her theme song. She did remarkably well, considering the damage that had been caused by her prolonged period of insulin shock less than a year before.

Smith said she knew her fans were concerned about her and that she was trying "with the Good Lord's help" to bounce back from the problems she was having with her voice and her walking. She told her public: "We have had a wonderful forté [she meant rapport], the public and myself. . . You've got to be honest with [the public], you can't lie. Now, of course, an awful lot of 'em are upset because I have been ill. It is perfectly normal for a person to be ill, no matter who they are or what they do. You have a time in your life when you can't do what you want to do."

She went into some detail about the nature of her illness, saying part of it was laryngitis, "a terrible bugaboo for any singer." She also said she had fallen in the bathtub, injuring her spine and making it difficult to walk. She ended by saying, "I'm fighting like crazy, with God's help, and I think that eventually I'll come out of it all right . . . but it's gonna take time."

All of this was said slowly and rather haltingly. Ray Katz asked Lyn Duddy to have her sing some songs. Duddy said that her voice had lowered considerably and that she did not have nearly the range she had before. Unfortunately, she was indeed fighting a losing battle and would never again perform before the public.

Smith and the Gelosis returned to New York that September, and she lived alone in her 39th floor apartment that winter without incident. In April 1978, however, she fell, breaking the humerus bone of her left arm. She spent a couple weeks in Lenox Hill Hospital and in May was taken to Lake Placid by Gelosi to convalesce at the Uihlein Center, operated by the sisters of the Catholic church.

Smith's mind was deteriorating, and she was very demanding on the staff. She was given daily walking therapy, but she clearly was not herself and called for attention day and night. It was too much for the staff to cope with, and it was clear that she could not remain there indefinitely. It had been Smith's wish to live out her days there should she become incapacitated, but it was not to be.

Sal and Nancy Gelosi enjoyed the summer at Camp Sunshine to be close to Smith. Near the summer's end they took her back to New York, where help was hired to care for her in her apartment. Pat Castledine, who resumed her frequent weekend visits, noted that around Christmastime Smith began to act strangely. She was slipping in her personal grooming, and she ceased attending Mass regularly. Her spoken responses were not always appropriate. She was failing so much mentally that on July 23, 1979, her family had her declared mentally incompetent to handle her affairs. Her two nieces, Kathryn Rodriguez and Suzanne Andron, were named conservators of her estate, along with attorney Richard Becker, son of business manager Sanford Becker.

All of Smith's relatives already lived in, or were about to move to, Raleigh, North Carolina. They decided to relocate her there in October 1979. The conservators added a codicil to her will, reducing Sal Gelosi's inheritance drastically. Gelosi fought it in court and a compromise was reached. The conservators hired Pat Castledine to be a resident companion for Smith in Raleigh.

For a time they all lived together there: Helena, her daughter Suzanne and her family, Pat Castledine and Kathryn. Eventually a ranch house in a secluded area was found, and Kathryn and Pat moved into it. By the time she was taken to Raleigh, Smith could no longer walk by herself. Her legs were mobile, but she had developed spinal arthritis and was too weak to walk without help. When they went out, she either stayed in the car or was placed in a wheelchair. She now weighed only 135 pounds, had lost her full face and her "presence." She stared blankly and seldom smiled.

Before many weeks had passed, Smith and Castledine were suddenly and unexpectedly joined by niece Kathryn Rodriguez and her family. Conditions were tumultuous and stressful as Helena and her daughters took turns suing one another, all of it being reported in the media. Many of Smith's possessions were sold at auction, as the conservators were saying that she didn't have enough money left to pay her bills.

In November, 1980, Father Raymond Wood, a longtime friend and fellow Kate Smith fan and collector, and I spent a few days with Smith and Castledine. (By this time the Rodriguez family had been evicted by the court.) We were shocked at the change in Kathryn's appearance since we had last seen her. One evening we took them to a local steak house for dinner. Pat had called ahead to make the reservation and to notify the maître d' that Kate Smith was coming in a wheelchair. The entire restaurant staff was ready and waiting to greet the celebrity as Smith was wheeled down the red carpet. She reacted by smiling, waving, and saying hello back to them. The maître d' brought a large piece of paper and a felt-tipped pen, asking Miss Smith to autograph it for his mother, a devoted fan. She did so with a flourish, just like old times.

Smith's affliction was diagnosed as "organic brain syndrome, reflecting generalized cerebral arteriosclerosis." It took a strong stimulus such as the restaurant scene to briefly bring back some semblance of the Kate Smith of old. Her only recognizable feature was her voice, weak though distinctively hers. Her enunciation was as crystal clear as ever, and when she could be persuaded to sing a chorus of "God Bless America" she was right on key. The haunting question was whether she comprehended what went on around her. When it was time for us to leave, she wished us a safe flight.

THE TELEVISION ACADEMY (EMMY) Awards Committee had contacted Ray Katz to have Smith make an appearance at the end of the three-hour show in September 1982. Members of her family were under court order not to travel with her, so she, her physician, Castledine, and a household aide were flown to Los Angeles in a private plane.

Shortly before 8 P.M. (PDT) a film montage of Smith's career was shown on the television screen. Then she appeared, a frail old woman in a wheelchair, a mere shadow of her former self. Kate was outfitted in a yellow and orange gown she had worn on television. She was overly made up and wore an unbecoming brown hairpiece. She was wheeled onto the enormous stage of the Pasadena Civic Auditorium by Bob Hope. As the television camera scanned the audience of celebrities, there were looks of horror and teary eyes. Smith had a habit of subconsciously reaching down and rubbing her right leg, so her shoulders had to be harnessed to the wheelchair.

The press reported, "Looking frail but aware, the 75 year-old singer was pushed onto the stage by Bob Hope. She joined the singing of 'God Bless America' and wiped a tear from her eye at the conclusion of the Irving Berlin song." Hope whispered something to her and she threw a kiss to the audience. She received no award and the program ended.

On October 26, 1982, Smith was wheeled out before the television cameras again. This time it was at the Raleigh Civic Center and the occasion was very different and very special. President Reagan had come to present her the highest award that can come to an American civilian: the Medal of Freedom. A group of private citizens had prevailed upon Senator John Warner, of what was presumed to be her home state of Virginia, to nominate her in a letter to the president.

This time she was dressed appropriately, wearing a black dress, a fur cape, and a large orchid, and her hair was attractively set. Reagan himself wheeled her onto the small stage, where a select audience was assembled. He read the following citation:

> The voice of Kate Smith is known and loved by millions of Americans, young and old. In war and peace, it has been an inspiration. Those simple but deeply moving words, "God Bless America," have taken on added meaning for all of us because of the way Kate Smith sang them. Thanks to her they have become a cherished part of all our lives, an undying reminder of the beauty, the courage, and the heart of this great land of ours. In giving us a magnificent, selfless talent like Kate Smith, God has truly blessed America.

Smith remained mute and seemed to be oblivious of what was taking place. Helena Steene stood and thanked the President on her sister's behalf, as Kathryn neither spoke nor made a gesture of any sort.

Each year saw America's Songbird's health slowly deteriorate. In November 1985, her right leg and foot became gangrenous, necessitating removal just above the knee. Her seventy-ninth birthday, which would be her last, was especially sad. Her only significant response that day came when the large birthday cake was brought in. She blew out the candles on cue, then I suggested we all sing "God Bless America." She joined in, mouthing the words, so I called for "When the Moon Comes Over the Mountain," and again she joined in. Then she faded. We had given her one last moment in the limelight, so to speak, and she savored it.

A malignant lump was found in Kathryn's left breast, and on May 9 a mastectomy was performed. About a month later Kathryn took a bad fall, having been left alone in her bedroom, and fractured two cervical vertebrae. She was placed in a restrictive neck brace and released two days later.

Tuesday afternoon, June 17, Kate Smith stopped breathing and was pronounced dead. Her physician said that the fall contributed to, but did not cause, her death. Two days later a funeral Mass was celebrated at Our Lady of Lourdes Church in Raleigh. Then her body was flown to Washington for a second funeral Mass on Saturday at St. Matthew's Cathedral. Her flag-draped coffin rested in the same spot where John F. Kennedy's had. She was eulogized by Father Salmon, who had baptized her in 1965. He asked the 750 mourners to join in singing "God Bless America." There was not a dry eye in the cathedral.

Smith's family intended to bury her in the Washington cemetery where her ancestors are buried until Castledine, Gelosi, and business manager Sanford Becker reminded them that it was her wish to rest in St. Agnes Cemetery at Lake Placid. After a family feud, the body was taken to be temporarily placed in a refrigerated vault at the North Elba, New York, cemetery. (The village of Lake Placid is located in the town of North Elba.)

Back in 1973 Smith had sent identical letters to Helena, Becker, and Gelosi, designated executors of her will, specifying her wish to be entombed in a mausoleum of pink or rose granite. She had a fear of being underground, even in death. A highly publicized battle ensued between her family and St. Agnes Church, and was not resolved until November 1987. Kathryn's wish was finally granted and a fitting memorial service was conducted at the church, followed by the blessing of the pink granite mausoleum.

MEANWHILE, THE PHILADELPHIA FLYERS HOCKEY TEAM had commissioned Marc Mellon of New York City to sculpt an eight-foot high bronze statue of Kate Smith to repose to the left of the parking lot entrance to the Spectrum. Mellon based the pose, in large part, on a videotape of the ending of "God Bless America" at one of her four live appearances there; she is looking upward, with arms outstretched. The statue was unveiled at an elaborate noonday ceremony on the day of the Flyers' opening game, October 8, 1987.

Bernie Parent, Bobby Clark, and other 1974-75 team members were among the invited guests, as were surviving members of Kate Smith's family. Pat Castledine and I were invited, also. Entire classes of school children were bused in for this prestigious patriotic occasion. The Boy Scouts of America, financial benefactors of the song for nearly fifty years, were represented by a troop from the Philadelphia Council. "God Bless America" was rendered by the Valley Forge Military Academy band and glee club. A letter from President Reagan was read. It stated in part:

> Kate Smith was a patriot in every sense of the word. She thrilled us all many times with her stirring rendition of "God Bless America." Kate sang the song with a love that made it her own—a fact fans of the Philadelphia Flyers Hockey Club will appreciate, because they considered her their good luck charm.
>
> It is truly appropriate that during the Bicentennial of the Constitution we take time to remember Kate Smith, who made us all proud to be Americans. No one who heard her sing will ever forget the vitality she brought to her music. America was indeed blessed by God to have Kate Smith become a special part of our lives.

An inspiring and well-researched address was given by Flyers president Jay Snider, son of owner Ed Snider.

As the impressive statue was unveiled on that windy day, the American flag flew briskly against the blue autumn sky. It was a stirring moment. Brass plaques to its left and right tell of the life of America's Songbird and the story behind the anthem. It is an altogether fitting memorial to the woman whose rendition of "her song" guided the team to victory.

LET US CLOSE WITH A PLEASANT MEMORY from a warm, humid Saturday in early August of 1974. Kate Smith had been invited to give two outdoor concerts at the Allentown Fair in Pennsylvania. She had never attended a fair, she said, and had never given an outdoor concert.

Several of her friends were with her for the occasion. Father Wood celebrated Mass for all of us in Smith's motel room, then she treated us to brunch. Seated at the head of the table, she entertained us with light-hearted stories about her life and career.

The covered stage looked out on an array of bleacher seats. Just before 6 P.M., the time of Smith's first performance, the skies opened and there was a cloudburst, complete with thunder and lightning. The crowd ran for cover. By 6:30 the storm was over and a small audience gathered for a delightfully informal concert. Smith gave her all and adapted her remarks to the small crowd. She was wearing glasses and so could see her audience clearly for the first time.

The second show began at 9:30 P.M. By then the bleacher seats had dried and the weather was improving. Partway through the show Smith suddenly exclaimed, "Oh, folks, turn around and look at the beautiful moon!" The clouds had parted and there shone the full moon in all of its splendor. She took the occasion to render her perennial theme song, "When the Moon Comes Over the Mountain." It was a moment to hold forever.

> I'll see you in the morning sun
> And when the night is new,
> I'll be looking at the moon,
> But I'll be seeing you.*

---

*"I'll Be Seeing You," by Sammy Fain and Irving Kahal. © 1938 by Williamson Music Co. Copyright renewed. Used by permission. All rights reserved.

Discography

The matrix number is embossed in wax between label and innermost groove. It is often followed by a dash and take number, when known. A song is frequently recorded several times; each recording is referred to as a *take*. Sometimes more than one take is released. This is especially true of Kate Smith's Harmony, Velvet Tone, Diva, and Clarion records. Recording dates are not repeated for each song listed.

Matrix No.	Record No.	Title	Date Recorded
		— VICTOR —	
Test (no #)	Rejected	Mary Dear	Sept. 16, 1926
Test (no #)	Rejected	The Little White House	
Test (no #)	Rejected	Jersey Walk	
BVE-36396–1, 2, 3	Rejected	The Little White House	Oct. 7, 1926
BVE-36397–1, 2	Rejected	Mary Dear	
BVE-36398–1, 2, 3	Rejected	Jersey Walk	
		— COLUMBIA —	
W142884–2	810-D	The Litte White House	Oct. 28, 1926
W142885–3	810-D	Mary Dear	
W142886–	Rejected	Jersey Walk	

Note: Piano accompaniment by composer James Hanley.

W143476–3	911-D	One Sweet Letter from You	Feb. 14, 1927
W143477-3	911-D	I'm Gonna Meet My Sweetie Now	

Note: Accompanied by the Charleston Chasers.

W144233–1	1348-D	In the Evening	May 26, 1927
W144234–5	1132-D	Just Another Day Wasted Away	

Note: Piano accompaniment by James Hanley.

W144522–5	Rejected	Worryin'	May 28, 1927

Matrix No.	Record No.	Title	Date Recorded

— C O L U M B I A (continued) —

Matrix No.	Record No.	Title	Date Recorded
W144523–6	1348-D	A Little Smile, A Little Kiss	May 28, 1927
W144524–4	1132-D	Clementine (From New Orleans)	
W148806–2	Har. 970-H VT 1970-V Diva 2970-G	He's a Good Man to Have Around	July 12, 1929
W148807–3	Har. 970-H VT 1970-V Diva 2970-G MGM 1043-P	Maybe—Who Knows?	
H148937W–3	Har. 999-H VT 1999-V Diva 2999-G MGM 1050-P, 1073-P	Moanin' Low	Aug. 27, 1929
H148938W–1	Har. 999-H VT 1999-V Diva 2999-G MGM 1052-P, 1073-P, 1087-P, 1093-P	Waiting at the End of the Road	
H149457W–1	Har. 1050-H VT 2050-V Diva 3050-G MGM 1087-P	I May Be Wrong	Nov. 1, 1929
H149458–1	Har. 1050-H VT 2050-V Diva 3050-G	Love (Your Magic Spell Is Everywhere)	
H149651W–1	Har. 1069-H VT 2069-V Diva 3069-G MGM 2014-P	Chant of the Jungle	Nov. 29, 1929
H149652W–2	Har. 1069-H VT 2069-V Diva 3069-G MGM 2011-P	That Wonderful Something	
H149722W–	Unissued	St. Louis Blues	Dec. 13, 1929
H149723W–	Unissued	Frankie and Johnny	
H150447W–2	Har. 1170-H VT 2170-V Diva 3170-G	Sharing	May 20, 1930
H150448W–2	Har. 1170-H VT 2170-V Diva 3170-G Clar. 5015-C	Dancing with Tears in My Eyes	
H150631W–1	Clar. 5015-C	Don't Let Me Hold You, Baby Mine	July 8, 1930
H150632W	Har. 1191-H(3) VT 2191-V(1) Diva 3191-G(3) Clar. 5074-C	I Don't Mind Walkin' in the Rain	
H150633W–1	Har. 1191-H VT 2191-V Diva 3191-G Clar. 5038-C	Swinging in a Hammock	

Matrix No.	Record No.	Title	Date Recorded
H150634W–1	Clar. 5038-C	You'll Be Coming Back to Me	July 8, 1930
H150835W	Har. 1216-H(4) VT 2216-V(4) Diva 3216-G(1)	Maybe It's Love	Sept. 23, 1930
H150836W	Har. 1216-H(2) VT 2216-V(2) Diva 3216-G(4) Clar. 5074-C	You'll Never Know, Sweetheart	
H150937W	Har. 1236-H(2) Diva 3235-G Clar. 5124-C(3)	Here Comes the Sun	Nov. 6, 1930
H150938W	Har. 1235-H(2) VT 2235-V(1) Diva 3235-G Clar. 5123-C	I Got Rhythm	
H150958W–2	Clar. 5124-C	Morning, Noon, and Night	
H150959W–1	VT 2235-V Clar. 5123-C		
H151247W–2	Har. 1280-H VT 2293-V Clar. 5228-C	Overnight	Jan. 29, 1931
H151248W–1	Har. 1280-H VT 2292-V Clar. 5227-C	Reaching for the Moon	
H151251W–	VT 2293-V Clar. 5228-C	Grievin'	
H151252W–1	VT 2292-V Clar. 5227-C	You Don't Want Me Anymore	
H151419W–	Unissued	You Didn't Have to Tell Me	March 13, 1931
H151420W–1	Har. 1303-H VT 2344-V Clar. 5278-C	Wabash Moon	
H151421W–2	Clar. 5279-C	Now's the Time	
H151422W–	Unissued	At Dusk	
H151449W–2	VT 2344-V Clar. 5278-C	Dinah Lee from Tennessee	March 20, 1931
H151450W–1	Har. 1303-H Clar. 5279-C	You Didn't Have to Tell Me	
W365025H–3	Har. 1347-H VT 2423-V Clar. 5359-C	Makin' Faces at the Man in the Moon	
W365026H–3	Har. 1347-H VT 2423-V Clar. 2423-C	When the Moon Comes Over the Mountain	
W151735–3	Col. 2516-D	If I Have to Go on Without You	Aug. 17, 1931
W151736–1	Col. 2516-D	When the Moon Comes Over the Mountain	

Note: Released with both black and blue labels (identical).

W151786–2	Col. 2539-D	You Call It Madness	Sept. 15, 1931
W151787–2	Col. 2539-D	I Don't Know Why (I Just Do)	

Note: This and both versions of "When the Moon Comes Over the Mountain" contain spoken introduction, "Hello everybody, this is Kate Smith."

Matrix No.	Record No.	Title	Date Recorded

— C O L U M B I A *(continued)* —

W365031–2	Har. 1371-H VT 2448-V Clar. 5384-C	Shine On, Harvest Moon*	Sept. 15, 1931
W365032–2	Har. 1371-H VT 2448-V Clar. 5384-C	I Apologize*	

*Vocalist named as Ruth Brown *(nom de disc)*.

W151866–1	Col. 2563-D	That's Why Darkies Were Born	Oct. 28, 1931
W151867–1	Col. 2563-D	Tell Me with a Love Song	

Note: Released with both black and blue labels (identical).

W365038–	VT 2465-V(1) Clar. 5405-C(2)	You Try Somebody Else	
W365039–2	VT 2465-V Clar. 5405-C	Goodnight Sweetheart	
W152031–	Col. 2578-D	Too Late	Dec. 8, 1931

Note: With Guy Lombardo and His Royal Canadians. Two different takes—1 and 2— released with same label.

W152032–2	Col. 2578-D	River, Stay 'Way from My Door	

Note: With Guy Lombardo and His Royal Canadians.

W365048–3	VT 2483-V Clar. 5423-C	River, Stay 'Way from My Door	Dec. 10, 1931
W365049–2	VT 2483-V Clar. 5423-C	All of Me	
W365059–3	VT 2512-V Clar. 5452-C	Just Friends	Jan. 28, 1932
W365060–3	VT 2512-V Clar. 5423-C	Between the Devil and the Deep Blue Sea (Blues in My Heart interpolated)	
W152096–3	Col. 2605-D	In the Baggage Coach Ahead	
W152099–3	Col. 2605-D	Twenty-One Years	
W152121–2	Col. 2624-D	Snuggled on Your Shoulder	March 1, 1932
W152122–2	Col. 2624-D	Love, You Funny Thing!	
W100606–1	Col. 2637-D	My Mom	March 4, 1932
W100607–1	Col. 2637-D	(In the Gloaming) By the Fireside	
W255000–1	Col. 18000-D	Medley from *Face the Music*: Soft Lights and Sweet Music (Smith); Let's Have Another Cup of Coffee (The Three Nitecaps); On a Roof in Manhattan (Jack Miller)	March 22, 1932
W255001–2	Col. 18000-D	Medley from *Hot-Cha*: You Can Make My Life a Bed of Roses (Smith); Say (The Three Nitecaps); There I Go Dreaming Again (Jack Miller)	

Note: First in a short series of "Longer Play" 10" 78s. Label reads "Ben Selvin and His Orchestra." Released in both black and blue wax. Appears nonbreakable (vinyl?).

Matrix No.	Record No.	Title	Date Recorded
260001–4	Col. 56000-D	"Kate Smith Presents a Memory Program": Old Folks at Home; Grandfather's Clock; Songs My Mother Taught Me; Seeing Nellie Home	May 18, 1932

Note: This record is indeed a miniature program, with opening and closing signatures and spoken introduction to each song. Reverse side: "Ted Lewis Presents a Miniature Dance Program." Blue label; released in both black and blue wax.

— BRUNSWICK —

B13045-A-1	6497	Pickaninnies' Heaven	Feb. 9, 1933
B13046-A-4	6496	Twenty Million People	
B13047-A-3	6496	My Queen of Lullaby Land	
B13048-A-1	6497	Moon Song	

Note: Orchestra conducted by Victor Young. All songs from Smith's feature Paramount picture, *Hello Everybody!*

— DECCA —

38928-A	288-A	The Continental★	Oct. 31, 1934
38937-A	277-A	College Rhythm★	Nov. 1, 1934
38938-A	277-B	Let's Give Three Cheers for Love★	
38939-A	288-B	When My Ship Comes In	
38940-A	276-A	I'm Growing Fonder of You	
38941-A	276-B	Stay as Sweet as You Are	

★With the Three Ambassadors vocal trio. Orchestra conducted by Jack Miller.

— RCA VICTOR —

BS-017776-1	25760	When the Moon Comes Over the Mountain★ (Collins Special)	Dec. 28, 1937
BS-017777-1	25752	There's a Gold Mine in the Sky (with the Girls)	
BS-017778-1	25760	You're a Sweetheart	
BS-017779-1	25752	Bei Mir Bist du Schoen	
BS-035319-1	26198	God Bless America (with mixed chorus)	March 21, 1939
BS-035320-2	26198	The Star Spangled Banner (with mixed chorus)	
BS-035321-1	26214	It's Never Too Late	
BS-035322-1	26214	I Cried for You	
BS-035753-1	26235	Don't Worry 'Bout Me	April 17, 1939
BS-035754-1	26245	If I Had My Way	
BS-035755-1	26235	And the Angels Sing	
BS-035756-1	26245	If I Didn't Care	

★With the Three Ambassadors. Orchestra conducted by Jack Miller.

Matrix No.	Record No.	Title	Date Recorded

— COLUMBIA —

WCO-26522A-5	35398A	The Woodpecker Song	Feb. 15, 1940
WCO-26523A-	35413B	So Long	
WCO-26524A-7	35398B	I'm Stepping Out with a Memory Tonight	
WCO-26525A-	35413A	When You Wish Upon a Star	
CO27242-1	35996B	Lamplight	April 30, 1940
CO27243-1	35486A	Imagination	
CO27344-1	35486B	Make Believe Island	
CO27345-	Unissued	I Haven't Time to Be a Millionaire	
CO27273-1	35501A	The Lord Done Fixed Up My Soul	May 9, 1940
CO27274-1	35502B	You Can't Brush Me Off	
CO27275-1	35501B	You're Lonely and I'm Lonely	
CO27276-1	35502A	It's a Lovely Day Tomorrow	
WCO26959-	35564A	Can't Get Indiana Off My Mind	June 26, 1940
WCO26960-2	35638A	Trade Winds	
WCO26961-1	35638B	Good Night Again	
WCO26962-	35564B	Maybe	
CO27632-27637	Unissued	Little Johnny Appleseed (album)	July 12, 1940

Note: Undoubtedly sold to MGM Records and released as Album 34.

CO28528-2	Philco 7	Kate Smith and Ted Collins for Philco	Sept. 1940

Note: Smith sings a few bars of "When the Moon Comes Over the Mountain" and part of her record of "Trade Winds."

CO28836-1	35778A	A Nightingale Sang in Berkeley Square	Oct. 9, 1940
CO28837-1	35778B	Two Dreams Met	
CO28838-1	35802B	Along the Santa Fe Trail	
CO28839-1	35822A	Somewhere	
CO28897-1	35802A	The Last Time I Saw Paris	Oct. 16, 1940
CO28898-1	35822B	My Buddy	
CO28899-1	35791B	Silent Night, Holy Night	
CO28900-1	35791A	Adeste Fideles	
CO29536-1	35965A	It's Sad but True	Jan. 22, 1941
CO29537-1	36046B* 37138	Macushla	
CO29538-1	36045B*	When Day Is Done**	
CO29539-1	36048A*	The Rosary	
CO29540-1	36047B*	Thine Alone	
CO29541-1	35965B	Love Is	
CO29670-1	35996A 36498	We're All Americans	Feb. 10, 1941
CO29671-1	36015A	A Little Old Church in England	
CO29672-1	36047A*	The Sunshine of Your Smile	
CO29673-1	36046A*	Your Eyes Have Told Me So	
CO29674-1	36048B*	Kiss Me Again	
CO29675-1	36045A*	When the Moon Comes Over the Mountain**	

Matrix No.	Record No.	Title	Date Recorded

*These eight sides made up the first released Kate Smith album, "Kate Smith U.S.A.," Album C-50. **Also released by Sears, Roebuck Co. as Silvertone 605.

Matrix No.	Record No.	Title	Date Recorded
CO29770–1	36015B	It All Comes Back to Me Now	Feb. 19, 1941
CO29771–1	36043B	I Do, Do You?	
CO29772–1	36043A	Two Hearts That Pass in the Night	
CO29773–1	36247	Dancing in a Dream with You	
CO30606–1	36210	You and I	June 5, 1941
CO30607–2	36220	Don't Cry, Cherie	
CO30608–1	36210	Until Tomorrow	
CO30609–1	36220	Will You Still Be Mine?	
CO30716–1	36272	Time Was	June 19, 1941
CO30717–1	36247	Wasn't It You?	
CO30718–1	36524	Somebody Loves Me	
CO30719–1	36272	Along 'Bout Sundown	
CO31626–1	36448	The White Cliffs of Dover	Oct. 30, 1941
CO31627–1	36448	Rose O'Day	
CO31628–1	36443	A Merry American Christmas	
CO31629–1	36443 36524	My Melancholy Baby	
CO31774–1	36468	The Shrine of St. Cecilia	Nov. 19, 1941
CO31775–1	36674	Time on My Hands	
CO31776–1	36686	Embraceable You	
CO31777–1	36468	I Don't Want to Walk Without You	
CO31982–1	36511	America, I Love You*	Dec. 16, 1941
CO31983–1	36511	The Star Spangled Banner*	
CO31984–1	36498	They Started Somethin'*	
CO31985–1	36489	Dear Mom	
CO31986–1	36489	On the Street of Regret	
CO31987–1	36686	If I Had My Way	
CO31988–1	36674	Shine On, Harvest Moon	
CO32194–1	36514	She'll Always Remember	Jan. 13, 1942
CO32195–1	36514	When the Roses Bloom Again	
CO32196–1	Unissued	The Sweetheart of Sigma Chi	
CO32197–	Unissued	Memories of You	
CO32436–1	36540	This Time*	Feb. 12, 1942
CO32437–1	36540 37522	The Marine's Hymn*	
CO32438–1	36534	Blues in the Night	
CO32439–1	36534	How Do I Know It's Real?	
CO32577–1	36569	There Are Rivers to Cross	March 9, 1942
CO32578–1	36552	I Threw a Kiss in the Ocean	
CO32579–1	36552	Somebody Else Is Taking My Place	
CO32580–1	36569	We'll Meet Again	
CO32662–1	36581 37522	After Taps	April 8, 1942
CO32663–2	36577	One Dozen Roses	
CO32664–1	36581	Here You Are	
CO32665–1	36577	A Soldier Dreams (of You Tonight)	

Matrix No.	Record No.	Title	Date Recorded

— C O L U M B I A *(continued)* —

CO32821–1	36605	This Is Worth Fighting For	May 20, 1942
CO32822–1	36605	My Great, Great Grandfather	
CO32823–1	36609	Wonder When My Baby's Coming Home	
CO32824–1	36609	Old Sad Eyes	
CO32925–1	36618	Be Careful, It's My Heart	June 18, 1942
CO32926–1	36628	A Boy in Khaki—A Girl in Lace	
CO32927–1	36618	He Wears a Pair of Silver Wings	
CO32928–1	36628	I've Got a Gal in Kalamazoo	

*With the Kate Smith Singers. The American Federation of Musicians recording ban with Columbia (and Victor) Records was in effect from August 1, 1942, until November 13, 1944. Kate Smith made no records during that period.

VP-	V-Disc 24B	Wait for Me, Mary (Air check)	Feb. 26, 1943
VP-212	V-Disc 88B	In a Friendly Little Harbor (Air check)	Oct. 15, 1943
CO33812–1	36759	Don't Fence Me In*	Nov. 15, 1944
CO33814–1	36759	There Goes That Song Again	
CO33815–1	Unissued	(All of a Sudden) My Heart Sings	
CO34271–2	36783	Just a Prayer Away*	Feb. 9, 1945
CO34272–1	Unissued	Poor Little Rhode Island*	
CO34273–1	36783	All of My Life	
CO34622–1	36807	Question and Answer	April 25, 1945
CO34623–1	36807	Can't You Read Between the Lines?	
CO34755–1	36821	And There You Are	
CO34756–1	36821	Say It Over Again	
CO34851–1	36871	Tumbling Tumbleweeds*	June 1, 1945
CO34852–1	36832	On the Atchison, Topeka, and the Santa Fe*	
CO34853–1	36832	Johnny's Got a Date with a Gal in New York*	
CO34973–1	36839	Dearest Darling*	June 14, 1945
CO34974–1	36871	Just a Little Fond Affection*	
CO34977–1	36839	Some Sunday Morning†	
CO35505–1	36915	Here Comes Heaven Again	Dec. 13, 1945
CO35506–1	36915	Somebody's Walking in My Dreams	
CO35638–1	36950	If I Had a Wishing Ring	Jan. 17, 1946
CO35639–1	36950	Seems Like Old Times	
CO35841–1	36963	I Didn't Mean a Word I Said	Feb. 14, 1946
CO35842–1	36963	Sioux City Sue*†	

*With vocal quintet Four Chicks and Chuck.   †Also included on Japanese Columbia record #34977.

CO36064–1	36991	And Then I Looked at You	April 9, 1946
CO36065–1	36991	Pretending	
CO36095–1	37139	That's an Irish Lullaby*	April 17, 1946
CO36096–1	37136	Molly Malone*	

Matrix No.	Record No.	Title	Date Recorded
CO36097–1	37136	Where the River Shannon Flows*	April 17, 1946
CO36200–1	37137	A Little Bit of Heaven*	April 23, 1946
CO36201–1	37138	When Irish Eyes Are Smiling*	
CO36202–1	37137	Mother Machree*	
CO36203–1	37139	My Wild Irish Rose*	
(CO29537–1)	37138	Macushla* (Reissue of CO36046B)	

*Album C-116, "Kate Smith Sings Songs of Erin," was reissued on 10" LP Cl-6031 (LP592) as well as in a 45 rpm boxed set.

— M G M —

Note: Matrix and record numbers are the same.

Matrix No.		Title	Date Recorded
10003A–4		Anniversary Song	April 20, 1947
10003B–4		If I Had My Life to Live Over*	
30331-30334		"Between Americans," Narrative Album, by Norman Corwin: #7A	Spring 1947
10024A–2		After Graduation Day	May 1947
10024B–1		Dreams Are a Dime a Dozen*	
10028A–4		Tallahassee*	
10028B–1		Ask Anyone Who Knows	
10041A–1		Tomorrow*	June 19, 1947
10041B–1		Feudin' and Fightin'*	
10096A–1		White Christmas	Fall 1947
10096B–4		The Christmas Song	
10113A–1		It Had to Be You	
10113B–3		Dancing with Tears in My Eyes	
10125A–2		Now Is the Hour (with vocal quartet)	
10125B–3		I'll Never Say "I Love You"	
10157A–2		Long After Tonight	Winter 1947
10157B–3		Miracle of the Bells	
	Unissued	Dirty Face, Dirty Hands	Dec. 13, 1947
	Unissued	Little Man, You've Had a Busy Day	
	Unissued	It's a Sin to Tell a Lie	Jan. 6, 1948
	Unissued	Will You Love Me in December?	
	Unissued	I'm Tired of Everything But You	Jan. 19, 1948
10338A–		Tell Me (Tell Me Why)**	
10338B–		Till We Meet Again	
	Unissued	Mean to Me	Jan. 22, 1948
	Unissued	Tea for Two	Jan. 29, 1948
	Unissued	I Wonder Where My Baby Is Tonight	Feb. 24, 1948
	Unissued	I Never Knew	March 2, 1948
10498A–1		Memory Lane	
30025A–2		God Bless America (with chorus)	Early 1948
30101B–2***			

Matrix No.	Record No.	Title	Date Recorded

— M G M (continued) —

30025B–5		Bless This House (with chorus)	Early 1948
30059A–1		Foggy River†	
30059B–2		Cool Water†	
30060A–1		Tears on My Pillow†	
30060B–1		It's a Sin†	
30061A–2		Red River Valley†	
30061B–1		Down in the Valley†	
30062A–1		You Are My Sunshine†	
30062B–3		It Makes No Difference Now†	
	Unissued	It's Been a Long, Long Time	March 30, 1948
	Unissued	Good Bye, Good Luck, God Bless You	March 31, 1948
	Unissued	If I Had You	
	Unissued	When Your Hair Has Turned to Silver	
10220A–		When I Lost You**	April 12, 1948
10220B–		Easter Parade	
	Unissued	Bye Bye Blues	
	Unissued	I'll Walk Alone	
	Unissued	I'm in the Mood for Love	
10356A–1		A Rosewood Spinet	Winter 1949
10356B–2		Far Away Places (with Elm City Four)	
10388A–		Dreamy Old New England Moon (with Elm City Four)	Spring 1949
10388B–		Because You Love Me	
10439A–		A Million Miles Away	
10439B–1		I Promise	
10498B–1		Over the Hillside	
10529A–1		I Only Have Eyes for You	Oct. 3, 1949
10529B–1		Please Don't Talk About Me When I'm Gone	
30473A–		Beautiful Dreamer††	1949
30473B–		Jeanie with the Light Brown Hair††	
30474A–		Nellie Was a Lady††	
30474B–		My Old Kentucky Home††	
30475A–		Massa's in De Cold, Cold Ground††	
30475B–		Oh! Susanna††	

*With vocal quintet Four Chicks and Chuck. **Orchestra conducted by Bill Stegmeyer. ***In album 23, "Big City" with various artists. †In album 22, "Kate Smith Sings Songs of the Hills and Plains." ††In album 106, "Kate Smith Sings Songs of Stephen Foster."

Note: The following test pressings from the MGM period lack dates.

		Almost Like Being in Love	1947
		I Know That You Know	
		I'll See You in My Dreams	
		I Wonder What's Become of Sally	

Matrix No.	Record No.	Title	Date Recorded
		June Night	1947
		That Old Feeling	
		When Your Lover Has Gone	1948

— N A T I O N A L —

47-S-689	9138	The Lord's Prayer (with chorus)	1951
XX-1	9138	Ave Maria (with chorus)	
NSC-650-3	9139	The Same Lord (with chorus)	
NSC-651-5	9139	Little Bitty Baby (with chorus)	
47S-479-2B	9140	The Sweetheart of Sigma Chi	Feb. 25, 1948(?)
47S-497-2B	9140	You Tell Me Your Dream	Jan. 6, 1948(?)

Note: On 9140, orchestra conducted by Bill Stegmeyer.

Long Playing 10" Albums

— N A T I O N A L —

KS-1, 3001A	3001A	"REMINISCING WITH KATE SMITH"	
		Let Me Call You Sweetheart	Feb. 25, 1948
		Three O'Clock in the Morning	April 9, 1948
		After the Ball	Feb. 27, 1948
		Meet Me Tonight in Dreamland	April 9, 1948
KS-2, 3001B	3001B	Down by the Old Mill Stream	Feb. 24, 1948
		My Gal Sal	?
		(On) Moonlight Bay	April 5, 1948
		Just Awearying for You	?
KS-3, 3002A	3002A	"ALL TIME GREATS BY KATE SMITH"	
		Star Dust	?
		The Lord's Prayer	Jan. 20, 1948
		A Perfect Day	?
		Music, Maestro, Please	April 9, 1948
KS-4, 3002B	3002B	Sleepy Lagoon	March 20, 1948
		Till the End of Time	?
		Ave Maria	?
		Because	March 24, 1948
KS-5, 3003A	3003A	"SONGS TO REMEMBER BY KATE SMITH"	
		Jealous	?
		Lonesome and Sorry	April 8, 1948
		The One I Love	?
		I'll Never Be the Same	?
KS-6, 3003B	3003B	Linger Awhile	?
		Cheatin' on Me	Feb. 20, 1948
		You're Driving Me Crazy	?

Matrix No.	Record No.	Title	Date Recorded

— NATIONAL *(continued)* —

I'm Sorry I Made You Cry   March 25, 1948

Note: Nearly all Kate Smith National recordings were made during her tenure with MGM.

— CAPITOL —

H1-515-D3	H-515	"KATE SMITH: TV CURTAIN CALLS"	
20325		(Our) Love Is Here to Stay*	Jan. 25, 1954
20326		It Could Happen to You*	
20327		But Not for Me*	
20328		The Nearness of You*	
20329		The Very Thought of You*	Jan. 26, 1954
20330		They Can't Take That Away from Me*	
20331		Love Walked In*	
20332		If I Had You	
Unissued on 10" LP			
20364		'S Wonderful*	May 24, 1954
20365		You	
20366		Somebody Loves Me*	
20367		Who Cares?	
20368		The Best Things in Life Are Free	May 26, 1954
20369		Ridin' High	
20370		Just One of Those Things	
20371		You Do Something to Me	

*Available on Capitol cassette #4XL-9448.

Long Playing 12" Albums

— CAPITOL —

Note: All Capitol records are arranged and conducted by Nelson Riddle.

T-515   "KATE SMITH: TV CURTAIN CALLS"

Note: A 1955 reissue of H-515, plus: 'S Wonderful, You, Who Cares?, Ridin' High. Also available on Curb compact disc D2-77475.

T-854   "KATE SMITH"

Note: A 1957 reissue of T-515, with "Somebody Loves Me" replacing "Ridin' High."

— KAPP —

	KL/KS-1082	"THE FABULOUS KATE"	Early 1958
J90P-1475-2		All the Way*	
		Just in Time*	
		It Don't Mean a Thing	
		Thinking of You	
		The Beat O' My Heart*	
		Yes Indeed!*	

Matrix No.	Record No.	Title	Date Recorded

J90P-1476–2   High on a Windy Hill   Early 1958
Mr. Wonderful*
Love Is a Many Splendored
   Thing*
Comes Love*
Wish You Were Here*
The Huckle-Buck

Note: Orchestra conducted by Frank Hunter, except for "Yes Indeed!" and "The Huckle-Buck," conducted by George Siravo.
*Available on MCA cassette MCAC-20479: "KATE SMITH: LOVE IS A MANY SPLENDORED THING."

— T O P S —

               L-1672   "THE GREAT KATE"   Fall 1959
L-1672A   Come Rain or Come Shine
Ghost of a Chance
You'd Be So Nice to Come
   Home To
I Concentrate on You
Tenderly
Side by Side
L-1672B   Who's Sorry Now?
I'll Be Seeing You
People Will Say We're in
   Love
So Beats My Heart for You
Don't Worry 'Bout Me
Getting Sentimental Over
   You

Note: Orchestra conducted by Alex Deane.

               L-1673   "KATE SMITH SINGS   Fall 1959
                                   HYMNS AND SPIR-
                                   TUALS"
L-1673A   Old Time Religion
Rock of Ages
Sometimes I Feel Like a
   Motherless Child
Nearer, My God, to Thee
Swing Low, Sweet Chariot
The Lord's Prayer
L-1673B   Git on Board, Little Children
Sweet Hour of Prayer
Onward, Christian Soldiers
The Old Rugged Cross
Nobody Knows the Trouble
   I've Seen
God Be with You Till We
   Meet Again

Note: Orchestra conducted by Alex Deane.

               L-1677   "CHRISTMAS WITH   Fall 1959
                                   KATE"
L-1677A   Deck the Halls

Matrix No.	Record No.	Title	Date Recorded

— T O P S *(continued)* —

		White Christmas	Fall 1959
		Hark, the Herald Angels Sing	
		The First Noel	
		O Come All Ye Faithful	
		Santa Claus Is Coming to Town	
L-1677B		Joy to the World	
		O Little Town of Bethlehem	
		God Rest Ye Merry, Gentlemen	
		It Came Upon a Midnight Clear	
		Silent Night	
		Jingle Bells	

Note: Also available on compact disc: Laser Light 15414: "Kate Smith Christmas."

	L-1705	"KATE SMITH SINGS GOD BLESS AMERICA"	Fall 1959
L-1705A		God Bless America	
		Moonlight in Vermont	
		Yellow Rose of Texas / Deep in the Heart of Texas	
		Stars Fell on Alabama	
		Back Home Again in Indiana	
L-1705B		Oklahoma	
		Beautiful Ohio	
		In Old New York / Sidewalks of New York	
		Carolina Moon	
		My Old Kentucky Home	

Note: Orchestra conducted by Bill Stegmeyer.

	L-1706	"KATE SMITH SINGS FOLK SONGS"	Fall 1959
L-1706A		Wreck of the Old '97	
		Scarlet Ribbons	
		Cool Water	
		Blue Tail Fly	
		Kisses Sweeter Than Wine	
L-1706B		He's Got the Whole World in His Hands	
		Greensleeves	
		Down in the Valley	
		Sixteen Tons	
		On Top of Old Smokey	

Note: Orchestra conducted by Bill Stegmeyer. All five Tops albums are said to have been recorded in one week's time.

— R C A   V I C T O R —

| | LPM/LSP 2819 | "KATE SMITH AT CARNEGIE HALL" | Nov. 2, 1963 |
| PHRS-6382-1S | | Who Cares? | |

Matrix No.	Record No.	Title	Date Recorded
		I'll Be Seeing You	Nov. 2, 1963
		Please / Don't Blame Me /	
		Fine and Dandy	
		Moon River	
		What Kind of Fool Am I?	
PHRS-6383-1S		As Long as He Needs Me	
		How Deep Is the Ocean	
		Margie / Carolina Moon /	
		When Your Lover Has	
		Gone	
		This Is All I Ask	
		God Bless America	
		When the Moon Comes Over	
		the Mountain	

Note: Orchestra conducted by Skitch Henderson. Available on RCA Camden cassette
  CAK-2587.

	LPM/LSP 2921	"THE SWEETEST	April 6, 8, 9,
		SOUNDS"	1964
RPRM-4053-1S		The Sweetest Sounds	
		Just in Time	
		Days of Wine and Roses	
		My Coloring Book	
		I Wanna Be Around	
		I Wish You Love	
RPRM-4054-1S		More	
		Make Someone Happy	
		Lollipops and Roses	
		I Left My Heart in San Fran-	
		cisco	
		He Loves Me	
		If Ever I Would Leave You	

Note: Arranged and conducted by Peter Matz.

	LPM/LSP 3308	"A TOUCH OF MAGIC"	Sept. 29, 30,
RPRM-4242-1S		Love Is a Many Splendored	Oct. 1, 1964
		Thing	
		Call Me Irresponsible	
		Now I Have Everything	
		It Was So Beautiful	
		'Til Tomorrow	
		Temptation	
RPRM-4243-1S		Danke Schoen	
		You're Nobody 'Til Some-	
		body Loves You	
		I Gotta Right to Sing the	
		Blues	
		Too Close for Comfort	
		Lazy River	
		Climb Ev'ry Mountain	

Note: Arranged and conducted by Peter Matz.

	LPM/LSP 3445	"HOW GREAT THOU	June 7–9, 1965
		ART"	
SPRM-3667-1S		It Is No Secret	
		Until Then	

Matrix No.	Record No.	Title	Date Recorded

— R C A   V I C T O R *(continued)* —

		Were You There?	June 7–9, 1965
		Beautiful Isle of Somewhere	
		The Touch of His Hand on Mine	
		How Great Thou Art	
SPRM-3668-1S		It Took a Miracle	
		May the Good Lord Bless and Keep You	
		I May Never Pass This Way Again	
		I Asked the Lord	
		I See God	
		The Lord's Prayer	

Note: Arranged and conducted by Glenn Osser.

	LPM/LSP 3535	"THE KATE SMITH AN-NIVERSARY ALBUM"	Feb. 18, 19, 21, 1966
TPRM-2825-2S		Medley: When the Moon Comes Over the Mountain, Seems Like Old Times, All the Things You Are	
		Medley: What's New?, Wrap Your Troubles in Dreams, Long Ago (and Far Away)	
		Medley: September in the Rain, A Nightingale Sang in Berkeley Square, The Old Lamplighter	
		Medley: How Are Things in Glocca Morra, The White Cliffs of Dover, Don't Sit Under the Apple Tree	
TPRM-2826-4S		Medley: Symphony, I Didn't Know What Time It Was, Don't Fence Me In	
		Medley: Somebody Else Is Taking My Place, That Old Feeling, There Goes That Song Again	
		Medley: Once in a While, You'd Be So Nice to Come Home To, Some Sunday Morning	
		Medley: Deep Purple, Along the Santa Fe Trail, Don't Take Your Love from Me	

Note: Arranged and conducted by Peter Matz.

	LPM/LSP 3607	"THE KATE SMITH CHRISTMAS ALBUM"	June 7–9, 1966
TPRS-4287-1S		The Christmas Song	
		Do You Hear What I Hear?	
		Medley: Deck the Halls, Joy	

Matrix No.	Record No.	Title	Date Recorded

		to the World, It Came	June 7–9, 1966
		Upon a Midnight Clear	
		Silver Bells	
		I Heard the Bells on Christ-	
		mas Day	
TPRS-4288-5S		White Christmas	
		Happy Birthday, Dear Christ	
		Child	
		Christmas Eve in My Home	
		Town	
		It's Beginning to Look Like	
		Christmas	
		Medley: The First Noel, Si-	
		lent Night, O Holy Night	

Note: Arranged and conducted by Peter Matz. Also available on compact disc: 07863-33607-2 and cassette: 53607-4.

Matrix No.	Record No.	Title	Date Recorded
	LPM/LSP 3670	"KATE SMITH TODAY"	June 28–30,
TPRM-6629-1S		Somewhere, My Love	1966
		Yesterday	
		My Best Beau	
		Daydream	
		I Do, I Do	
		Who Can I Turn To?	
TPRM-6630-1S		The Impossible Dream	
		Strangers in the Night	
		The Ballad of the Green	
		Berets	
		On a Clear Day	
		The Shadow of Your Smile	
		If He Walked Into My Life	

Note: Arranged and conducted by Peter Matz.

Matrix No.	Record No.	Title	Date Recorded
	LPM/LSP 3735	"JUST A CLOSER WALK	Nov. 21–23,
		WITH THEE"	1966
TPRS-6726-3S		Just a Closer Walk with Thee	
		Take My Hand, Precious	
		Lord	
		When I Get to the End of the	
		Way	
		The Door Is Open	
		Room at the Cross for You	
		Ten Thousand Angels	
TPRS-6727-3S		God Is Love	
		An Evening Prayer	
		I Love to Tell the Story	
		Heaven Came Down and	
		Glory Filled My Soul	
		Why Should He Love Me So?	
		Beyond the Sunset	

Note: Arranged and conducted by Glenn Osser.

Matrix No.	Record No.	Title	Date Recorded
	LPM/LSP 3821	"KATE SMITH HERE	March 21–23,
		AND NOW"	1967
UPRS-0363-6S		Anyone Can Move a Moun-	
		tain	

Matrix No.	Record No.	Title	Date Recorded

— RCA VICTOR (continued) —

		That's Life	March 21–23,
		Don't Say Goodbye	1967
		What Makes It Happen?	
		What Is a Woman?	
		I'll Take Care of Your Cares	
UPRS-0364-4S		All	
		Theme from *The Sand Pebbles*	
		(And We Were Lovers)	
		Sherry!	
		My Cup Runneth Over	
		The Splendor of You	
		Pillow Warm (on 8-track car-	Dec. 17, 1964
		tridge only)	

Note: Arranged and conducted by Claus Ogerman.

	LM/LSC 2991	"KATE SMITH / BOSTON	June 8–9, 1967
		POPS / ARTHUR FIED-	
		LER / AMERICA'S FA-	
		VORITES"	
URRS-1585-2S		If It Were Up to Me	
		Danny Boy	
		April in Paris	
		Thine Alone	
		Be My Love*	
		Kiss Me Again	
URRS-1586-3S		Brazil	
		Because*	
		Strange Music	
		For You Alone	
		All the Way	
		When Day Is Done	

Note: Kate Smith was the first vocalist to record with the Boston Pops.
*Also available on compact disc 09026-62578-2.

	LPM/LSP-3870	"SOMETHING SPECIAL:	July 18, 19, 21,
		KATE SMITH"	1967
UPRS-0393-5S		I Think I Like You	
		You Wanted Someone to	
		Play With	
		If You Leave Me Now	
		Love Me Forever	
		A Fool There Was	
		Born Free	
UPRS-0394-2S		Now I Know	
		More and More	
		Someone to Love	
		If You're Not There	
		Misty Blue	

Note: Arranged and conducted by Glenn Osser.

	LSP-4031	"MAY GOD BE WITH YOU"	May 8–10,
WPRS-3977-1S		Say a Little Prayer	1968
		Bless This House	
		Precious Memories	

Matrix No.	Record No.	Title	Date Recorded
		Peace in the Valley	May 8–10,
		My Lord Is Near Me All the Time	1968
		You'll Never Walk Alone	
WPRS-3978-1S		Pass Me Not (O Gentle Savior)	
		Known Only to Him	
		I Believe in Miracles	
		He Touched Me	
		May God Be with You	

Note: Arranged and conducted by Glenn Osser.

Matrix No.	Record No.	Title	Date Recorded
	LSP-4105	"SONGS OF THE NOW GENERATION"	October 22–24, 1968
WPRS-5664-1S		Gentle on My Mind	
		Didn't We?	
		Little Green Apples	
		That's the Way I'll Come to You	
		The "Thank You" Song	
		Yesterday I Heard the Rain	
WPRS-5665-1S		By the Time I Get to Phoenix	
		This Girl's in Love with You	
		Honey	
		Here, There, and Everywhere	
		Mr. Clown	

Note: Arranged and conducted by Peter Matz.

– G U I D E P O S T S –

Matrix No.	Record No.	Title	Date Recorded
	GP-102A	"GUIDEPOSTS TO FREEDOM: KATE SMITH AND NORMAN VINCENT PEALE"	May 1964
R3PM-7798-1		The Sacrifice	
		The Wasp	
		Four Brothers	
		Freedom Is a Barefoot Boy (with Peale)	
		God Bless America (from RCA LPM-2819)	
R3PM-7799-1		It Happened in a Coffeeshop	
		One Small Life	
		Declaration of Dependence (with Peale)	
		The Invasion—When America Prayed	
		The Lord's Prayer (with organ accompaniment)	

Note: All are narrations except "God Bless America" and "The Lord's Prayer." Recorded at RCA Victor's New York studios for *Guideposts* magazine.

Note: The following 4 LPs contain broadcast material:

Matrix No.	Record No.	Title	Date Recorded

— SUNBEAM —

	P-510	"KATE SMITH'S GOLDEN YEARS OF BROAD- CASTING"	
P-510A		I Surrender Dear	1943
		It Was So Beautiful	
		Small Fry	1938
		God Bless America	1943
		The White Cliffs of Dover	1942
		Blues in the Night	
		It's Been a Long, Long Time	1945
		September Song	1946
P-510B		Kerry Dances	1943
		Wait for Me, Mary	
		Fresh as a Daisy	
		Why Don't You Do Right?	
		These Foolish Things	1945
		God Bless America	1943
P-510C		Knee Deep in Star Dust	1941
		How About You?	1942
		Deep in the Heart of Texas	
		Johnny Doughboy Found a Rose in Ireland	
		Comin' in on a Wing and a Prayer	1943
		I'll Be Seeing You	1944
		How Are Things in Glocca Morra	1946
P-510D		If	1951
		The Best Things in Life Are Free	1954
		Medley: Little Old Lady; It's a Lonesome Old Town; Smile, Darn You, Smile; I'll Always Be in Love with You; Home	1960
		I Have Dreamed	1975
		Mame (with Kids Next Door)	1969
		The Way We Were	1975

— SONGBIRD —

KES-1A	KES-1	"KATHRYN ELIZABETH SMITH: THE LADY AND HER MUSIC"	
		Getting to Know You	1951
		The Day After Forever	1944
		One Dozen Roses	1942
		Medley: Mexicali Rose, As Time Goes By, I Had the Craziest Dream	1943
		I Talk to the Trees	1951

Matrix No.	Record No.	Title	Date Recorded
		My Dreams Are Getting Better All the Time	1945
		I Don't Want to Walk Without You	1952
		Saturday Night	1944
		I'll Walk Alone	1948
KES-1B		Wonderful, Wasn't It?	1951
		The Old Lamplighter	1946
		After Graduation Day	1952
		Love Is a Many Splendored Thing	1958
		How Will He Know?	1952
		Medley: The Summer Knows, Song Sung Blue, Didn't We?	1973
		You and Me Against the World	1975
		When the Moon Comes Over the Mountain	1973
	KES-2	"KATE SMITH: MUSIC, MAESTRO, PLEASE"	
KES-2A		Music, Maestro, Please	1952
		This Time It's Real	1938
		Don't Take Your Love from Me	1944
		Suddenly It's Spring	
		This Is Worth Fighting For	1951
		I Only Have Eyes for You	1960
KES-2B		When Day Is Done	1946
		I Hear a Rhapsody	1943
		Boy of Mine	1947
		Time After Time	1960
		Strange Music	1945
		I Love You (from "Mexican Hayride")	1944
		Granada	1960
		Climb Ev'ry Mountain	1966
		Upon My Lips a Song	1960
	KES-3	"A MERRY AMERICAN CHRISTMAS: KATE SMITH"	
KES-3A		A Merry American Christmas	1941
		White Christmas	1943
		"The Christmas Whale" (narration)	1945
		When My Ship Comes In	1934
		The Christmas Song	1960
		O Come, All Ye Faithful	1940
		Toyland	1941
KES-3B		Skater's Waltz (Winter Waltz)	1950
		I'll Be Home for Christmas	1943
		Little Bitty Baby	1951
		"There Really Is a Santa Claus, Isn't There?" (narration)	1949

Matrix No.	Record No.	Title	Date Recorded

— SONGBIRD *(continued)* —

| | | Medley of Winter Songs (with Bing Crosby) Christmas Eve in My Home Town | 1966 |
| | | Ave Maria | 1942 |

Note: Available on Songbird cassette KES-3C.

45 RPM Singles

— CAPITOL —

| | EBF-515 | "TV Curtain Calls"—same as H-515; two-record album | |

— KAPP —

| J90W-8463 | K-237X | The Huckle-Buck (from KL-1082 LP) | |

Note: Disc jockey record. Label reads simply "Kate." Both sides same.

— TOPS —

| E-6018 | 45-5319-A | God Bless America (from LP L-1705) | |
| E-6019 | 45-5319-B | The Music of Home (from *Greenwillow*) | Early 1960 |

— RCA VICTOR —

PHKM-6314-9S	47-8285	In the Summer of His Years	Nov. 29, 1963
PHKM-6315-2S	47-8285	God Bless America (from LPM-2819)	
PHKM-6322	47-8279	What Kind of Fool Am I? (from LPM-2819)	
PHKM-6323	47-8279	As Long as He Needs Me (from LPM-2819)	
RPKM-6906-1	Unissued	Heart to Heart	Dec. 17, 1964
RPKM-6907-1	Unissued	Love, You're Playing Favorites	
RPKM-6909-1	Unissued	Think Spring!	
TPA1-2819	Unissued	A Nightingale Sang in Berkeley Square	Feb. 18, 1966
TPKM-2829-2	Unissued	To Wait for Love	Feb. 21, 1966
TPKM-4275-2	47-9007	Happy Birthday, Dear Christ Child (from LPM-3607)	
TPKM-4276-2	47-9007	Christmas Eve in My Home Town	
TPKM-6623-2	47-9014	If He Walked into My Life (from LPM-3670)	
TPKM-6625-2	47-9014	I Do, I Do (from LPM-3670)	

Matrix No.	Record No.	Title	Date Recorded
UPKM-0348-1	47-9217	Anyone Can Move a Mountain (from LPM-3821)	Feb. 21, 1966
UPKM-0352-2	Unissued	Never Let Me Know	March 21, 1967
UPKM-0353-2	Unissued	San Juan	March 22, 1967
UPKM-0360-1	47-9217	Don't Say Goodbye (from LPM-3821)	
WPKM-2714-3S	47-9495	Masquerade	Feb. 16, 1968
WPKM-2715-2	Unissued	Time	
WPKM-2717-2	Unissued	Nothing Lasts Forever	
WPKM-2718-3S	47-9495	Something to Live For	
WPKM-5671-3	47-9680	The "Thank You" Song (from LSP-4105)	
WPKM-5675-3	47-9680	Gentle on My Mind (from LSP-4105)	

— ATLANTIC —

ST-A-28362-SP	45-3022	A Perfect Love	Nov. 1973
ST-A-28363-SPP	45-3022	Smile, Smile, Smile	

Selected LP Album Reissues

COLUMBIA HARMONY   HL 7393   1966
Ten Columbia 78s from 1940–46: **"When the Moon Comes Over the Mountain."** *Side 1:* When the Moon Comes Over the Mountain; On the Atchison, Topeka, & Santa Fe; Make-Believe Island; The Woodpecker Song; Seems Like Old Times. *Side 2:* There Goes That Song Again (alternate take); Time on My Hands; Here Comes Heaven Again; I'm Stepping Out with a Memory Tonight; Maybe.

TEE-VEE RECORDS   TV-1057   1981
Sixteen Columbia 78s from 1940–46 (special television offer): **"The Incomparable Kate Smith."** *Side 1:* Seems Like Old Times; When the Moon Comes Over the Mountain; I've Got a Gal in Kalamazoo; Shine On, Harvest Moon; Don't Fence Me In; When You Wish Upon a Star; Be Careful, It's My Heart; The Marine's Hymn. *Side 2:* The Star Spangled Banner; My Melancholy Baby; On the Atchison, Topeka, & The Santa Fe; I Don't Want to Walk Without You; America, I Love You; Blues in the Night; Maybe; God Bless America (later recording).

COLUMBIA ENCORE   P14360   1982
Twelve Columbia 78s from 1940–44: **"When the Moon Comes Over the Mountain."** *Side 1:* Imagination; Make-Believe Island; A Nightingale Sang in Berkeley Square; Two Dreams Met; The Last Time I Saw Paris; When the Moon Comes Over the Mountain. *Side 2:* When Day Is Done; Don't Fence Me In (alternate take); Blues in the Night (alternate take); I've Got a Gal in Kalamazoo; My Heart Sings (unissued in USA as 78); God Bless America (later recording).

CBS SPECIAL PRODUCTS: **"Kate Smith: Her Classic CBS Records"**   1986
Side 1: God Bless America (recorded later); The White Cliffs of Dover; There Goes That Song Again; The Woodpecker Song; The Last Time I Saw Paris; A Nightingale Sang in Berkeley Square; I'm Stepping Out with a Memory Tonight; Maybe. *Side 2:* If I Had My Way; Shine On, Harvest Moon; Somebody Else Is Taking My Place; I've Got a Gal in Kalamazoo; When You Wish Upon a Star; We'll Meet Again; On the Atchison, Topeka, & The Santa Fe.
Note: Comes with RCA Special Products LP **"Kate Smith: Her Famous RCA Records"** (see below).

MGM   E-3487   1957
Twelve MGM 78s from 1947–49: **"Kate Smith: Memory Lane."** *Side 1:* Memory Lane; Now Is the Hour; Dancing with Tears in My Eyes; Far Away Places; Tears on My Pillow; Anniversary Song. *Side 2:* Till We Meet Again; Dreamy Old New England Moon; I Only Have Eyes for You; If I Had My Life to Live Over; When I Lost You; Beautiful Dreamer.
Note: Reissued in 1964 as **"The Very Best of Kate Smith,"** with "God Bless America" replacing "Memory Lane," #E/SE-4220.

RCA VICTOR   **"The Best of Kate Smith"**   LPM/LSP-3970   1967
Side 1: When the Moon Comes Over the Mountain; That's Life; Born Free; The Impossible Dream; Climb Ev'ry Mountain; I Left My Heart in San Francisco. *Side 2:* You're Nobody 'Til Somebody Loves You; Medley: Somebody Else is Taking My Place, That Old Feeling, There Goes That Song Again; Theme from *The Sand Pebbles*; God Bless America.
Note: Also available on cassette #AYK1-3845 and compact disc 0763-53845-2.

"The Best of Kate Smith: Sacred"   LSP 4258   1969
Side 1: Were You There?; How Great Thou Art; It Took a Miracle; Take My Hand, Precious Lord; Ten Thousand Angels. *Side 2:* God Is Love; I Love to Tell the Story; Pass Me Not; He Touched Me; The Lord's Prayer.

"Kate Smith: A Legendary Performer"   CPLI-2661   1978
One of a beautifully packaged series, with artist's drawing suitable for framing, plus a 12"×12" illustrated biographical booklet. *Side 1:* When the Moon Comes Over the Mountain; I'll Be Seeing You; Medley: Please, Don't Blame Me, Fine and Dandy; Medley: How Are Things in Glocca Morra, The White Cliffs of Dover, Don't Sit Under the Apple Tree. *Side 2:* Anyone Can Move a Mountain; Medley: Margie, Carolina Moon, When Your Lover Has Gone; Danke Schoen; This Is All I Ask; God Bless America / When the Moon Comes Over the Mountain.

"Kate Smith: Her Famous RCA Records"   #DVK1-0752
(RCA Special Products)   1986
Side 1: When the Moon Comes Over the Mountain; Moon River; Somewhere My Love; Yesterday; Misty Blue; Honey; Beautiful Isle of Somewhere; Bless This House. *Side 2:* April in Paris; I'll Be Seeing You; White Christmas; More; When Day Is Done; May the Good Lord Bless and Keep You; Climb Ev'ry Mountain.
Note: Comes with Columbia LP **"Kate Smith: Her Classic CBS Records"** (see above).

READER'S DIGEST RECORDS
In 1981 a boxed set of six LPs, all from RCA Victor LPs, was reissued, including a fine illustrated 12"×12" booklet.

"America's Favorite: Kate Smith"   RCA Custom RD4A-029

In 1983 a *Reader's Digest* LP titled **"Kate Smith Sings Inspirational Favorites"** was released, #RDA-012/D, containing:
Side 1: Climb Ev'ry Mountain; I Believe in Miracles; Born Free; The Impossible Dream; Danny Boy; Anyone Can Move a Mountain. *Side 2:* An Evening Prayer; Ten Thousand Angels; It Took a Miracle; Say a Little Prayer; Pass Me Not; God Is Love.

BOOK OF THE MONTH RECORDS
"Kate Smith—Hello Everybody!"   Boxed set #6667   3 LPs, mostly of vintage Columbia 78s (1926–46), released in 1982. Also on two cassettes.

SUNBEAM
"Kate Smith Sings 'God Bless America'"   HB-307   1974
Reissue of sixteen 78s: six RCA Victor and ten Columbia. *Side 1:* When the Moon Comes Over the Mountain (Collins special); You're a Sweetheart; I Cried for You; Bei Mir Bist Du Schoen; Sioux City Sue; Seems Like Old Times; Maybe; America, I Love You. *Side 2:* God Bless America; The Sunshine of Your Smile; On the Atchison, Topeka, & Santa Fe; Rose O'Day; My Melancholy Baby; Somebody Loves Me; Can't Get Indiana Off My Mind; The Star Spangled Banner.

"Miss Kate Smith" MFC-13 1975
Reissue of sixteen Columbia 78s from 1926–31. *Side 1:* When the Moon Comes Over the Mountain; The Little White House; One Sweet Letter from You; I'm Gonna Meet My Sweetie Now; He's a Good Man to Have Around; Moanin' Low; Waiting at the End of the Road; Just Another Day Wasted Away. *Side 2:* I May Be Wrong; Sharing; I Got Rhythm; Wabash Moon; Grievin'; Shine On, Harvest Moon; I Apologize; Good Night, Sweetheart.

"Sincerely, Kate Smith" P-516 1984
Reissue of thirteen 78s dating from 1930–34, plus audition disc from 1934. *Side 1:* I Don't Know Why; That's Why Darkies Were Born; "Face the Music" Medley; River, Stay 'Way from My Door; Too Late; You Don't Want Me Anymore; I Don't Mind Walkin' in the Rain. *Side 2:* An Old Fashioned Waltz; Pickaninnies' Heaven; College Rhythm; When My Ship Comes In; Medley from "Hot-Cha"; Dancing with Tears in My Eyes; The Continental.

Compact Discs

RCA VICTOR
"Kate Smith: Songs of Faith and Inspiration" RD 194-C 1988
Note: Available only as a premium when ordering *Reader's Digest* Mormon Tabernacle Choir CD set.
May the Good Lord Bless and Keep You; My Cup Runneth Over; I May Never Pass This Way Again; The Door Is Open; Peace in the Valley; How Great Thou Art; It Is No Secret; Just a Closer Walk with Thee; I Love to Tell the Story; Beyond the Sunset.

PICKWICK reissue of Tops recordings.
"Kate Smith: God Bless America" PMTD 16007 1989
Oklahoma; Carolina Moon; In Old New York / Sidewalks of New York; Moonlight in Vermont; Down in the Valley; Scarlet Ribbons; On Top of Old Smokey; My Old Kentucky Home; Kisses Sweeter Than Wine; Stars Fell on Alabama; The Yellow Rose of Texas / Deep in the Heart of Texas; Blue Tail Fly; Beautiful Ohio; Back Home in Indiana; Greensleeves; God Bless America.
Note: Reissued on LaserLight label with different cover, #15 380, in 1991.

PROARTE. Eighteen 78s from 1929–39.
"Kate Smith: God Bless America" CDD 518 1990
When the Moon Comes Over the Mountain; Tell Me with a Love Song; Waiting at the End of the Road; Moanin' Low; I Don't Mind Walking in the Rain; Maybe It's Love; I Got Rhythm; Held by the Spell of the Moon; Kate Smith Presents a Memory Program; You Try Somebody Else; All of Me; River Stay 'Way from My Door; Too Late; I Don't Know Why; Twenty Million People; When My Ship Comes In; When the Moon Comes Over the Mountain (Collins Special swing version); God Bless America.
Note: Also available on cassette #PCD-518.

CURB. All twelve songs from Capitol T-515 plus "God Bless America" (RCA Victor, 1939).
"The Best of Kate Smith" #D2-77475 1991
Note: Also available on cassette #D4-77475.

GOOD MUSIC COMPANY **"The Golden Voice of Kate Smith"** #KSK 1991
Reissue of Pickwick CD: "Kate Smith: God Bless America," plus broadcast recordings of: When Your Lover Has Gone (edited); How Many Hearts Have You Broken?; Saturday Night; Don't Fence Me In; The Trolley Song; and 1941 Columbia record of "When the Moon Comes Over the Mountain" (edited).
Note: Also available on cassettes.

COLUMBIA (CBS/SONY). Reissue of fifteen Columbia 78s from 1940–46 plus "Memories of You," previously unissued.
"Kate Smith: 16 Most Requested Songs" #46097 1991
When the Moon Comes Over the Mountain; On the Atchison, Topeka, & The Santa Fe; When You Wish Upon a Star; I've Got a Gal in Kalamazoo; Tumbling Tumbleweeds; Be

(COLUMBIA *continued*)   Careful, It's My Heart; Imagination; Time Was; My Melancholy Baby; Memories of You; Somebody Loves Me; The Last Time I Saw Paris; One Dozen Roses; My Buddy; Embraceable You; We'll Meet Again.
Note: Also available on cassette #CT 46097.

TAKE TWO RECORDS. Reissue of twenty 78s dating from the thirties.
"Kate Smith: Emergence of a Legend"   #TT-401   1991
Maybe It's Love; You'll Never Know, Sweetheart; Here Comes the Sun; Now's the Time; You Didn't Have to Tell Me; Makin' Faces at the Man in the Moon; If I Have to Go on Without You; When the Moon Comes Over the Mountain; You Call It Madness; River, Stay 'Way from My Door; Snuggled on Your Shoulder; Love, You Funny Thing!; By the Fireside; Twenty Million People; My Queen of Lullaby Land; The Continental; There's a Gold Mine in the Sky; Bei Mir Bist Du Schoen; It's Never Too Late; I Cried for You.

LASERLIGHT. Reissue of fifteen Tops recordings from 1959.
"Kate Smith Christmas"   #15414   1991
Deck the Halls; White Christmas; Hark the Herald Angels Sing; The First Noel; O Come All Ye Faithful; Santa Claus Is Coming to Town; He's Got the Whole World in His Hands; Greensleeves; Joy to the World; O Little Town of Bethlehem; God Rest Ye Merry, Gentlemen; Moonlight in Vermont; It Came Upon a Midnight Clear; Silent Night; Jingle Bells.

Cassettes Only

SONGBIRD KES-6C   **"Kate Smith on the Air: The Fabulous Forties—Volume 1"** 1990.
Side 1: I'm Stepping Out with a Memory Tonight; A Nightingale Sang in Berkeley Square; I Don't Want to Set the World on Fire; The G.I. Jive; Long Ago (and Far Away); Lucky to Be Me; But Beautiful. *Side 2:* Tess's Torch Song; Paper Doll; Every Time We Say Goodbye; You'd Be So Nice to Come Home To; Wonder When My Baby's Coming Home; I'll Be Seeing You.

STAR LINE #SLC-61010   **"Kate Smith: First Lady of Song"**
Same contents as TOPS "God Bless America" LP.

RCA Special Products #DVK1-0752   **"Home Town Christmas: Bing Crosby and Kate Smith"**
Side 1 by Bing Crosby. *Side 2* by Kate Smith: Medley: Deck the Halls, Joy to the World, It Came Upon a Midnight Clear; Silver Bells; I Heard the Bells on Christmas Day; Christmas Eve in My Home Town; It's Beginning to Look Like Christmas.

DEMAND PERFORMANCE   **"The Great Kate"** #DPC-716
Eight from TOPS LP of the same name: *Side 1:* You'd Be So Nice to Come Home To; Tenderly; People Will Say We're in Love; Don't Worry 'Bout Me. *Side 2:* I Concentrate on You; Side by Side; So Beats My Heart for You; I'm Getting Sentimental Over You.

Filmography

Kate Smith—Songbird of the South. Vitaphone short subject #817. June 29, 1929. Released in 1930.
After an introduction by the Vitaphone Orchestra, Kate Smith sings "Carolina Moon" and "Bless You Sister" in a drawing room setting. One reel Ca.10 minutes.

Newsreel. August 26, 1931. Kate Smith is shown with a large group of World War I veterans and a piano outside the Brooklyn, New York, navy hospital, singing "When the Moon Comes Over the Mountain." Ca.1 minute.

Rambling Round Radio Row. The first in a series of twelve Vitaphone short subjects. No. 1408. Ca. April 1932. With Jerry Wald, Sid Garry, the Boswell Sisters, Abe Lyman, Stoopnagle and Budd, Nat Brusiloff, Jack Miller, and Kate Smith. The last three are in the last scene. Brusiloff was bandleader and violinist, Miller was pianist, Smith sings "Whistle and Blow Your Blues Away." Ca.10 minutes.

Paramount Pictorial. Ca. May 1932. Three vignettes: a biologist shows animals from the Gobi Desert; autumn trees and leaf-raking; "Ted Collins: Talent Scout," includes Cliff Ukulele Ike" Edwards, pianist Jack Miller, and Kate Smith, who sings a chorus of "When Work Is Through" and part of "When the Moon Comes Over the Mountain." Ca.10 minutes.

The Big Broadcast. Paramount, 1932. Kate Smith has a four-minute cameo in this feature picture starring Bing Crosby and Stuart Erwin. In her cameo, made in Paramount's Astoria, New York, studio, she sings a few bars of "When the Moon Comes Over the Mountain," then "It Was So Beautiful." July (?) 1932.

Hello Everybody! Paramount, 1933. Kate Smith's only feature picture, filmed in Hollywood November–December 1932 and released January 1933. Director: William A. Seiter. Story by Fannie Hurst. Screenplay by Dorothy Yost and Lawrence Hazard. Music composed by Arthur Johnston and Sam Coslow. Costars are Randolph Scott (Hunt Blake), Sally Blane (Kate's sister Lily), Charley Grapewin (farmhand Jed), with Julia Swayne Gordon (Mother Smith), Jerry Tucker (Bobby), Marguerite Churchill (Bettina), William B. Davidson (Mr. Parker), George Barbier (Mr. Blair), Paul Kruger (Mr. Lindle), Fern Emmett (Ettie), Irving Bacon (Joe), Frank Darien (Mr. Thompson), Edward Davis (Mr. Eldredge), Russell Simpson (Horton), and Ted Collins as himself. Ca.70 minutes. Smith sings part of "When the Moon Comes Over the Mountain," as well as "Moon Song," "Out in the Great Open Spaces," "Twenty Million People," "Pickaninnies' Heaven," a chorus of "Dinah" (followed by a memorable Charleston dance), and "My Queen of Lullaby Land." Nat Brusiloff is shown conducting the orchestra in the "Central Park Casino" simulated scene.

Hollywood on Parade. No. 11, Paramount, June 1933. Produced by Lewis Lewyn. Cast: Jackie Searle, Charles Ray, Barbara Stanwyck, Jane Withers, Fifi D'Orsay, Frank Fay, Arline Judge, Wesley Ruggles, Kate Smith, Ted Collins. Ted Collins appears in a radio station set and talks with Kate Smith, who sings "Here Lies Love" (from *The Big Broadcast*). Ca. 12 minutes.

America Sings with Kate Smith. Columbia, 1942. Ted Collins introduces the picture (though he is not seen). Kate Smith gives patriotic messages, sings "We're All Americans," "The Caissons Go Rolling Along," "The Marines' Hymn," and "America, I Love You." Jack Miller conducts the orchestra. The second chorus of each song is to be sung by Smith and the theatre audience and lyrics are shown. Ca.12 minutes.

This Is the Army. Warner Bros., 1943. All Irving Berlin musical. Smith's five-minute cameo was filmed on or about May 1, 1943, in Hollywood. It is a simulation of her radio introduction of "God Bless America." She sings the verse and three choruses. Regarded as a highlight of this most important World War II musical. Color.

Note: Columbia Pictures in 1974 edited and compiled eight vintage short subjects into *The Three Stooges Follies.* Included was *America Sings with Kate Smith* as the finale.

It has been reported that Kate Smith in 1932 made a short subject film of her Columbia record, *Kate Smith Presents a Memory Program*, including "Old Folks at Home," "Grandfather's Clock," "Songs My Mother Taught Me," and "Seeing Nellie Home."

Kate Smith appears in an unknown number of newsreels, including one in 1945 with Mayor Fiorello LaGuardia, singing "Sidewalks of New York."

Several cartoons have included caricatures or mentions of Kate Smith, including the 1934 color cartoon "Toyland Broadcast" (MGM) and a "Snoopy" cartoon. In the Vitaphone short subject "Nutville" (1932), the Radio Ramblers do a takeoff of Kate Smith singing her theme song.

APPENDIX C

Broadcast History

Radio

Kate Smith was heard from time to time over local radio stations in the Washington, D.C., area during the period 1923–26. Her first network broadcast was Thursday, April 4, 1929, in an NBC coast-to-coast special broadcast starring Sophie Tucker, Ted Lewis, and Nick Lucas.

"Freddy Rich's Rhythm Kings." 5:45–6 P.M. Mondays. Winter, 1930-31.

"Kate Smith Sings." NBC, 11:30–11:45 P.M. Tu, Th. March 17–April 23, 1931. She first used her theme song, "When the Moon Comes Over the Mountain," on these broadcasts. Sustaining.

"Kate Smith Sings." CBS, 7:45–8 P.M. M, W, Th, Sat. First broadcast Sunday, April 26, 1931. Sustaining. Moved to 7–7:15 P.M. as of May 24, replacing Morton Downey. On six days a week through Sept. 12.

"Kate Smith and Her Swanee Music." CBS, 8:30–8:45 P.M. M, W, Th, Sat. Sept. 14– Nov. 28, 1931. Sponsor: LaPalina Cigars (Congress Cigar Co.).
From Dec. 1, 1931–June 2, 1932, M, Tu, W, Th.
From June 6–Dec. 28, 1932, M, Tu, W.
From Jan. 3–June 1, 1933, Tu, W, Th.
From June 5–Sept. 13, 1933, M, Tu, W.
From Sept. 18–Oct. 31, 1933, Sustaining.

"Kate Smith and Her Swanee Music." CBS, 8–8:15 P.M. M, Th, F. Sustaining. July 16– Nov. 26, 1934.

"Kate Smith's Matinee Hour." CBS, 3–4 P.M. Wednesdays. Variety show. Sept. 26–Dec. 26, 1934. Sustaining. Bob Trout, announcer.

"Kate Smith's New Star Revue." CBS, Mondays, 8:30–9 P.M. Variety and talent search. Sponsor: Hudson-Terraplane Motor Car Co. Dec. 24, 1934–May 27, 1935.

"Kate Smith's Hour." May 30–Sept. 5, 1935. CBS, Thursdays, 8–9 P.M. Variety hour. Sustaining.

"Kate Smith's Coffee Time." CBS, 7:30–7:45 P.M. Tu, W, Th. Oct. 1, 1935–June 25, 1936. June 30–Sept. 10, 1936, Tu, Th. Sponsor: Great Atlantic & Pacific Tea Co. Red Circle, Bokar, Eight O'Clock Coffees.

Note: A one-hour A & P all-star special was broadcast Sunday, March 15, 1936, from 8–9 P.M. to "test the waters" for a weekly hour variety program.

"Kate Smith's A & P Bandwagon." CBS, 8–9 P.M. Thursdays. Sept. 17, 1936–June 24, 1937. Variety hour. Sponsor: A & P Coffees.

"Kate Smith Hour." CBS, 8–9 P.M. Thursdays. Rebroadcast to West Coast 12 P.M.–1 A.M. Sponsor: General Foods (Swansdown Cake Flour and Calumet Baking Powder). Announcer: André Baruch. Variety hour.

Sept. 30, 1937–June 23, 1938, and Sept. 29, 1938–June 29, 1939.

Moved to Fridays, 8–8:55 P.M. Oct. 6, 1939–June 28, 1940; Sept. 20, 1940–June 27, 1941; Oct. 3, 1941–June 26, 1942; Sept. 18, 1942–Jan. 1, 1943. Advertising General Food products Grape Nuts cereal, Jell-O.

Reduced to 25 minutes (8:30–8:55 P.M. Fridays) Jan. 8–June 25, 1943. Resumed 8–8:55 P.M. Oct. 1, 1943–June 9, 1944.

Moved to Sundays, 7–8 P.M. Sept. 17, 1944–June 10, 1945. Advertising Jell-O and Sanka.

"Kate Smith 'Speaking Her Mind.'" CBS, 3:30–3:45 P.M. M, W, F. Commentary program. April 4–June 17, 1938. Sustaining.

From Oct. 4, 1938–May 27(?), 1939, 12–12:15 P.M. Tu, Th, Sat. Sponsor: General Foods (Diamond Crystal Shaker Salt).

From Oct. 2, 1939, to the end of its run, **"Kate Smith Speaks"** was broadcast M–F 12–12:15 P.M., 52 weeks per year. CBS: Oct. 2, 1939–June 20, 1947, sponsored by General Foods.

From June 23, 1947–June 15, 1951, Mutual. Various sponsors. *Note:* Broadcast from tiny studio in boathouse at Camp Sunshine, Lake Placid, summers 1940–50.

"Kate Smith Sings." CBS, Fridays, 8:30–8:55 P.M. Sept. 14, 1945–June 28, 1946. Advertised Postum, a General Foods beverage. Moved to Sun., 6:30–7 P.M. Oct. 6, 1946–June 29, 1947. *Note:* All music program with no audience Sept. 14–Dec. 28, 1945. Variety show with audience after that.

"Kate Smith Sings." Mutual, Sept. 20, 1948–April 22, 1949. Sponsor: Flagstaff Jellies and others. Kate Smith and Ted Collins act as disc jockeys playing Kate Smith records. Continued 1949–51 (dates uncertain).

"Kate Smith Calling." ABC, Mondays 9–11 P.M. Combination of commentary, music, and Smith making telephone calls to listeners. Sept. 1949–June 1950.

"Kate Smith Show." NBC, 12:05–1 P.M. Oct. ?, 1951–Sept. ?, 1952. Mixture of commentary by Kate Smith and Ted Collins, Kate Smith records, and occasional guests. Broadcast from Lake Placid summer 1952.

"Kate Smith Show." Mutual, 10:05–10:30 A.M. M–F. Description same as above NBC program. Jan. 6, 1958–Jan. 2, 1959. Sponsored mainly by Scranton Lace Co. and Reader's Digest Condensed Books.

GUEST APPEARANCES

1. NBC Special. Thurs., April 4, 1929.
2. "Saks and Company." CBS. Mon., May 26, 1930.
3. Introduced "You'll Never Know, Sweetheart" on the air. CBS. Wed., Oct. 22, 1930.
4. "Rudy Vallée Fleischmann Sunshine Hour." NBC. Thurs., Oct. 30, 1930.
5. "The Roxy Gang." NBC. Mon., Nov. 3, 1930.
6–7. "Ludwig Baumann Hour." NBC. Nov., Dec., 1930.
8–9. "Rudy Vallee Fleischmann Sunshine Hour." NBC. Thurs., Jan. 8, 1931, Thurs., April 9, 1931.
10–11. "Walter Winchell and Guest Artist." CBS. Thurs., July 9, Tues., Oct. 27, 1931.
12. "Mobilization for Human Needs." CBS. Sun., Nov. 1, 1931.
13–14. "Meet the Artist" (Winchell). CBS. Tues., Aug. 30, 1932, May 31, 1933.
15. "Studebaker Champions Hour." CBS. Mon., Dec. 25, 1933.
16. American Red Cross Roll Call. CBS. Sun., Nov. 9, 1935. M.C.
17–19. American Red Cross. CBS. W–F, Jan. 27–29, 1937. Flood relief.
20. "Nash Speed Show." CBS. Sun., Feb. 13, 1937.
21. "Richard Himber Show." NBC. Mon., April 26, 1937, Guest M.C.
22. "Robert Benchley Show." CBS. Thurs., Feb. 24, 1938.

23. "Jack Benny Program." NBC. Sun., March 27, 1938.
24. "Benny Goodman's Camel Caravan." CBS. Sat., Oct. 22, 1938.
25. "Aunt Jenny's Real Life Stories." CBS. Fri., Oct. 6, 1939. Via telephone.
26. "Bob Hope Pepsodent Show." NBC. Tues., April 1, 1941.
27. "Command Performance." Armed Forces Radio (AFRS). March 15, 1942. Program #3. M.C. Kate Smith was heard on numerous Armed Forces broadcasts, including "Command Performance" and "Mail Call," weekly 30-minute variety shows, and the 15-minute musical program, "Personal Album."
28. "Spirit of '42." CBS. Sun., April 17, 1942.
29. "Coca Cola Program." With André Kostelanetz and His Orchestra. Sun., May 30, 1943. Sang "My Heart at Thy Sweet Voice."
30. "We, the People." CBS. Sun., May 21, 1944. Sang "We're All Americans."
31. "Philco Radio Hall of Fame." Sun., May 28, 1944. Sang "G.I. Jive."
32. "It Pays to Be Ignorant." NBC. Fri., Dec. 8, 1944. Guest, with Ted Collins.
33. "We, the People." CBS. Mon., May 14, 1945. With Irving Berlin.
34. "Tribute to the late Major Glenn Miller." NBC. Sun., June 3, 1945.
35. "Al Smith Memorial Drive." Wed., Oct. 31, 1945.
36. "Philco Radio Hall of Fame." Sun., Dec. 2, 1945. Sang "It's Been a Long, Long Time"; "If I Loved You"; "God Bless America." Told children's story "The Christmas Whale."
37. "Sister Kenny Fund Program." Saturday, Nov. 16, 1946. With Bing Crosby and Ted Collins. Sang "Somewhere in the Night" and "You Keep Coming Back Like a Song."
38–39. "It Pays to Be Ignorant." January 1947. Smith substituted for Lulu McConnell for at least two weeks when McConnell was ill.

Note: Kate Smith appeared on several "Here's to Veterans" and "Guest Star" programs from the mid-forties through the fifties.

Television

Kate Smith appeared on the first CBS experimental television program. The date was Tuesday, July 21, 1931, from 10–10:45 P.M. The station was W2XAB.

"The Kate Smith Hour." A live daytime variety hour. NBC. 4–5 P.M. M–F for three seasons:
Sept. 25, 1950–June 22, 1951.
Sept. 10, 1951–June 6, 1952.
Sept. 8, 1952–June 5, 1953.
M–F 3–4 P.M. Sept. 21, 1953–June 18, 1954.

"The Kate Smith Evening Hour." A live prime time variety hour. NBC, Wed. 8–9 P.M. Sept. 19, 1951–June 11, 1952. Sponsors: Reynolds Aluminum, Norge, B. T. Babbitt (Bab-O), Congoleum-Nairn.

"The Kate Smith Hour." ABC, 9–10 P.M. Sunday, April 28, 1957. A one-time special commemorating Kate Smith's 26th anniversary in broadcasting. Sponsor: Youngstown Kitchens.

"The Kate Smith Show." All music show. CBS, 7:30–8 P.M. Mondays, Jan. 25–July 18, 1960. Last live show June 6; six shows repeated June–July. Sponsors: Whitehall Pharmaceuticals and Boyle-Midway Division of American Home Products Corporation.

"The Kate Smith Show." Columbia Screen Gems. Feb., 1969. A one-time syndicated special. Local sponsors.

"Kate Smith: Remembrances and Rock." Filmed by Columbia Screen Gems. 1973. A one-time syndicated special. Local sponsors.

GUEST APPEARANCES

1. "Milton Berle Texaco Star Theatre." NBC. Tues., Nov. 13, 1951.
2–3. "Stage Show," starring Tommy and Jimmy Dorsey. CBS. Sat., March 12, and Sat., May 7, 1955.

4–7. "Toast of the Town" (Ed Sullivan Show). CBS. Sun., Dec. 4, 1955, April 29, 1956 (25th anniversary), May 27, 1956, June 24, 1956.

8–10. "Ed Sullivan Show." CBS. Sun., Oct. 7, 1956, Dec. 9, 1956, Jan. 13, 1957.

11–12. "Jackie Gleason Show" (guest hostess). CBS. Sat., March 16 and April 14, 1957.

13–14. "Ed Sullivan Show." CBS. Sun., Oct. 6, Nov. 10, 1957.

15. "The Big Record," starring Patti Page. CBS. Wed., Dec. 11, 1957.

16–17. "The Perry Como Show." NBC. Sat., March 1 and Dec. 13, 1958.

18. "The Eddie Fisher Show." NBC. Tues., Jan. 6, 1959.

19–20. "Tennessee Ernie Ford Show." NBC. Thurs., Jan. 15 and Jan. 22, 1959.

21. "Garry Moore Show." CBS. Tues., April 7, 1959.

22. "Startime Show." NBC. Tues., Oct. 6, 1959. Special.

23. "Once Upon a Christmastime." NBC. Dec. 9, 1959. Special Christmas musical fantasy.

24–25. "Tennessee Ernie Ford Show." NBC. Thurs., Dec. 17, 1959, and Dec. 22, 1960.

26–28. "Ed Sullivan Show." CBS. Sun., Jan. 21, June 24, Oct. 21, 1962.

29. "Andy Williams Show." NBC. Thurs., Jan. 3, 1963.

30. "Ed Sullivan Show." CBS. March 3, 1963.

31. "Jack Paar Show." NBC. Fri., April 26, 1963.

32–34. "Ed Sullivan Show." CBS. Sun., May 19, Aug. 4 (taped), Oct. 6, 1963.

35. "Jack Paar Show." NBC. Fri., Nov. 1, 1963.

36. "What's My Line?" CBS. Sun., Nov. 3, 1963. Mystery guest.

37. "Ed Sullivan Show." CBS. Sun., Jan. 19, 1964.

38. "ABC Hollywood Palace." Sat., Feb. 29, 1964.

39. "Jack Paar Show." NBC. Fri., Dec. 25, 1964.

40. "ABC Hollywood Palace" (hostess). Sat., Jan. 23, 1965.

41. "Ed Sullivan Show." CBS. Sun., Oct. 10, 1965.

42. "Dean Martin Show." NBC. Thurs., Nov. 11, 1965.

43. "ABC Hollywood Palace" (hostess). Sat., Jan. 8, 1966.

44–45. "Dean Martin Show." NBC. Thurs., Feb. 10 and 24, 1966.

46. "NBC Tonight Show," starring Johnny Carson. Mon., April 4, 1966.

47. "Ed Sullivan Show." CBS. Sun., May 15, 1966.

48. "NBC London Palladium Show." Fri., June 6, 1966. Hostess.

49. "Dean Martin Show." NBC. Thurs., Oct. 20, 1966.

50. "Andy Williams Show." NBC. Sun., Oct. 30, 1966.

51. "NBC Tonight Show," starring Johnny Carson. Thurs., Dec. 1, 1966.

52. "ABC Hollywood Palace." Sat., Dec. 24, 1966.

53. "Dean Martin Show." NBC. Thurs., Jan. 19, 1967.

54. "ABC Hollywood Palace." Sat., March 11, 1967. Hostess.

55. "Smothers Brothers Comedy Hour." CBS. Sun., Oct. 15, 1967.

56. "Dean Martin Show." NBC. Thurs., Nov. 23, 1967.

57. "Jackie Gleason Show." CBS. Sat., Dec. 30, 1967.

58. "Kraft Music Hall." NBC. Wed., Oct. 2, 1968.

59. "Beautiful Phyllis Diller Show." CBS. Sun., Oct. 20, 1968.

60. "Smothers Brothers Comedy Hour." CBS. Sun., Nov. 10, 1968.

61. "Jonathan Winters Show." CBS. Wed., Nov. 27, 1968.

62. "Rowan and Martin's Laugh-In." NBC. Mon., Dec. 30, 1968.

63. "What's It All About, World?" ABC. Thurs., March 6, 1969.

64. "Dean Martin Show." NBC. Thurs., March 20, 1969.

65. "Kraft Music Hall." NBC. Wed., April 16, 1969.

66. "Jim Nabors Hour." CBS. Thurs., Oct. 21, 1969.

67. "Jimmy Durante Presents the Lennon Sisters." ABC. Fri., Nov. 21, 1969.

68. "Andy Williams Show." NBC. Sat., Jan. 17, 1970.

69. "Dean Martin Show." NBC. Thurs., Feb. 12, 1970.

70. "Honor America Day." Wed., July 4, 1970. Morning and afternoon.

71. "Jim Nabors Hour." CBS. Thurs., Oct. 1, 1970.

72. "Andy Williams Show." NBC. Sat., Nov. 7, 1970.

73. "Lawrence Welk Show." ABC. Sat., Jan. 23, 1971.

74. "Pearl Bailey Show." ABC. Sat., Feb. 20, 1971.

75. "Sonny and Cher Show." CBS. Mon., Jan. 17, 1972.
76. "NBC Tonight Show." Mon., April 2, 1973. Hostess.
77. "Entertainer of the Year Awards" (American Guild of Variety Artists). CBS. Sat., Jan. 26, 1974.
78–82. "Mike Douglas Show." Westinghouse. Mon.–Fri., May 13–17, 1974. Cohost.
83. "Smothers Brothers Show." NBC. Mon., Jan. 20, 1975.
84–85. "Tony Orlando and Dawn Show." CBS. Wed., Jan. 29, 1975, and Wed., March 19, 1975.
86. "Cher Show." CBS. Sun., April 27, 1975.
87. "NBC Tomorrow Show" (Tom Snyder, host). NBC. Thurs., June 19, 1975.
88. "Tony Orlando and Dawn Show." CBS. Wed., Oct. 1, 1975.
89. Howard Cosell's "Saturday Night Live." ABC. Sat., Oct. 25, 1975.
90. "Donny and Marie (Osmond) Special." ABC. Sun., Nov. 16, 1975.
91. "Tony Orlando and Dawn Show." CBS. Wed., Dec. 10, 1975.
92. "Tournament of Roses Parade." ABC, CBS, NBC. Thurs., Jan. 1, 1976. Grand Marshal.
93. Rose Bowl Game. Thurs., Jan. 1, 1976. Sang "God Bless America" at opening ceremonies.
94. "Tony Orlando and Dawn Show." CBS. Wed., Feb. 4, 1976.
95. "Donny and Marie Show." ABC. Fri., Feb. 20, 1976.
96. "Mac Davis Show." ABC. Thurs., April 1, 1976.
97. "Women of the Year Awards Show." Thurs., April 8, 1976.
98. "Hollywood Squares." Wed., May 12, 1976. She was on for a week leading up to this date.
99. "Stars and Stripes Show." Wed., June 30, 1976. Two hour special for bicentennial from Oklahoma City.
100. "Emmy Awards Show." Tues., Sept. 19, 1982.

APPENDIX D

Sheet Music

These songsheets contain Kate Smith's picture on the cover. Where a number in square brackets follows a title, there are two or more variations of the cover. Where a date is missing, the date is not known.

After Awhile (1945)
After Taps (1942)
All Ashore (1938)
All That I'm Asking Is Sympathy (1929)
Aloha Beloved (1932)
Alone at a Table for Two (1935)
Along a Texas Trail (1937)
Along 'Bout Sundown (1941)
Always Yours (1944)
An Apple Blossom Wedding (1947)
And Then Your Lips Met Mine (1930)
An Old Fashioned Home in New Hampshire (1931)
An Old Fashioned Waltz (There's Nothing Like) (1934)
An Old, Old Man (1933)
At Your Beck and Call (1933)

Bless Your Heart (1933)
Blue Again (1930)
The Blue Bugle Call (1932)
Blue Skies Are 'Round the Corner (1938)
By a Little Bayou (1932)
(In the Gloaming) By the Fireside (1932)
By the River Ste. Marie (1931)

Cabin in the Carolines (1938)
Cabin in the Cotton (1932)
Cabin in the Sky (1940)
Call of the Canyon (1941)
Can't Get Indiana Off My Mind (1940)
Can't We Dream a Midsummer's Dream? (1935)
Can't You Read Between the Lines (1945)

Carolina Moon (1927)
Carolina Sweetheart (1938)
Christmas Eve in My Home Town (1951)
The Clouds Will Soon Roll By (1932)
Colorado Moon (1933)
Concerto for Two (1941)
Connecticut (Is the Place for Me) (1946)
Crying Myself to Sleep (1930)
Cupid's Holiday (1931)

Daddy's Letter (1942)
Dancing in a Dream with You (1941)
Darn That Dream (1939)
Day In, Day Out (1939)
Deep Water
Did Your Mother Come from Ireland? (1936)
Don't Blame Me (1933)
Don't Cry, Cherie (1941)
Don't Do Anything I Wouldn't Do (1933)
Don't Forget Me in Your Dreams
Don't Worry, Mom (1944)
Down by the Old Mill Stream (1931)
Dream a Little Dream of Me (1931)
Dreams Are a Dime a Dozen (1946)

Foggy River (1948)
For All We Know (1934)
Funny Little Snowman (1938)

The Glory of Love (1936)
God Bless America [3, no pic] (1939)
Goodnight, My Love (1936)
Goody Goody (1936)
Guilty (1931)

272

The Harbor of Home Sweet Home (1933)
Have It Your Way, Foolish Heart (1938)
Heart-Breaker (1933)
Heavenly Hideaway (1942)
Heaven Only Knows (1933)
Hello Beautiful (1931)
Here Comes the Navy (1943)
Here Comes the Sun (1930)
Here Lies Love (1932)
He Wears a Pair of Silver Wings (1942)
Hiawatha's Lullaby (1933)
Hi-Ho-Lack-a-Day (What Have We Got to Lose?)
Hikin' Down the Highway (1931)
Hold Me (1933)
Hold Up Your Hands in the Name of the Law of Love (1932)
Home (1931)
How's Your Uncle? (1931)
Hurry Home (1938)

I Believe in Miracles (1934)
I Came Here to Talk for Joe (1942)
I Can't Lose That Longing for You (1936)
I Couldn't Tell Them What to Do (1933)
I Do, Do You? (1941)
I Don't Know Why (I Just Do) (1931)
I Don't Mind Walking in the Rain (1930)
I Double Dare You (1937)
I Had a Pal on Guadalcanal (1942)
I Hate Myself for Being So Mean to You (1934)
I May Be Dancing with Somebody Else (1933)
I Never Mention Your Name (1943)
I Still Get a Thrill (1930)
I Surrender Dear (1931)
I Take to You (1941)
I Touched a Star (1941)
I Wake Up Smiling [2] (1933)
I Want the Whole World to Love You (1936)
I Want to Dream by the Old Mill Stream (1931)
I Was True, That's Why I'm Blue (1931)
I Wonder, I Wonder, I Wonder (1947)
I Wouldn't Change You for the World (1931)
If I Didn't Care (1939)
If I Feel This Way Tomorrow, Then It's Love (1940)
If I Had My Life to Live Over (1939)
If I Had My Way (1939)
If I Have to Go on Without You (1931)
If You Were Only Mine (1932)
I'll Be Faithful (1933)

I'll Follow You (1932)
I'll Get Along Somehow
I'll Keep the Lovelight Burning (1942)
I'll Never Be the Same (1932)
I'll See You Later in Slumberland (1931)
I'll Take You Home Again, Kathleen (1932)
I'm All Dressed Up with a Broken Heart (1931)
I'm Alone Because I Love You (1930)
I'm Getting Sentimental Over You (1932)
I'm Just a Fool in Love with You (1930)
I'm Stepping Out with a Memory Tonight (1940)
In a Little Blue Canoe with You (1932)
In the Chapel in the Moonlight [2] (1937)
In the Dreamy Hills of Home Sweet Home (1932)
In the Hills of Old Missouri (1932)
In the Little White Church on the Hill (1933)
In the Mission by the Sea (1937)
Indiana Sweetheart (1931)
It'll Take a Little Time
It Might Have Been a Different Story (1933)
It's a Sin to Tell a Lie (1936)
I've Found What I Wanted in You (1931)
I've Got an Invitation to a Dance (1935)

Johnny Doughboy Found a Rose in Ireland (1942)
Johnny's Got a Date with a Gal in New York (1945)
Just a Crazy Song (Hi-Hi-Hi) (1931)
Just a Kid Named Joe (1938)
Just a Little Fond Affection [2] (1945)
Just a Little Home for the Old Folks (1932)
Just Once Too Often (1934)
Just a Prayer Away (1945)
Just a Year Ago Tonight (1933)
Just Dreaming ('Til You Come Home) (1943)
Just Say Aloha (1936)

Kate (Have I Come Too Early Too Late?) (1947)
Knee-Deep in Stardust (1941)

The Lamp of Memory (1929)
Last Night a Miracle Happened (1938)
The Last Time I Saw Paris (1940)
Lawd, You Made the Night Too Long (1933)
Lazy Day (1931)
Let's Make Up (1933)
Let's Sail to Dreamland (1938)

Let's Tie the Old Forget-Me-Not (1938)
Let That Be a Lesson to You (1932)
Lies (1931)
Lights Out [3] (1935)
Linger a Little Longer in the Twilight (1932)
A Little Bit Independent (1933)
Little Did I Know (1943)
Little Lady Make-Believe (1938)
A Little Less of Moonlight
A Little Old Shack in the Mountains (1933)
A Little on the Lonely Side (1944)
Little Skipper (1939)
Little White Lies (1930)
Lost in a Fog (1934)
Lovable (1932)
Love Letters in the Sand (1931)
Love, You Funny Thing! (1932)
Lying in the Hay (1932)

Ma and Pa (Send Their Sweetest Love) (1932)
Make Believe Island (1940)
Makin' Faces at the Man in the Moon (1931)
Many Happy Returns of the Day (1931)
Marching Along Together [2] (1933)
Maybe (Flynn & Madden) (1935)
Maybe (C. Lombardo, Loeb, Kogen) (1937)
The Mem'ry of a Rose (Australian) (1940)
A Million Dreams
Moon Song (That Wasn't Meant for Me) (U.S., Engl.) (1933)
Mother Indiana (1931)
My First Thrill [2] (1935)
My Prayer (1939)
My Queen of Lullaby Land (1932)
My Whole Day Is Spoiled (1934)

New Dreams for the Old Folks
A Nightingale Sang in Berkeley Square (1940)
Now That I Need You, You're Gone (1931)
Now That It's All Over
The Nurse's Prayer (1948)

Oh! What a Thrill (1931)
An Old Fashioned Home in New Hampshire (1931)
The Old Kitchen Kettle (1932)
Old Playmate (1931)
The Old Spinning Wheel (1934)
Ole Faithful (1934)
On a Coconut Island (1936)

On a Little Dream Ranch (1937)
On the Other Side of the Rainbow (1945)
On the Wrong Side of the Fence (1934)
The One Rose [3] (1936)
One Sweet Letter from You (1927)
The Oregon Trail (1935)
Out in the Great Open Spaces (1933)
Over the Hillside (1949)

Pals of the Little Red School (1931)
Paradise Lane (1933)
Peg O' My Heart (1913)
Pickaninnies' Heaven (1932)
Please (U.S. & Austr.) (1932)
Please Forgive Me
Pretending (1946)
Prove It by the Things You Do (1945)
Put on an Old Pair of Shoes (1935)
Put Your Heart in a Song (1936)

Question and Answer (1945)

Rain (1934)
Red Sails in the Sunset [2] (1936)
The River's Takin' Care of Me (1933)
Robins and Roses (1936)
Rock Me in the Cradle of Kalua (1931)
Rocky Mountain Rose (1931)
Roll on, Mississippi, Roll On

A Sailboat in the Moonlight (1937)
Seems Like Old Times (1945)
Shake Hands with a Millionaire (1933)
She'll Always Remember (1942)
She Shall Have Music (1936)
Shine on, Harvest Moon (Australian) (1908)
Sleep, Come on and Take Me (1932)
Sleepy Hollow Home (1931)
The Smiths and the Jones' (1942)
Smoke from a Chimney (1938)
So at Last It's Come to This (1932)
A Soldier Dreams (1942)
So Long (1940)
So Many Memories (1937)
Somebody Else Is Taking My Place (U.S. & Austr.) (1938)
Someone Else's Sweetheart (1943)
Somewhere in Old Wyoming (1930)
Southern Moon (1931)
South of the Border (1939)
Stars Fell on Alabama (1934)
Summer Souvenirs (1938)
Sundown in Peaceful Valley (1936)
Sun-Kissed Days and Moon-Kissed Nights (1943)
Swanee Cradle Song (1933)
Swanee River Home
Sweet and Lovely [2] (1931)

Tell Me with a Love Song (1931)
Tell Me with Your Kisses (1936)
Tell-Tales (1931)
That Daddy and Mother of Mine (1932)
That's Where I Came In (1946)
There Are Rivers to Cross [2] (1942)
There's a Cabin in the Pines (1933)
There's a Cowboy Ridin' Thru the Sky (1942)
There's a Gold Mine in the Sky (1937)
There's a Harbor of Dreamboats (1943)
There's a Ray of Sunshine (1943)
There's Something in Your Eyes (1931)
These Foolish Things Remind Me of You (1936)
They Gave Him a Gun to Play With (1938)
They'll Be All Coming Back Bye and Bye (1943)
They'll Sing LaMarsellaise Again [photo on back] (1944)
This Time It's Real (1938)
Throw Another Log on the Fire (1933)
Till Tomorrow (1932)
Timber [2] (1936)
Time on My Hands (1930)
Tiny Little Fingerprints (1931)
Trust in Me (1936)
Try a Little Tenderness (1933)
Trying to Forget (1931)
Tumbling Tumbleweeds (1934)
Twenty Million People (1932)
Two Hearts That Pass in the Night (1941)
Two Little Fishes and Five Loaves of Bread (1944)

Violins Were Playing (1943)
The Voice in the Old Village Choir (1932)

Wabash Moon (1931)
Waiting at the End of the Road (1929)
Wake Up and Sing! [2] (1936)
Walkin' My Baby Back Home (1930)
We'll Meet Again (1942)
Were You Sincere? (1931)
We're All Americans [2, one w/o photo] (1940)
We've Come a Long Way Together (1939)
What Did You Do with It? (You Took My Heart) (1931)

What Have We Got to Lose? (1933)
What Is It? (1931)
What More Can I Do? (1931)
What Will I Tell My Heart? (1937)
When a Pal Bids a Pal Goodbye (1932)
When It's Moonlight in Sunshine Valley (1933)
When the Crimson Snow of Russia Is White Again (1942)
When the Moon Comes Over the Mountain [theme] (1931)
When the Poppies Bloom Again (1936)
When the Roses Bloom Again [2] (1942)
When the Sun Goes Down in My Home Town (1932)
When Work Is Through (1932)
Where the Mountains Meet the Sea (1934)
Where the Sunset Turns the Ocean's Blue to Gold (1932)
While the Rest of the World Is Sleeping (1933)
Whistling in the Dark (1931)
The White Cliffs of Dover [2] (1941)
Why Can't This Go on Forever? (1932)
Why Dance? [2] (1931)
Why Don't You Do Right? (1942)
Wild Honey (1934)
Will You Remember Tonight Tomorrow? (1938)
Wonder When My Baby's Comin' Home (1942)
Won't You Say Hello? (1933)
The Woodpecker Song (1940)
Wrap Your Troubles in Dreams (1931)

Yarza Buncha Yacka Larry (1941)
You Can't Pull the Wool Over My Eyes (1936)
You Knew Just What You Were Doing (1946)
You'll Never Go to Heaven (If You Break My Heart) (1936)
You'll Never Know, Sweetheart (1930)
You Made Me Care (1939)
You're Gonna Lose Your Gal (1933)
You're a Heavenly Thing (1935)
You're Nobody 'Til Somebody Loves You [photo on back] (1944)
You've Got Everything (1933)
(You Were Only) Passing Time with Me (1930)

APPENDIX E

Stage Appearances

1. *Honeymoon Lane.* Opened Monday, September 20, 1926, at the Knickerbocker Theatre, New York City. Ran 364 performances. Produced by Abraham L. Ehrlanger. Book, lyrics, and music by Eddie Dowling and James Hanley. Staged by Edgar McGregor. Dances by Bobby Connolly. Musical Director: Arthur Lange.

Kate Smith had a small part, cast as Tiny Little. She sat on stage until near the end of the show, then she did a "specialty," singing and dancing the Charleston to "Half a Moon." She was then joined by Johnny Marvin (as Honey Duke) and the Uke Girls for "Jersey Walk." After a dance specialty by Lorraine Webb, she sang "Mary Dear." Just before the finale she sang "The Little White House." She recorded the latter three songs, the last two comprising her first record, Columbia 810-D. "Jersey Walk" was never released.

The show previewed in Atlantic City and at the Garrick Theatre in Philadelphia from late August to mid–September, 1926.

The show was one of the most successful of the 1926-27 Broadway season. It went on tour, playing major cities from coast to coast for a second year; Smith traveled with the road company. She was the sensation of the show, cast as an overweight buffoon.

2. *Hit the Deck.* Shubert-Belasco Theater, New York. Two weeks beginning Sunday, January 6, 1929. Produced by Charles Emerson Cook. Book by Herbert Fields. Music by Vincent Youmanns. Lyrics by Leo Robbins and Clifford Gray. Staged by Edward P. Bower. Dances and ensembles by Frank Gallagher. Musical director: Vincent J. Colling. Presented by the Savoy Musical Comedy Company with Kate Smith.

Act I, Scene 2 was essentially a specialty by Kate Smith: presumably song-and-dance. In Act II, Scene 2 she appeared in blackface as Mammy Lavinia, singing the hit of the show, "Hallelujah."

This was a revival of the 1927 musical production. Kate Smith said she also did it in summer stock that year.

3. *Honeymoon Lane.* Shubert-Belasco Theater, New York. Week beginning Sunday, January 20, 1929. Produced by Charles Emerson Cook. Book, lyrics, and music by Eddie Dowling and James Hanley. Staged by Vance Leonard. Dances and ensembles by Frank Gallagher. Musical director: Vincent J. Collins. Presented by the Savoy Musical Comedy Company with Kate Smith. (May have lasted more than one week.)

Kate Smith reprised her role as Tiny Little exactly as she did in the original production. This time Honey Duke was played by Robert Carbaugh.

4. *Flying High.* Apollo Theatre, 42nd Street, west of Broadway. Opened Monday, March 3, 1930. Ran 357 performances. Produced by George White. Starred Bert Lahr and Oscar Shaw. Book by B. G. DeSylva, Lew Brown, and Jack McGowan. Songs by B. G. DeSylva, Lew Brown, and Ray Henderson. Staged by Bobby Connolly. Settings by Joseph Urban. Orchestra directed by Al Goodman. Costumes designed by Charles LaMaire. Book staged by Edward Clark Lilley.

Kate Smith was again a buffoon, playing Pansy Sparks, girlfriend of Rusty Krause. In

276

Act I she and Lahr sang "The First Time for Me." Just preceding the act's finale she belted out "Red Hot Chicago" with the Gale Quadruplets and Ensemble. In the middle of Act II, Smith sang "I'll Get My Man." Later she reprised the lovely ballad, "Without Love," her most memorable song in the show. Show was biggest hit of the season.

5. Kate Smith sang and danced on stage many times between 1929 and 1933 at such New York locations as the Palace, the Capitol, the RKO, and Paramount theatres. She also appeared at the Steel Pier in Atlantic City and in Philadelphia. Her vaudeville production, *The Swanee Revue,* played in major eastern cities, then went on the road from November 1933 to June 1934, playing in major cities from coast to coast.

6. Central Park Casino. In the spring of 1932, Kate Smith sang and danced on the stage of the Central Park Casino for several weeks, with Eddy Duchin's orchestra.

7. Madison Square Garden. On September 30, 1935, Kate Smith starred in an A & P gala on stage at Madison Square Garden, New York, to inaugurate her two-year radio series for A & P Coffees.

8. Carnegie Hall. November 2, 1963. One-night concert produced by Durgom-Katz Associates. Songs selected by Ted Collins and Lyn Duddy. 46-piece orchestra conducted by Cedric (Skitch) Henderson. Twenty-member chorus directed by Will Irwin. Recorded by RCA Victor.

9. Fontainebleu Hotel, Miami, Florida. Concerts in LaRonde. February 17–25, 1964. Twenty-nine-piece orchestra conducted by Jerry Bresler. Pianist: Lyn Duddy.

10. Carousel Theatre, West Covina, California. With the Young Americans and comedian George Gobel. January, 1966.

11. Concerts in the South in 1968. Orchestra conducted by Mitchell Ayres. Comedy by Pat Paulsen. Nashville Municipal Auditorium, Tennessee, Friday, March 15, 1968; Knoxville Auditorium, Tennessee, Saturday, March 16, 1968; Jacksonville Civic Auditorium, Florida, Friday, March 22, 1968; Atlanta Civic Center, Georgia, Saturday, March 23, 1968; Greensboro Coliseum, North Carolina, Friday, April 5, 1968.

12. Toledo Masonic Auditorium, Ohio. Saturday, March 13, 1971. With Toledo Symphony Orchestra. Benefit for widows of Masons and orphan children.

13. Wichita, Kansas. April 1971.

14. John Ascuaga's Nugget Hotel, Sparks, Nevada. June 28–July 12, 1972. Two concerts daily. Orchestra conducted by Jerry Bresler. With the Kids Next Door.

15. Arie Crown Theatre, McCormick Place, Chicago. Sunday, May 13, 1973. Two Mother's Day concerts. Orchestra conducted by Jerry Bresler with eight Kids Next Door.

16. John Ascuaga's Nugget Hotel, Sparks, Nevada. May 24–June 13, 1973. Two concerts daily. Orchestra conducted by Jerry Bresler with the Kids Next Door.

17. Allentown Fair, Pennsylvania. Saturday, August 3, 1974. Two performances on an outdoor stage. Orchestra conducted by Jerry Bresler. Comedy by Jud Strunk.

18. Latin Casino, Cherry Hill, New Jersey. December 9–15, 1974. Two concerts daily. Orchestra conducted by Jerry Bresler with the Kids Next Door. Comedy by Soupy Sales.

19. Temple University, Ambler, Pennsylvania. July 6, 1975. With the Pittsburgh Symphony Orchestra.

20. Mill Run Theatre, Niles, Illinois. Monday, November 24–Sunday, November 30, 1975. With George Gobel, comedian.

21. Van Wezel Auditorium, Sarasota, Florida. Monday and Tuesday, March 10–11, 1976. Orchestra conducted by Jerry Bresler.

Bibliography

Books

Bergreen, Laurence. *As Thousands Cheer: The Life of Irving Berlin*. New York: Viking, 1990, Chapters 8 and 15.

Costello, Chris. *Lou's on First*. New York: St. Martin's, 1981, Chapter 4. Abbott & Costello on the Kate Smith Hour.

Gala Kate Smith Birthday Party. Souvenir program. May 4, 1936. Given by A & P Managers' Benefit Association in Washington, D.C.

Gala Kate Smith Party. Souvenir program. Great Atlantic and Pacific Tea Company. September 30, 1935. Held at Madison Square Garden to inaugurate radio series for A & P coffees.

Green, Stanley. *Broadway Musicals of the Thirties*. New York: Da Capo Press, 1971, Chapters 1–3.

Gross, Ben. *I Looked and I Listened*. New Rochelle, New York: Arlington House, 1970, Chapter 8 and 9.

Hayes, Richard K. (ed.). *Kate Smith on Television: A Log*. Cranston, R.I.: Kate Smith/God Bless America Foundation, 1992.

_____ (ed.). *Kate Smith on the Radio: A Log*. Cranston, R.I.: Kate Smith/God Bless America Foundation, 1992.

_____ (ed.). *Kate's Letters to Bessie: 1933–1937*. Cranston, R.I.: Kate Smith/God Bless America Foundation, 1990. Collection of letters and postcards written to Bessie Phillips, a teenage fan in Pennsylvania.

_____ (ed.). *Pages from Aunt Minnie's Diary: 1933–1938*. Cranston, R.I.: Kate Smith/God Bless America Foundation, 1989. Minerva Klinge of Washington, D.C., details her visits with Kate Smith in New York.

Lahr, John. *Notes on a Cowardly Lion*. New York: Knopf, 1969, Chapter 4. Bert Lahr and Kate Smith in "Flying High" on Broadway.

Merton, Robert K. *Mass Persuasion: The Psychology of a War Bond Drive*. New York: Harper and Brothers, 1946. Psychological analysis of Kate Smith's September 21, 1943, radio war bond drive, produced by Columbia University.

Parish, James Robert, and Michael R. Pitts. *The Hollywood Songsters*. New York: Garland, 1991, pp. 670–76.

Pitts, Michael R. *Kate Smith: A Bio-Bibliography*. Westport, Conn.: Greenwood, 1988. An extensive and useful 261-page reference on all aspects of Kate Smith's career.

Portrait of a Great American. New York: Columbia Broadcasting System, 1943. Booklet with statistics and highlights of Kate Smith's career.

Smith, Kate. *Kate Smith's "Company's Coming" Cookbook*. Englewood Cliffs, N.J.: Prentice-Hall, 1958.

_____. *Living in a Great Big Way*. New York: Blue Ribbon Books, 1938. Illustrated autobiography.

————. *Stories of Annabelle.* Kansas City, Mo.: Tell-Well Press, 1951. A 26-page children's book based on television hour segment.
————. *Upon My Lips a Song.* New York: Funk & Wagnall, 1960. Illustrated autobiography.

Articles

Alexander, Jack. "Philosopher at Work." *The Saturday Evening Post,* August 15, 1942.
Allan, Alfred K. "Big Voice, Big Heart." *Columbia* (Knights of Columbus magazine), July 1966.
"America's Singer Smith Dead at 79." *The Hollywood Reporter,* June 18, 1986.
"And Now It's Kate Smith–Ted Collins, Incorporated." *Radio Guide,* November 30, 1935. Pastel portrait on cover.
Arnold, Maxine. "Hi Ya, Kate!" *Movie-Radio Guide,* August 1943.
Bennetts, Leslie. "Kate Smith: Philadelphia's Lady Luck." *Philadelphia Evening Bulletin,* June 13, 1974.
Black, Meredith. "The Indestructible Kate Smith." *Buffalo Evening News,* April 19, 1969.
Boal, S. "Why Kate Sings to Millions." *Coronet,* June 1953.
Boehnel, William. Review of "Hello Everybody!" *New York World Telegram,* January 30, 1933.
Bowers, Franklin L. "Why Isn't Kate Smith on the Air?" *Radioland,* July 1934.
"Brotherhood Award ceremonies in Chicago: Kate Smith holds press conference to criticize CBS' censoring of 'Kate Smith Speaks.'" *Los Angeles Times,* June 11, 1947.
Bundy, June. "Kate Smith TV Hour reviewed." *Variety,* October 9, 1950.
"Can Kate Smith Find Love?" *Radio Stars,* June 1936.
Carnegie Hall concert review. *Los Angeles Times,* November 4, 1963.
"Carrying On in a Large Way." *St. Louis Post-Dispatch,* July 2, 1939.
Carskadon, Tom. "Kate Smith—and Her Svengali." *Radioland,* November 1937.
Church, Peter. "Kate Stays Contemporary." *Reno Evening Gazette & Nevada State Journal,* June 1, 1973.
Cole, Hilda. "What's Happened to Kate Smith?" *Radio Stars,* May 10, 1934.
Collins, Frederick L. "The Answer to the Kate Smith Riddle." *Liberty,* June 8, 1940.
Collins, Ted. "I Know Kate Smith." *Tower Radio.* October 1934.
————. "Kate Smith, the Fat Girl Everybody Loves." *Radio Pictorial,* June 11, 1937.
————. "Kate Smith's Inside Story—By Her Manager." *Radio Guide,* October 16–22, 1932.
————. "What Makes a Hit Song?" *Song Parade,* July 1941.
"Columbia Pictures Plans USO Benefit Musical Film Short Starring Kate Smith." *Los Angeles Times,* April 29, 1942.
"Cooking for Christmas with Kate." *Radio Stars,* January 1938.
Dill, Larry. "Kate Smith: 'I Thank God for My Voice.'" *National Catholic Press,* March 21, 1976.
Dyer, Richard. "Kate—Everybody's Favorite Auntie." *Boston Globe,* December 30, 1975.
Edwards, John. "Why Kate Smith Is Afraid of Love." *Radio Mirror,* June 1936.
"Flyers Unveil Statue Honoring Kate Smith." *The Philadelphia Inquirer,* October 9, 1987.
Gardner, Christopher. "Long-Play Record." *New York Sunday News,* November 26, 1967.
Hanley, Jack. "Camera-Mad Kate Smith." *Popular Photography,* February 1938.
————. "No More Movies!" *Radio Guide,* February 1938.
Harper, Lorne. "Hello Everybody." *Popular Songs,* July 1935.
Hart, Gene. "God Bless Kate." *Philadelphia Daily News* special supplement. 1992.
Hartley, Grace. "Kate Smith Not Only Likes, but Cooks Southern Foods." *Atlanta Journal,* March 23, 1968.
Hecht, Marion. "Katherine, Kate, or Kated, Inc." *Radio Dial,* November 14, 1935.
Heggie, Barbara. "Star-Spangled Kate." *Woman's Home Companion,* May 1946.
"Hello Everybody!" (film review). *New York Daily News,* January 28, 1933.
"Hello Everybody!" (film review). *New York Evening Post,* January 30, 1933.
"Hello Everybody!" (film review). *New York Sun,* January 31, 1933.

"Hello Everybody!" (film review). *New York Times,* January 30, 1933.
Hopper, Hedda. "The Magic of Kate Smith." Sunday newspaper magazine, April 12, 1959.
"How Kate's Calorie Countdown Paid Off." *Today's Health,* June 1960.
"The Indomitable Kate Smith." *Tune In,* May 1943.
Johnson, Jack F. "Kate Smith—The Gift of Radiance." (Spokane) *Spokesman-Review Sunday Magazine,* March 12, 1967.
"Josephine Baker and 'Ethel and Albert' make debuts on Kate Smith Evening Hour." *Los Angeles Times,* November 2, 1951.
"Kate and Ted—It's Fun on Payday." *TV Forecast,* May 24, 1952.
"Kate Behind the Mike." *Movie-Radio Guide,* December 3–9, 1941.
"Kate Smith." In *Current Biography,* Nov. 1965.
"Kate Smith Accepts Chairmanship of Sister Kenny Infantile Paralysis Fund Drive." *Los Angeles Times,* August 8, 1946.
"Kate Smith at Carnegie Hall" album review. *Audio,* November 1964.
"Kate Smith—Back in the Swim Again." *Ladies' Home Companion,* February 1960.
"Kate Smith Calls." *Los Angeles Times,* June 29, 1950.
"Kate Smith Chats." *Variety,* October 11, 1939.
"Kate Smith Comments on 'God Bless America'." *New York Times,* June 15, 1940, section 4, p. 2.
"Kate Smith Finds Fame a Bit Irksome." *Radio Guide,* February 14–20, 1932.
"Kate Smith Goes to Hollywood." Two-part story, *Movie-Radio Guide,* May 31 and June 6, 1941.
"Kate Smith Has a Finger on the Nation's Pulse." *Tune-In,* July 1945.
"Kate Smith Is 'Just Folks'." *Baltimore & Phio Magazine,* May 1938.
"Kate Smith Loses Belongings in Fire." *Los Angeles Examiner,* February 20, 1934.
"Kate Smith Marks 25th Year on Air; to Slow Down." *Chicago Sun-Times,* April 20, 1956.
"Kate Smith Performance for King and Queen at White House." *Los Angeles Times,* June 9, 1939.
"Kate Smith Saved from Kidnap Attempt!" *TV Picture Life,* August 1966.
"Kate Smith—She Lives Alone and Likes It." *Radio Guide,* Part 1: April 1–7, 1939; part 2: April 8–14, 1939.
"Kate Smith—She's in Better Shape than Ever." *Ladies' Circle,* October 1969.
"Kate Smith Speaks." *Newsweek,* June 23, 1967. She criticizes CBS's censoring of editorial comments.
"'Kate Smith Speaks' voted top daytime radio program." *Movie-Radio Guide,* December 25, 1942.
"The Kate Smith Story—Song and Devotion." *Chicago American,* April 30, May 1 and 2, 1956. International News Service story.
"Kate Smith Takes 'A' Train to Carnegie Hall to Wow Partisan House." *Variety,* November 4, 1963.
"Kate Smith Tells You How to Sing for Radio." *Radioland,* April 1934.
"Kate Smith Tends Store." UPI, September 10, 1967. Story about godmother's shop in Lake Placid.
"Kate Smith, the Girl the Nation Loves." *Song Hits,* May 1946.
"Kate Smith the Last to 'Stop the Show'." *Variety,* October 7, 1926.
"The Kate Smith Touch." *Radio-TV Mirror,* February 1951. Photo essay.
Kate Smith to Visit President Truman Regarding Red Feather Drive. *Los Angeles Times,* October 2, 1946.
"Kate's Appeal." *Time,* September 21, 1943. Article about 18-hour radio war bond marathon.
Kent, Arthur. "The Girl Who Came Back." *Radio Guide,* August 11, 1934.
Kerrison, Ray. "Kate Smith Disgrace." *New York Post,* December 11, 1986.
————. "They Won't Let Kate Smith R.I.P." *New York Post,* January 6, 1987.
"Kin Conspired to Make Money Off Kate Smith, Sister Testifies." *Philadelphia Evening Bulletin,* August 28, 1980.
Kish, Frances. "Homespun Happiness." *TV-Radio Mirror,* March 1952.
————. "Many Happy Returns." *Radio-TV Mirror,* May 1954.
Kling, Ruth. "Everyone's Vocalist." *New York Sunday News,* July 20, 1969.

_____. "She Has Personality Plus." *New York Sunday News*, June 29, 1969.

Knight, Ray. "The Modern's Her Dish, Too." *Jacksonville Journal*, March 21, 1968.

Leitschuh, Jan. "Kate Smith, the Legend." *Raleigh Times*, March 17, 1986.

Lewis, Richard Warren. "The 'God Bless America' Girl at 59." *TV Guide*, April 5, 1969.

Linden, Sarah. "Kate Smith—The Woman Who Made a Bargain with God." *Movie Mirror*, November 1969.

Lowry, Cynthia. "Kate Smith—A Star Is Reborn." *Chicago Tribune*, November 3, 1969.

McAndrew, John, "Star Studded Shellac—Kate Smith U.S.A." *Record Research*, Spring 1964, Issues 60–62. Three-part review of Kate Smith's recording career.

Molloy, Paul. ". . . and the Return of Kate Smith, Dozens of Pounds Lighter." *Showcase/Chicago Sun-Times*, May 6, 1973.

Morrison, Walter. "Kate Smith Comes Back—Has She Ever Been Away?" *Chicago Tribune*, May 15, 1973.

Mulholland, Blane. "The Bright New Feather In Kate Smith's Cap." *Radio Stars*, December 1934.

Nelson, Don. "Tune Smith." *New York Sunday News*, May 29, 1960.

Obituary of Ted Collins. *Los Angeles Times*, May 28, 1964.

"The Odd Couple." *Los Angeles Times*, December 10, 1973. Kate Smith teams with Dr. John to make a record.

Parker, Jerry. "Kate Smith Is Back in the Limelight." *Newsday*, August 26, 1974.

Pearson, Dan. "She'll Sing Up a Storm Come Rain or Come Shine." *Allentown Morning Call*, August 3, 1974.

"Philadelphia Flyers and Kate Smith's Record of 'God Bless America'." *Sports Illustrated*, January 31, 1972.

Piper, Peter. "Beware of Hollywood." *Radio Stars*, September 1934.

"Premiere of Kate Smith Hour on Television Reviewed." *Los Angeles Times*, September 26, 1950.

"The Presidency—Out of the Fog." *Time*, June 26, 1939. Article includes Eleanor Roosevelt's visit to the Kate Smith Hour and discussion of White House musicale.

"President Reagan Gives Kate the Medal of Freedom." *New York Times*, October 27, 1982.

"President Thanks Kate Smith." *New York Times*, February 11, 1932.

"Radio's Own Life Story." *Radio Mirror*, June 1950. Brief history of radio entertainment programs, including those of Kate Smith.

Reddy, John. "Kate Smith's Alter Ego." *Coronet*, September 1944.

"Sad Songs, Family Disputes for Kate Smith." *Washington Post*, August 28, 1980.

Schaefer, Marilyn. "Philadelphia Honors Kate Smith." *Philadelphia Evening Bulletin*, December 11, 1974.

Scheuer, Philip K. "'Hello Everybody!' reviewed." *Los Angeles Times*, January 30, 1933.

Senger, Sofia. "Kate Smith—Lonely Songbird." *Radio Guide*, March 30, 1935.

"Singer's Belongings Auctioned." *Raleigh Times-Picayune*, November 30, 1986.

"Singing Lady Who Likes People." *New York Times Magazine*, January 16, 1944.

Smith, Kate. "Behind the Scenes on My Show." *TV Show*, October 1951.

_____. "Hello Everybody! This Is Kate Smith Speaking." *Liberty*, September 24, 1932.

_____. "I Speak for Myself." *Radio Mirror*, May, June, and July 1934. Three part biographical story.

_____. "I'm Back to Stay!" *TV-Radio Mirror*, June 1966.

_____. "My American Credo." *Reader's Digest*, April 1939.

_____. "My Visit with Their Majesties." *Radio Guide*, July 1–7, 1939.

_____. "Radio Singing as a Profession." The Grolier Society: *Book of Knowledge 1948 Annual*.

_____. "Shake Hands with the Champions." *Radio Stars*, January 1936.

_____. "This Is My Life." *Radio-TV Mirror*, June 1951.

_____. "Why Dean Martin Is the Man I Love." *TV-Radio Mirror*, May 1968.

_____ and Dena Reed. "Try Asking God." *Journal of Living*, November 1950.

"The Songbird of the South." *Movie-Radio Guide*, April 26–May 2, 1941.

"Songbird of the South Takes to the Air Again." *Newsweek*, September 8, 1934.

"A Sophie Tucker Rival." *New York Times*, October 31, 1926, Section 8, p. 4.

"Southern Singer a Star Finder." *Newsweek*, March 2, 1935.

Tate, Bob. "The Spectator" (column featuring a review of Kate Smith's concert). *Jacksonville Journal*, March 23, 1968.

Temple, Mary. "Kate Smith—Star in His Hands." *TV-Radio Mirror*, January 1953.

"10 Big Years Before the Mike for Kate Smith and Jack Benny." *Newsweek*, June 5, 1941.

"Ten Minutes 'Til Air Time." *Radio Stars*, April 17, 1938. Rotogravure photo essay.

"Thanks for List'nin'." *New York World Telegram*, 1941.

Towner, Leslie. "Why Kate Smith Never Married." *Radio Album*, July 1949.

"Troubled Kate Smith Gets Flood of Fan Mail." *Baltimore Morning Sun*, September 3, 1980.

"TV's Richest Woman." *Look*, April 6, 1954.

Wald, Jerry. "Will Kate Quit?" *Radio Stars*, September 1933.

Wells, Peggy. "Kate Smith's Path to Glory." *Radio Stars*, February 1932.

West, Stephen. "The Most Popular Woman Singer in Radio Cannot Read a Note." *The Etude*, May 1942. A conference with Kate Smith.

Wharton, Don. "God Bless America." *Look*, December 7, 1940.

Wolters, Larry. "Kate Gives Manager a Big Hand." UPI, April 1956.

Additional Reference Materials

Articles written by members of the Kate Smith USA Friends Club in its official journal, *Our Kate*. These are from thirteen volumes, dating from 1968 to 1975.

"Kate Smith Speaks" scripts transcribed from bound volumes by the author.

Personal correspondence. Letters from Kate Smith to Minerva Klinge, William Freeh, Jr., Charles L. D'Imperio, and the author.

Radio and television programs in the author's collection.

Taped interviews with Kate Smith by the author on January 7 and July 31, 1971.

Index